WINDOWS XP
HACKS

Other Microsoft Windows resources from O'Reilly

Related titles

Amazon Hacks
Google Hacks
eBay Hacks
TiVo Hacks

Wireless Hacks
Mac OS X Hacks
Linux Server Hacks

Hacks Series Home

hacks.oreilly.com is a community site for developers and power users of all stripes. Readers learn from each other as they share their favorite tips and tools for Mac OS X, Linux, Google, Windows XP, and more.

Windows Books Resource Center

windows.oreilly.com is a complete catalog of O'Reilly's Windows and Office books, including sample chapters and code examples.

oreillynet.com is the essential portal for developers interested in open and emerging technologies, including new platforms, programming languages, and operating systems.

Conferences

O'Reilly & Associates brings diverse innovators together to nurture the ideas that spark revolutionary industries. We specialize in documenting the latest tools and systems, translating the innovator's knowledge into useful skills for those in the trenches. Visit *conferences.oreilly.com* for our upcoming events.

Safari Bookshelf (*safari.oreilly.com*) is the premier online reference library for programmers and IT professionals. Conduct searches across more than 1,000 books. Subscribers can zero in on answers to time-critical questions in a matter of seconds. Read the books on your Bookshelf from cover to cover or simply flip to the page you need. Try it today with a free trial.

WINDOWS XP
HACKS

Preston Gralla

O'REILLY®

Beijing · Cambridge · Farnham · Köln · Paris · Sebastopol · Taipei · Tokyo

Windows XP Hacks
by Preston Gralla

Published by O'Reilly & Associates, Inc., 1005 Gravenstein Highway North,
Sebastopol, CA 95472.

O'Reilly & Associates books may be purchased for educational, business, or sales pro-
motional use. Online editions are also available for most titles (*safari.oreilly.com*). For
more information, contact our corporate/institutional sales department: (800) 998-9938
or *corporate@oreilly.com*.

Editors:	Nancy Kotary and Lorrie LeJeune	Production Editor:	Darren Kelly
Series Editor:	Rael Dornfest	**Cover Designer:**	Hanna Dyer
Executive Editor:	Dale Dougherty	**Interior Designer:**	David Futato

Printing History:

August 2003:   First Edition.

ISBN: 0-596-00511-3
[C]

Contents

Credits

About the Author

Preston Gralla is the author of more than 20 books about computers and the Internet, which have been translated into 15 languages. He has been writing about technology since the dawn of the PC age, and has been an editor and columnist for many national newspapers, magazines and web sites. He was the founding editor of *PC Week*; a founding editor, then editor, then editorial director of *PC/Computing*; and executive editor for ZDNet/CNet. Preston has written about technology for numerous magazines and newspapers, including *PC Magazine, Computerworld, CIO Magazine, Computer Shopper,* the *Los Angeles Times, USA Today,* the *Dallas Morning News* (where he was a technology columnist), and many others. He has been a columnist for ZDNet/CNet and is currently a columnist for TechTarget.com. His commentaries about technology have been featured on National Public Radio's *All Things Considered*, and he has won the award for the Best Feature in a Computer Publication from the Computer Press Association. Under his editorship, *PC/Computing* was a finalist for General Excellence from the National Magazine Awards. He lives in Cambridge, MA, with his wife and two children—although his daughter has just fled the nest for college. Between writing books, articles, and columns, he swims, plays tennis, goes to the opera, and contemplates the ram's skull hanging on the wall of his office.

Contributors

The following people contributed their hacks, writing, and inspiration to this book:

- Eric Cloninger was one of the original contributors to the Palm OS, working on tools for software developers. After 15 years in the Real

World, Eric decided that living in a small town in Oklahoma wasn't so bad after all. When he's not writing software, Eric enjoys spending time with his family, tinkering with his John Deere tractor, and watching tornadoes roll across the plains. While he doesn't miss the traffic in the Big City, he does occasionally yearn for a Spicy Tuna Roll.

- Jim Foley, a.k.a. The Elder Geek (*http://www.theeldergeek.com*), owns and operates a small consulting and web design firm in Cambridge, NY, that specializes in the integration of Windows XP technology into home and business environments. He is also the creator and owner of The Elder Geek on Windows XP, a web site that strives to provide relevant information related to Windows XP, including a notification service and Windows XP forum to keep readers informed of the latest XP tips, troubleshooting, and update developments.

- Scot Finnie (*http://www.scotsnewsletter.com*) is a noted book and magazine article author who has been writing about computers, technology, and other subjects since 1983. His articles have appeared in *PC Magazine*, *PC World*, *Computerworld*, *Popular Science*, *Popular Mechanics*, and a long list of other magazines. He's the author of the biweekly email newsletter Scot's Newsletter, the editor of TechWeb.com, and one of the founding editors of SecurityPipeline.com and StoragePipeline.com. Catch up with Scot at his web site, ScotsNewsletter.com.

- Wei-Meng Lee is an experienced author and developer specializing in .NET technologies. He was awarded the Microsoft .NET Most Valuable Professional (MVP) award in 2003. Besides .NET development, Wei-Meng maintains a keen interest in wireless technologies and has coauthored many books and articles on mobile applications development and XML technologies. He is the author of *Windows XP Unwired* (O'Reilly & Associates, Inc.).

- Margaret Levine Young has coauthored many books, including *The Internet for Dummies*, *Windows XP: The Complete Reference*, *UNIX for Dummies*, *Internet: The Complete Reference*, and *Poor Richard's Building Online Community*. She has a B.A. in Computer Science from Yale and lives in Vermont.

Acknowledgments

Any book is a cooperative venture, and this one was more so than many. Thanks to Nancy Kotary, who corralled the burgeoning project that always seemed on the verge of escaping from the barn, and managed to whip it into shape and get it into print with good grace and even better humor. Thanks to Rael Dornfest for his laser-like focus on making sure that every hack was exceedingly useful and moved well beyond the obvious. Laurie Petrycki and Dale Dougherty offered valuable advice and feedback in the early stages of writing. Many thanks to Tim O'Reilly, who entrusted me with this project, albeit in a very different form when it was first conceived, and who gave very targeted advice and pointers in the important early phases of writing.

Thanks also to the production team at O'Reilly: Brian Sawyer, Lorrie LeJeune, Darren Kelly, Ellen Troutman-Zaig, Jamie Peppard, Mary Agner, James Quill, Robert Romano, and Jessamyn Read.

As always, thanks to my family. Lydia put up with my usual diet of late-night deadlines, and Mia let me get my work done when we were on her grand audition tour for college ballet programs. As for Gabe, his advice and recommendations on which hacks to cover was an enormous help. We'll get the DivX tip in next time, Gabe!

Preface

Windows XP marks the biggest change to the Windows OS since the advent of Windows 95. It combines the stability of the NT/2000 operating system with the user-friendliness and hardware support of the consumer Windows line—and it does so literally, because those two operating systems have been combined for the first time in XP. Although there are two versions of XP— Home Edition and Professional Edition—the differences between them are relatively minor and have to do primarily with security and administrator tools. Under the hood, they're the same OS.

XP marks several other change as well. DOS is no longer a part of the underlying OS, although it's still available as a command prompt. Multimedia and graphics have been built into the operating system more directly than before and are no longer treated as an afterthought. And, cosmetically, XP has been given a makeover, in both the way it looks (rounded windows and almost cartoonish at times) and the way it works.

All this is good news for would-be operating system hackers. Because of the operating system's greater stability, those who work under the hood of XP can concentrate on actually getting work done and making the OS more effective, rather than trying to fix its shortcomings. Because of the richer interface and greater support for graphics and multimedia, you can more easily change the way the operating system works and looks. And, because the OS offers a variety of tools for recovering from errors, you can hack to your heart's content without worrying that you'll damage the OS beyond recognition.

This collection is based on the hands-on, real-world experience of those who in many cases have been using PCs well before any version of Windows even existed. They have wrestled with each new version of Windows as it was released, and found ways to take advantage of every nook and cranny of the operating system. When XP came out, they applied that hard-earned knowledge to it as well, and came up with ways to take advantage of the myriad new features of the operating system.

The results is 100 hacks that are useful, frequently entertaining, and will save you countless hours at the keyboard. Whether you want to speed up your PC, customize XP's interface, hack your wired and wireless network, get more out of the Web, make better use of email, use the Registry to bend the operating system to your will, or use XP for countless other useful tasks, you'll find what you're looking for here. And each hack doesn't just show you *how* to do something; it also teaches *why* it works. Each hack is a starting point, rather than an ending point, so that you can apply the knowledge you've gained to create new hacks of your own. Try it out—who knows, in the next edition of this book, you may get a hack of your own published.

How to Use This Book

You can read this book from cover to cover if you like, but each hack stands on its own, so feel free to browse and jump to the different sections that interest you most. If there's a prerequisite you need to know about, a cross-reference will guide you to the right hack. If you're not familiar with the Registry yet, or want a refresher, you might want to spend some time in Chapter 7, to get a good grounding.

How This Book Is Organized

This book is not a mere tips-and-tricks compendium that tells you where to click, where to drag, and what commands to type. It takes advantage of XP's flexibility and new features, recognizes that there are specific tasks you want to accomplish with the operating system, and offers you bite-sized pieces of functionality that you can put to use in a few minutes. It also shows how you can expand on their usefulness yourself. To give you this kind of help, the book is organized into 12 chapters:

Chapter 1, *Startup and Shutdown*
> With XP, startup and shutdown can mean much more than turning on your PC or selecting "Shut Down" form the start menu. With hacks in this chapter, you can change the picture that appears on the startup screen, speed up the sometimes endless startup and shutdown processes, hack the Registry to control many different aspects of startup and shutdown, customize multiboot options, and much more.

Chapter 2, *The User Interface*
> XP lets you change the way it looks and works more than any other version of Windows, and this chapter shows how to do it. Want a speedy, stripped-down version of the OS? It's in here. Want to build your own

themes and find thousands more online? It's in here as well. So are hacks for controlling the Control Panel, Start Menu, and Taskbar; creating transparent windows; and building your own cursors and icons. The hacks don't stop there, so interface hackers may want to head here first.

Chapter 3, *Windows Explorer*

Windows Explorer provides a basic window into XP and lets you manage files and folders, among other tasks. When hacked, it does much more as well. This chapter shows how to customize folder icons and balloon tips, improve the context menu, find files fast by mastering the indexing service's query language, get more disk space by using NTFS compression, keep your PC secure with encryption, and more.

Chapter 4, *The Web*

You probably spend a significant portion of your computing life on the Web, so why not make the most of it? Want to find information fast, straight from your browser, without having to head off to sites like Google? This chapter teaches you how to do it. You can also kill popups, stop spyware, surf anonymously without a trace, and speed up file downloads. If you host your own web site, you'll find out secrets of using the built-in Internet Information Services (IIS) web server. There are many more hacks here as well.

Chapter 5, *Networking*

XP was built for networking, and this chapter shows you how to take full advantage of it. Tweak your DNS settings for faster Internet access, go "war driving" to find WiFi wireless networks to which you want to connect, extend the reach of your own WiFi network, use command-line tools for trouble-free network operations, or build firewalls and punch holes through them. This chapter helps you get the most out of XP's powerful, built-in ability to connect.

Chapter 6, *Email*

Email is both the greatest productivity-booster and time-waster known to humankind. This chapter ensures that you'll stop wasting time, and get more out of email. Slam spam, open blocked file attachments in Outlook and Outlook Express, get better email software, and retrieve Web-based email using a normal email client. There's all that and more here.

Chapter 7, *The Registry*

If you're going to hack XP, you'll need to use the Registry. It's that simple. This chapter goes beyond merely teaching you how to use the Registry and how it's organized (although it covers that in detail as well). It also shows you how to hack the Registry itself—for example, by offering hacks on how to use *.reg* files to edit the Registry safely, and how to track and restore Registry changes.

Chapter 8, *Basic Utilities*

XP comes with a basic suite of built-in utilities, with the emphasis on *basic*. But you can hack these basic utilities so that they're much more useful powerhouses. Store multiple clips on the Clipboard, extend your real estate with virtual desktops, build a better backup strategy, take better screenshots, or use a universal instant messenger. As you'll see in this chapter, there's a lot more you can do with XP's utilities than you ever thought you could.

Chapter 9, *Applications*

An operating system needs applications in order to do much of its work. In this chapter, you'll see how to hack XP applications. Have older Windows applications that have a hard time running under XP? This chapter shows you how to make sure they run. You can also use command-line shortcuts to customize how each application runs, open and create Microsoft documents without Microsoft Office, and more.

Chapter 10, *Graphics and Multimedia*

In XP, Windows gets serious about multimedia and graphics for the first time. In this chapter, you'll see how to get the most out of them, with hacks for saving streaming audio to your PC, making videos with Movie Maker, sharing music without the spyware, and easy image conversion.

Chapter 11, *System Performance*

No matter how fast your PC is, it's not fast enough. This chapter show you ways to hack XP to juice up its performance. Get the most out of your RAM, use the Performance Console to speed up system performance, use a variety of Registry hacks to make XP run faster, and more.

Chapter 12, *Hardware*

By itself, an operating system can't do a thing; it needs hardware to run on. In this chapter, you'll see how to use XP to hack your hardware. Remap your keyboard, set up a direct cable connection between PCs for a quick-and-dirty network, uncover "hidden hardware" with the Device Manager, and get better resolution on your laptop and your LCD screen. And yes, there are more hacks here as well.

Conventions Used in This Book

I use the following font conventions in this book:

Italic

Used to indicate new terms, URLs, filenames, file extensions, directories, and folders.

Constant width

    Used to show code examples, verbatim searches and commands, the contents of files, and the output from commands.

Constant width bold

    Used in examples and tables to show commands or other text that should be typed literally.

Constant width italic

    Used in examples, tables, and commands to show text that should be replaced with user-supplied values.

Color

    Used to indicate a cross-reference within the text.

Pay special attention to notes set apart from the text with the following icons:

    This icon indicates a tip, suggestion, or a general note. It contains useful supplementary information or an observation about the topic at hand.

    This icon indicates a warning or note of caution.

The thermometer icons, found next to each hack, indicate the relative complexity of the hack:

 beginner   moderate   expert

How to Contact Us

We have tested and verified the information in this book to the best of our ability, but you may find that features have changed (or even that we have made mistakes!). Please let us know about any errors you find, as well as your suggestions for future editions (we take these seriously), by writing to:

    O'Reilly & Associates, Inc.
    1005 Gravenstein Highway North
    Sebastopol, CA 95472
    (800) 998-9938 (in the U.S. or Canada)
    (707) 829-0515 (international/local)
    (707) 829-0104 (fax)

You can also send us messages electronically. To be put on the mailing list or request a catalog, send email to:

info@oreilly.com

To ask technical questions or comment on the book, send email to:

bookquestions@oreilly.com

The web site for *Windows XP Hacks* lists examples, errata, and plans for future editions. You can access this page at:

http://www.oreilly.com/catalog/winxphks

For more information about this book and others, see the O'Reilly web site:

http://www.oreilly.com

Got a hack? To explore Hacks books online or to contribute a hack for future titles, visit:

http://hacks.oreilly.com

CHAPTER ONE

Startup and Shutdown

Hacks #1–7

Possibly the most overlooked part of XP is the way people start up and shut down their systems. How much do *you* think about startup and shutdown? Probably not much. Press a button to start your PC, click on a few buttons to shut it down, and that's it.

In fact, there's a lot you can do to get more productive—and to have a little customization fun—when using startup and shutdown. You can create boot menus and choose from customized startup options; you can create your own bootscreen; you can perform automated tasks every time you shut down your PC; you can eliminate unnecessary programs and services from starting to increase the speed of your PC. In this chapter, you'll learn all that, plus other ways to master and customize system startup and shutdown.

HACK #1 Customize Multiboot Startup Options

Edit or create a startup menu that lets you choose which operating system to boot into in multiboot systems, or create a menu that lets you choose different startup options for your single operating system if you have only XP installed.

If you've installed another operating system (in addition to XP) on your system, your PC starts up with a multiboot menu, which allows you to choose which operating system you want to run. The menu stays live for 30 seconds, and a screen countdown tells you how long you have to make a choice from the menu. After the 30 seconds elapse, it boots into your default operating system, which is generally the last operating system you installed.

You can customize that multiboot menu and how your PC starts by editing the *boot.ini* file, a hidden system file, to control a variety of startup options, including how long to display the menu, which operating system should be the default, whether to use the XP splash screen when XP starts, and similar features. And as you'll see later in this hack, you can also use the file to create a startup menu that will allow you to choose from different versions of your operating system—for example, one that you'll use for tracking down startup problems, and another for starting in Safe Mode.

The *boot.ini* file is a plain text file found in your root *C:* folder. You might not be able to see it, because it's a system file, and if you can see it, you might not be able to edit it, because it's a read-only file. To make it visible, launch Windows Explorer, choose View → Tools → Folder Options → View and select the radio button "Show Hidden Files and Folders." To make it a file you can edit, right-click on it in Windows Explorer, choose Properties, uncheck the Read-Only box, and click OK.

Editing Files

To edit the file, open it with a text editor such as Notepad. Following is a typical *boot.ini* file for a PC that has two operating systems installed on it—Windows XP Home Edition and Windows Me:

```
[boot loader]
timeout=30
default=multi(0)disk(0)rdisk(0)partition(1)\WINDOWS
[operating systems]
multi(0)disk(0)rdisk(0)partition(1)\WINDOWS="Microsoft Windows XP Home
Edition" /fastdetect
multi(0)disk(0)rdisk(0)partition(2)\WINNT="Windows 2000 Professional" /
fastdetect
```

As you can see, there are two sections in the file: [boot loader] and [operating systems]. To customize your menu and startup options, edit the entries in each section. Before editing *boot.ini*, make a copy of it and save it under a different name (such as *boot.ini.old*), so that you can revert to it if you cause problems when you edit the file.

Following are details about how to edit the entries in each section:

[boot loader]

> This section controls how the boot process works; it specifies the default operating system and how long a user has to make a selection from a boot menu, if a boot menu has been enabled. The timeout value specifies, in seconds, how long to display the menu and wait for a selection before loading the default operating system. If you want a delay of 15 seconds, for example, enter 15 for the value. Use a value of 0 if you want the default operating system to boot immediately. If you want the menu to be displayed indefinitely and stay onscreen until a selection is made, use a value of -1. The default value specifies which entry in the [operating system] section is the default operating system. (The default

value is used even if there is only one operating system in the [operating system] section.) To change the default operating system, edit the setting, in our example, to default=multi(0)disk(0)rdisk(0)partition(2)\WINNT.

So, in our example, if you change the menu settings so that the screen appears for 10 seconds before loading the default operating system, and the default operating system is Windows 2000 Professional, the section reads:

```
[boot loader]
timeout=10
default=multi(0)disk(0)rdisk(0)partition(2)\WINNT
```

[operating system]

This section specifies which operating systems are present on the computer, and detailed options for each one. XP uses the Advanced RISC Computing (ARC) path to specify the location of the boot partition. In our example, the ARC path is:

```
multi(0)disk(0)rdisk(0)partition(1)\WINDOWS
```

The first parameter, which identifies the disk controller, should be 0. The second parameter, the disk parameter, should also be 0. The rdisk parameter specifies the disk number on the controller that has the boot partition. The numbers start at 0. So, if you have three hard disks installed and the second hard disk has the boot partition, the setting is rdisk(1). The partition parameter identifies the partition number of the boot partition. Partitions start with the number 1. The final section, which in our example is \WINDOWS, specifies the path to the folder where the operating system is installed.

To the right of the ARC path in the example is ="Microsoft Windows XP Home Edition" /fastdetect. The words within quotes are what will appear on the boot menu next to the entry. To customize the text on the menu you can change these words to whatever you wish—for example, "My Favorite Operating System." The /fastdetect switch disables the detection of serial and parallel devices, which allows for faster booting. The detection of these devices isn't normally required in XP, because the functions are performed by plug-and-play drivers, so as a general rule it's a good idea to use the /fastdetect switch. The /fastdetect switch is only one of many switches that can be used in the *boot.ini* file to customize how the operating system loads. Table 1-1 lists others you can use.

Table 1-1. Switches for boot.ini

Switch	What it does
/BASEVIDEO	Starts XP using the standard VGA driver. It's most useful if you can't boot normally because of a video driver problem.
/BOOTLOG	Logs information about the boot process to the *ntbtlogl.txt* file in the *C:\Windows* folder.
/CRASHDEBUG	Loads the debugger at boot, but the debugger remains inactive unless a crash occurs.
/DEBUG	Loads the debugger at boot and runs it.
/FASTDETECT	Disables the detection of serial and parallel devices.
MAXMEM:*n*	Specifies the maximum amount of RAM that XP can use.
/NOGUIBOOT	Does not allow the XP splash screen to load during boot.
/NODEBUG	Stops the debugger from loading.
/SAFEBOOT:switch	Forces XP to boot into the safe mode specified by the switch parameter, which can be minimal, network, or minimal(alternate shell). In minimal safe mode, only the minimum set of drivers necessary to start XP are loaded. In network safe mode, networking drivers are loaded in addition to the minimum set of drivers. In minimal(alternate shell) the minimum set of drivers are loaded and XP boots into the command prompt.
/SOS	Displays the name of each driver as it loads and gives descriptions of what is occurring during the boot process. It also offers other information, including the XP build number, the service pack number, the number of processors on the system, and the amount of installed memory.

When you've finished editing the *boot.ini* file, save it. The next time you start your computer, its settings will go into effect.

In our example, if we want the menu to appear for 45 seconds, the default operating system to be Windows 2000, and the XP splash screen to be turned off when we choose to load XP, the *boot.ini* file should look like this:

```
[boot loader]
timeout=45
default=multi(0)disk(0)rdisk(0)partition(2)\WINNT
[operating systems]
multi(0)disk(0)rdisk(0)partition(1)\WINDOWS="Microsoft Windows XP Home
Edition" /fastdetect /noguiboot
multi(0)disk(0)rdisk(0)partition(2)\WINNT="Windows 2000 Professional" /
fastdetect
```

Create a Startup Menu Even if You Have Only One Operating System

Even if you have only one operating system, you can create a boot menu that will let you choose to load your operating system with different parameters.

For example, for menu choices, you might have your normal operating system; a mode that lets you trace any startup problems; and Safe Mode. To give yourself the option of operating systems with different parameters, create separate entries for each new operating system choice. For example, for the version of the operating system that traces potential startup problems, you could create this entry:

```
multi(0)disk(0)rdisk(0)partition(1)\WINDOWS="Trace Problems XP Home Edition"
/fastdetect /bootlog /sos
```

This entry creates a startup log and also displays information about the drivers and other operating system information as it loads.

For the version of the operating system that loads in Safe Mode but that still allows networking, you could create this entry:

```
multi(0)disk(0)rdisk(0)partition(1)\WINDOWS="Safe Start XP Home Edition" /
fastdetect /safeboot:network
```

The *boot.ini* file would look like this, assuming that you want the menu to display for 30 seconds and you want normal XP startup to be the default:

```
[boot loader]
timeout=30
default=multi(0)disk(0)rdisk(0)partition(1)\WINDOWS
[operating systems]
multi(0)disk(0)rdisk(0)partition(1)\WINDOWS="Microsoft Windows XP Home
Edition" /fastdetect
multi(0)disk(0)rdisk(0)partition(1)\WINDOWS="Trace Problems XP Home Edition"
/fastdetect /bootlog /sos
multi(0)disk(0)rdisk(0)partition(1)\WINDOWS="Safe Start XP Home Edition" /
fastdetect /safeboot:network
```

> If you're leery of using a text editor to edit *boot.ini* directly, you can use the System Configuration Utility **[Hack #4]** instead. Type msconfig at a command prompt or the Run box and click on the BOOT.INI tab, shown in Figure 1-1. You'll be able to add several switches (but not as many as you can if you edit the *boot.ini* file yourself using a text editor).

See Also

- Create Multiple Startup Profiles with Advanced Startup Manager **[Hack #5]**

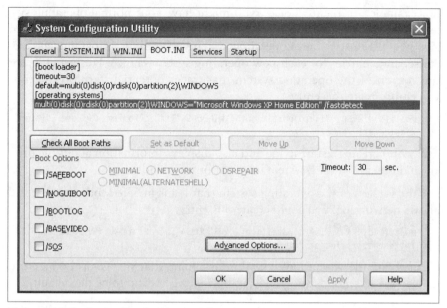

Figure 1-1. The System Configuration Utility

Change the Picture that Appears on the XP Startup Screen

You're not stuck with XP's default splash logo on the startup screen—use any picture or logo of your choosing.

One of the nice things about XP is how malleable it is. Don't like the way it looks? No problem—change it. Take my splash screen, please!

Many people, myself included, would prefer to see a more interesting splash screen (also called the startup screen) than the default gives you on start-up. You can change your splash screen to any of hundreds that have been created, or make one of your own—for example, with your picture or company logo on it.

To choose from already created splash screens, go to *http://www.themexp.org* and click on Boot Screens. You'll find over a thousand of them, organized by categories such as Sports, TV/Movies, and so on. Being a fan of Jack London's *The Call of the Wild*, I use a picture of huskies for my splash screen. You can see it pictured in Figure 1-2. Nice way to greet the new day, don't you think?

Once you've found the image you want to use as your splash screen, download it. It will be downloaded as a *.zip* file. I create a general folder for all my

Figure 1-2. Every time I start up my PC, I can imagine myself in the wilds of Alaska

boot screen files, called *C:\Bootscreens*, and then for each bootscreen I download I create a new folder—in this instance, *C:\Bootscreens\Wild*.

> It's possible that something will go wrong with your new boot screen, so before making the change, create a System Restore point by choosing Control Panel → Performance and Maintenance → System Restore and following the instructions. If something goes wrong, you can revert to that restore point.

Unzip the contents of the *.zip* file into the folder. There will be one or more files, including *ReadMe* files. The boot screen itself, however, will be named *ntoskrnl.exe*. If you have XP Service Pack 1 installed, you may have to use a different file, named *ntoskrnlSP1.exe*, that may also be in the downloaded *.zip* file. Check the documentation of the file you download to make sure. If you're not sure if you have Service Pack 1 installed, it's easy to find out. Right-click on My Computer, and choose Properties → General. Your version of the operating system will be displayed. If you have Service Pack 1, it will say so on that screen.

The *ntoskrnl.exe* file is an executable file that contains the XP bootscreen. During the boot process, XP executes this file, found in *C:\Windows\System32*, which in turn displays the bootscreen graphic. So, to change your bootscreen, replace your existing *ntoskrnl.exe* file with the one you just downloaded. But wait: there's more.

You might think that all you have to do is copy the new *ntoskrnl.exe* over the existing one and then restart your computer in order for the changes to take effect. That's not quite the case, though. You first have to get around a feature of Windows XP that protects system files from being overwritten. Windows File Protection automatically replaces certain files with the original XP version of the file if they've been replaced, and *ntoskrnl.exe* is one of those files. However, if you make the change in Safe Mode, Windows File Protection won't kick in and you can safely copy the file.

> Windows File Protection protects many other files, not just *ntoskrnl.exe*. Also included are *.dll, .exe, .fon, .ocx, .sys, .tff* files, and, depending on your system, other file types such as *.ax, .cpl, .cpx, .dll, .exe, .fon,. inf, .ocx, .rsp, .sys, .tff,* and *.tlb*.

Reboot your PC and press F8 immediately to get into Safe Mode. Now go to the *C:\Windows\System32* folder and find the *ntoskrnl.exe* file. Copy it to another folder or rename it as a backup so that you can revert to it when you no longer want to use your new bootscreen, or if something goes wrong when you install the new screen. Now copy the new *ntoskrnl.exe* file into *C:\Windows\System32*. (If you have to use the *ntoskrnlSP1.exe* file, rename it to *ntoskrnl.exe* first, and then copy it over.)

Reboot your computer again but don't go into Safe Mode this time. Your new splash screen will now appear every time you start your PC. To revert to your old splash screen, repeat the steps, copying your original *ntoskrnl. exe* file over your new one.

Choose from Multiple Splash Screens on Startup

Depending on my mood, I might not want to be greeted by huskies every morning. There are times when I want to be greeted by the normal startup screen, and other times when I want to see Andy Warhol's famous painting of Marilyn Monroe, or Al Pacino from the movie *Scarface*, all available from *http://www.themexp.org*. So I've made a startup menu that lets me choose which graphic should be my startup screen.

To create a startup menu, first download all the screens you want to use. Then rename the *ntoskrnl.exe* or *ntoskrnlSP1.exe* of each so that the filename describes the screen, for example, *ntospacino.exe, ntosmonroe.exe,* and *ntosspongebob.exe*. Copy them each into *C:\Windows\System32*. Don't touch the existing *ntoskrnl.exe* file there; you'll keep that as one of your options. Because you're not changing that file, you don't have to boot into Safe Mode to make any of these changes.

Following the instructions in "Customize Multiboot Startup Options" [Hack #1], create a multiboot screen by editing your *boot.ini* file. In the [operating systems] section of the *boot.ini* file, create a new entry for each of the screens from which you want to choose. Copy the existing primary XP entry and append /kernel=*newbootscreenfilename.exe* to the end of it, where *newbootscreenfilename.exe* is the filename of the bootscreen you want to use for that entry. Also edit the description so that it describes the bootscreen. For example, if the primary entry is:

```
multi(0)disk(0)rdisk(0)partition(1)\WINDOWS="Microsoft Windows XP Home
Edition" /fastdetect
```

you would create this entry for the Sponge Bob startup screen:

```
multi(0)disk(0)rdisk(0)partition(1)\WINDOWS="Sponge Bob Startup Screen" /
fastdetect /kernel=ntosspongebob.exe
```

Create as many entries as you want in the [boot loader] section. My *boot.ini* file looks like this:

```
[operating systems]
multi(0)disk(0)rdisk(0)partition(1)\WINDOWS="Microsoft Windows XP Home
Edition" /fastdetect
multi(0)disk(0)rdisk(0)partition(1)\WINDOWS="Huskies Startup Screen" /
fastdetect /kernel=ntosspongebob.exe
multi(0)disk(0)rdisk(0)partition(1)\WINDOWS="Pacino Startup Screen" /
fastdetect /kernel=ntospacino.exe
multi(0)disk(0)rdisk(0)partition(1)\WINDOWS="Marilyn Monroe Startup Screen"
/fastdetect /kernel=ntosmonroe.exe
```

Whenever you start up XP now, you'll be able to choose from your normal startup screen or any of the others you've put on the menu. If you have a laptop, for example, you might set up a menu that lets you choose a business-like startup screen at work and a more entertaining one at home.

Build a Startup Screen from Any Graphic

So far this hack has shown you how to use a startup screen that someone else built. But you're not limited to that; you can turn any graphic into a startup screen, using BootXP (downloadable from *http://www.bootxp.net*). It's shareware and free to try, but it costs $7.95 if you decide to keep using it.

The program will convert graphics from many different formats to a bootscreen graphic, use it as your bootscreen, or build a boot menu for you so that you can choose from multiple bootscreens. That way, you don't have to edit the *boot.ini* file yourself.

It's a surprisingly simple program to use. Select a graphic that you want to use as a bootscreen, and then click a button to convert it to the 640×480-pixel, 16-color bitmap startup screen standard. Preview the graphic, and if it's what you want, tell the program to set it as your bootscreen. The program provides a variety of options, including choosing a different progress bar that alerts you XP is loading, restoring your original startup screen, or randomizing your bootscreen so that it randomly selects one you've created each time you boot. You can also use the program to download already created startup screens from *http://www.bootxp.net*.

See Also

- Create Your Own XP Themes and Find Thousands Online [Hack #14]

HACK #3 Speed Up Boot and Shutdown Times

Shorten the time it takes for your desktop to appear when you turn on your PC, and make XP shut down faster as well.

No matter how fast your PC boots, it's not fast enough. Here's a hack to help you get to your desktop more quickly after startup, and to let you walk away faster after shutdown.

The quickest way to speed up boot times is to use the free Microsoft utility *BootVis.exe*. Although it's intended primarily for developers, anyone can use it to analyze their boot times and see where there are slowdowns. More important, the tool will also automatically make system changes to speed up your boot time, so you don't need to go into a lengthy analysis of where your slowdowns are and how to solve them.

Depending on your system and how it's set up, you may see only a moderately faster startup time, or you may speed up boot time dramatically. I've seen reports of improvements ranging from a little over 3 seconds to more than 35 seconds. The improvements I found on my systems were moderate—7 seconds faster on one, and 10 seconds faster on another. Think of all the things you could accomplish with another 10 seconds in the day!

The *BootVis* utility traces boot time metrics and then displays the results in a variety of graphs showing total boot time, CPU usage, disk I/O, driver delays, and disk utilization. Download it from *http://www.microsoft.com/hwdev/platform/performance/fastboot/BootVis.asp* and extract it into its own folder. Go to the folder and double-click on *BootVis.exe*. To analyze how your system boots, choose Trace → Next Boot. (Choose Trace → Next Boot + Driver Delays if you want to trace delays caused by drivers as well as your normal boot sequences.) Tell the program how many times to reboot and run the test (the more times it runs, the more accurate the results, although the longer the test takes to run). Click OK, and your system will reboot. After you log on after the reboot, you'll see this message:

```
1 Please WAIT for Bootvis to launch!
```

Don't do anything yet; the program is working, even though it doesn't appear to be doing anything. After a while, you will see the screen shown in Figure 1-3. Soon after that the results appear, as shown in Figure 1-4.

Figure 1-3. BootVis alerts you that it is working

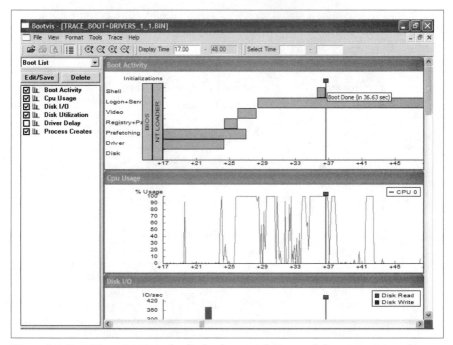

Figure 1-4. BootVis activity graphs display how much time each bootup activity takes

A series of graphs outline boot activity and loading time. The Boot Activity graph, shown in Figure 1-4, is the most important and details all aspects of the boot, including how much time each boot activity takes. Hover your mouse over an activity, such as Driver, and a balloon tip will appear, telling how much time that activity takes to load. To see the total boot time, hover your mouse over the rectangle at the top of a solid black line, and your total boot time will be displayed in a balloon tip, as shown in Figure 1-4.

The pictures and graphs are pretty, but the truth is, you don't really need them, because the utility will automatically make changes to speed up your boot time. To have the utility speed up your boot time, choose Trace → Optimize System and click Reboot Now when a prompt appears. Your system will shut down, reboot, give you the same initial prompt as when it's analyzing your system, but then alert you that it's reorganizing your boot files for faster startup. When the alert goes away, you can use your computer as you would normally. If you want to determine your increase in boot speed, run BootVis again and compare the new boot time to your previous boot time.

Enable Quicker Startups with a Boot Defragment

There's another way to speed up XP startup: make your system do a boot defragment, which will put all the boot files next to one another on your hard disk. When boot files are in close proximity to one another, your system will start faster.

On most systems, boot defragment should be enabled by default, but it may not be on yours, or it may have been changed inadvertently. To make sure that boot defragment is enabled on your system, run the Registry Editor [Hack #68], and go to:

    HKEY_LOCAL_MACHINE\SOFTWARE\Microsoft\Dfrg\BootOptimizeFunction

Edit the Enable string value to Y if it is not already set to Y. Exit the Registry and reboot. The next time you reboot, you'll do a boot defragment.

I've found many web sites recommending a way of speeding up boot times that may in fact slow down the amount of time it takes to boot up, and will probably slow down application launching as well. The tip recommends going to your *C:\WINDOWS\Prefetch* directory and emptying it every week. Windows uses this directory as a way of speeding up launching applications. It analyzes the files you use during startup and the applications you launch, and creates an index to where those files and applications are located on your hard disk. By using this index, XP can launch files and applications faster. So, by emptying the directory, you are most likely slowing down launching applications. In my tests, I've also found that after emptying the directory, it takes my PC a few seconds *longer* to get to my desktop after bootup.

Speed Up Shutdown Times

It's not only startup times that you'd like to speed up; you can also make sure that your system shuts down faster. If shutting down XP takes what seems to be an inordinate amount of time, here are a couple of steps you can take to speed up the shutdown process:

Don't have XP clear your paging file at shutdown
> For security reasons, you can have XP clear your paging file (*pagefile.sys*) of its contents whenever you shut down. Your paging file is used to store temporary files and data, but when your system shuts down, information stays in the file. Some people prefer to have the paging file cleared at shutdown, because sensitive information such as unencrypted passwords sometimes ends up in the file. However, clearing the paging file can slow shutdown times significantly, so if extreme security isn't a high priority, you might not want to clear it. To shut down XP without clearing your paging file, run the Registry Editor and go to:
>
> ```
> HKEY_LOCAL_MACHINE\SYSTEM\CurrentControlSet\Control\Session Manager\
> Memory Management
> ```
>
> Change the value of `ClearPageFileAtShutdown` to 0. Close the Registry and restart your computer. Whenever you turn off XP from now on, the paging file won't be cleared, and you should be able to shut down more quickly.

Turn off unnecessary services
> Services take time to shut down, so the fewer you run, the faster you can shut down. For information on how to shut them down, see "Halt Startup Programs and Services" **[Hack #4]**.

HACK #4   Halt Startup Programs and Services

Increase your PC's performance and speed up startup times by shutting off applications and services that you don't need.

One of the best ways to speed up your PC without having to spend money for extra RAM is to stop unnecessary programs and services from running whenever you start your PC. When too many programs and services run automatically every time you start up your system, startup itself takes a long time, and too many programs and services running simultaneously can bog down your CPU and hog your memory.

Some programs, such as antivirus software, should run automatically at startup and always run on your computer. But many other programs, such as instant messenger software, serve no purpose by being run at startup. And while you need a variety of background services running on your PC in order for XP to function, there are many unnecessary services that run on startup. For example, on many systems, the Wireless Zero Configuration Service runs to automatically configure a WiFi (802.11) network card, even though no such card is present in the system.

Eliminating Programs that Run at Startup

Stopping programs from running at startup is a particularly daunting task, because there is no single place you can go to stop them all. Some run because they're put in the *Startup* folder, others because they're part of logon scripts, others because of Registry settings and so on. But with a little bit of perseverance, you should be able to stop them from running.

Cleaning out the Startup folder. Start by cleaning out your *Startup* folder. Find it in *C:\Documents and Settings\<User Name>\Start Menu\Programs\Startup,* where *<User Name>* is your Windows logon name. Delete the shortcuts of any programs you don't want to run on startup. As with any shortcuts, when you delete them, you're only deleting the shortcut, not the program itself. (You can also clear out the startup items by going to Start → Programs → Startup and right-clicking on items you want to remove.) Next, clean out your *Scheduled Tasks* folder. Go to *C:\WINDOWS\Tasks*, and delete the shortcuts of any programs that you don't want to run automatically on a schedule.

> You can bypass all the programs in your *Startup* folder on an as-needed basis. To stop XP from loading any programs in the *Startup* folder, hold down the Shift key during boot-up. No programs in the *Startup* folder will run, but the items will still remain there, so that they will start up as they would normally the next time you boot.

Using the System Configuration Utility. Taking the previous steps will stop the obvious programs from running at startup, but it won't kill them all. The best tool for disabling hidden programs that run on startup is the System Configuration Utility, shown in Figure 1-5. To run it, type msconfig at a command prompt and press Enter. (If that doesn't work, first do a search for *msconfig.exe*, and then when you find the file, double-click it.)

To stop a program from running at startup, go to the Startup tab in this utility and uncheck the box next to the program. It can sometimes be difficult to understand what programs are listed on the Startup tab. Some, such as America Online, are clearly labeled. But often, you'll see a phrase or collection of letters, such as *fs20*. That's the name of the running file—in this case, *fs20.exe*, which is Free Surfer mk II, an excellent free popup killer [Hack #33]. As you can see from the picture, I've chosen to let this useful tool run on startup.

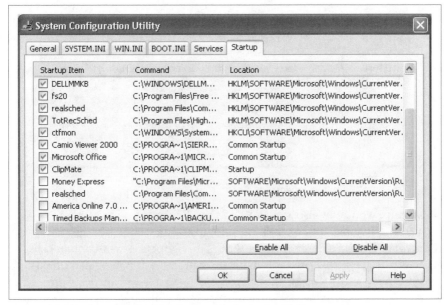

Figure 1-5. The Startup tab of the System Configuration Utility

To get more information about a listing, expand the width of the Command column near the top of the Startup tab. Expand it enough and you'll see the startup command that the program issues, including its location, such as *C:\Program Files\Free Surfer\fs20.exe*. The directory location should be another hint to help you know the name of the program.

When stopping programs from running at startup, it's best to stop them one at a time rather than in groups. You want to make sure that you're not causing any system problems by stopping them. So stop one and restart your PC. If it runs fine, then stop another and restart. Continue doing this until you've cleared all the programs you don't want to run automatically.

Each time you uncheck a box and restart your PC, you'll get a warning, shown in Figure 1-6, that you've used the System Configuration Utility to disable a program from starting automatically. If you don't want to see that warning, disable it by checking the box in the dialog itself.

After you've used the System Configuration Utility to identify programs that run on startup, you may want to try disabling them from with the programs themselves. So run each program that starts automatically, and see if you can find a setting that allow you to halt it from running on startup.

Using the Registry to Halt programs running on startup. Even the System Configuration Utility won't necessarily let you identify and kill all programs that run

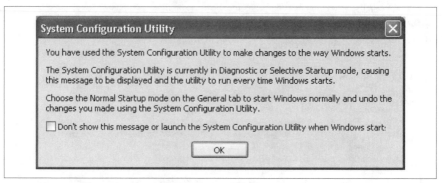

Figure 1-6. Disabled program warning

on startup. You may also need to hack the Registry to disable them. To do so, run the Registry Editor [Hack #68] and go to HKEY_CURRENT_USER\Software\ Microsoft\Windows\CurrentVersion\Run. The right pane will contain a list of some of the programs that automatically run at startup. The Data field tells you the path and name of the executable so that you can determine what each program is. Right-click on any program you don't want to run, and choose Delete. That will kill any programs that run specific to your logon. To kill programs that run for every user of the system, go to HKEY_LOCAL_MACHINE\ SOFTWARE\Microsoft\Windows\CurrentVersion\Run and follow the same instructions for deleting other programs you don't want to run at startup.

Disabling Services that Run at Startup

Constantly running in the background of XP are services—processes that help the operating system run, or that provide support to applications. Many of these services launch automatically at startup. While you need many of them, there are also many that aren't required and that can slow your system down when they run in the background.

You can disable services at startup by using the System Configuration Utility, similar to the way that you halt programs from running at startup, except that you use the Services tab instead of the Startup tab. But the System Configuration Utility doesn't necessarily list every service that launches on startup. A bigger problem is that disabling services is more of shot in the dark than disabling programs. When you disable a program, you can get a sense of what the program does. But when you disable a service through the System Configuration Utility, there's often no way to know what it does.

A better way of disabling services at startup is via the Services Computer Management Console, shown in Figure 1-7. Run it by typing services.msc at the command prompt. The Services Computer Management Console includes a description of all services, so that you can know ahead of time whether a particular service is one you want to turn off. It also lets you pause the service, so that you can test out your machine with the service off to see whether it's needed or not.

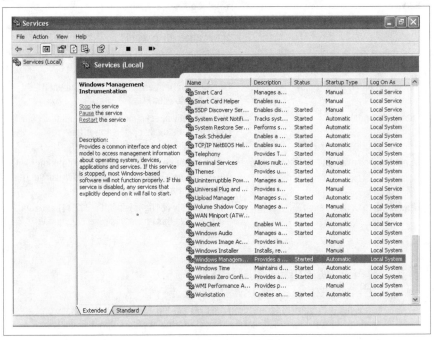

Figure 1-7. The Services Computer Management Console

After you run the console, click on the Extended tab. This view will show you a description of each service in the left pane when you highlight the service. The Startup Type column shows you which services launch on startup—any services with "Automatic" in that column. Click on that column to sort together all the services that automatically launch on startup. Then highlight each of those services and read the descriptions.

When you find a service you want to disable, right-click on it and choose Properties. In the Properties dialog box that appears, choose Manual from the "Startup type" drop-down list. The service won't start automatically from now on, but you can start it manually via the console. If you want the service disabled so that it can't be run, choose Disabled. To test the effects of turning off the service, turn off any services that you don't want to run by clicking "Stop the service" in the left pane, or by right-clicking on the service and choosing Stop.

Table 1-2 lists some common services you might want to halt from running at startup.

Table 1-2. Services you might want to turn off

Service	What it does
Portable Media Serial Number	Retrieves the serial number of a portable music player attached to your PC.
Task Scheduler	Schedules unattended tasks to be run. If you don't schedule any unattended tasks, turn it off.
Uninterruptible Power Supply	Manages an Uninterruptible Power Supply (UPS) connected to your PC.
Automatic Updates	Automatically checks for Windows updates. (You can check manually by going to *http:// windowsupdate.microsoft.com*.)
Telnet (service available on XP Pro only)	Allows a remote user to log in to your computer and run programs. (This will not be found on all versions of XP Pro.)
Wireless Zero Configuration Service	Automatically configures a WiFi (802.11) network card. Disable this only if you're not using a WiFi network card.

HACK #5 Create Multiple Startup Profiles with Advanced Startup Manager

If you need to start different programs on startup, depending on what you need to do on your PC, create different startup profiles with this startup utility.

With the hacks covered in this chapter, you can customize how XP starts up. But there's one thing these hacks won't be able to do for you—create different startup profiles. For that, you need downloadable software.

Let's say, for example, you have a laptop that you sometimes run attached to a keyboard, monitor, and an always-on Internet connection, and other times you travel with it, so it is not connected to the Internet. When you use it when you travel, you use it primarily in airplanes, airports, and other places where you typically aren't connected to the Internet. You also run a piece of monitoring software that will send a signal to a call center if your laptop is stolen. You don't need to run that software when you're not on the road.

Ideally, you would have one set of programs that run automatically at home and another set of programs that run when you're on the road. At home, you might want instant messenger software and file sharing software to load at startup; on the road, you don't want that software to load automatically, but you do want your monitoring software to load.

Advanced StartUp Manager—a piece of shareware from Ray's Lab (*http://www.rayslab.com*), shown in Figure 1-8—lets you create multiple startup profiles so that you can have separate profiles for your laptop at home and the road—or for any other purpose. It's free to try, but it costs $19.95 if you decide to keep it.

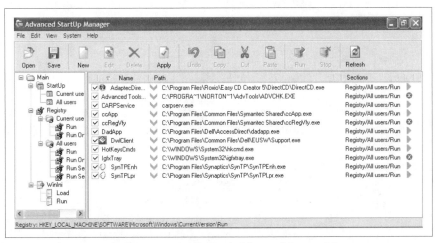

Figure 1-8. Create multiple startup profiles with Advanced Startup Manager

In addition to creating a profile for traveling and one for home, you may want to create other profiles. For example, when you want to play games, you'll want to start your system with a minimal number of services and programs running in the background, so you'll create a profile that disables a variety of services, such as the Indexing service, the Task Scheduler, and the Themes service that lets you apply themes to your PC. If you frequently need to troubleshoot your network, you'll want to create a network-troubleshooting profile that automatically starts networking analysis software, such as QCheck. [Hack #57].

To create a profile, add all the programs you want to run on startup, by having them start from the *Startup* folder, the Registry, or the *Win.ini* file. Where you want them to start from is up to you. To add a program, just highlight where you want it to run from, choose File → Add Program, and choose the program's executable file. You can add switches, if you want, in the Flags field of the screen you use to add the program. You can also choose whether the program should run for just one specific user or for all users of the machine. To delete a program from the profile, right-click on it and choose Delete.

When you have built a profile with all the programs you want to run at startup, save it by choosing File → Backup Configuration as, and then choosing a name for the profile. Create as many profiles as you want. To load a profile, choose File → Open Backup, and choose the profile you want to load. After you've loaded a profile, the next time you start your computer it will load with that startup software. Be aware that this means you can't choose a profile when you boot your system. You have to run Advanced StartUp Manager before you exit XP, choose the profile you want to run next time you start XP, and then exit.

See Also

- OSL 2000 (*http://www.osloader.com*) lets you boot from up to 100 separate operating systems (including multiple copies of XP or other versions of Windows), lets you boot from a second hard disk, and offers a variety of other features, such as an automatic boot timer. It's shareware and free to try, but it costs $25 if you decide to continue using it.

- For software to customize shutdowns, try Shutdown Now! (*http://wsw.dworld.de*). It gives you just about every option you can imagine for shutdown. You can specify applications to launch or documents to load automatically before shutdown, schedule shutdowns, perform actions such as ejecting and loading CDs on shutdown, empty directories on shutdown, and the list goes on. It's shareware and free to try, but if you keep using it you're expected to pay $19.50.

- For a free shutdown manager, try Switch Off (*http://yasoft.km.ru/eng/switchoff*), a simple shutdown utility that runs in your system tray. It lets you schedule shutdowns and perform other tasks on shutdown, such as locking your workstation, and it also lets you do any of them quickly from the system tray. It's not nearly as powerful as Shutdown Now!, but it's free.

Miscellaneous Startup and Shutdown Hacks
HACK #6

A grab bag of ways to customize the way you start up and shut down your system.

There are many small ways that you can control the way you start up and shut down your PC. This grab bag of four hacks shows you the best of them.

Create One-Click Shutdown and Reboot Shortcuts

Turning off or rebooting XP involves a several-step process: click the Start menu, choose Shut Down, and then select Shut Down or Restart. If you want, however, you can exit or reboot much more quickly, by creating a shortcut that enables one-click shutdowns. You can also use the shortcut to customize the shutdown or reboot—for example, by displaying a specific message or automatically shutting down any programs that are running.

First, create a shortcut on your desktop by right-clicking on the desktop, choosing New, and then choosing Shortcut. The Create Shortcut Wizard appears. In the box asking for the location of the shortcut, type shutdown. After you create the shortcut, double-clicking on it will shut down your PC.

But you can do much more with a shutdown shortcut than merely shut down your PC. You can add any combination of several switches to do extra duty, like this:

```
shutdown -r -t 01 -c "Rebooting your PC"
```

Double-clicking on that shortcut will reboot your PC after a one-second delay and display the message "Rebooting your PC." The shutdown command includes a variety of switches you can use to customize it. Table 1-3 lists all of them and describes their use.

I use this technique to create two shutdown shortcuts on my desktop—one for turning off my PC, and one for rebooting. Here are the ones I use:

```
shutdown -s -t 03 -c "See you later!"
shutdown -r -t 03 -c "You can't get rid of me that quickly!"
```

Table 1-3. Switches you can use with shutdown

Switch	What it does
-s	Shuts down the PC.
-l	Logs off the current user.
-t *nn*	Indicates the duration of delay, in seconds, before performing the action.
-c "*messagetext*"	Displays a message in the System Shutdown window. A maximum of 127 characters can be used. The message must be enclosed in quotation marks.
-f	Forces any running applications to shut down.
-r	Reboots the PC.

Automatically Turn On Num Lock, Scroll Lock, and Caps Lock

When you start your PC, Num Lock, Scroll Lock, and Caps Lock don't automatically toggle on. You can automatically turn each of them on or off whenever your PC starts, for all accounts on the PC. As a practical matter, most people probably want to have only Num Lock automatically turned on, but this Registry hack gives you the power to force any combination of keys on or off. Run the Registry Editor [Hack #68] and go to HKEY_USERS\.Default\ Control Panel\Keyboard. Find the String value InitialKeyboardIndicators. By default, it is set to 0, which means that Num Lock, Scroll Lock, and Caps

Lock are all turned off. Set it to any of the following values, depending on the combination of keys you want turned on or off:

0   Turns off Num Lock, Caps Lock, and Scroll Lock

1   Turns on Caps Lock

2   Turns on Num Lock

3   Turns on Caps Lock and Num Lock

4   Turns on Scroll Lock

5   Turns on Caps Lock and Scroll Lock

6   Turns on Num Lock and Scroll Lock

7   Turns on Caps Lock, Num Lock, and Scroll Lock

Exit the Registry. When you restart, the new setting will take effect.

Stop Error Messages from Displaying on Startup

If you constantly see an error message that you can't get rid of—for example, from a piece of software that didn't uninstall properly and continues to give errors on startup—you can disable it from displaying on startup. Run the Registry Editor and go to HKEY_LOCAL MACHINE\SYSTEM\CurrentControlSet\Control\Windows. (This key holds a variety of Windows system settings, such as the location of your system directory.) Create a new DWORD called NoPopupsOnBoot and give it a value of 1. Exit the Registry and reboot for the setting to take effect. To disable it, either delete the DWORD value or give it a value of 0.

Give More Time for Processes to Close at Shutdown

When you shut down Windows, XP gives each process, service or application 20 seconds to close before the operating system turns off the computer. If the process, service, or application doesn't shut down within 20 seconds, a dialog box appears, prompting you to either wait 20 more seconds, immediately end the process, service, or application, or cancel shutdown.

If this dialog box appears frequently, you may be running an application, service, or process that often takes more than 20 seconds to close. To solve the problem, you can increase the amount of time that XP waits to display the dialog box so that the dialog box will no longer appear. To do so, run the Registry Editor and go to HKEY_CURRENT_USER\Control Panel\Desktop. Look for the String value WaitToKillAppTimeout. Edit the value by entering the amount of time you want XP to wait before displaying the dialog box, in milliseconds. The default is 20000, or 20 seconds. If you want XP to wait 25 seconds, enter the value of 25000. Exit the Registry and reboot.

Control User Logins by Hacking the Registry

Make better use of the XP login screen.

If there is more than one user account on your system, or if you've set up XP to require logins, you'll have to log in to XP before you can begin to use it. But you needn't stay with the default XP login rules; you can use a single Registry key to customize how you log in. For example, you can display custom text before login, and you can remind anyone with an account on the PC to change their password a certain number of days prior to the password's expiration.

To control logon options, run the Registry Editor [Hack #68] and go to the HKEY_ LOCAL_MACHINE\SOFTWARE\Microsoft\Windows   NT\CurrentVersion\Winlogon subkey, which contains a variety of logon settings (as well as some settings not having to do directly with logons). Following are the most important values you can edit to customize logons.

DontDisplayLastUserName

This setting lets you control how the system logon dialog box is used. If this String value is present and set to 1, all users will have to enter both their username and password in order to log on. If the value is 0, the name of the last user to log on will be displayed in the system logon dialog box.

DefaultUserName

This String value contains the name of the last user who logged on. It will be displayed only if the DontDisplayLastUserName value is not present or is set to 0.

LegalNoticeCaption

This String value, used in concert with the LegalNoticeText value, displays a dialog box prior to logon that contains any text you want to display. (The text doesn't have to be a legal notice, but this value is often used for that purpose.) The box has a title and text. The LegalNoticeCaption value will be the dialog box's title.

LegalNoticeText

This String value, used in concert with LegalNoticeCaption, contains the text that you want to be displayed inside a dialog box displayed prior to logon.

PasswordExpiryWarning

This DWORD value lets you display a warning message to users a certain number of days before their passwords are set to expire. It lets you determine how many days ahead of time the warning should be issued.

To edit the value, click on the decimal button and enter the number of days.

ShutdownWithoutLogon

This String value enables or disables a button on the XP logon dialog box that lets the system be shutdown. A value of 1 enables the button (so that it is shown); a value of 0 disables the button (so that it is not shown).

Shell

This String value really doesn't have to do with logons, but it's one you should know about. It determines the shell—the user interface—that will be used by XP. The default is Explorer.exe, but it can be another shell as well—for example, the Program Manager from older Windows versions. Type in the name of the program—for example, Progman.exe for Program Manager, or Taskman.exe for the Task Manager.

AutoRestartShell

This DWORD value doesn't have to do with logons either, but it's another good one to know. It sets whether to automatically restart the Windows shell if the shell crashes. A value of 1 automatically restarts the shell. A value of 0 tells XP not to restart the shell, forcing you to log off and then back on again to restart it.

Now that the Startup and Shutdown are under control, let's move on to the user interface, in Chapter 2.

The User Interface

Hacks #8–20

The Windows XP makeover was the biggest change Microsoft made to the Windows interface since it moved from Windows 3.1 to Windows 95. Rounded-edge windows, large, cartoon-like icons, and a completely redesigned Control Panel are just a few of the most obvious changes. It's not merely the way XP looks that has been changed, but how it works as well. It's based on a more stable kernel and finally gets rid of its DOS-based heritage.

But let's face it: XP's interface isn't perfect. As shipped, its cartoonish user-friendliness may help newbies, but it can frustrate power users. XP's graphical user interface (GUI) need not be one-size-fits-all, though. Under the hood, there are countless changes you can make to the way it looks and functions. In this chapter, you'll learn how to hack your way to a better GUI—one that reflects your own preferences, not the market-driven designs of Microsoft engineers.

HACK #8 Customize the GUI with TweakUI

Want to bend XP's interface to your will without getting your hands into the Registry or having to excavate through menus three levels deep? Then get this supremely useful freebie from Microsoft and create your own customized version of XP.

There are countless ways to customize XP's interface, including Registry hacks and menus and options hidden four layers deep. But if you're the kind of person who lives in the express lane, juices up on double espressos, and wants to hack away at the interface fast, then you need TweakUI (Download it for free from Microsoft at *http://www.microsoft.com/windowsxp/pro/ downloads/powertoys.asp*. It's part of a suite of free, unsupported utilities from Microsoft called XP PowerToys, but it's far and away the best one.) It lets you tweak not only the interface, as the title suggests, but also many other system settings, such as how Internet Explorer's search works, whether to automate your logon upon system startup, and whether to enable CD autoplay so that the CD immediately starts up whenever you pop it into your drive. In this hack, you'll learn how to use it and apply that knowledge to create a speedy, stripped-down version of XP. Figure 2-1 shows TweakUI in action, customizing the display of thumbnail pictures in Windows Explorer.

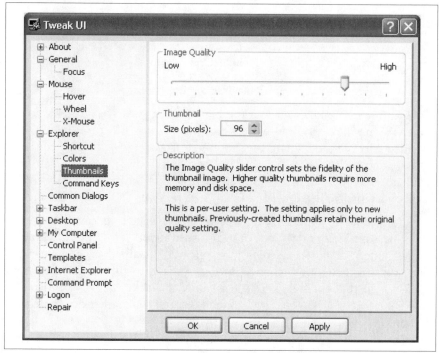

Figure 2-1. Customizing the size and quality of thumbnails in Windows Explorer

I don't have room to show you all the ways you can hack the user interface with TweakUI, but here are some of the highlights:

- The General section lets you control XP's animated effects, fades, and shadowing. Also worthwhile in that section is "Show Windows version on desktop." Check the option and it displays, in the lower-right portion of your screen, your exact version of XP—for example, "Windows XP Home Edition Build 2600.xpsp2.021108-1929(Service Pack 1)," as shown in Figure 2-2. I find it useful for knowing whether I need to add XP Service Packs, or for providing the information to tech support if I have an operating system problem that needs to be solved. You'll have to log off or restart your PC before it will display your version.

Windows XP Home Edition
Build 2600.xpsp1.020828-1920 (Service Pack 1)

Figure 2-2. Displaying your exact version and build of XP on your desktop

 You can also force the operating system to display your exact version and build of XP on your desktop by using a Registry hack. Run the Registry Editor **[Hack #68]**. go to HKEY_CURRENT_ USER\Control Panel\Desktop, and find the DWORD value PaintDesktopVersion. Change the value to 1. Exit the Registry and reboot. To remove the version and build number, change the value back to 0. In beta versions of XP, the value was turned on by default, but when the product shipped, it was turned off.

- Hide Desktop icons that apparently can't be deleted from the Desktop, such as the Internet Explorer, Microsoft Outlook, My Computer, My Documents, My Network Places, and the Recycle Bin. To do this, go to the Desktop section and uncheck the boxes next to the icon you want to vanish. You won't have to log off for the changes to take effect. (You can force the Registry to do the same thing: see "Remove "Unremovable" Desktop Icons" **[Hack #13]**.)

- In the Explorer section, customize the Taskbar and Desktop by enabling or disabling balloon tips and determining which programs will be allowed to show up on the Frequently Used Programs list, among other customizations.

- Customize how Windows Explorer looks and functions by controlling the quality of image thumbnails; changing the way that shortcuts look; determining whether to include Help, Recent Documents, and Logoff on the Start menu; and many similar options.

There's a lot more as well—to find it all, download it and try it all out.

Create a Speedy, Stripped-Down Interface with Tweak UI

While it may be fun to use TweakUI to fiddle with the UI, its real power becomes apparent when you use it to create your own customized XP interfaces. For example, you may be the type who is concerned about only one thing when you use your PC: pure functionality. You want to get your work done fast, and you don't want to be bothered by the extra frou-frous that XP throws in your way and that slow down your system. Here's how to create a speedy, stripped-down interface using TweakUI:

Turn off animations, fades, and similar features

Animations and fades are pretty, but they require system resources and slow down your system. You can turn off a wide variety of these animations and fades from the General section of TweakUI. Uncheck the boxes next to all of them, such as Enable menu animation, Enable menu selection fading, Enable tooltip animation, and the many others listed there.

Speed up right-click menu displays, hovers, and other mouse actions

If you want menus to appear with absolutely no delay when you right-click on an object or icon, go to the Mouse section and move the Menu speed slider all the way to the left. Test how fast the menus will display by right-clicking on the test icon. From this section, you can also increase your mouse sensitivity so that it responds more quickly to your clicks and drags. In the Mouse sensitivity section, decrease the numbers next to Double-Click and Drag, and see the results by double-clicking the test icon.

The Mouse section also lets you change the mouse's sensitivity to "hovering"—for example, displaying a tool tip when you hover your mouse over an icon. To speed up the hover display, highlight Hover underneath the Mouse section, then decrease the numbers next to Hover sensitivity and Hover time. Test out your settings using the test icon.

Decrease the image quality of thumbnails in Windows Explorer

Windows Explorer uses up RAM when it displays thumbnails, which can slow down your system, because the RAM could instead be used for your applications or the operating system itself. Use TweakUI to give thumbnails the minimum amount of RAM only. Go to the Explorer\Thumbnails section and in the Image Quality area, move the slider all the way to the left, to the lowest setting for image quality. Decrease the thumbnail size, in pixels.

You can also completely turn off thumbnails so that they aren't displayed in Windows Explorer. From Windows Explorer, choose View → Details, or choose View → List.

Delete unnecessary desktop icons

Desktop icons take up RAM, and clutter your interface, so you want as few of them as possible on your desktop if you want a stripped-down version of XP. You can delete most desktop icons, but some of them such as Outlook and Internet Explorer apparently can't be deleted. However, TweakUI lets you delete them. Go to the Desktop section and uncheck the boxes next to the icons that you want off the Desktop, as shown in Figure 2-3. (You can force the Registry to do the same thing—see "Remove "Unremovable" Desktop Icons" [Hack #13].)

Hide Control Panel applets

The Control Panel is filled with applets that you will rarely, if ever, use, and they clutter up the interface, making it more difficult to find the applets you do want to use. To hide applets, go to the Control Panel section and uncheck the boxes next to the applets that you want to hide. (You can force the Registry to do the same thing—see "Control the Control Panel" [Hack #9]. That hack also shows you how you can run the applets, even after you've removed their icons.)

Clean up the right-click "New" menu

When you right-click on the desktop and choose New, you can automatically create a new document by choosing from a submenu. That submenu may offer many choices of which document types to create, depending on the applications you have installed on your PC, and how those applications handle their installation process. In many instances, those choices may be little more than clutter, because you may rarely need to create new documents of certain types. Strip down that submenu to the essentials, so that it has only those document types that you frequently create. Choose Templates, and uncheck the boxes next to the document types you rarely create. For example, most people rarely use the Briefcase [Hack #30], but that is one of your choices, so remove that unless you regularly move files using it. (For a hack on how to add power to the right-click context menu in Explorer, see "A Power User's Hidden Weapon: Improve the Context Menu" [Hack #29].

Enable autologon

If you're the primary person who uses your PC, you can enable autologon so that you're logged in automatically when the system starts and don't have to log on manually each time. Choose Autologon from the Logon section, check the box next to "Log on automatically at system startup," and make sure that your username, domain, and password are correct.

Control the Control Panel

Whether you're a fan of the new Control Panel or not, there's a lot you can do to make it more palatable—like hiding applets you never use, re-categorizing the ones you do use, and displaying all applets in a simple-to-use cascading menu.

When I first started using XP, one of the things that annoyed me most was its new Control Panel. Yes, the big new icons for running applets are certainly pretty, but the Control Panel's several-layer organization forces you to click far too many times in order to get to the applet that you want. And its clutter of applets that I rarely if ever use make it even more difficult and confusing.

My first reaction was to click on the Switch to Classic View button, to do away with the new design, but the Classic View has its problems as well: its long, alphabetized list of thumbnails is just as difficult to navigate as the new Control Panel.

The solution? Start by cleaning up the Control Panel, hiding applets that you rarely if ever use. Note that when you hide the applets, you can still use them; you just won't see their icons in the Control Panel.

In this hack, you'll not only find out ways that you can control the Control Panel—you'll also see how you can apply that knowledge to create different customized Control Panels.

Hide Unused Applets with the Registry

To hide unused applets using the Registry, run the Registry Editor [Hack #68] and go to HKEY_LOCAL_MACHINE\SOFTWARE\Microsoft\Windows\CurrentVersion\ Control Panel\don't load.

The key, as its name implies, determines which Control Panel applet icons are not loaded into the Control Panel. You'll still be able to run those applets from the command line after you hide them (as explained later in this hack); you just won't be able to see their icons in the Control Panel.

To hide an applet, create a new String value whose name is the filename of the applet that you want to hide. For example, to hide the Mouse Control dialog box, the String value would be *main.cpl*. See Table 2-1 for a list of Control Panel applets and their filenames.

Table 2-1. Control Panel applets and their filenames

Applet	Filename
System Properties	*sysdm.cpl*
Display Properties	*desk.cpl*
Network Connections	*ncpa.cpl*
Accessibility Options	*access.cpl*
Add or remove programs	*appwiz.cpl*
Add Hardware Wizard	*hdwwiz.cpl*
Internet Properties	*Inetcpl.cpl*
Region and Language Options	*intl.cpl*
Game Controllers	*joy.cpl*
Mouse Properties	*main.cpl*

Table 2-1. Control Panel applets and their filenames (continued)

Applet	Filename
Sound and Audio Devices	*mmsys.cpl*
User Accounts	*nusrmgr.cpl*
ODBC Data Source Administrator	*odbccp32.cpl*
Power Options Properties	*Powercfg.cpl*
Phone and Modem Options	*telephon.cpl*
Time and Date Properties	*timedate.cpl*
Speech Properties	*sapi.cpl*

Create separate String values for each applet you want to hide, then exit the Registry. The applets will vanish from the Control Panel. To make hidden applets appear again, delete its string value from this same registry key.

Hide Unused Applets with XP Pro's Group Policy Editor

If you have XP Professional, you don't need to get your hands dirty with the Registry to hide unused applets; you can instead use XP Professional's exceedingly useful Group Policy Editor to accomplish the same task. The Group Policy Editor is primarily used for setting network and multiuser policies and rights, but it can also be used to customize the way that XP looks and works. (For example, to use it to hack away at the Start Menu and Taskbar, see "Hack the Start Menu and Taskbar" [Hack #10].) Run the Group Policy Editor by typing gpedit.msc at the Run prompt or command line.

Once you've run it, go to User Configuration\Administrative Templates\ Control Panel, the section that handles the Control Panel. As you can see when you get there, you can do a lot more than hide the Control Panel's unused applets in this section of the Group Policy Editor; you can also control many other aspects of how the Control Panel looks and functions.

Now right-click on "Show only specified Control Panel applets," and choose Properties. You'll see the screen pictured in Figure 2-3.

Get ready for a bit of counterintuitive selecting. To disable Control Panel applets, you must choose the Enabled radio button, because you're enabling the feature to show only certain Control Panel applets. Strange, but true.

When you do this, you'll hide *all* applets in the Control Panel, which is a bit draconian. If you don't want to see any applets at all for some odd reason, you're now done; just click OK. But you'll most likely want to show some applets, so to add them, click the Show button. The Show Contents screen appears. Click Add, and you're ready to list all the Control Panel applets that you want to appear. For each item that you want to appear, type in its

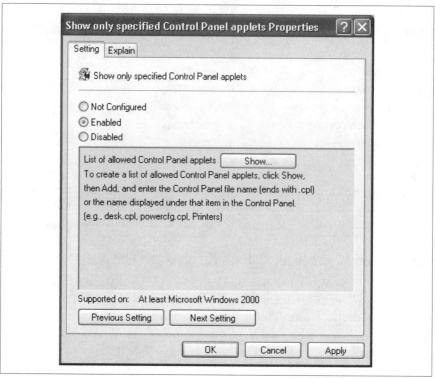

Figure 2-3. Disabling Control Panel applets in the Group Policy Editor

Control Panel filename, which you can find in Table 2-1. For example, if you want the Date and Time dialog box to appear, type in `timedate.cpl`.

You can also use TweakUI [Hack #8] to hide Control Panel applets.

When you've listed all the Control Panel applets that you want to appear, click OK and exit the Group Policy Editor. Only the applets that you've chosen to display will now appear in the Control Panel.

This technique is most useful when you're hiding most applets in the Control Panel and want to display only a few. There's another way to use the Group Policy Editor to hide applets, and it's better suited for when you want to hide only a few applets. In User Configuration\Administrative Templates\ Control Panel, double-click on "Hide specified Control Panel applets" and choose Enabled. After you click on Enabled, choose Show → Add and type in its Control Panel filename (which you can find in Table 2-1) for each applet that you want to hide. Click OK on each dialog box that appears. When you exit the Group Policy Editor, the specified applets will no longer appear in the Control Panel.

To customize other aspects of how the Control Panel works, follow the same instructions as outlined previously—right-clicking on the item you want to change, choosing Properties, and then picking your options.

How to Run Hidden Applets

Hiding applets cleans up the Control Panel, but leaves you with another problem—what to do if you need to run an applet whose icon you've hidden? It's simple to do. At the Run box or command line, type in the name of the applet you want to run—such as `Inetcpl.cpl` for the Internet Properties applets and press Enter. See Table 2-1 for a list of filenames.

Recategorize Control Panel Applets

Hiding applets goes only partway toward cleaning up the Control Panel. You can also recategorize applets and put them in any category you want. For example, by default, the Mouse Properties applet can be found in the Printers and Other Hardware category, but if you'd prefer that it instead be found in Accessibility Options, you can move it there.

To put any applet into any category you want, you need two pieces of information: the filename of the applet (for example, *main.cpl* for the Mouse Properties dialog box), and the Registry value for each Control Panel category (for example, 0x00000007 (7) for Accessibility Options.) For filenames of each applet, see Table 2-1. For the Registry value for each Control Panel category, see Table 2-2. With these two pieces of information in hand, you can recategorize any or all Control Panel applets.

Table 2-2. Control Panel categories and their Registry value data

Control panel category	Value data
Accessibility Options	0x00000007 (7)
Add or Remove Programs	0x00000008 (8)
Appearance and Themes	0x00000001 (1)
Date, Time, Language and Regional Options	0x00000006 (6)
Network and Internet Connections	0x00000003 (3)
Other Control Panel Options	0x00000000 (0)
Performance and Maintenance	0x00000005 (5)
Printers and Other Hardware	0x00000002 (2)
Sounds, Speech, and Audio Devices	0x00000004 (4)
User Accounts	0x00000009 (9)
No category	0xffffffff

To recategorize a Control Panel applet, run the Registry Editor [Hack #68] and go to HKEY_LOCAL_MACHINE\SOFTWARE\Microsoft\Windows\CurrentVersion\Control Panel\Extended Properties\{305CA226-D286-468e-B848-2B2E8E697B74}2. The key {305CA226-D286-468e-B848-2B2E8E697B74}2 is the container that holds all Control Panel categories. (Remember that it's safest to back up your Registry first [Hack #71].

Now find the Registry key of the applet that you want to recategorize. The filename of the applet will appear on the end of the key; for example, %SystemRoot%\system32\main.cpl is the Mouse Properties dialog box. Turn to trusty Table 2-1 for a list of other filenames for Control Panel applets.

Change the key's DWORD value to the value of the Control Panel category into which you want the applet to appear, as detailed in Table 2-2. For example, if you want the applet to appear in the Performance and Maintenance category, give it a value of 5. The value will then be displayed in the Registry as 0x00000005(5).

When you're done, exit the Registry. The applet will now appear in the new category.

Display Control Panel Applets in a Cascading Menu

If you're a "just the facts ma'am" type, then you'll want to bypass the Control Panel altogether. Rather than clicking on effete icons, you can instead force XP to display Control Panel applets in a cascading menu when you choose Control Panel from the Start button, as shown in Figure 2-4.

To force the Control Panel to display as a cascading menu, right-click on the Taskbar and choose Properties → Start Menu. Click the Customize button and choose the Advanced tab. In the Control Panel heading, choose "Display as a menu." Press OK twice.

Build Customized Control Panels

Armed with all this Control Panel hackery, you can build customized Control Panels. For example, you can build a Control Panel for computer newbies, which would hide the more technical applets and categories. Hide the applets in the Network and Internet Connections category, the Performance and Maintenance category, and the Sounds, Speech, and Audio Devices category—that way, newbies can't get into trouble by making changes that will affect the system in unexpected ways.

For system administrators, group all system-type applets into a single category, such as Network and Internet Connections. You'd probably want to keep all the existing applets there, but also add the Administrative Tools,

Figure 2-4. Turning the Control Panel into a cascading menu for quick access to applets

Scheduled Tasks, and System applets to it, as well as the Printers and Faxes applet. (If the administrator has to handle other hardware, such as scanners, add the Scanners and Cameras applet as well.)

For those who like to hack their systems and want instant, stripped-down access to customization tools, take all the applets that are now in Network and Internet Connections, and all those in Performance and Maintenance, and group them into the Appearance and Themes category. Then force the Control Panel to display as a cascading menu, and all of the hackery-type applets will be available instantly, because the Appearance and Themes category is at the top of the cascading menu and all the relevant applets will be available directly from it.

HACK #10 Hack the Start Menu and Taskbar

XP Professional's Group Policy Editor gives you instant access to changing more than three dozen interface settings. Here's how to use it to create your own personalized Start Menu and Taskbar.

XP Professional's Group Policy Editor does more than just customize the Control Panel [Hack #9]; it gives you control over many aspects of XP's interface as well—in particular, the Start Menu and Taskbar. In fact, it gives you quick access to over three dozen separate settings for them.

Run the Group Policy Editor by typing gpedit.msc at the Run prompt or command line. Go to User Configuration\Administrative Templates\Start Menu and Taskbar. As you can see in Figure 2-5, the right pane displays all the settings you can change. If you click on the Extended tab at the bottom of the screen, you'll be shown a description of the setting that you've highlighted, along with an explanation of each of the options. Settings you can customize include showing the My Pictures icon, the Run menu, and the My Music icon on the Start Menu; locking the Taskbar so that it can't be customized; and many others. To change a setting, double-click on it and choose the options from the menu it displays, as outlined in "Control the Control Panel" [Hack #9].

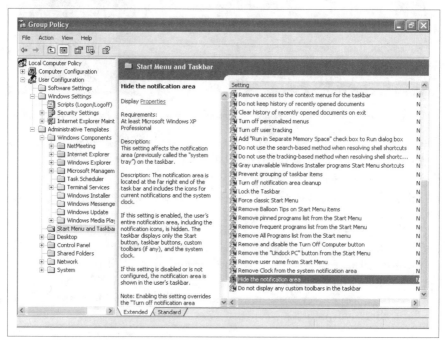

Figure 2-5. Customizing the Start Menu and Taskbar in the group policy editor

There's not room in this hack to go into detail about each of the settings you can change, so I'll tell you about some of my favorites. I've never been a big fan of My Documents, My Pictures, and My Music. In fact, I never use those folders, so there's no point having them on the Start Menu. The settings in the Group Policy Editor let you get rid of them.

If you share your PC with other people, the Group Policy Editor is a great way to make sure that no one can change the Start Menu and Taskbar except you. So when you have the Start Menu and Taskbar working the way you like, they'll stay that way until you want to change them. Enable "Prevent changes to Taskbar and Start Menu Settings," and no one will be able to change their settings except you. Select "Remove Drag-and-drop context menus on the Start Menu," and no one except you will be able to remove or reorder items on the Start Menu. You can even stop anyone else from shutting down Windows by selecting "Remove and prevent access to the Shut Down command." (Of course, they can still shut down your PC the old-fashioned way: using the power switch.)

Among the many entries here are a lot of pointless ones, by the way. You can remove the Log Off entry on the Start Menu, for example, which certainly isn't high on my list of must-haves. But who knows, you may want to do that or any of the many other changes the Group Policy Editor allows. Go in there yourself and muck around; you'll find plenty to change.

Hack the Taskbar with TweakUI

TweakUI [Hack #8] can be used to hack the Taskbar to a limited degree. Go to its Taskbar section, and you can disable or enable balloon tips, and enable or disable warnings when you're low on disk space. Underneath the Taskbar section, you'll find a Grouping subsection that controls how Taskbar "grouping" works. When you run too many programs with too many files open, all can't fit individually on the Taskbar. So, XP groups files from the same application with each other. For example, if you have four Word files open, it shows only a single icon for Word on the Taskbar, with the number 4 inside it. Click on the icon, and a list of all four files pops up. You can then choose which to open. TweakUI lets you control how that grouping works; you can decide whether to first group applications with the most windows, or instead first group applications that you use the least. You can also choose to group all applications with two or more windows open, three or more windows open, and so on.

Clean Up the Most Frequently Used Programs List

HACK
#11

Make this infrequently used tool useful. Ban programs from the Most Frequently Used Programs List, change the number of programs on the list, or do away with it altogether to make more room for the Pinned Programs List.

Windows keeps track of programs you use frequently and puts them on the Most Frequently Used Programs List, which appears on the new Windows

XP–style Start Menu (not the Classic-style Start Menu) between the Pinned Items List at the top and the All Programs link at the bottom. The Most Frequently Used Programs List is a quick way to access programs you use often. But the rules for when programs appear on that list and disappear from the list are murky at best, and there appears to be no logic to what programs appear there.

There is some hidden logic, however. XP bans a variety of programs from the list. If any of the following words or phrases are included in the program's shortcut name, the program will be excluded from the list: Documentation, Help, Install, More Info, Readme, Read me, Read First, Setup, Support, What's New.

Additionally, the following executables are excluded from the list: *Setup.exe*, *Install.exe*, *Isuninst.exe*, *Unwise.exe*, *Unwise32.exe*, *St5unst.exe*, *Rundll32.exe*, *Explorer.exe*, *Icwconn1.exe*, *Inoculan.exe*, *Mobsync.exe*, *Navwnt.exe*, *Realmon.exe*, and *Sndvol32.exe*.

Banning Programs from the List

There may be other programs you'd like to ban from the list, not just those that XP bans by default. Just because you use a program a time or two doesn't mean that you want it in on the Start Menu's Most Frequently Used Programs List. You can ban programs from the list using a Registry hack.

Run the Registry Editor [Hack #68] and go to HKEY_CLASSES_ROOT\Applications. Underneath this key, you'll find a series of subkeys, each of which represents an application. The primary purpose of these subkeys, as you'll see later in this hack, is to determine whether the program appears on the Open With dialog box that appears whenever you try to open an unknown file type. But you can also add a value to any of the subkeys which will ban programs from appearing on the Most Frequently Used Programs List.

Look for a subkey that is the executable name of the application that you want to ban from the list—for example, visio.exe for the Visio business illustration program. Once you find the application's subkey, create a new String value for that subkey, named NoStartPage. Leave the value blank. Exit the Registry. You may have to reboot in order for the setting to take effect and the program to be banned from the list.

Another use for HKEY_CLASSES_ROOT\Applications. While you're rooting around in HKEY_CLASSES_ROOT\Applications, you may want to hack the Open With dialog box (shown in Figure 2-6) that appears whenever you try to open an unknown file type. Each application's subkey in HKEY_CLASSES_ROOT\

`Applications` controls whether that particular application will show up on the dialog box.

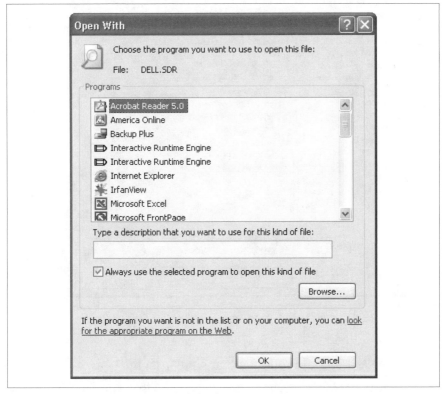

Figure 2-6. Hacking the Open With dialog box

If you want to ban a particular program from the Open With dialog box, look for the application's subkey underneath `HKEY_CLASSES_ROOT\ Applications`, add a `String` value named `NoOpenWith`, and leave the value blank.

Ban programs from the Most Frequently Used Programs List with TweakUI. If you don't want to muck around in the Registry, you can ban programs from the Most Frequently Used Programs list using TweakUI. (To learn how to download, use and run TweakUI **[Hack #8]**. Run TweakUI, and choose Task-bar → XP Start Menu. You'll see the screen shown in Figure 2-7, with a list of programs and checks next to most or all of them.

Each program with a check next to it will be allowed to appear on the Most Frequently Used Programs List. To stop a program from appearing on the list, uncheck the box and click OK.

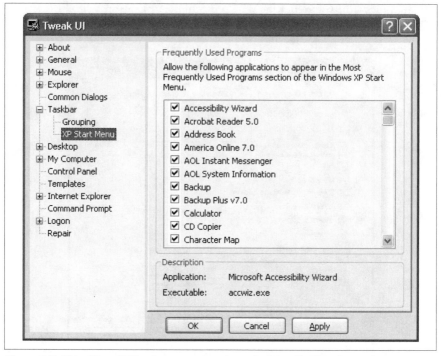

Figure 2-7. Using TweakUI to ban programs from the Most Frequently Used Programs List

Change the Number of Programs that Appear on the List

By default, the Most Frequently Used Programs List has room for six programs, but you can change that default and have more or fewer programs appear. Right-click on the Start button and choose Properties → Customize → General. The Customize Start Menu dialog box, shown in Figure 2-8, appears. To customize the number of programs to include on the list, edit the "Number of programs on Start menu" box. You can choose any number between 0 and 30. Be aware, though, that depending on your screen resolution and whether you're using large or small icons, the entire list might not appear if you choose a large number. No matter how high your resolution is, for example, don't expect there to be room for 30 programs.

Make Room for the Pinned Programs List

The Pinned Programs List, just above the Most Frequently Used Programs List on the XP-style Start Menu, gives you instant access to any program you want. You, rather than the operating system, decide what programs go there. To add a program to it, drag the program's icon or filename to the

Figure 2-8. Customizing the number of programs on the Most Frequently Used Programs List

Start Menu, and when the menu pops up, drag it to the spot on the list where you want it to appear.

This list makes a lot more sense than the Most Frequently Used Programs list: after all, you know better than XP what programs you want within easy reach. So, do what I do: kill the Most Frequently Used Programs List as a way to make more room for the Pinned Programs List. When you kill the Most Frequently Used Programs List, there will be a big blank space between the Pinned Programs List and the All Programs button. Drag programs to fill that space; the shortcuts will stay there until you delete them.

You can kill the Most Frequently Used Programs List with a Registry hack. Run the Registry Editor [Hack #68] and go to HKEY_CURRENT_USER\Software\ Microsoft\Windows\CurrentVersion\Policies\Explorer. Create a new DWORD called NoStartMenuMFUprogramsList and give it a value of 1. You'll have to reboot or log off and back on for the setting to take effect. When it does, the nice big blank space will be left for you to fill with pinned programs.

Rename and Change "Unchangeable" Desktop Icons and System Objects

To create the perfect XP interface, you want to be able to give every desktop icon and system object the name and icon of your choice. Here's how to do it—even to objects that appear to be unchangeable.

Interface hackers (myself included) are a details-oriented bunch. We want to be able to control every part of the interface so that it reflects our personality. That means being able to choose our own icons for desktop items and system objects, give new names to system objects, and create our own balloon tips—for example, adding a balloon tip to the Recycle Bin saying "Take Out the Trash!"

But it's not as simple as you might think. Microsoft has a way of protecting its own. For example, it won't let you change the text and balloon tips associated with a variety of system objects, such as the Recycle Bin, Outlook, Internet Explorer, My Computer, and My Network Places.

You can normally change both the name and the balloon text (text that appears when you hover your mouse over the icon) of all the icons on your desktop, but you can't change these. Normally, to change the name and balloon text of an icon, you first right-click on the icon and choose Properties. To change the name of the icon, you choose the General tab and, in the box at the top, type in the name that you want to appear beneath the icon.

Then, to change the balloon text, you click on the Shortcut tab and in the Comment box type in the text that you want to appear. When you're ready to make the change, click OK. The icon name and balloon text should now be changed.

But when you try to do this for system objects such as Outlook, Internet Explorer, My Computer, and Network Neighborhood, it won't work. The proper options don't appear when you right-click on them and choose Properties.

There are ways, however, to change them in any way that you want, so that you can create your own personalized XP interface.

The Registry to the Rescue

The Registry is your best tool for personalizing XP. It will let you change both the text and balloon tip associated with system objects. First, you need to know the object's class ID (CLSID), which uniquely identifies each system object. Table 2-3 lists the CLSIDs for common desktop objects.

Table 2-3. CLSIDs for desktop objects

Desktop object	CLSID
My Computer	{20D04FE0-3AEA-1069-A2D8-08002B30309D}
Recycle Bin	{645FF040-5081-101B-9F08-00AA002F954E}
Microsoft Outlook	{00020D75-0000-0000-C000-000000000046}
Internet Explorer	{FBF23B42-E3F0-101B-8488-00AA003E56F8}
The Internet	{3DC7A020-0ACD-11CF-A9BB-00AA004AE837}
My Network Places	{208D2C60-3AEA-1069-A2D7-08002B30309D}
Briefcase	{85BBD920-42A0-1069-A2E4-08002B30309D}
Dial-Up Networking	{992CFFA0-F557-101A-88EC-00DD010CCC48}

Armed with the proper CLSID, it's easy to change the name and balloon text of system objects. First, use Table 2-3 to find the CLSID for the object whose name or balloon text you want to change. Then run the Registry Editor [Hack #68] and go to HKEY_CLASSES_ROOT\CLSID, a key that lets you change characteristics of system objects, and highlight the CLSID whose name or balloon text you want to change. For example, for My Computer, highlight the subkey HKEY_CLASSES_ROOT\CLSID\{20D04FE0-3AEA-1069-A2D8-08002B30309D}. Keep in mind that HKEY_CLASSES_ROOT\CLSID has many CLSIDs listed under it, so it might take you a while to find the proper subkey.

Once you find the right subkey, if you want to edit the name of the object, open the Default value and type in the text that you want to appear underneath the object. If you want to edit the balloon text for the object, open the InfoTip value and type in the text that you want to appear as balloon text. Once you're done, exit the Registry and reboot.

You may also be able to force the changes to take effect without rebooting. After you exit the Registry, go to your Desktop and press F5 to refresh the screen. The new names and balloon tips might now appear.

Change the Desktop Icons of System Objects

You can hack objects besides names and balloon with this method. You can also change the desktop icons of system objects that appear to have unchangeable icons.

First, using Table 2-3, find the CLSID for the object whose icon you want to change. Then run the Registry Editor, go to HKEY_CLASSES_ROOT\CLSID, and look for the CLSID subkey from Table 2-3 for the object whose icon you want to change. Open the subkey and then the DefaultIcon subkey under that. For example, to change the icon for My Computer, open the subkey HKEY_CLASSES_ROOT\CLSID\{20D04FE0-3AEA-1069-A2D8-08002B30309D}\DefaultIcon.

Change the Default value to the path of the icon that you want displayed. Exit the Registry. You may have to reboot in order for the new settings to take effect.

> Some people aren't able to change their icons using this method. Instead of editing HKEY_CLASSES_ROOT\CLSID, they have to edit HKEY_CURRENT_USER\Software\Microsoft\Windows\ CurrentVersion\Explorer\CLSID\, and that does the trick.

Remove "Unremovable" Desktop Icons
#13
To create your own customized XP interface, you need to be able to remove certain desktop icons. A Registry hack lets you remove any you want, including those apparently protected by XP.

Creating the perfect, customized XP interface doesn't only mean changing icons; it also means removing them. For example, many power users look down their nose at America Online, and yet, on many systems, that icon can't be removed easily.

America Online isn't the only icon protected this way; many others are as well. Which desktop icons are protected on your system will depend on your exact version of XP (for example, SP-1) and the manufacturer of your PC. The Recycle Bin is protected on all versions, but the America Online icon is protected on some systems, and not on others.

To customize XP to your liking, you'll want to be able to delete these protected icons. To do so, you'll need a Registry hack. Run the Registry Editor [Hack #68] and go to HKEY_LOCAL_MACHINE\SOFTWARE\Microsoft\Windows\ CurrentVersion\Explorer\Desktop\NameSpace. Here's where you'll find various special desktop icons. They're not listed by name, but instead by CLSID—for example, {645FF040-5081-101B-9F08-00AA002F954E} for the Recycle Bin. Table 2-3 in "Rename and Change "Unchangeable" Desktop Icons and System Objects" [Hack #12] lists CLSIDs of common desktop objects, so use it to find the CLSID of the icon you want to delete.

To remove an icon from the desktop, simply delete the key of the icon—for example, {645FF040-5081-101B-9F08-00AA002F954E} for the Recycle Bin. Then exit the Registry, go to your Desktop, and press F5 to refresh the screen. The Recycle Bin icon should now be gone.

> On some systems, the icons may not be deleted immediately. Instead, after making the Registry change, you might have to right-click on the icon and choose Delete.

Some CLSIDs in HKEY_LOCAL_MACHINE\SOFTWARE\Microsoft\Windows\ CurrentVersion\Explorer\Desktop\NameSpace can be deleted from the desktop without having to go through this procedure, but when you try to delete them they may give you a special warning message. For example, when you try to delete Microsoft Outlook from the Desktop, you get the warning message "The Outlook Desktop icon provides special functionality and we recommend that you do not remove it." If you'd like, you can edit that message to display whatever you want. In the CLSID's subkey—for example, {00020D75-0000-0000-C000-000000000046} for Microsoft Outlook—you'll find the value Removal Message. Edit this value to whatever text you want, and your warning message will appear whenever someone tries to delete the icon.

Keep in mind that when you remove desktop icons you're removing only icons, not the underlying feature or program. So, the Recycle Bin still works even if you remove its icon. To open the Recycle Bin, go to C:\RECYCLER and open the folder inside it. To restore an item that's been deleted, right-click on it and choose Properties → Restore. Delete items as you would any other item.

> Some manufacturers make America Online an unremovable desktop icon. If that's the case with your PC and you want to remove it, delete the CLSID {955B7B84-5308-419c-8ED8-0B9CA3C56985}. America Online will still work, but its icon will no longer be on the desktop.

HACK #14
Create Your Own XP Themes and Find Thousands Online

Customize the way XP looks and sounds, and dress it up with themes from the best sites on the Internet.

Themes control just about every part of the way XP looks and sounds, including its background wallpaper, colors, icons, cursors, sounds, fonts, screen saver, and the visual style of its windows and buttons. By default, your computer uses the basic Windows XP theme, which some people refer to as *Luna* because it was called that during XP's development. You can apply countless themes to XP, though it only ships with two: the basic Windows XP theme and the Windows Classic theme—a more stolid-looking theme, based on older versions of Windows, that uses rectangular windows and solid colors.

To change between themes, right-click on the desktop and choose Properties → Themes. Choose the theme you want to use from the drop-down list, as shown in Figure 2-9. Click on OK, and the theme will be applied.

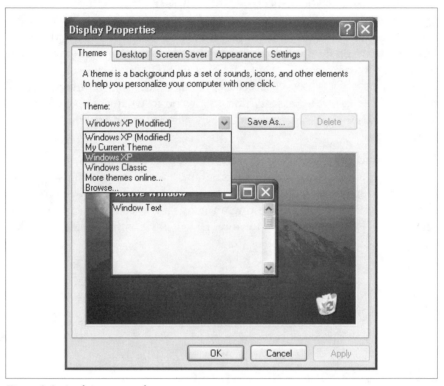

Figure 2-9. Applying a new theme

Note that if you choose "More themes online..." from the drop-down list, you won't actually be able to get more themes online, so choosing that option is a bit of a bait-and-switch. When you choose it, you'll be sent to a web page suggesting that you buy Microsoft Plus! for Windows XP. There's no need to buy it if you're looking to use more themes, though. Instead, you can make your own and get thousands more online from non-Microsoft sites.

Roll Your Own Themes

If you're like me (and most other people), you won't be happy with the basic themes that come with XP. What good is an operating system, after all, if you can't bend it, twist it, and make it your own?

There's no single, central place you can go to make themes in XP. Instead, you'll have to customize each part of XP individually and then roll it all up into a single theme. Once your system is using all the elements of your theme, save the theme with the following instructions.

Start off by right-clicking on the desktop, choosing Properties, and then customizing your desktop using the following tabs:

Desktop

Lets you customize the desktop background and color, as well as which system icons should appear on your desktop.

Screen Saver

Lets you choose a screen saver and control its functions and features. It also adjusts power controls for your monitor.

Appearance

Lets you customize the colors, style, and font size for windows, toolbars and buttons. It also controls effects, such as whether to use fade effects, whether to show shadows under menus, how to smooth the edges of screen fonts, and similar effects.

Settings

Lets you choose your screen resolution, color quality, and to choose advanced features such as the screen refresh rate.

Next, customize your mouse pointers by typing `main.cpl` in the Start → Run box and pressing Enter. The Mouse Properties dialog box will appear, allowing you to choose a preset pointer scheme or select individual pointers you want as part of your theme.

To choose system sounds for your theme, type `mmsys.cpl` from the Run box and press Enter. The Sounds and Audio Devices properties dialog box will appear. Click on the Sounds tab and choose a preset sounds scheme or select individual sounds for different system and program events.

When you're finished customizing, go back to the Themes tab of the Display Properties dialog box, choose Save As, and save the theme to either *My Documents* or to *C:\Windows\Resources\Themes*. You can now use the theme as you can any other.

Get XP Themes Online

This has been a rather roundabout way of creating your own themes. And face it, few of us (including myself) are visual artists or sound artists. So, even better than rolling your own themes is going online and choosing from thousands you can download for free from many Internet sites. Some people make themes and post them as a hobby, many companies create themes as a way to market products, and movies and TV shows frequently create themes as a way to get free publicity.

Or course, there are many themes you can find online that may violate copyright laws; people create themes using characters, sounds, and people from popular entertainment and then post them online for others to use. The entertainment companies' lawyers will tell you the themes are illegal; on the other hand, others say that the themes fall under the fair use provisions of the copyright laws. Who's right? I don't know, and at this point, I'm not even sure that the courts do. As to which themes you can download and use, let your conscience be your guide.

A few popular theme sites are *http://www.themeworld.com*, *http://www.topthemes.com*, and *http://www.themexp.org,* and the themes section of the download site *http://www.tucows.com.* In addition, many general software download sites include theme sections. Movie studios are good places to find themes, as are web sites created for movies.

Depending on the theme that you download, you may have to install it differently, so check with the site from which you download, or check within the download itself. As a general rule, though, to use a theme that you download, install it into the *C:\Windows\Resources\Themes* folder. Typically, a file with the extension *.theme* will be installed into that directory, and all the associated art, sound, icon, wallpaper, and cursor files will be installed into a subfolder of *C:\Windows\Resources\Themes.* Once you've installed the new theme, choose it as outlined previously in this hack.

These are a few of my favorite themes. My hard disk is too full of themes to list them all, but I'll give you some of my current and all-time favorites that I found online. I favor several Wallace & Gromit themes from the *http://www.topthemes.com* site. (If you haven't come across them before, Wallace & Gromit are hilariously understated claymation animations from the Oscar-winning animator Nick Park.)

I must say, though, that, being an opera fan, my favorite theme of all time is the one I found on *http://www.themeworld.com,* based on Verdi's opera *Don Carlo.* There's nothing like starting up your computer in the morning and being greeted by the sweeping sounds of one of the most dramatic operas of all time. I can almost see the Grand Inquisitor making his way onstage, preparing to burn an idolater or two at the stake. Figure 2-10 shows the wallpaper from the theme, which was chosen to match the mood of the opera. Other elements include the Startup sound taken from the orchestral prelude of the opera's last act, the Shutdown sound from the last seconds of the opera, and many other sounds and icons.

Figure 2-10. The wallpaper from the Don Carlo theme, based on the Verdi opera

See Also

- Style-XP, shareware from TFT Soft LLC at *http://www.tgtsoft.com* manages your themes, lets you automatically rotate them on a schedule, and lets you easily customize them, among other features.

 ## Give XP a Makeover with WindowBlinds

HACK #15

Control freaks, rejoice. With the powerful WindowBlinds utility, you no longer need to suffer with plain, common GUI elements such as the standard toolbars and scrollbars. You can modify and skin Windows to your heart's content.

In the years immediately following World War II, Bill Levitt realized that GIs needed homes. He planned and built a community outside New York City that he called Levittown. There were two models of home in Levittown and there was very little distinction between them. Levittown was the first "cookie cutter" community and remains the epitome of that term.

The Windows XP user interface is a "cookie cutter" experience. Frequently, users don't bother to replace the *Bliss* (green field and blue sky) background, and it's even more rare for someone to change the Windows XP standard menu or colors. Fortunately, you don't have to settle for the same desktop as the guy in the next office. One way you can customize your Windows XP experience is to use themes **[Hack #14]**. An even better way is to use a software package called WindowBlinds to "skin" (customize many aspects together) the user interface.

WindowBlinds is created by a company called Stardock and can be downloaded from their web site at *http://www.stardock.com*. It is sold by itself (for $19.95) or as part of a larger package called Object Desktop (for $49.95). There is also a free trial available from their web site.

> If you use a P2P client to download software, be warned that there is a common virus that spreads itself by pretending to be an installer for WindowBlinds. Make sure you've got the real thing. The virus is passed around only through Kazaa and other P2P apps. The smartest thing to do and the best way to avoid the virus is to pay for this software!

After you install WindowBlinds, you will not notice any immediate changes. Activate the software via Control Panel → Display Properties → Appearance tab.

WindowBlinds makes several changes to the Appearance settings, as shown in Figure 2-11. The Add button allows you to search for and add skins to the "Windows and buttons" popup and the Delete button removes skins from the popup. The small icon button to the right of the "Windows and buttons" drop-down box leads you the Skin Studio web site (discussed a little later in this hack).

Choose a skin from the "Windows and buttons" drop-down list. If a skin has more than one "subdesign," you can choose those from this dialog as well. A subdesign of a skin might be the same thing in different colors; a skin might look good in brown, green, and blue, so the author could include all three subdesigns in the package.

WindowBlinds includes a number of skins when the software is installed. One of the more interesting skins is called Colony. The Colony skin shows some of the abilities of WindowBlinds. Choose Colony from the popup and press the Apply button. Notice the textured areas around the window borders, the customized menu bars, and the smooth buttons on the taskbar. These are things that make WindowBlinds more useful than Windows XP themes and manually changing each aspect of the interface yourself.

Press the button labeled WindowBlinds when you have a skin selected for the WindowBlinds Advanced Configuration screen (shown in Figure 2-12).

Figure 2-11. Display settings with WindowBlinds installed

From this screen, you can modify almost any part of the user interface that WindowBlinds modifies.

By clicking on "Basic Settings," you can allow the skin to change the standard window buttons, the taskbar and toolbar buttons, as well as menu borders, progress bar controls, and the status bar—or any subset of these options (perhaps you want your own window buttons, for example). You can also allow the skin to change the background and have custom sounds. If, for some reason, you don't want to allow the skin to override any part of the user interface, you can change it from this screen. When you are satisfied with the changes you have made, click "Apply changes" on the left of the screen.

Some skins look nice on the desktop but might not look so hot when viewed in another program. For example, some skins do not handle fonts correctly, which might interfere with word processing. WindowBlinds includes the ability to change its behavior for individual programs by clicking on the "Per Application" item on the left side of the screen. From this screen, you can add programs to the list and modify their behavior individually.

Figure 2-12. WindowBlinds Advanced Configuration screen

Downloading Skins from the Internet

The most popular programs today allow users to customize Windows. Around this notion, users have created independent web sites to share their ideas and their creations. One such web site is WinCustomize, at *http://www.wincustomize.com*.

The WinCustomize web site is free. If you find a skin that you like, you need only click on the Download link to download it to your computer. However, if you want to access some of the advanced features, you must register with the web site. There is no cost to register, but there are different levels of access, depending on your level of participation or willingness to pay. There is an advantage to registering with the web site; you are given better search tools, which is useful, considering that there are over 2,000 custom skins available for download!

WinCustomize is associated with Stardock, the makers of WindowBlinds and Object Desktop, and therefore it has the most skins for their software. If you aren't finding what you want, you might look at some of these other web sites:

http://www.lotsofskins.com
http://www.skinbase.org
http://www.velocityart.com
http://www.deskmod.com
http://www.deviantart.com

Each of these sites sports different features, but they all provide skins for various programs. The DeviantArt web site is unique in that it is more interested in digital art as an art form rather than simply pushing skins out the door. Some of the artwork on the site may not be suitable for everyone, but if you are interested in the digital medium, then this would be a good site to investigate.

Creating Your Own WindowBlinds Skins

If you can't find a skin that suits your tastes, you can create your own skin for WindowBlinds. Not only can you create a skin from scratch, you can also modify existing skins as you wish using SkinStudio. SkinStudio can be downloaded from the Stardock web site for free, but you are reminded that you should register the software.

Creating a skin from scratch is not a simple project. As with most facets of our life, practice in the art of making skins makes perfect. There are many elements of the Windows user interface that can be modified, and you will need good tools and advanced skills to make your own skin look correct. Instead of jumping into this at the deep end, let's learn from those who have perfected the art, by modifying an existing skin.

One of my favorite WindowBlinds skins is called Liquid2, which emulates the Macintosh OS X user interface (I'm a closet Mac user). One of the aspects of Liquid that I do not like is that the start button has the word "Liquid" on it. I would prefer something a little more familiar, like the word "Start."

I used Photoshop to create the image in Figure 2-13. The Start button template consists of five separate subimages in the same file, each subimage being 57×23 pixels. The first subimage is the normal image, the next is when the button is pressed, followed by the disabled image, the focused image, and the default image. Once I am happy with the button, I need to save it somewhere I can access it. Since it is going to be part of the Liquid skin, I save the file as *C:\Program Files\Stardock\Object Desktop\WindowBlinds\ Liquid2\StartButtonNew.bmp*.

Figure 2-13. The replacement Start button with five subimages

Now that we have a suitable image, it's time to use SkinStudio to modify the skin. Bring up the skin browser (File → Edit). The skin browser looks different than the standard file browser. Click on the box next to WindowBlinds Skins, locate the skin named Liquid2, and press the Edit button.

Figure 2-14 shows the edit window for the Liquid2 skin. The box in the top left is for exploring the many different elements in the user interface. The box in the top middle is for previewing the skin. The box in the top right is for modifying individual attributes of the user interface. The box in the lower left gives you help and allows you to zoom in on portions of the screen. In the lower right is another editor for individual attributes.

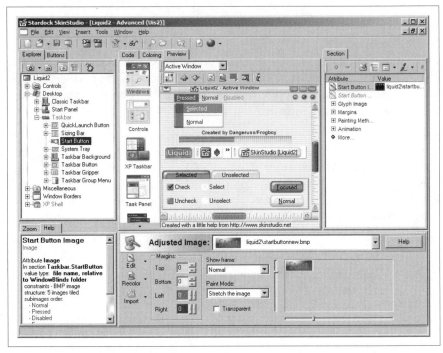

Figure 2-14. The SkinStudio editor

To replace the Start button, click on the box next to Desktop in the Explorer box, then click on Taskbar and finally Start Button, as shown in Figure 2-14. In the lower right, click on the popup next to the words Adjusted Image. Inside the list should be our new Start button named *StartButtonNew.bmp*. After you choose the new button, click the XP Taskbar button in the Preview area.

Once you are happy with the modified skin, press the Save button on the toolbar (the third button from the left). Saving a skin does not make it active. To make the skin active, press the Apply button on the toolbar (the seventh button from the left). The new Start button should now show up on the taskbar. If you press the button, the darker colored image should appear as long as the mouse button is pressed.

SkinStudio is a very complicated program with many settings that you can modify. The official documentation is rather limited, but there is an excellent tutorial that covers SkinStudio at *http://www.aleksyandr.com/tutorial.htm.*

—*Eric Cloninger*

Hacking Your Way Through the Interface

Use Registry hacks to make a grab-bag of great interface changes.

Hidden in the mazes of the Registry are countless ways to hack XP's interface. Here are some of my favorites.

Hide All Icons in the Notification Area

The System Tray, also called the Notification Area, is the small area on the far-right side of the Taskbar, in which utilities and programs that run in the background, such as antivirus software, show their icons.

I don't find it a particularly intelligent use of screen real estate, so I'd prefer not to see the icons there. To hide them, run the Registry Editor [Hack #68] and go to HKEY_CURRENT_USER/Software/Microsoft/Windows/CurrentVersion/ Policies/Explorer. Among other things, this key controls the display of objects throughout XP. Create a new DWORD called NoTrayItemsDisplay. Assign it a value of 1. (A value of 0 will keep the icons displayed.) Exit the Registry and reboot.

While you're at the HKEY_CURRENT_USER/Software/Microsoft/Windows/ CurrentVersion/Policies/Explorer key, you can also delete the My Recent Documents icon on the Start menu. Create a new DWORD called NoRecentDocsMenu. Assign it a value of 1. (A value of 0 will keep the icon displayed.) Exit the Registry and reboot.

Hide Only Certain Icons in the Notification Area

You might like to display some icons in the notification area but hide others. If so, you can hide icons on a case-by-case basis. You'll do it by delving through menus, though, not by hacking the Registry. Right-click on the Taskbar and choose Properties → Taskbar. The Taskbar and Start Menu Properties dialog box appears. This dialog box, as the name implies, lets you control how the Taskbar and Start Menu look and function.

In the Notification area of the dialog box, check the box next to "Hide inactive icons," then click Customize. The Customize Notifications dialog box appears, as shown in Figure 2-15.

Figure 2-15. Hiding inactive icons

Click on the program's listing in the Behavior column, and choose from the drop-down menu to hide the icon when the program is inactive, always hide it, or never hide it. Click OK twice. Your changes will take immediate effect.

Add Specific Folders to the Open Dialog Box

When you use certain Windows applications (such as Notepad) to open a file, on the left side of the Open dialog box are a group of icons and folders (such as My Documents, My Recent Documents, Desktop, My Computer, and My Network) to which you can navigate to open files.

Good idea, bad implementation. Do you really keep documents in My Computer? Unlikely, at best. It would be much more helpful if you could list only those folders that you use, and if you could choose to put *any* folder there, not just ones XP decides you need.

In fact, you can do it, with a Registry hack. It'll let you put just the folders of your choosing on the left side of the Open dialog box. Note that when you do this, it will affect XP applications such as Notepad and Paint that use the Open and Save common dialog boxes. However, it won't affect Microsoft Office applications and other applications that don't use the common dialog boxes.

If you want to change the dialog "frequently used" folders for Microsoft Word, try Woody Leonhard's Place Bar Customizer, one of many useful utilities from *http://www.wopr.com.*

Run the Registry Editor and go to HKEY_CURRENT_USER\Software\Microsoft\ Windows\CurrentVersion\Policies\comdlg32. This is the key that determines how common dialog boxes are handled. You're going to create a subkey that will create a customized location for the folders, and then give that subkey a series of values, each of which will define a folder location.

To start, create a new subkey underneath HKEY_CURRENT_USER\Software\ Microsoft\Windows\CurrentVersion\Policies\comdlg32 called Placesbar, and create a String value for it named Place0. Give Place0 a value of the topmost folder that you want to appear on the Open dialog box—e.g., C:\Projects.

Next, create another String value for Placesbar called Place1. Give it a value of the second folder that you want to appear on the Open dialog box. You can put up to five icons on the Open dialog box, so create new String values up to Place4 and give them values as outlined in the previous steps. When you're done, exit the Registry. You won't have to reboot for the changes to take effect. Figure 2-16 shows an example of an Open dialog box customized this way.

If you want no folders to appear in common open dialog boxes, you can do that as well. In HKEY_CURRENT_USER\Software\Microsoft\Windows\ CurrentVersion\Policies\comdlg32 create a new DWORD value called NoPlacesBar and give it a value of 1. Exit the Registry. If you want the folders back, either delete NoPlacesBar or give it a value of 0.

Turn Off System Beeps

To me, system beeps that my PC makes when it encounters certain system errors are like balloon tips—gnat-like annoyances that I can do without. So I turn them off using a Registry hack. Run the Registry Editor, go to HKEY_ CURRENT_USER\Control Panel\Sound, and find the Beep and ExtendedSounds String values. Set each value to No. Exit the Registry and reboot. The beeps will no longer sound.

Use Your Own Graphic for Your User Account

This one isn't a Registry hack, but I couldn't resist putting it in here since it's one of the more useful ways to customize the interface. The Windows XP graphic for your user account on the Start Menu may not be to your taste, and your choice of other graphics to display there isn't particularly

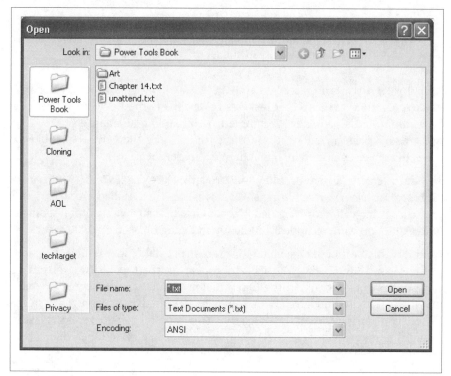

Figure 2-16. A customized Open dialog box

inspiring, either. After all, not everyone wants to be pictured as a rubber ducky, a snowflake, or a pair of horses.

But you're not limited to XP-supplied pictures for your user account: you can use any picture in *.gif*, *.jpg*, *.png*, or *.bmp* format. In this hack, I'll show you how to use your own picture.

To change your User Account picture to any one that you want, from Control Panel choose User Accounts, then pick the account you want to change and choose "Change my picture" → "Browse for more pictures." Navigate to the picture you want to use and click on OK. Figure 2-17 shows the screen you'll use to change your picture; it also shows the customized User Account picture I use during the winter holiday season.

If you have a digital camera or scanner attached to your PC, a button will show up on the screen shown in Figure 2-17 that lets you take a picture with the camera, or scan a picture with the scanner, and then immediately use that picture for your user account.

For those interested in saving keystrokes, there's a quicker way to get to the screen letting you customize your picture. From the Windows XP–style Start menu, click on your picture, and the screen appears.

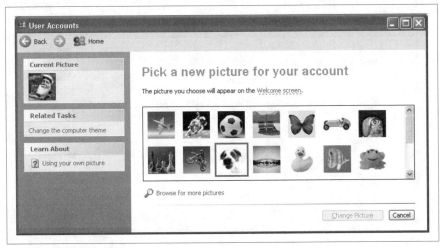

Figure 2-17. Changing your User Account picture

Remove "Uninstallable" XP Utilities

HACK #17

Think you can't uninstall Windows Messenger, WordPad and similar components? Think again. This hack shows you how.

Windows has always had a problem with uninstalling software, and it's particularly poor at uninstalling its own utilities, such as WordPad or Windows Messenger. Uninstalling these utilities can free up hard disk space if your hard disk is starting to fill up. And if you never use Windows Messenger, you most likely will want to uninstall it, because the program frequently launches itself automatically even after you've shut it down repeatedly, kind of like Dracula returning from the dead. It won't bother you any longer if you uninstall it.

To remove XP utilities and components, you normally choose Control Panel → Add or Remove Programs → Add/Remove Windows Components to get to the Windows Component Wizard, shown in Figure 2-18. To uninstall a utility or component, just follow the wizard's instructions.

Ah, but there's a catch. A number of Windows utilities and components—notably Windows Messenger and WordPad—don't show in the Windows Component Wizard, so there's no apparent way to uninstall them. But you can, in fact, remove these components. XP has a Setup Information file that controls what appears in the Windows Component Wizard. If you edit this file, you can force these components to appear in the Wizard, and you can then remove them as you would any others.

To start, use Notepad or another text editor to open the Setup Information file, *sysoc.inf*, which is generally found in the *C:\WINDOWS\INF* folder. For safety's sake, make a backup of the file before editing it, so you can revert to it

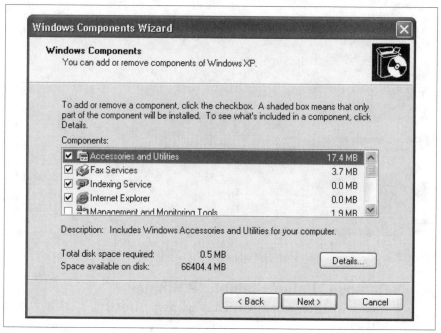

Figure 2-18. The Windows Component Wizard

if you need to. You should also set up a System Restore point before making the changes. To set up a System Restore point, choose Control Panel → Performance and Maintenance → System Restore and then follow the instructions.

C:\WINDOWS\INF is a hidden folder, so if you want to view its contents, you will have to enable hidden folders by going into Windows Explorer and choosing Tools → Folder Options → View and choosing Show Hidden Files and Folders.

When you open the file, look for the line describing the program you want to uninstall. Lines in the file have the format:

```
program=program.dll,OcEntry,program.inf,,numeral
```

Programs that are uninstallable all have the word hide (or HIDE) embedded in the string. When this word is included in the string, the program won't show up in the Windows Component Wizard. The Pinball game entry, which doesn't show up in the wizard, looks like this:

```
Pinball=ocgen.dll,OcEntry,pinball.inf,HIDE,7
```

To force it to show up in the wizard, remove the word hide from the entry that refers to the component that you want to remove. For example, if you want to remove Pinball, edit its entry to this:

```
Pinball=ocgen.dll,OcEntry,pinball.inf,,7
```

Save the *sysoc.inf* file, then run the Windows Component Wizard. The component will now show up in the wizard. Remove it as you would any other component.

Keep in mind that not all of the entries in *sysoc.inf* are as easy to understand as Pinball and WordPad. For example, if you want to remove Windows Messenger, look for the entry that starts with the text msmsgs. If you want to remove the Accessibility Wizard, look for the entry for AccessOpt. Table 2-4 lists the "uninstallable" programs their entries in the *sysoc.inf* file.

Table 2-4. "Uninstallable" programs and their sysoc.inf entries

Entry	What entry refers to
AccessOpt	Accessibility Wizard
MultiM	Multimedia components, including Media Player, Volume Control, and Sound Recorder
CommApps	Communications components, including Chat, Hyperterminal, and Phone Dialer
AutoUpdate	Windows Automatic Update
TerminalServer	Terminal Server
dtc	Distributed Transaction Coordinator
dom	COM+
WBEM	Windows Management Instrumentation
Pinball	Pinball game
MSWordPad	WordPad
msmsgs	Windows Messenger

You may run into a few gotchas when trying to remove "uninstallable" components. On some systems, you simply won't be able to remove Windows Messenger, because Windows Messenger won't show up on the Windows Component Wizard even after you edit the *sysoc.inf* file. And some components, such as Terminal Server, will show up in the wizard if you edit the *sysoc.inf* file, but the wizard still won't let you uninstall them.

Hide Components You Don't Want to Be Uninstalled

You can use this same technique in reverse to hide components you don't want to be uninstalled accidentally. Simply put the word HIDE in the proper place in the entry that you don't want to show up in the Windows Component Wizard. For example, if you want to hide the uninstall entry for the fax utility, edit its entry by changing:

```
Fax=fxsocm.dll,FaxOcmSetupProc,fxsocm.inf,,7
```

to:

```
Fax=fxsocm.dll,FaxOcmSetupProc,fxsocm.inf,HIDE,7
```

Create Transparent Windows

#18   Make any XP window transparent and control the amount of transparency for each.

One of the cooler new interface features of XP is the ability to use transparent or semitransparent windows, in which the background can show through the current window. But there's a problem with that feature: very few programs take advantage of transparency, and there is no way built into XP for you to make windows transparent. So, to a great extent, the feature is worthless.

However, a number of downloadable programs tap into that XP capability and let you make any window transparent. My favorite is Glass2K (*http://www.chime.tv/products/glass2k.shtml*), because it's small, it's simple, and above all, it's free. It doesn't muck around with your system by making Registry changes or installing .dlls. It's just run an executable file, and with it you can make any window transparent. When it's running, go to the window you want to make transparent, and press Ctrl-Shift and a number from 0 to 9. 9 makes the window the least transparent, 1 makes it the most transparent, and 0 sets it so that it's solid, with no transparency. You can also right-click on a window, and select the degree of transparency from the program's pop-up menu. The window will keep that degree of transparency as long as you run the program and keep the transparency setting. Figure 2-19 shows the results of making windows transparent with the program.

Trans-XP is another downloadable that lets you make windows transparent. It's shareware, and is free to try, but costs $14.95 if you decide to keep it. It's available from *http://www.totalidea.com*.

The downloadable version limits you to having only three transparent windows.

Another similar program is Actual Transparent Windows. It's also shareware and is free to try, but it costs $19.95 if you decide to keep it. It's available from *http://www.actualtools.com*.

If you're looking for an all-in-one tool that lets you make countless interface tweaks, including making any window transparent, try Tweak-XP, from *http://www.totalidea.com*. In addition to giving you transparency, it lets you hide programs on the Start Menu, and create your own folder icons. It also offers a variety of optimization tools, as well as utilities such as a pop-up ad blocker, a Registry cleaner, Zip file repairer and much more. It's shareware and free to try, but you're expected to pay $29.95 if you keep using it.

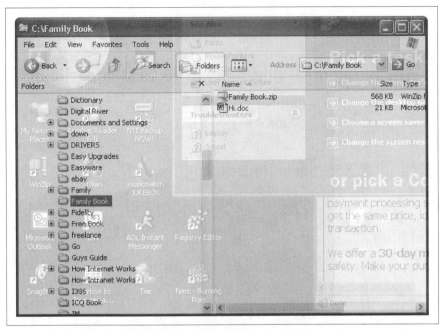

Figure 2-19. Making any windows transparent with Glass2K

There's one drawback to using transparent windows: it takes up processing power and RAM, so it may slow down your system. The fewer transparent windows you create, the less processing and RAM are used, so handle transparent windows with care.

Make Your Own Cursors and Icons

Don't settle for the icons and cursors that Microsoft built for you. Roll your own with downloadable software.

If you're not happy with the cursors and icons that XP ships with, don't despair. You can easily make your own with Microangelo, from *http:// www.microangelo.us*. It's shareware and free to try, but if you continue using it, you're supposed to pay $54.95. You can create animated icons or regular icons—in both the standard 32-pixel and large 48-pixel sizes—and a variety of cursors as well. Use paint-type tools and build your icons and cursors on a grid, as shown in Figure 2-20. A preview is available, so you can see the effects of what you do as you work.

What I find most useful about the program is that you can import existing cursors, icons, or other graphics, edit them, and then save the edited ver-

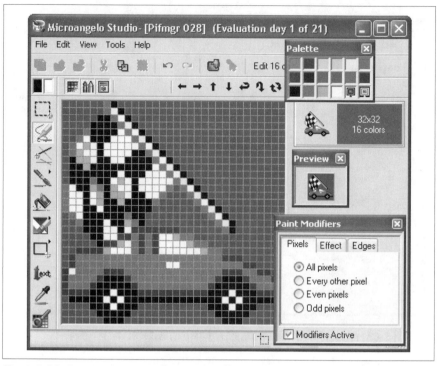

Figure 2-20. Creating an icon with Microangelo

sion. I'm no great artist, so I find editing existing graphics much easier than creating ones from scratch. The fine art of pixel placement in tiny icon images can be trickier than expected.

For a big selection of cursors, get CursorXP Free from *http://www. windowblinds.net*, the same company that makes the interface-customizing program WindowBlinds [Hack #15]. CursorXP Free is free, as the name implies. Install it, and a new CursorXP tab is added to the Mouse Properties dialog box, shown in Figure 2-21.

The Mouse Properties dialog box lets you choose from a variety of new cursors that ship with the program. By clicking on the Options/Configure button at the bottom of the dialog box you can also customize how each cursor works and looks. (The button toggles between Options and Configure, depending on whether you click on the Configure button at the top of the dialog box.) You can also import cursors that you've created with Microangelo or another program.

Figure 2-21. Customizing cursors with CursorXP Free

If you want a more powerful version of the program that includes special effects—the ability to colorize cursors, add trail effects, and more—you can try CursorXP Plus from the same site. The Plus version costs $10 to register.

If you want to create cursors from scratch, your best bet is Axialis AX-Cursors (*http://www.axialis.com*). It's shareware and free to try, but it costs $14 if you decide to keep using it. In addition to drawing tools, it lets you convert any existing graphic into a cursor. It also lets you do a screen capture and convert what you've captured to a cursor, and it includes an exceptionally wide range of cursor-editing tools. To give you a sense of its power, I'll create a cursor from scratch and make it larger than normal. If you have a parent with poor eyesight, you can make custom cursors that he can easily see.

Since I'm not artistically inclined, I'm not going to use the program's drawing tools. Instead, I'm going to search the Internet for a graphic that I'll start with, then have AX-Cursors automatically turn it into a cursor. Then I'll resize it to be very large.

A rocket is a good shape for a cursor, so I search for a drawing of one by doing a Google image search by going to *http://www.google.com*, clicking on images, and then searching for the word rocket. Rather than a photograph, I find a bold-looking drawing of a rocket, with a limited number of colors; that will make the best cursor. Figure 2-22 show the results of the search. I'm going to use the rocket in the lower-right portion of the screen as a starting point.

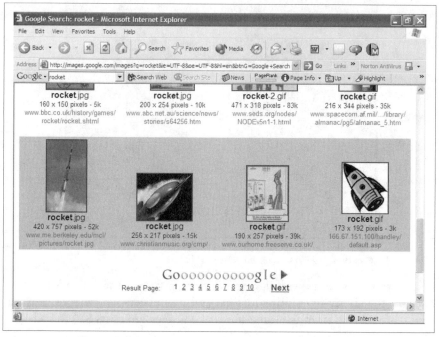

Figure 2-22. Finding a graphic using Google image search

I save the graphic to my hard disk by clicking on it to see the full-size graphic, then right-clicking on the large image, choosing Save As, and saving it to my disk. AX-Cursors can import graphics only in a handful of format: *.bmp*, *.jpg*, *.dib*, and *rle*. In this case, I have a *.gif* file. So, before importing it, I convert it to a *.jpg* file [Hack #86].

Now I run AX-Cursors. I want to create a large cursor, so I first set the cursor size by choosing Draw → New Image Format. I have the option of saving it as an icon of 32×32, 48×48, 64×64, or 72×72. I choose the largest size and the 256-color option.

Next I choose Draw → Import Bitmap, and choose the rocket image that I've just saved. The program lets me crop the image so that I can just import part of it, but in this instance I want the whole thing, so I don't crop it. I can also set the cursor's transparency. In this instance, because the cursor is going to be for someone with eyesight problems, I choose no transparency. After I'm done, the picture is converted into a cursor that I can edit, as shown in Figure 2-23. Notice that you're given tools to edit the cursor in the middle of the screen. In the right side of the screen, you can see a picture of the original graphic.

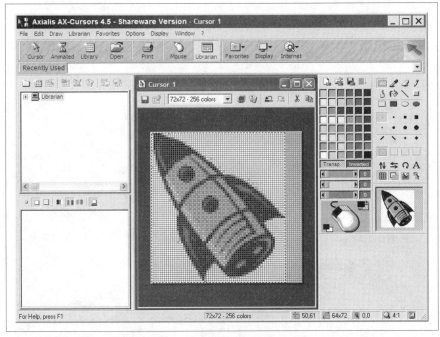

Figure 2-23. Converting the image into a cursor

The cursor looks good to me, so I save it by choosing File → Save. It's now ready to be used. So I exit the program, choose Control Panel → Printers and Other Hardware → Mouse → Pointers → Browse and choose the icon I've just created. It's done; you can see it in action in Figure 2-24.

Figure 2-24. The completed cursor in action

See Also

- For a collection of more than 7,000 free icons you can download and use, go to *http://www.iconarchive.com*. Also see *http://www.iconbazaar.com* for a collection of free icons.

- For a collection of free cursors to download and use, go to *http://www.1freecursors.com*. Note that some cursor and icon sites use a lot of pop-up ads. To get rid of them, see Stop Pop Ups, Spyware, and Web Bugs **[Hack #33]**.

Windows XP to Windows 2000: Retro is Cool
Don't like those cute XP graphics? Here's how to make Windows XP look more like Windows 2000.

Sometimes, no matter how much you tweak, you still don't like what you see. After sampling the hacks in this chapter, I decided that I didn't care for the cartoon-like graphical look of Windows XP (see Figure 2-25).

Figure 2-25. Windows XP desktop

Since XP is so customizable, it only took a few seconds to make my start menu and desktop look like the old standby Windows 2000.

First, let's change that cluttered XP start menu (see Figure 2-26) to a classic Start menu.

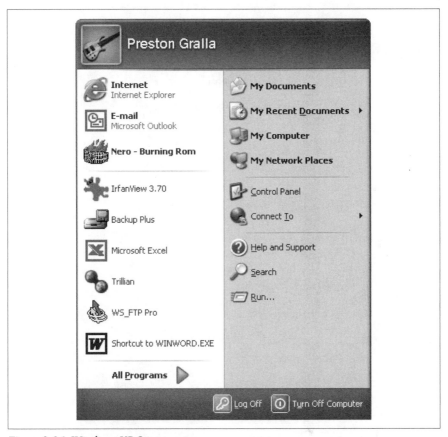

Figure 2-26. Windows XP Start menu

Right click anywhere on the taskbar at the bottom of the screen and select Properties from the popup menu. Go to the top of the window and select the Start Menu tab. Click the button for Classic Start menu. While you're in this tab you also have the option of customizing the Classic Start menu. Choose Customize to add or remove programs from your start menu, enable options such as drag and drop, or display Favorites. Hit OK and your start menu will now look like the one shown in Figure 2-27, just like Windows 2000.

Now that you've cleaned up the Start menu, it's time to change the look of your desktop. Though it's not a necessary step to making your desktop look like Windows 2000, your notification area (the lower right-hand corner near

Figure 2-27. The lean and mean Classic Start menu running on Windows XP

the clock) will be a lot neater if you go back to the Taskbar tab, and uncheck Hide inactive icons. Windows 2000 doesn't have the graphical features of XP, so hiding the icons before switching over is a good idea.

Right click anywhere on the desktop and choose Properties from the popup menu. Select the Themes tab and under Themes, scroll down to Windows Classic. Hit OK and your desktop will now look like the one shown in Figure 2-28.

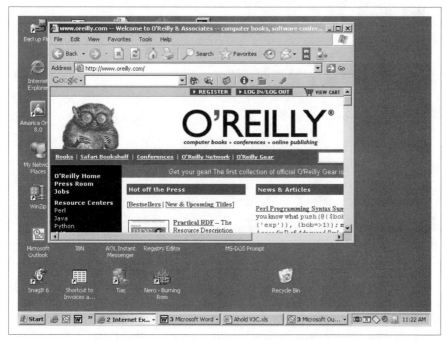

Figure 2-28. Back to the past: Windows Classic theme running on Windows XP

Your desktop now has the icons, the window setup, the Start menu, and the general look and feel of Windows 2000.

—Lorrie LeJeune

CHAPTER THREE

Windows Explorer
Hacks 21–32

You use Windows Explorer every day, probably many times a day, without giving it much thought. You open it, view some files, delete others, drag a few around to different folders, and then you're back on your way.

But there's a lot of ways that Explorer can make your life easier. For example, you can use it to hide files by encrypting them, give yourself more hard disk space by compressing files, and easily find the files you want by using the indexing service and its query language. And there are ways to hack Explorer to make it much easier to use—for example, by customizing its right-click context menu. In this chapter, I'll show you how to do all that and more.

HACK #21 Generating Folder and File Listings for Printing or Editing

Longtime PC users and former Mac users alike are often shocked when they realize that there's no easy, built-in option to print a list of files in a folder. This hack creates a context-menu right-click option to create such a list, which you can then edit, copy, paste, and—most usefully—print.

How many times have you been browsing through directories in Windows Explorer and wished you could generate a text file or printout listing the files and folders? It seems like such a simple request that it's amazing the option isn't available. You don't believe me? Right-click on a folder and see for yourself if there is an option to list or print the structure. There isn't, but there is a workaround that doesn't require any third-party software. Here's how to create a context menu item [Hack #29] that, when clicked, generates a printable (and editable) text-file listing of the selected directory.

To create the entry in the context menu it's necessary to first create a *batch file*. A batch file is a text file that contains a sequence of commands for a computer operating system and uses the *.bat* extension. The format for the *.bat* file is:

```
dir /a /-p /o:gen >filelisting.txt
```

The name of the *.txt* file can be whatever you like. In this example, I've used *filelisting.txt*, but it could just as easily be *filelist*, *listoffiles*, *namedfiles*, or even *Wally* if you enjoy the bizarre in your filenaming schemes. Once you've decided on the filename, create the file in Notepad, as shown in Figure 3-1.

Figure 3-1. Creating a batch file in Notepad

Save the file in your *WINDOWS* folder as shown in Figure 3-2, making sure to use the *.bat* extension and not the default *.txt* extension. It's important to set "Save as type" to All Files and "Encoding:" to ANSI.

Now that we have the *.bat* file created, the next step is to make it functional and easily accessible by integrating it into the context menu that opens when a right click is executed. Open Windows Explorer and choose Tools → Folder Options → File Types tab → Folder → Advanced → New, to open the New Action box shown in Figure 3-3.

In the Action box, type the name that you want to appear in the context menu. Once again, you have wide latitude in choices; something like Create File Listing will probably be most useful, but you can name yours something more confusing if you like. Browse to the location of the *.bat* file you created, and select it in the box labeled "Application used to perform action." Click OK, and you'll see that Create File Listing (or whatever you chose as an action name) has been added as one of the Actions in the Edit File Type window, as shown in Figure 3-4. Do the standard Windows dance of clicking OK again to close all the open windows.

That's it! Congratulations. You've created a new item on the context menu that's ready to go to work. So, now that's it there, what can you do with it?

Open up Windows Explorer. Navigate to whatever folder you want to use as the basis for the file list, and right-click to open the context menu. Click on

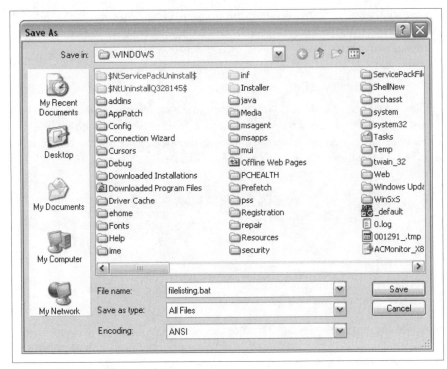

Figure 3-2. Saving file listing.bat

Figure 3-3. Creating a new action for the context menus

the Create File Listing item (see Figure 3-5), and the list will be generated and displayed at the bottom of the open Notepad window as *filelisting.txt*. Figure 3-6 shows the file listing generated from the Sample Music folder shown in Figure 3-5. Since it is a text file, it can be fully edited, copied, pasted, printed, and so on for any purpose.

Figure 3-4. The revised Edit File Type box with your new action

Figure 3-5. Your new context-menu action: Create File Listing

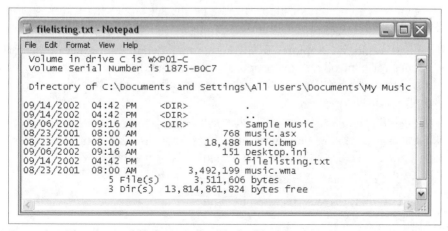

Figure 3-6. The generated file listing, all ready for editing and printing

If for any reason you want to remove the Create File Listing entry from the context menu, you must edit the Registry [**Hack #68**]. Navigate to HKEY_CLASSES_ROOT\Folder\shell\Create_File_Listing and delete the Create_File_Listing key in the left pane. Close regedit and reboot to complete removal.

Alternative Method for Users of Outlook XP

If you happen to be a user of Outlook XP, there is another method available for printing directory listings that requires no system modifications. Using the Outlook Bar, you can generate a nicely formatted listing with a few mouse clicks:

1. Open Microsoft Outlook.
2. Choose View → Outlook Bar → Other Shortcuts.
3. The three default selections listed are My Computer, My Documents, and Favorites. Select one and navigate the tree until the directory is displayed in the right pane.
4. When the display matches what you'd like to print, click the printer icon on the Outlook toolbar.

—Jim Foley

H A C K
#22   Control Windows Explorer with Command-Line Shortcuts

Create customized Explorer views from the command line, and save your favorite views in desktop shortcuts.

I rarely open Windows Explorer in its default view. Instead, I generally want to open it at a specific location, with a specific set of viewing features—for example, with the Folders bar in the left side on or off.

I launch Windows Explorer from the command line, along with a set of switches for controlling how it opens. I also create desktop shortcuts out of these command-line launches, so that my favorite views are always only a couple of clicks away.

For example, when I want to open Windows Explorer to the *C:\Power Tools Book\Hacks* subfolder only, with no folders above it, and using the Folders bar, I open the command prompt and issue this command:

```
explorer /e,/root,c:\Power Tools Book\Hacks
```

When I do that, the view pictured in Figure 3-7 appears.

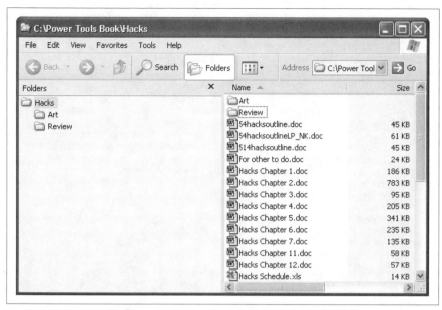

Figure 3-7. Opening Windows Explorer to a specific folder with a specific view

Compare that view with my default view that I get when I launch Windows Explorer the normal way (shown in Figure 3-8). Not only does the Explorer view in Figure 3-7 open to a specific subfolder, but it also shows no folders above it. In contrast, Figure 3-8 shows the entire structure of my hard disk and opens to *C:*. I use the view in Figure 3-7 when I want to work exclusively on a specific subfolder and want to get to it quickly.

This is just one of the many uses for launching Windows Explorer from the command line with switches; no doubt you'll be able to find other uses for it. You'll be able to use it not only on the command line and with desktop shortcuts, but also if you run scripts and batch programs.

The syntax for running Explorer from the command line with switches is:

```
explorer [/n] [/e] [,root,object] [[,/select],subobject]
```

You don't have to use switches; you can type `explorer` by itself, though doing that launches your default Explorer view.

Here is an explanation of how to use the switches and syntax:

/n

Opens Windows Explorer without displaying the Folders bar, the tree structure of the hard drive. Instead, it launches the view shown in Figure 3-9.

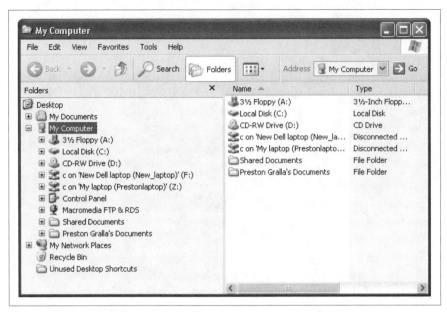

Figure 3-8. My default for launching Windows Explorer

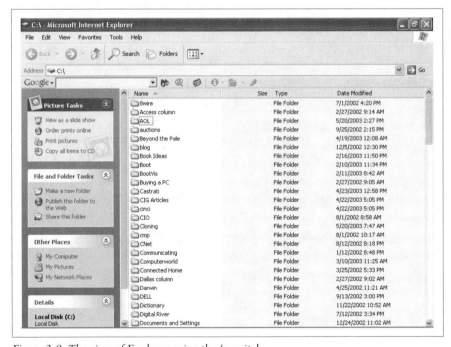

Figure 3-9. The view of Explorer using the /n switch

/e
> Opens Windows Explorer displaying the Folders bar.

/root,*object*
> Opens Windows Explorer to a specific object, such as a folder, without displaying the folders above it, as shown in Figure 3-7. You can also use Global Unique Identifiers with this switch, as explained later in this hack.

[[/select],*subobject*]
> Opens Windows Explorer to a specific file or folder that is then highlighted or expanded. You can use the subobject switch only without the /select parameter. When you include the /select parameter, the branches are not expanded, the folder is highlighted, and the subobject is highlighted in the right pane.

Create Desktop Shortcuts for Explorer

Typing command-line shortcuts can quickly give you a case of carpal tunnel syndrome, so a better idea is to run them as desktop shortcuts. Right-click on the desktop, choose New → Shortcut, and in the location box type the Explorer command-line syntax you want to use. Click Next and give the shortcut a descriptive name—for example, "Hacks folder"—and click OK.

Using Global Unique Identifiers (GUIDs) with Command-Line Switches

You might want to open Explorer to certain system folders—for example, to My Network Places. To do so, run explorer from the command line and follow it by a space, two colons, and the Global Unique Identifiers (GUIDs) that identify specific system folders, like this:

```
explorer ::{208D2C60-3AEA-1069-A2D7-08002B30309D}
```

That command opens Windows Explorer to My Network Places.

If you're using switches, similarly put a space and two colons in front of the GUID, like this:

```
explorer /e, ::{208D2C60-3AEA-1069-A2D7-08002B30309D}
```

You can use GUIDs in desktop shortcuts, batch files, and scripts, as well as at the command line. Table 3-1 lists the GUIDs for various system folders.

Table 3-1. GUIDs for system folders

Folder name	GUID
My Computer	{20D04FE0-3AEA-1069-A2D8-08002B30309D}
My Network Places	{208D2C60-3AEA-1069-A2D7-08002B30309D}
Network Connections	{7007ACC7-3202-11D1-AAD2-00805FC1270E}

Table 3-1. GUIDs for system folders (continued)

Folder name	GUID
Printers and Faxes	{2227A280-3AEA-1069-A2DE-08002B30309D}
Recycle Bin	{645FF040-5081-101B-9F08-00AA002F954E}
Scheduled Tasks	{D6277990-4C6A-11CF-8D87-00AA0060F5BF}

Empower Windows Explorer with PowerDesk

Supplanted by this most powerful utility, Windows Explorer will no longer draw curses or contribute to increased Macintosh sales.

I'm guessing that you have a Leatherman multitool. No hacker worth his weight in solder would leave home without it. In fact, I'll go further and guess that you have at least two. You probably have a large one that you keep in your glove box and a small one that you carry with you at all times, even to weddings (just in case). If I'm correct—or if you're wondering where to buy such a useful tool—then you will love PowerDesk.

PowerDesk is the multitool of utilities. This beast is no mere Swiss Army Knife. There's no unnecessary toothpick, leather punch, or nail file here; it's a pair of vise grips with four screwdrivers, a strong blade, wire cutters, pliers, an Allen wrench, a corkscrew, and a bottle opener. It's the software that those guys on *Junkyard Wars* would use if they put down their cutting torch and picked up a computer.

OK, maybe I'm being melodramatic, but PowerDesk really is a useful utility for your computer. PowerDesk combines much of the functionality of Windows Explorer, the old Windows File Manager, WinZip, and a host of other programs. If you find yourself with more than one program open for manipulating files, you probably need PowerDesk. While many of the features of PowerDesk are available in Windows XP, PowerDesk puts them all in one convenient location. PowerDesk also runs on older versions of Windows, which may not have the advanced file-handling features that Windows XP has.

PowerDesk is available from VCOM at *http://www.v-com.com/product/pd_ind.html*. PowerDesk Pro sells on the VCOM web site for $39.95. You can also download an evaluation version that has fewer features.

When you install PowerDesk on your computer, the installer will ask you if you want to associate ZIP and other archive files with PowerDesk. If you already use a ZIP file manager, such as WinZip, you might not want to allow PowerDesk to handle these types by default. After installing PowerDesk, you should not need to restart your computer.

While PowerDesk is a separate application, it is integrated into Windows Explorer, so you have access to many of its features even when you aren't running it. In Windows Explorer, if you right-click with the mouse you will see a submenu called PowerDesk, where you have access to many of Power-Desk's functions.

When you start PowerDesk, you will be faced with a window that looks similar to the one shown in Figure 3-10. As you click around PowerDesk, most of the things you see should look familiar. Those that aren't so familiar are grouped well, so they are easy to find and understand.

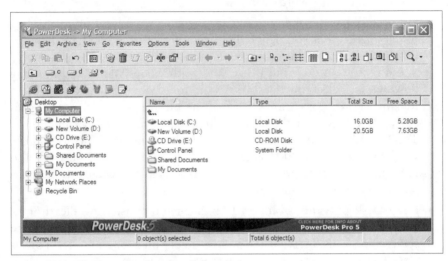

Figure 3-10. The PowerDesk main window

Each of the toolbars that shows up in PowerDesk is configurable. Use the Options → Customize Toolbar menu item to modify the toolbars as you wish. The bottom toolbar in Figure 3-10 is called the Launchbar and is similar to the Quick Launch area of the Windows XP Taskbar. You add programs by dragging icons onto the Launchbar and dropping them.

When you restart PowerDesk, you are placed back at the location you were when you left. I find this to be such a simple, yet useful, feature. If you create a shortcut to PowerDesk, you can force it to open at a specific location by putting the name of the directory after the program name in the Target field of the shortcut properties.

PowerDesk has so many features that we could spend an entire chapter of this book describing them, and even then there would be things we'd miss. So, I'm going to give a brief summary of the coolest features and leave the rest as an exercise for the reader:

- Most of the features of the Windows Explorer are available from the File and Tools menus. You can open, delete, and rename files. You can map network drives, format diskettes, and empty the trash.

- PowerDesk provides Move To and Copy To icons on the main toolbar, context menu, and File menu for moving and copying files to a specific location. You can recreate this functionality [Hack #27] in Windows Explorer without using PowerDesk.

- The File Finder feature provides many options for finding files on your computer. You can have PowerDesk search for Microsoft Word documents beginning with the word "Hack," modified in the last three days, and containing the word "wireless."

- PowerDesk has the ability to find and rename a group of files according to parameters that you define. For example, let's say you have a bunch of digital photographs from your trip to Belize. The digital camera doesn't know you went to Belize, and neither does Windows XP. Using PowerDesk, select the files you want to rename and choose File → Rename. PowerDesk shows a list of the files to be renamed and gives you a place to rename the files something like *Belize 2003 Vacation.JPG*. The first file will be named *Belize 2003 Vacation.JPG*, the second file will be named *Belize 2003 Vacation (1).JPG*, and so on. PowerDesk also has a more powerful group-rename feature that uses wildcards and pattern matching to find files and choose their new names.

- PowerDesk provides a built-in FTP client for transferring files from a remote file server (much like WinFTP). The connection to the remote server appears as if it were just another folder on your computer. Power-Desk FTP can even resume interrupted downloads.

- You can convert image files between the numerous available formats with File → Convert Picture Format.

- Security-conscious users will appreciate the Destroy File feature. This feature not only deletes a file from the filesystem, but it also wipes the disk drive where the file existed. Needless to say, using this feature will also prevent *you* from recovering the file, so don't test it out on your favorite photo from the Belize vacation.

- If you are truly security-conscious, do not use the Encrypt/Decrypt feature of PowerDesk. Details on the algorithm they use are not available. In the security world, it's common practice to describe how your cryptography works and rely on the strength of the key to protect the data. PowerDesk does allow you to choose 56-bit DES encryption for your data, but 56-bit encryption is the bare minimum these days. Do you want to trust your financial data to the bare minimum? I didn't think so.

- PowerDesk manages ZIP file archives as well as files that are stored using the older UUENCODE format.

- For copying files between two locations, use the Dual Pane view. This view displays two independent file browsers side-by-side, so you can easily copy files from one to the other without worrying about other windows getting in your way.

- If you find yourself managing the same set of files on two different disks, the Compare Folders feature is a great time saver. Select the folder that you want to compare, and let PowerDesk find the other folder and compare the contents.

- I run a network at home, and not all of our computers run Windows XP. PowerDesk provides a level playing field between the different versions of Windows so that I can always be assured that I have the tools I need on every computer I use.

There is so much more to PowerDesk than the few pages in this book. If the things you've read here interest you, download the evaluation version and try it for yourself.

—Eric Cloninger

HACK #24 Better File Rename
Rename multiple files quickly and easily.

I hate to admit it, but sometimes I'm impatient. Why should I waste my time doing the same thing over and over again? If you've ever had to rename more than one file at a time, you know how foolish it is to have to click, pause, click again, type the new name, hit Enter, and then *repeat for each file*, just to rename them—especially if there's some sort of pattern to what you're doing. Unix expatriates will find this procedure especially annoying after using powerful wildcards and other Unix pattern-matching syntax. Better File Rename (well worth the $15 shareware registration fee from *http://www.publicspace.net/windows/BetterFileRename/*) does all you might imagine a file-renaming utility would do and more. It's conveniently accessed via the context menu, a right-click away from any group of selected files.

Figure 3-11 displays some of the options for renaming files based on pattern or placement in the filename (beginning or end of filename). For each pattern or placement option, you get a powerful set of variables and settings to choose from so that you can rename files in all sorts of ways, quickly and easily.

One of the ways to use this utility is to append a prefix to a list of files that all belong to the same project but begin with entirely different filenames (such as a list of figures for a book). It's also especially useful for digital camera owners who don't like the numerical or other automatically generated

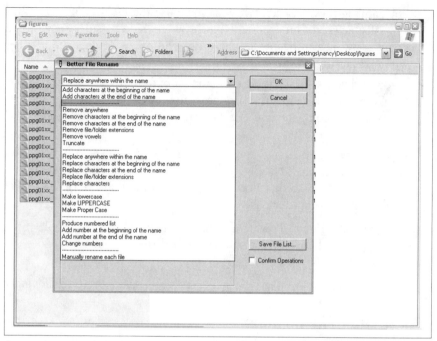

Figure 3-11. Better File Rename options

names for your files. While you might remember that a bunch of pictures with random numbers for filenames are pictures of your daughter, appending her name to each filename in one step with Better File Rename is easier than trying to remember such details or doing the painfully slow click-and-rename dance for each one. You can also change a whole list of filenames from upper- to lowercase, and vice versa. The pattern-replacement and automatic successive-numbering options are especially useful. Impatient control freaks, rejoice!

—Nancy Kotary

HACK #25 Find Files Faster by Mastering the Indexing Service's Query Language

Got a hard disk filled with many files, and no easy way to find what you want quickly? Use the Indexing Service and its query language to get what you want fast.

Packrats like me (and my editor) have a hard time finding exactly what they want on their hard disk. I have thousands of files there, some dating back close to ten years, that I dutifully copy to a new system every time I upgrade my hardware. After all, who knows when I might need to find the list of books I planned to take out of the library in 1986?

XP's Search Companion is too slow and the kinds of searches it can perform are fairly limited. It can't find files based on properties such as when the file was last printed or the word count of a file, or using a sophisticated search language.

The Indexing Service, first used with the Microsoft Internet Information Services (IIS), is a far more powerful tool. It can perform searches hundreds of times faster and includes an exceedingly sophisticated query language you can use for performing searches. It works by indexing the files on your disk, and then, when you do a search, it queries that index rather than searching through your entire hard disk. The indexes that the service creates are called *catalogs*.

By default, the Indexing Service is turned off. To activate it, first run the Search Companion by choosing Start → Search[→ For Files or Folders]. From the Search Companion, choose Change Preferences → With Indexing Service. If the With Indexing Service option isn't available, and instead you see Without Indexing Service, it means that the Indexing Service is already turned on.

When you activate the Indexing Service, it won't immediately be available. It first has to build an index, which can take a substantial amount of time, depending on the amount of files on your hard disk, and your processor speed. It's best to start the Indexing Service and leave your computer on overnight so that it can complete indexing.

To turn off the Indexing Service from the Search Companion, choose Change Preferences → Without Indexing Service. When you do that, you'll use the normal Search Companion. The index will remain intact; when you do a search, you just won't search through it. You can always turn the index back on when you want.

Using the Indexing Service's Query Language

The Indexing Service's query language is a sophisticated language, letting you search on file properties—such as the author of documents or the number of bytes in a document—and also uses Boolean operators and other search criteria.

The language uses tags to define search criteria. For example, to search for the phrase "That dog won't hunt," the query would be:

```
{phrase} That dog won't hunt {/phrase}
```

There are two basic ways to search for text in the query language, using either phrase or freetext. A phrase search searches for the exact words in the exact order, like this:

```
{phrase} old dog barks backwards {/phrase}
```

The search results will include only files whose text includes that exact phrase.

A freetext expression search looks for any words in the phrase and returns files that have any one of the words in the phrase. It works like the Boolean OR operator. So, the query:

```
{freetext} old dog barks backwards {/freetext}
```

returns many more searches than the phrase query, since it returns results that contain any of the words in the phrase.

Searching Using Properties

The Indexing Service's query language's power is contained in the way it can search not just for text, but also for document properties. The syntax for searching using properties in a query is:

```
{prop name=property name} query {/prop}
```

where *property name* is the name of the property, such as those listed in Table 3-2, and *query* is the text you're searching for. For example, to search for all documents last edited by Preston Gralla, you would enter:

```
{prop name=DocLastAuthor} Preston Gralla {/prop}
```

Queries can use * and ? wildcard characters, as well as Unix-style regular expression queries (for more on regular expressions, see *Mastering Regular Expressions* from O'Reilly). In order to use these wildcards, you must use the {regex} tag, like this:

```
{prop name=filename} {regex} *.xl? {/regex} {/prop}
```

The Indexing Service indexes not just the text of each document, but also all the summary information associated with each document. (To see summary information for any document, right-click on it and choose Properties → Summary.) In addition to searching for properties in the summary, you can also search for the properties found in Table 3-2, which lists the most important properties you can use to search.

Table 3-2. Important properties for searching via the Indexing Service

Property	Description
Access	The last time the document was accessed.
All	All available properties. Works with text queries, but not numeric queries.
AllocSize	The total disk space allocated to the document.
Contents	The contents of the document.
Created	The time the document was created.

Table 3-2. Important properties for searching via the Indexing Service (continued)

Property	Description
Directory	The full directory path in which the document is contained.
DocAppName	The name of the application in which the document was created.
DocAuthor	The author of the document.
DocByteCount	The number of bytes in the document.
DocCategory	The type of document.
DocCharCount	The number of characters in the document.
DocComments	Comments made about the document.
DocCompany	The name of the company for which the document was written.
DocCreatedTime	The time spent editing the document.
DocHiddenCount	The number of hidden slides in a PowerPoint document.
DocKeyWords	The key words in the document.
DocLastAuthor	The name of the person who last edited the document.
DocLastPrinted	The time the document was most recently printed.
DocLineCount	The number of lines contained in the document.
DocLastSavedTm	The time that the document was last saved.
DocManager	The name of the manager of the document's author.
DocNoteCount	The number of pages with notes in a PowerPoint document.
DocPageCount	The number of pages in the document.
DocParaCount	The number of paragraphs in the document.
DocPartTitles	The names of document parts, such as spreadsheet names in an Excel document or slide titles in a PowerPoint slide show.
DocRevNumber	The current version number of document.
DocSlideCount	The number of slides in a PowerPoint document.
DocTemplate	The name of the document's template.
DocTitle	The title of the document.
DocWordCount	The number of words in the document.
FileName	The filename of the document.
Path	The path to the document, including the document filename.
ShortFileName	The 8.3-format name of the document.
Size	The size of the document, in bytes.
Write	The date and time the document was last modified.

Searching Using Operators and Expressions

The query language also lets you use a variety of operators and expressions for both text and numbers:

EQUALS *and* CONTAINS *operators*

> When you're creating a query using text, you can use the EQUALS and CONTAINS operators to narrow your search. Use the EQUALS operator when you want the exact words matched in the exact order, like this:
>
> ```
> {prop name=DocTitle} EQUALS First Draft of Final Novel {/prop}
> ```
>
> This query finds all documents with the title "First Draft of Final Novel." The query wouldn't find a document with the title "Final Draft of First Novel" or "First Draft of Novel." The EQUALS operator works like the phrase expression.
>
> Use the CONTAINS operator when you want to find any of the words in the document, in the same way you would use the freetext expression.

Relational operators

> Use relational operators when you're searching using numbers:
>
> =   Equal to
>
> != Not equal to
>
> <   Less than
>
> <= Less than or equal to
>
> >   Greater than
>
> >= Greater than or equal to

Date and time expressions

> You can use the following formats when searching using dates and times:
>
> ```
> yyyy/mm/dd hh:mm:ss
> yyyy-mmmm-dd hh:mm:ss
> ```
>
> You can also use date and time expressions in combination with relational operators—for example, to look for files that were created within the last two days:
>
> ```
> {prop name=Created}  >-2d  {/prop}
> ```
>
> Table 3-3 lists the date and time abbreviations you can use.

Table 3-3. Date and time expressions that work with relational operators

Abbreviation	Meaning	Abbreviation	Meaning
Y	Year	D	Day
Q	Quarter	H	Hour
M	Month	N	Minute
W	Week	S	Second

Boolean operators

> The query language also uses the Boolean operators detailed in Table 3-4.

Table 3-4. Boolean operators used by the Indexing Service's query language

Boolean Operator	Long Form	Short Form
AND	&	AND
OR	|	OR
Unary NOT	!	NOT
Binary NOT	&!	AND NOT

Use the unary NOT when you're searching using numbers rather than text. For example, to search for all documents that do not have seven PowerPoint slides, use the query:

```
{prop name=DocSlideCount} NOT = 7 {/prop}
```

Use the binary NOT to narrow a search, by combining two properties in a query. For example, to search for all documents with an author of "Preston Gralla" that are not titled "Chapter 10", use this query (on one line):

```
{prop name=DocAuthor} Preston Gralla  {/prop} NOT {prop
name=DocTitle} Chapter 10  {/prop}
```

Alternative verb forms

You can use the double-asterisk wildcard to search for alternative forms of verbs in a document. For example, the query:

```
{prop name=Contents} run** {/prop}
```

returns all documents with the word "ran" or the word "run."

Ranking the Order of Search Results

If you're doing a search likely to return many results, you'll want the most relevant searches to appear at the top of the results, and the least relevant to appear at the bottom. You can determine the relative importance of each term in your search and have the results weighted by that importance, by using the weight tag. Note that it does not get a closing tag:

```
{weight value = n} query
```

The value parameter ranges between 0.000 and 1.000.

If you are searching for the three terms, "fire," "ice," and "slush," and you want to weight "fire" most heavily, "ice" second most heavily, and "slush" least heavily, you can use this syntax (on a single line) in your query:

```
{weight value=1.000}fire AND {weight value=.500}ice AND {weight value=.
250}slush
```

Editing the Indexing Service's "Noise" Filter

You can force the Indexing Service to ignore more words when you search, or you can have it ignore fewer words, simply by editing a text file. In a text file called *noise.eng*, usually found in *C:\Windows\System32*, you can find the list of words that the Indexing Service ignores. (The extension *.eng* is for English. Noise filters from other languages can be found as well—for example, *noise.deu* for German, *noise.fra* for French, and so on.)

The *noise.eng* file contains common articles, prepositions, pronouns, conjunctions, various forms of common verbs, and similar words. Open it in Notepad or another text editor, add words that you want it to ignore, and delete files that you don't want it to ignore. Then save the file, and the Indexing Service will follow your new rules.

Hiding Folders and Files with the Encrypting File System
HACK #26

Protect all the information on your PC from prying eyes, using XP Professional's built-in encryption scheme.

If you have Windows XP Pro, you can use the Encrypting File System (EFS) to encrypt your files so that no one else can read them.

Home Edition users won't be pleased to know that EFS isn't available for Windows XP home users.

EFS lets you encrypt only the files and folders of your choice; you can encrypt a single file or folder, or all of your files and folders. Encrypted files and folders show up in Windows Explorer as green, so you can tell at a glance which have been encrypted. You can work with encrypted files and folders transparently. In other words, after you encrypt them, you open them and close them as you normally would any other file. They're decrypted on the fly as you open them, and then decrypted as you close them. You're the only person who can read or use the files. Encryption is tied to your account name, so even other accounts on the same computer won't be able to read or use them, unless you specifically grant access to certain accounts.

Each time you encrypt a file, EFS generates a random number for that file called the file encryption key (FEK). EFS uses that FEK to encrypt the file's contents with variant of the Data Encryption Standard (DES) algorithm, called DESX. (DESX features more powerful encryption than DES.) The FEK itself is encrypted as well, using RSA public key–based encryption.

EFS does have a few minor limitations you should be aware of:

- EFS works only on NTFS volumes. If you have a FAT or FAT32 volume, you'll have to convert it to NTFS if you want to use EFS [Hack #31].
- EFS won't work on compressed files. [Hack #31]. You'll have to decompress them if you want to encrypt them. Similarly, if you want to compress an encrypted file, you'll have to decrypt it.
- EFS can't compress files in the *C:\Windows* folder or any files marked with the System attribute.

When you work with encrypted files and folders, they seem to behave like any other files on your hard disk. In fact, though, their behavior is somewhat different, and you may notice files you thought were encrypted suddenly become decrypted for no apparent reason. So, before you turn on encryption, you should understand the common actions you can take with encrypted files and folders, and what the results will be. Table 3-5 lists what you need to know.

Table 3-5. How encrypted files and folders behave

Action	Result
Move or copy unencrypted files into an encrypted folder.	The files are automatically encrypted.
Move or copy encrypted files from an encrypted folder to an unencrypted folder.	The files remain encrypted.
Move or copy encrypted files from an encrypted folder to a non-NTFS volume.	The files are decrypted, though you are first given a warning and a chance to cancel the move or copy operation.
Back up files using XP's backup utility.	The backed-up files and folders remain encrypted.
Rename an encrypted file.	The file remains encrypted after it is renamed.
Delete an encrypted file.	The restorable file in the Recycle Bin remains encrypted.

Encrypting Files and Folders

To encrypt a file or folder, right-click on the folder or file and choose Properties → General → Advanced. The Advanced Attributes dialog box appears, as shown in Figure 3-12.

 If no Advanced button appears on the Properties dialog box, it means that you aren't using NTFS, so you can't use encryption.

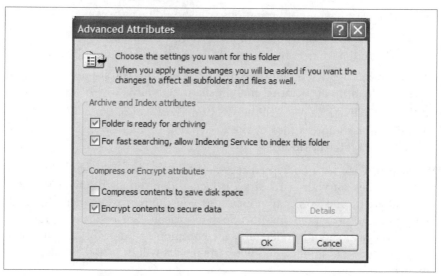

Figure 3-12. Encrypting files or folders using the Advanced Attributes dialog box

Check the box next to "Encrypt contents to secure data." Note that you can't check both this box and the "Compress contents to save disk space" box. You can either compress the item or encrypt it, but not both.

Click OK and then OK again. If you're encrypting a folder, the Confirm Attributes Changes dialog box appears, as shown in Figure 3-13. You have a choice of encrypting the folder only, or encrypting the folder plus all subfolders and all the files in the folder and subfolders. If you encrypt the folder only, none of the files currently in the folder will be encrypted, but any new files you create, move, or copy into the folder will be encrypted.

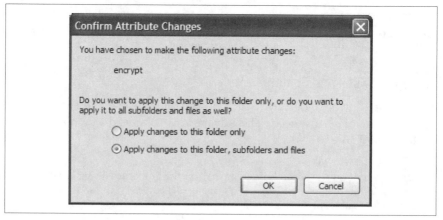

Figure 3-13. Encrypting the folder only, or all the subfolders and files as well

If you're encrypting a file in an unencrypted folder, the Encryption Warning box will appear, as shown in Figure 3-14. You have the choice of encrypting the file only, or the file and the parent folder. As a general rule, you should encrypt the folder as well as the file, because if you encrypt only the file, you may accidentally decrypt it without realizing it. Some applications save copies of your files and delete the original; in those instances, the files become decrypted simply by editing them. If you encrypt the folder as well, all files added to the folder are encrypted, so the saved file is automatically encrypted. Click OK after you make your choice.

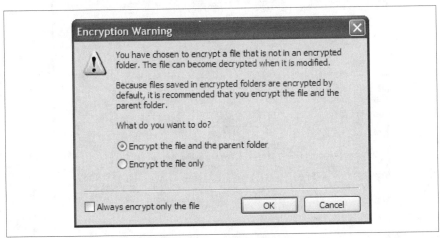

Figure 3-14. Encrypting the parent folder as well as the file

Note that you won't be able to encrypt every file on your system. Files that have the System attribute, as well as files located in *C:\Windows* and its sub-folders can't be encrypted.

Decrypting Files and Folders

You decrypt files and folders in the same way that you encrypted them. Right-click on the file or folder, choose Properties → Advanced, clear the check from the box next to "Encrypt contents to secure data," and click OK and then OK again.

Letting Others Use Your Encrypted Files

When you encrypt files, you can still share them with others and let them use them as if they were not encrypted—what XP calls "transparently." You'll be able to share them this way only with others users on the same computer or with others on your network. You designate who can use the files and who can't. To allow specified people to use your encrypted files, right-click on an unencrypted file and choose Properties → General → Advanced. The Advanced Attributes dialog box appears. Click Details. The Encryption Details dialog box appears, as shown in Figure 3-15. It lists all the users who are allowed to use the file transparently. Click Add.

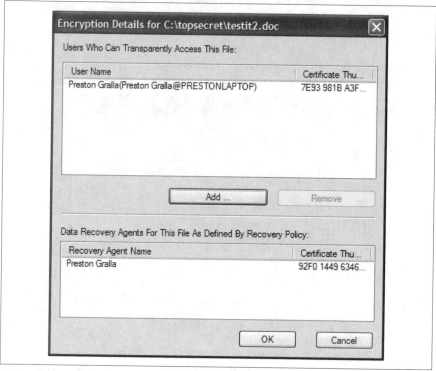

Figure 3-15. The Encryption Details dialog box

The Select User dialog box appears. Choose the user you want to be able to use your encrypted files, and click OK. Only users who have Encrypting File System certificates on the computer will show up on this list. The easiest way for someone to create a certificate is to encrypt any file; that automatically creates a certificate.

Encrypting and Decrypting from the Command Line

If you prefer the command line to a graphical interface, you can encrypt and decrypt using the *cipher.exe* command-line tool. To find out the current state of encryption of the directory you're in, type cipher without parameters at a command prompt. cipher tells you the state of the directory. For individual files, it lists a U next to files that are not encrypted, and an E next to those that are encrypted.

When used with parameters, cipher can encrypt and decrypt files and folders, show encryption information, create new encryption keys, and generate a recovery agent key and certificate.

To encrypt or decrypt a folder or file, use the complete path, filename (if you're acting on a file), and any appropriate switches, as outlined in Table 3-6. The /E switch encrypts folders or files, and the /D switch decrypts them. To perform the task on multiple folders or files, separate them with single spaces. For example, to encrypt the \Secret and \Topsecret folders, issue this command:

```
cipher /E \Secret \Topsecret
```

Note that you can use wildcards with the cipher command. Using the command line instead of the graphical interface is particularly useful for performing bulk or batch operations—for example, simultaneously encrypting or decrypting multiple folders or files, or types of files within folders. Let's say, for example, you want to encrypt every .doc file in the \Secret and \Topsecret folders, but not touch any other files in those folders. You issue this command:

```
cipher /E  /A \Secret\*.DOC  \Topsecret\*.DOC
```

Table 3-6 lists the most useful command-line switches for cipher. For more help, type cipher /? at the command line.

Table 3-6. Command-line switches for cipher

Switch	What it does
/A	Acts on individual files within folders.
/D	Decrypts the specified folder.
/E	Encrypts the specified folder.
/F	Forces encryption on all specified objects, including those that have already been encrypted.
/H	Displays all files in a folder, including those that have hidden or system attributes. By default, hidden or system attributes are not displayed when using the cipher command.
/I	Continues to perform the specified operation, even if errors are encountered. By default, cipher halts when errors are encountered.
/K	Creates a new file encryption key for the user running cipher. If this option is chosen, all the other options will be ignored.
/R	Generates an EFS recovery agent key and certificate, then writes them to a .pfx file (containing the certificate and a private key) and a .cer file (containing only the certificate).
/S	Performs the operation on the folder and all its subfolders.
/U	Updates the user's file encryption key or recovery agent's key on every encrypted file.

Table 3-6. Command-line switches for cipher (continued)

Switch	What it does
/U /N	Lists every encrypted file and does not update the user's file encryption key or recovery agent's key.
/Q	Lists only basic information about the file or folder.
/W	Wipes data from available, unused disk space on the drive. Normally, when a file is deleted in XP, only the entry in the filesystem table is deleted; the data itself remains untouched until another file overwrites it. This switch deletes all the data in those previously deleted files. It does not harm existing data.

HACK #27 Forcing Windows Explorer Into True Usefulness

A grab bag of ways to make better use of Explorer.

There are plenty of small ways you can hack Explorer to make your computing life more productive—for example, by hacking the right-click shortcut menu. Try out these hacks and see.

Add Shortcut Menu Items to Specific File Types

When you right-click on a file in Explorer, you get a shortcut menu that includes a list of programs with which you can open the file. But the programs that you want to open those files might not always be on the shortcut menu. It's easy to add new programs to that list. Let's say that you want to add a shortcut menu item that allows *.gif* files to be opened with the freeware graphics viewer IrfanView **[Hack #86]**. From Windows Explorer, choose Tools → Folder Options → File Types. In the Registered File Types list, select the file type for which you want to add a new shortcut menu item. In our example, we'll choose a GIF file. After this hack, any time you click on a file of this type, you'll get a new choice to open the file with.

Once you've chosen your file type, choose Advanced → New. You'll see the New Action dialog box shown in Figure 3-16.

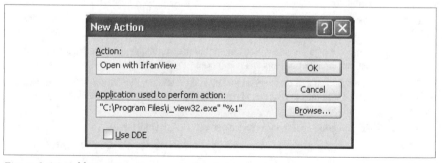

Figure 3-16. Adding a new program to the shortcut menu

In the Action box, type the text you want to appear on the shortcut menu—for example, Open with IrfanView. In the "Application used to perform action" box, enter the executable program you want to open the file with, including the full path. Surround it by quotation marks. Then leave a space and type in "%1". The "%1" is a placeholder; it will be used as a substitute for the name of the file on which you right-click. In our instance, the entire string looks like this:

```
"C:\Program Files\i_view32.exe" "%1"
```

Click OK. The change will take place immediately, and the new command will appear on the shortcut menu for the specified file type.

Add Global Shortcut Menu Items to All File Types

The previous section of this hack showed how to add shortcut menu items on a file-type-by-file-type basis. In other words, it will only be available on the shortcut menu for the one specific file type you specify. But you can also add that shortcut menu item to every type of file, by using a Registry hack. This is useful when you have a program that can open a wide variety of file types, and you don't want to have to go add a shortcut menu item for every one of those file types. I use the IrfanView graphics viewer for many different types of graphics, so I want it to show up on all those types. Although it will also show up on file types that I won't use it with, such as Word files, it's still worth putting it on the menu globally because of all the time I save by not having to add shortcut menu items over and over again for each file type.

Run the Registry Editor [Hack #68] and go to HKEY_CLASSES_ROOT*. Create a new subkey called Shell if it doesn't yet exist. The Shell subkey can control parts of the user interface. Create a new subkey under Shell and name it what your new command will be—for example, OpenWithIrfanView. For the default value of the new subkey, type in the text you want to appear on the shortcut menu—for example, Open with IrfanView. Create a new subkey named Command under the subkey that you just created. This subkey will contain the command string that you want to be executed to open the file. For the default value of the Command subkey, enter the command string you want to be executed when the shortcut menu item is chosen—for example:

```
"C:\Program Files\i_view32.exe" "%1"
```

Exit the Registry. The new shortcut menu item should be available immediately, though you may need to reboot in order for it to take effect.

Edit File Association Actions

You can use Windows Explorer to change how XP handles file types; for example, you can choose the default action when the file type is double-clicked upon, the application associated with the file type, the icon for the file type, and whether the extension should be displayed or hidden in Windows Explorer. To perform most of these actions, choose Tools → Folder Options → File Types, choose the file type for which you want to customize an action, then click Advanced. You'll see the screen shown in Figure 3-17.

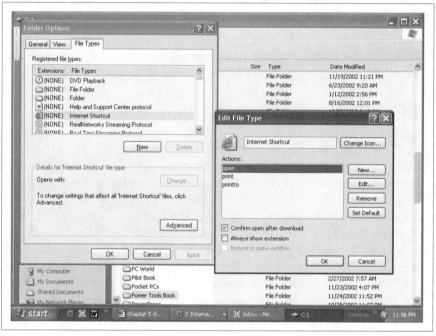

Figure 3-17. Editing file associations and their actions

From the Edit File Type dialog box, you can change the icon, edit the action to be taken on the file, and choose whether to display the file type in Windows Explorer. The dialog box is fairly self-explanatory. For example, click Change Icon to change the icon; to edit any action, highlight it and click Edit. If you want to change the application associated with the file, choose Tools → Folder Options → File Types, choose the file type whose association you want to change, click Change, and then choose the application you want to be associated with the file type in the same way as shown in Figure 3-16.

Remove Context Menu Items from Explorer

Explorer's menus can get messy at times. But you can use a Registry hack to clean it up a bit by removing two items from the Tools menu: Map Network Drive and Disconnect Network Drive. Run the Registry Editor and go to:

```
HKEY_CURRENT_USER\Software\Microsoft\Windows\CurrentVersion\Policies\Explorer
```

Create the DWORD entry NoNetConnectDisconnect. Give it a value of 1. Exit the Registry. You might have to reboot in order for the setting to take effect and the items to disappear from the menu. To place the items back on the Explorer menu, edit the value to 0, or delete the entry.

Organize the All Programs Menu with Explorer

If you're using the default Windows XP Start Menu view and you're not happy with the way your All Programs menu is organized, you can use Windows Explorer to modify it. The All Programs menu is nothing more than a collection of shortcuts found in two folders: the C:\Documents and Settings\ <Your Account>\Start Menu folder (where <Your Account> is your account name), and the C:\Documents and Settings\All Users\Start Menu folder. Items that you want to appear at the very top of the All Programs menu should be put in one of the /Start Menu folders (depending upon whether you want the item to appear only on your All Programs menu, or on all users' All Programs menu.) Items that you want to appear on the lower part of the All Programs menu should be put into the \Start Menu\Programs folder, again, depending on whether you want the item to appear only on your All Programs menu, or on all users' All Programs menu.

H A C K
#28   Customize Folder Icons and Balloon Text

Make it easier to recognize specific folders and remember their contents, by giving them their own pictures and identifying text.

All folders are not created equal; some are more important than others. Folders I use for writing books and articles, or for storing digital music, for example, are more vital to me than folders that hold tax records from eight years ago.

So I like to give myself visual clues when browsing my computer about what each folder holds and how important it is to me. I have so many folders on my hard disk that I can't always immediately recall the purposes of some of them, so for some I also create balloon text that describes the purpose of the folder when I hover my mouse over the folder.

To force a folder to display a specific icon and to have it display balloon text when you hover your mouse over it, create a Desktop.ini file in that folder. That file contains instructions on which icon to use and balloon text to display.

If you don't want to display customized balloon text, you can display an icon for any folder without having to create a *Desktop.ini* file yourself. Right-click on the folder you want to customize, choose Properties → Customize → "Change icon" and browse to the icon you want to use. When you do that, you'll automatically create a *Desktop.ini* file that will display the proper icon.

Before creating the file, choose the icon you want to use for the folder. Icons end in an *.ico* extension. You can also use *.bmp* bitmap files as icons. Make sure to note the name of the icon or bitmap, including its full path. If you want, create your own icon [Hack #19].

Not all icons are in *.ico* files, however. Many are part of entire icon libraries in *.dll* files. For example, you'll find hundreds of icons in the *shell32.dll* file found in *C:\WINDOWS\System32* folder. Each icon in a *.dll* file is assigned an index number, starting with 0. To use icons in *.dll* files, you'll need to know the index number for the specific icon. You won't be able to find out the index number by examining the file manually; instead, you'll need third-party software. Resource Tuner (*http://www.heaventools.com*) lets you examine the resources of any file and, among other things, will let you browse through the file's icons and show you their index numbers. It's shareware and free to try, but it costs $34.95 if you keep using it.

Figure 3-18 shows Resource Tuner, looking inside *Shell32.dll* and listing the index number for an icon.

For my *Music* folder, I'm going to use a *.bmp* file of cover art of the mezzo-soprano Cecilia Bartoli.

Now it's time to create the *Desktop.ini* file. Using a text editor like Notepad, create it in the folder you want to customize. I'm going to customize my *C:\ Music* folder, so that's where I create it. Here's what my file looks like:

```
[.ShellClassInfo]
IconFile=C:\MusicPics\Bartoli.bmp
IconIndex=0
InfoTip=The Best of Puccini, Donizetti, Verdi, and the Rest
```

The heading, [.ShellClassInfo], is required, so make sure to put that at the top of the file. The IconFile= entry should point to the file you want to use as an icon—and again, it can be an *.ico* file, a *.bmp* file, or an icon found in an icon collection, such as in a *.dll* file. Make sure to include the file's full path. The IconIndex= entry should point to the index number of the icon if the file is in an icon collection. If it's not in an icon collection, use the number 0. The InfoTip= entry should point to the text you want displayed as balloon text.

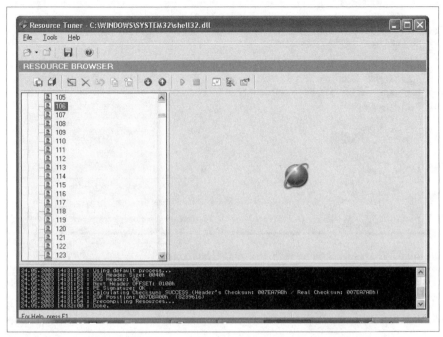

Figure 3-18. Using Resource Tuner to find the index number of an icon

After you create the *Desktop.ini* file, you need to define the folder you want to customize as a system folder, in order for it to be able to display the icon and balloon text. At the command prompt, issue the command attrib +s *foldername*, where *foldername* is the name of the folder you're customizing.

You're now done; the icon and balloon text should display. Figure 3-19 shows what mine looks like.

H A C K
#29 **A Power User's Hidden Weapon: Improve the Context Menu**

The context menu is an often underused tool. But with these four additions and edits to the menu, it'll turn into a powerhouse that you'll use every day.

Windows Explorer's right-click context menu is one of the most basic of all XP tools; it provides many shortcuts for whenever you want to take action on a file or a folder. But the right-click menu is missing several basic options, such as choosing a specific folder to which you want to move or copy the file you've highlighted, rather than just cutting or copying the file. And when you install new applications, they have a nasty habit of adding their own options that you'll rarely use in the right-click menu.

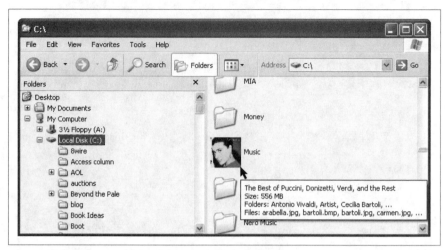

Figure 3-19. My Music folder with an icon and balloon text

The end result: a right-click context menu cluttered with options and lack-
ing several basic useful ones. But you can extend the power of the menu
with these four hacks.

Add "Copy To Folder" and "Move To Folder" Context Menu Options

I spend a lot of time copying and moving files between folders. More often
than not, when I click on a file in Explorer, I want to copy or move it to
another folder. That means I spend a good deal of time dragging files around
or copying and pasting them.

But with a Registry hack, you can save yourself time: you can add Copy To
Folder and Move To Folder options to the right-click context menu. When
you choose one of the options from the menu, you browse to any place on
your hard disk to copy or move the file to, and then send the file there. To
add the option, run the Registry Editor [Hack #68] and go to HKEY_CLASSES_
ROOT\AllFilesystemObjects\shellex\ContextMenuHandlers. shellex tells you
it's a shell extension key that lets you customize the user shell or the interface. Create a new key called Copy To. Set the value to {C2FBB630-2971-11d1-
A18C-00C04FD75D13}. Create another new key called Move To. Set the value to
{C2FBB631-2971-11d1-A18C-00C04FD75D13}. Exit the Registry. The changes
should take effect immediately. The Copy To Folder and Move To Folder
options will appear. When you right-click on a file and choose one of the
options, you'll be able to move or copy the file using a dialog box like the
one shown in Figure 3-20.

Figure 3-20. Specifying a destination using the Copy To Folder option

Add and Remove Destinations for the "Send To" Option

The right-click context menu does have one useful option, Send To, which allows you to send the file to any one of a list of programs or locations—for example, to a drive, program, or folder.

It would be nice to edit that list, adding new locations and programs and taking away existing ones that you never use. How locations and programs show up on the menu appears to be somewhat of a mystery, but, in fact, it's easy to hack. Go to *C:\Documents and Settings\<User Name>\SendTo*, where *<User Name>* is your user name. The folder will be filled with shortcuts to all the locations you find on your Send To context menu. To remove an item from the Send To menu, delete the shortcut from the folder. To add an item to the menu, add a shortcut to the folder by highlighting the folder, choosing File → New → Shortcut, and following the instructions for creating a shortcut. The new setting will take effect immediately; you don't have to exit Windows Explorer for it to go into effect.

Open the Command Prompt from the Right-Click Menu

I began computing in the days of DOS, and I still can't give up the command prompt. When it comes to doing down-and-dirty tasks like mass deleting or renaming of files, nothing beats it. I find myself frequently switching back and forth between Windows Explorer and the command prompt.

Often, when using Windows Explorer, I want to open the command prompt at the folder that's my current location. That takes too many steps: opening a command prompt and then navigating to my current folder. However, there's a quicker way: add an option to the right-click context menu that will open a command prompt at your current folder. For example, if you were to right-click on the *C:\My Stuff* folder, you could then choose to open a command prompt at *C:\My Stuff*.

To add the option, run the Registry Editor [Hack #68], then go to HKEY_LOCAL_ MACHINE/Software/Classes/Folder/Shell. Create a new key called Command Prompt. For the default value, enter whatever text you want to appear when you right-click on a folder—for example, Open Command Prompt. Create a new key beneath the Command Prompt key called Command. Set the default value to Cmd.exe /k pushd %L. That value will launch *Cmd.exe*, which is the XP command prompt. The /k switch puts the prompt into interactive mode. That is, it lets you issue commands from the command prompt; the command prompt isn't being used to issue only a single command and then exit. The pushd command stores the name of the current directory, and %L uses that name to start the command prompt at it. Exit the Registry. The new menu option will show up immediately. Note that it won't appear when you right-click on a file; it shows up only when you right-click on a folder.

> While many of us like fussing around with the Registry rather than doing things the easy way, there's also a way to add this option to your right-click context menu without editing the Registry. Download and install a free copy of Microsoft's "Open Command Window Here" PowerToy from *http://www.microsoft.com/windowsxp/pro/downloads/ powertoys.asp*. There are many other PowerToys on that page as well, and we cover them in other places in the book.

Clean Up the "Open With" Option

When you right-click on a file, one of the menu options is Open With, which provides a list of programs for you to open the file with. This list changes according to the type of file you're clicking. Depending on the file type, the lists can get long, because programs frequently add themselves to this list when you install them. Making things worse, there are times when the listed programs aren't applicable. For example, do you really want to open a *.bmp* bitmap graphics file with Microsoft Word? I think not.

You can clean up the Open With list by using a Registry hack. Run the Registry Editor and go to HKEY_CURRENT_USER\Software\Microsoft\Windows\ CurrentVersion\Explorer\FileExts. Look for the file extension whose Open

With list you want to edit and find its OpenWithList subkey—HKEY_CURRENT_
USER\Software\Microsoft\Windows\CurrentVersion\Explorer\FileExts\.bmp\
OpenWithList, for example. The subkey will have an alphabetical list of
String values. Open each value and examine the value data. It will be the
name of one of the programs on the Open With list (Winword.exe, for example). Delete any entry you don't want to appear. Don't delete the value data;
delete the String value listing. In other words, if the value data for the a
String value is Winword.exe, delete the entire string rather than just the value
data. Exit the Registry.

HACK #30 Take Your Work on the Go with Offline Files and the Briefcase

Two ways that road warriors can more easily take files with them when they
leave home or the office—and synchronize files back to their desktop PCs
when they return.

If you use a laptop on a corporate LAN, you might sometimes store files
on the network and forget to bring them home or with you on the road.
This frequently happens to people who, like me, are absent-minded on
occasion (or more than one occasion—after all, I once left my car keys in
the refrigerator).

If you have XP Professional, you can use its Offline Files feature to automatically synchronize folders from the LAN to your notebook so that whenever
you leave the office the latest version of your files will be available. To
enable the use of offline files, choose My Computer → Tools → Folder
Options → Offline Files tab (shown in Figure 3-21), and select the checkbox
next to Enable Offline Files.

> You won't be able to use Offline Files if you have enabled
> Fast User Switching. To turn off Fast User Switching, choose
> Control Panel → User Accounts → "Change the way users
> log on or off," uncheck the box next to Use Fast User
> Switching, and click Apply Options.

As you can see, there are a number of options on this tab for using offline
files. Here's what you need to know about each to take best advantage of
offline file synchronization:

Synchronize all offline files before logging off
    Make sure to choose this option. When you do, the most recent copies
    of files will automatically be copied to your laptop. If you don't choose
    this option, you'll get only a partial synchronization, which means that

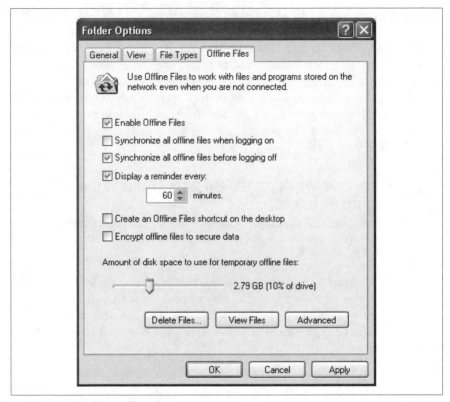

Figure 3-21. Enabling offline files

you won't have the latest version of all your files. Also, keep in mind that you have to log off or turn off your PC in order for this option to work. If you only physically disconnect your PC from the network, the files won't be copied.

Synchronize all offline files when logging on

If you choose this option, as soon as you connect back to the network, your files will be synchronized from your laptop back to the LAN. That means you won't be able to use them locally, and you'll have to use them on the LAN. If you don't choose this option, you'll be able to continue using your files locally and can then manually synchronize any folders you want to the LAN.

Display a reminder every...

If you've disconnected from the network, this option will automatically flash a balloon message at you, telling you at an interval of your choosing that you've been disconnected. More than anything, this is an annoying option and is useful only if you frequently disconnect from your LAN accidentally.

Create an Offline Files shortcut on the desktop
If you choose this option, XP creates a desktop shortcut to the *Offline Files* folder it creates when you enable the use of offline files.

Encrypt offline files to secure data
If you're concerned about the security of your files, choose this option. As the name implies, it will encrypt your offline files.

Amount of disk space to use for temporary offline files
When you use offline files, Windows caches files from the LAN onto your hard disk temporarily. This option lets you determine the exact amount of disk space to allocate to those temporary offline files.

After you've set up your laptop to use Offline Files, you next have to choose the specific folders on the server that you want to make available to you offline. Open Windows Explorer, right-click on the network folder, and choose Make Available Offline. If there are subfolders in the folder, you'll be asked whether you want to make those subfolders available as well.

After you do this, when you log off the network, the server copies to your laptop all the folders you've marked. They'll be available to you in the same way as any other folders are, via your applications, Windows Explorer, in My Computer, or My Network Places. Work with them on your laptop, and then, when you next connect to the network, they'll be synchronized to the network folders, depending on the options you've chosen.

On-Demand and Scheduled Synchronizations

If you'd like, rather than synchronize when you log off the network, you can synchronize manually on demand, or you can set up a schedule for automated synchronization. To synchronize on demand manually, in Windows Explorer choose Tools → Synchronize. From the dialog box that appears, select the items in the Logon/Logoff tab that you want to synchronize, and click Synchronize. To set up times to synchronize, use the On Idle and Scheduled tabs.

Use the Briefcase for Mobile File Transfers

Offline Files works only if you have XP Professional and if you have a local area network to which both your laptop and desktop connect. But if you need to synchronize files between two computers not on a network—even if you don't have XP Professional—there is still a way to way to synchronize files between computers: use the Briefcase. It's not as easy to use as Offline Files, but it still does the trick. It synchronizes files between your two machines by using removable media such as a CD or Zip drive.

Using floppy disks is not recommended, unless you have very few files or very tiny files that you need to transfer and have no other way of transferring them, such as email attachments.

To use the Briefcase to transfer files from a laptop to a desktop computer, first format the media you're going to use if it needs to be formatted. With the removable media in the drive, open Windows Explorer, click on the media's disk folder, and choose File → New → Briefcase. If you're going to be using more than one Briefcase at a time, rename the Briefcase with a descriptive name. The Briefcase is a folder, like any other folder on your computer. Open it, and then click Finish to close the dialog box that appears.

Copy into the Briefcase the files you're going to want to transfer to your laptop and keep synchronized between the two computers. You can copy files from different folders. If you've going to add files to the Briefcase over time, or if you expect the files in the Briefcase to grow, make sure to leave enough extra room on the disk. Eject the media from your desktop. (If you get an error message when trying to eject a CD, close Windows Explorer and then eject it.) Place the media in your laptop, and move or copy the Briefcase folder to the laptop's hard disk. Remember to move or copy the entire folder, not the individual files in the folder. Work on the files as you would normally. Add or delete files as well. When it's time to transfer the files back to your PC, copy the Briefcase from your laptop to removable media, and put the removable media in your desktop. Open the Briefcase folder.

To synchronize all the files back to your desktop, choose Briefcase → Update All and, from the Update Briefcase dialog box (shown in Figure 3-22), click Update. To synchronize individual files, select them, choose Briefcase → Update Selection, and click Update.

A Closer Look at the Briefcase

It's a good idea to examine the files in your Briefcase before you synchronize, so that you know the status of each. As you can see in Figure 3-23, you'll see whether each file has been updated and therefore needs to be updated on your current machine, or whether it was unchanged. The Briefcase folder also shows you the file's original location on the computer, as well as other details such as file size.

Right-click on any file in the Briefcase, and choose Properties → Update Status; you'll get updated information about each file. You can also perform the following tasks:

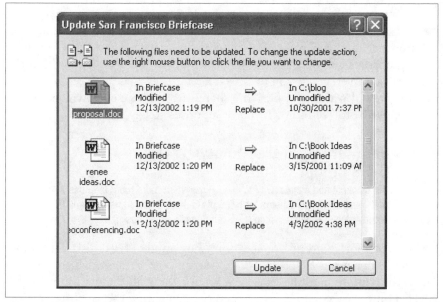

Figure 3-22. Synchronizing all the files in a Briefcase back to a desktop PC

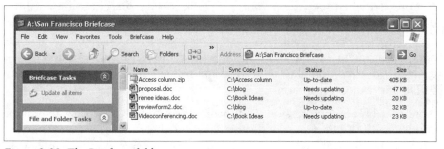

Figure 3-23. The Briefcase folder

Update

    This button updates the file. Only this file, and no others, will update.

Split from Original

    This button breaks the link between the Briefcase file and the file in the hard disk. You won't be able to do automatic updates. The file in the hard disk will be listed as an Orphan in the status field in the Explorer view. You can still copy the file, even though the automatic link no longer works.

Find Original

    This button opens the folder on your computer that holds the original file.

See Also

- Backer (*http://www.leanware.com/english/leanware.html*) is a combination backup/synchronization program that lets you synchronize your laptop data with a desktop PC or server. It also lets you synchronize with a server while you're traveling, transfer files between PCs, and archive old versions of files. It's shareware and free to download, but if you decide to keep using it you're supposed to pay $24.

HACK #31 Get More Hard Disk Space by Using NTFS Compression

The quickest and easiest way to give your system more room is to use XP's built-in compression scheme for NTFS disks. Here's how to use it—and how to convert your existing disk to NTFS if it doesn't already use it.

If you need more hard disk space, don't buy another hard disk right away. First, consider using NTFS (NT File System) compression, which can give significantly more hard disk space by compressing all the files on your PC. NTFS's on-the-fly compression capabilities can shrink the size of individual files and folders, or entire drives. When you use it, the files or folders will be compressed when they're on your hard disk to save space, but they will be decompressed automatically when you use them, and then compressed again when stored on your hard disk. This means that, unlike with a compression program such as WinZip (*http://www.winzip.com*), you don't have to deal with decompressing as well as compressing files. You can also easily turn compression on and off.

Note that NTFS compression isn't available with a FAT32 filesystem, so if you have a FAT32 system you'll first have to convert to NTFS, as explained later in this hack. If you're not sure which filesystem your volume uses, right-click on your volume in Explorer, choose Properties → General, and look for the information next to File System.

How much disk space can you save by using NTFS compression? That depends largely on the kinds of files you have on your system. Bit-mapped graphic files are very compressible, so you'll save quite a bit of hard disk space if you have many of them. Document files, such as Word files, are also reasonably compressible, while certain kinds of files, such as PDF (Adobe Acrobat) files, are barely compressible at all.

> If you use NTFS compression on a file, the file can't be encrypted using XP's encrypting capabilities, so be careful not to compress any files that you want to encrypt.

In tests on my own PC, I found that bit-mapped .*tif* graphic files were compressed by more than 80 percent—a folder full of them shrunk from 295 MB to 57 MB. Word files shrunk by 66 percent—a folder full of them shrunk from 131 KB to 44 KB. PDF files, by way of contrast, hardly compressed at all—a group of them shrunk by just over 6 percent, from 5.59 MB to 5.27 MB.

When you use compression, you may notice a slight drop in system performance. There may be a slight lag when opening or closing files, depending on the speed of your system, because the files have to be decompressed in order for you to open them and compressed when you save them. With newer systems, though, you probably won't notice a lag. On my now-aging 1.8 GHz desktop, for example, I don't see a difference between working with files that have been compressed and working with files that haven't been compressed.

You can use NTFS compression on individual files, folders, and entire disks. To use NTFS compression on a file or folder, right-click on the file or folder in Windows Explorer and choose Properties → General → Advanced. You'll see the screen shown in Figure 3-24.

Figure 3-24. Enabling compression on files and folders to save hard disk space

Check the box next to "Compress contents to save disk space," click OK, and click OK again when the Properties dialog box appears.

If you want to compress an entire drive, right-click on it in Windows Explorer, and choose Properties → General → "Compress drive to save disk space." You'll be asked for confirmation, and then every folder and file on the drive will be compressed, one after another. Depending on the size of the drive, the procedure can take several hours. You can continue to use XP while the compression takes place. During that time, however, you may be prompted to close a file you're working on, so that XP can compress it.

By default, XP visually differentiates between compressed files and decompressed files; compressed files are shown in blue. If for some reason your compressed files aren't blue, and you want them to be, from Windows Explorer, choose Tools → Folder Options → View, scroll down, and select the checkbox next to "Show encrypted or compressed NTFS files in color."

> Don't compress system files or *.log* files (files that contain logging information). If you do, your system can take a severe performance hit, because these files are in frequent background use and compressing and decompressing them constantly takes up CPU power. If these files are in folders that are compressed, you can decompress just those individual files by unchecking the "Compress contents to save disk space" box next to them. You can also decompress the folder in which they are located in the same way.

How Compressing Folders Affects Underlying Files

When you compress files in a folder, they are all, obviously, compressed. But things can get confusing when you mix compressed folders and decompressed folders on a hard disk, or when you have compressed files in decompressed folders and vice versa. What happens, for example, when you move a decompressed file into a compressed folder, or move a compressed file from a compressed folder into a decompressed folder? The possibilities can set your head spinning. Here are the rules that apply when you're mixing compressed and decompressed files and folders:

- Files copied into a compressed folder are automatically compressed.
- New files created in a compressed folder are automatically compressed.
- Files moved into a compressed folder from a separate NTFS volume are automatically compressed.
- Files moved into a compressed folder from the same NTFS volume retain their compression settings. So, if the file was compressed, it will remain compressed. If the file was not compressed, it will not be compressed.
- If you move a file from a compressed folder to a decompressed folder in the same NTFS volume, the file will remain compressed.
- If you move a file from a compressed folder to a decompressed folder on a different NTFS volume, the file will no longer be compressed.

- Files copied or moved from a compressed folder on an NTFS volume to a FAT32 volume are decompressed.
- Files attached to emails are decompressed.

Checking How Much Disk Space NTFS Compression Saves

When you compress a file or folder, it doesn't appear that you're actually saving any disk space; when you view a file listing in Windows Explorer, the size of the compressed files will remain the same as they were before compression. In fact, though, the files have been compressed and space has been saved. Explorer reports on only the decompressed file size, not the compressed file size. To see the compressed size of a file or folder, Right-click on it in Windows Explorer and choose Properties → General. You'll see two listings of the file size, one titled "Size" and the other titled "Size on disk". The "Size on disk" listing reports on the compressed size of the file, while the "Size" listing reports on the decompressed size, as shown in Figure 3-25.

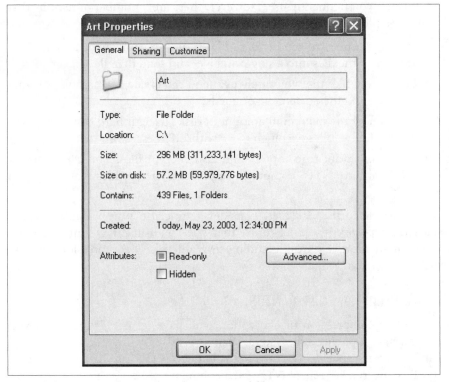

Figure 3-25. Viewing the true size of a compressed file

When to Use ZIP Files and When to Use NTFS Compression

Another way to gain extra space on your hard disk is to use XP's built-in ZIP capabilities. ZIP is an industry standard for file compression, and it compresses files much more effectively than NTFS does. In tests, I found that ZIP compression shrunk graphics files twice as effectively as NTFS compression—the resulting ZIP files were half the size of the NTFS-compressed files.

But that doesn't mean you should use ZIP compression all the time; there are times when using NTFS compression is a better bet. When files are ZIPped, for example, they can't be opened in their application by double-clicking on them. You first have to open the ZIP archive, and then double-click on the file. As a general rule, ZIPped files are not as convenient to use and handle as NTFS-compressed files. The exception is that ZIP lets you archive a group of files into a single folder, which you can then send to others via email or on disk.

What does this mean? On a day-to-day basis, NTFS compression is a better bet for files you frequently use. However, there are a number of reasons that to use ZIP files instead:

- When you need to send a large file or files to someone via email. You can zip all the files into a single archive, and send that along.

- For storing files that you rarely use. You can create ZIP archives to store the files, and then delete the originals.

- For gaining the maximum amount of disk space. If hard disk space is at a premium, you'll save much more with ZIP files.

- When you want to compress and also encrypt files. You can't encrypt files that have NTFS compression; you can encrypt files that have been ZIPped.

If you decide to use ZIP files, consider getting a copy of WinZip (*http://www.winzip.com*). It's easier to use than XP's built-in ZIP compression and offers many more features, including several levels of compression, built-in links to email, and much more.

Convert Your Hard Disk to NTFS

To use XP compression or encryption, you have to use NTFS. But if you instead have a previous filesystem, such as FAT32, you're not left out—you can convert it to NTFS. To convert a volume to NTFS, use XP's convert utility. To convert a volume to NTFS, at a command prompt, type:

```
convert d: /fs:ntfs
```

where d: is the volume you want to convert.

You can also use a number of parameters along with the utility:

/v

This runs the utility in verbose mode, which provides information about the volume being converted.

/nosecurity

This sets the security privileges on the converted disk so that its files and folders can be used by anyone.

/x

Use this parameter if you're on a network and want to make sure that another user cannot disrupt the conversion process by trying to access the drive while you're converting it. This parameter dismounts the drive from the network.

Hacking the Hack

If you convert to NTFS, here's a Registry hack for increasing its performance. Whenever you view a directory on an NTFS volume, the filesystem updates the date and time stamp to show the last time the directory has been accessed. If you have a very large NTFS volume, this continual updating process can slow system performance. You can use the Registry to disable automatic updating. Run the Registry Editor [Hack #68] and go to HKEY_LOCAL_MACHINE\SYSTEM\CurrentContolSet\Control\Filesystem. Look for NtfsDisableLastAccessUpdate. If it's not present, create it as a DWORD. Set the value to 1.

HACK #32 Put a Command-Line Prompt on Your Desktop

Command-line junkies always want the command prompt within easy reach. Here's how to put a command prompt directly on your desktop, so it's there whenever you need it.

If you use the command line regularly—for example, to launch Windows Explorer with shortcuts [Hack #22]—you'd like the command line within easy reach. In fact, you'd like it right on your desktop. XP has no built-in way to do that for you.

But there's a great free program called MCL (*http://www.mlin.net/MCL.shtml*) that runs as a small command line you can put anywhere on your desktop, as shown in Figure 3-26.

Use it as you would use the normal command line, including any normal switches that you use to launch programs.

Figure 3-26. Putting the command line right on your desktop with MCL

But MCL does more than just let you enter commands. It includes a number of other goodies that the XP command prompt doesn't, including these:

- It keeps a history of your last 100 commands, so you can easily reenter or edit any commands you've already typed.

- It includes an AutoComplete function that finishes your commands for you.

- It lets you launch URLs directly from the command line. If you type a URL, your default browser will open to that URL.

- It can be minimized to the System Notification area.

- It can be launched with a hot key. The default is Ctrl-Alt-M.

The program has a few eccentricities you'll have to keep in mind when using it. When executing a DOS command, you have to use the % prefix. For example, to copy a file from *C:\Favorite Files* to *C:\Summer*, you'd use this command:

```
%copy C:\Favorite Files\Gabecamp.doc C:\Summer\Gabecamp.doc
```

To open to a specific directory in Windows Explorer, precede the command with a $. So to open to *C:\Program Files*, you'd issue the command $C:\Program Files.

Command-line fans will also want to get a copy of 4NT (*http://www.jpsoft.com*). Run it instead of the normal command prompt and get countless new features, such as a command-line editor for modifying and reexecuting previous commands; the ability to copy, delete, and rename groups of files and directories with a single command; a built-in file viewer; the ability to select or include files by a variety of criteria, including date, time, and size; the ability to append descriptions (up to 511 characters) to files; and an exceedingly powerful batch language. It's shareware and free to try, but if you continue to use it, you're expected to pay $69.95.

See Also

- The free Command Prompt Explorer Bar (*http://www.codeproject.com/ csharp/CommandBar.asp*) lets you open a command-line toolbar from directly within Windows Explorer. It combines the command line with Windows Explorer navigation, so not only can you use the command line, but you can also navigate through your PC using Explorer.

The Web
Hacks 33–41

All of us live on the Web these days, and the demarcation between the operating system and the Web has gotten fuzzier with each iteration of Windows. XP has even more web-based tools built into it than its predecessors.

While Internet Explorer 6 betters all previous versions of the browser, it could still use some help. It doesn't give you much help when you want to protect your privacy or fight against annoyances like pop-up ads, for example. And its searching capabilities and offline display of web pages leaves much to be desired.

In this chapter, you'll find hacks to fix all that and more, including a great grab-bag of Registry hacks for Internet Explorer, a way to speed up file downloads, shortcuts for starting and running Internet Explorer, and more.

HACK #33 Stop Pop Ups, Spyware, and Web Bugs

You don't have to be victimized by obnoxious applications and behavior on the Internet. Fight back with these tips and tools.

Surfing the Web used to be such as simple, enjoyable experience. Go to the web site of your choice, enjoy the page, and head somewhere else.

No longer. At times, it now seems like a sleazy carnival midway, complete with flashing lights and loud music, barkers pleading at you to venture into the sideshows, scamsters promising you big payoffs if you try three-card monte, and no-goodniks lurking in the shadows.

For that, we have pop ups, spyware, and web bugs to thank. Pop ups are ads that, as the name implies, pop up over your browser, usually in a smaller window, and frequently contain flashing messages and other kinds of obnoxious come-ons. The infamous X.10 surveillance camera pioneered this insufferable form of advertising, and now it's everywhere.

Web bugs are invisible bits of data, frequently a single pixel in size (sometimes called "clear GIFs"), that can track all your activities on a web site and report them back to a server. Spyware is software that piggybacks onto your hard disk on the backs of other pieces of software, reports on your activities to ad servers, and then delivers ads to you based on what sites you visit. There's typically no way to know offhand that spyware has been installed on your system, because it lurks invisibly—hence the name. Even after you uninstall the program upon which it piggybacked, it could remain on your PC, reporting on your activities.

You don't have to be victimized, though. As you'll see in the rest of this hack, there are things you can do to keep your PC from resembling a virtual midway.

IE: Download Software to Stop Pop Ups

Internet Explorer has no built-in way to stop pop ups, but you can still kill them with downloadable software. There are many for-pay pop-up killers, but if you don't want to spend the cash, you can get an excellent one for free: EMS Free Surfer mk II, shown in Figure 4-1. It lets you set several levels of pop-up protection—you can block all pop ups or only those that appear to be unwanted—and you can turn it on and off with a click. It has other helpful tools as well, such as letting you shut every open instance of Internet Explorer with a single click, and it includes an add-in that will clean out your system cache and list of recently visited sites. Get it at *http://www.kolumbus.fi/eero.muhonen/FS/fs.htm*. (Don't confuse it with a related product, EMS Free Surfer Companion, which offers more features than the free versions and costs $20.)

Ditch IE: Use Opera or Mozilla to Stop Pop Ups

Here's one way to get rid of pop-up annoyances: skip Internet Explorer altogether! IE can't kill pop ups, but other browsers can. Both Opera and Mozilla include a built-in pop-up killer as a menu option.

Download Opera from *http://www.opera.com*. To enable its pop-up killer, choose File → Preferences → "Refuse pop-up windows". You can also have the program open pop-up windows in the background instead of on top of your browser.

Download Mozilla from *http://www.mozilla.org*. To enable its pop-up killer, choose Edit → Preferences → Privacy & Security → Pop-ups → and check "Reject pop-up windows."

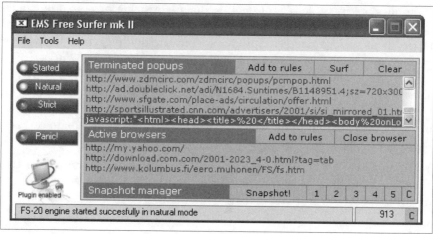

Figure 4-1. EMS Free Surver mk II

Stop Messenger Service Popups

In recent months, the most obnoxious pop ups of all have started to appear on computer users' screens—popups that aren't connected to a browser, appear even when you're not surfing the Web, and show up in a text-message window for no apparent reason. You've taken no conceivable action that could have caused them to appear, such as visiting a web site. And yet there they are.

These text pop ups use XP's Messenger service, which was designed for sending notifications over internal local area networks—for example, when a network administrator wants to notify network users that a server is about to go down, or when you're notified that a printer has completed a job of yours.

The Messenger service is not related to Windows Messenger, Microsoft's instant-messaging program.

But spammers took hold of the technology, and now blast out text pop ups to IP addresses across the Internet. How ubiquitous are these pop ups becoming? I recently bought a new laptop, and within 10 minutes of turning it on for the first time I had received my first Messenger service pop up.

To kill these pop ups, disable the Messenger service. Run the Services Microsoft Management Console by typing services.msc at a command prompt or the Run box and pressing Enter. Double-click on the entry for Messenger, choose Disabled as the Startup type from the screen that appears, and click OK. Pop ups will no longer get through. Unfortunately, neither will any network messages from administrators if you're on a LAN.

If you're running a router at home that allows you to block ports, you can kill these messages by disabling port 135. How you do this varies according to your router. To do it on a Linksys router, go to the router administrator screen and choose Advanced → Filters. In Filtered Private Port Range, choose Both, and for the range, type 135 twice. Click Apply. The pop ups should now be disabled.

Watch Out for Web Bugs

Web bugs are one of the more pernicious ways your online activities can be tracked, no matter which browser you're using. Sometimes, the web site the bugs send information to isn't the one that contains the web bug; for example, they may send information back to an online advertising network.

Web bugs are surprisingly common. The Cyveillance technology and analysis company found that their use grew nearly 500% between 1998 and 2001. Web bugs can send the following information back to a server:

- The IP address of your computer
- The URL of the page on which the web bug is located, so they know that you visited the page
- The time the web bug was viewed, so they know exactly when you visited the page
- The URL of the web bug image
- The type of browser that you have
- Your cookie values

A free piece of software called Bugnosis (*http://www.bugnosis.org*) will alert you whenever it comes across web bugs on pages you visit. It reports on the URL that the bug reports to, and, for some bugs, it will let you click on a link it creates so that you can send an email of complaint to the web site that runs the bug. It runs inside Internet Explorer.

> The last time I visited the site, it no longer had Bugnosis available, but promised it would be back soon. Be prepared that it might not be there when you visit.

The software can't actually protect you against web bugs, but it can alert you when you visit pages that use them. If you want your privacy protected when you surf the Web, your best bet is to surf anonymously [Hack #39].

Protect Yourself Against Spyware

Spyware has become increasingly controversial and increasingly popular, as developers of free software struggle to find a way to support themselves. Of late, spyware has been getting increasingly intrusive; some people call these more aggressive programs *scumware*. Scumware may change your default home page without telling you, or may even intervene when you're making a purchase online and redirect you to a different site.

There are several ways to protect yourself against spyware:

- Be vigilant about what you download. Ad-supported programs may include spyware, though not all do. Check out the "Index of Known Spyware" page run by Gibson Research at *http://grc.com/oo/spyware.htm* for a list of spyware programs. The only problem with that site is that it lists only the spyware components, and it's difficult to find out their names. A better bet is *http://www.spychecker.com*, which lets you type in the name of a program you downloaded and then tells you whether spyware piggybacks onto it.

- Use a personal firewall like ZoneAlarm [Hack #48]. A personal firewall will let you block any program on your system from contacting the Internet without your approval, so you can use it to block spyware. XP's Internet Connection Firewall doesn't have this capability, so you can't use it to block spyware.

- Get a spyware detector and eradicator. My favorite and the most popular is Ad-Aware, available for free from *http://www.lavasoft.de*. It does a thorough check of your system for spyware, finding not only program files, but also Registry entries and cookies, as shown in Figure 4-2. After it does a check, you can choose which of the spyware problems you want the program to fix, and it'll go about its work, deleting files, folders, and cookies, and fixing Registry entries. If you use file-sharing software, I highly recommend running Ad-Aware; many of these applications include spyware.

> Keep in mind that when you delete spyware, you may disable software as well, so it's a good idea to always create a Restore point before deleting spyware. Choose Control Panel → Performance and Maintenance → System Restore and follow the instructions. For example, if you remove the Cydoor spyware program, the Kazaa file-sharing program will no longer work. Alternatives to Kazaa include Shareaza (*http://www.shareaza.com*), a front-end to the popular Gnutella file-sharing network that also can hook into other file-sharing networks, such as the one that Kazaa uses.

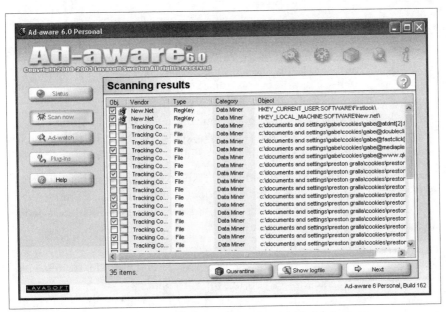

Figure 4-2. Finding and deleting spyware on your system with Ad-Aware

See Also

- Stop Hidden Fields in Word from Stealing Your Files and Information
  [Hack #85]
- File Sharing without the Spyware **[Hack #89]**

Take a Bite Out of Cookies

#34

Protect your privacy and keep your surfing habits to yourself with proper cookie handling.

Cookies are small text files that web sites put on your hard disk to personalize the site for you or to track and then record your activities on the site. Cookies have gotten a lot of press—most of it bad—but the truth is, not all cookie use is bad. As a means of site customization, they're a great way of helping you get the most out of the Web. They can also carry information about log-in names and passwords, which is a time-saver, since you won't have to log into each site every time you visit. If you delete all your cookies, you won't automatically get your Amazon wish list the next time you visit their site.

Cookies are big time-savers when it comes to logging you into web sites automatically, but they can also be security holes as well. If you use them to log you in automatically, anyone who uses your computer will be able to log into those sites with your username and password.

But cookies can also be used to track your online activities and identify you. Information about you, based on what cookies gather, can be put in a database, and profiles of you and your surfing habits can be created.

Because cookies can be privacy-invaders, XP gives you a number of ways to restrict how web sites place and use cookies on your PC. To understand how to restrict the ways cookies are used on your PC, you first need to understand three cookie-related terms:

First-party cookie
> A cookie created by the site you're currently visiting. These cookies are often used by sites to let you log on automatically—without having to type in your username and password—and customize how you use the site. Typically, these kinds of cookies are not invasive.

Third-party cookie
> A cookie created by a site other than the one you're currently visiting. Frequently, third-party cookies are used by advertisers or advertising networks. Some people (including me) consider these kinds of cookies invasive.

Compact privacy statement
> A publicly posted policy that describes the details of how cookies are used on a site—for example, detailing the purpose of cookies, how they're used, their source, and how long they will stay on your PC. (Some cookies are automatically deleted when you leave a web site, while others stay valid until a specified date.)

To protect your privacy, you also need to know the difference between implicit consent and explicit consent. *Explicit consent* means that you have specifically told a site that it can use personally identifiable information about you. It's the same as *opting in*. *Implicit consent* means that you haven't specifically told a site not to use personally identifiable information. It's the same as not having *opted out*, or specifically requesting to be taken off a list.

Internet Explorer lets you customize how it handles cookies. You can choose from six levels of privacy settings, from Accept All Cookies to Block All Cookies. When choosing, keep in mind that some sites won't function well or at all at the higher privacy settings, particularly if you choose to reject all cookies. I generally find that Medium High is a good compromise between protecting privacy and still being able to personalize web sites.

To customize your cookie settings in Internet Explorer, choose Tools → Internet Options → Privacy. Move the slider (shown in Figure 4-3) to your desired level.

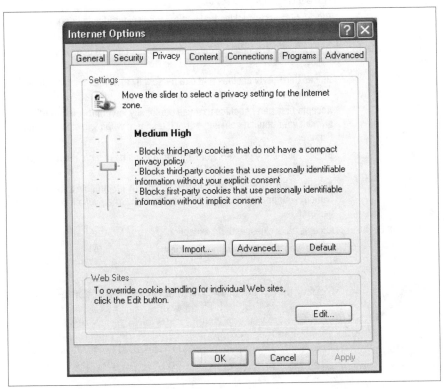

Figure 4-3. Customizing cookie settings in Internet Explorer

Table 4-1 shows how each setting affects Internet Explorer's cookie handling.

Table 4-1. Internet Explorer's privacy settings and your privacy

Setting	How the setting affects your privacy
Block All Cookies	Blocks all cookies, without exception.
	Does not allow web sites to read existing cookies.
High	Blocks cookies from all web sites that don't have a compact privacy policy.
	Blocks all cookies that use personally identifiable information without your explicit consent.

Table 4-1. Internet Explorer's privacy settings and your privacy (continued)

Setting	How the setting affects your privacy
Medium High	Blocks third-party cookies from sites that don't have a compact privacy policy.
	Blocks third-party cookies that use personally identifiable information without your explicit consent.
	Blocks first-party cookies that use personally identifiable information without your implicit consent.
Medium (Default)	Blocks third-party cookies from sites that don't have a compact privacy policy.
	Blocks third-party cookies that use personally identifiable information without your implicit consent.
	Accepts first-party cookies that use personally identifiable information without your implicit consent, but deletes them when you close Internet Explorer.
Low	Blocks third-party cookies from sites that don't have a compact privacy policy.
	Accepts third-party cookies that use personally identifiable information without your implicit consent, but deletes them when you close Internet Explorer.
Accept All Cookies	Accepts all cookies, without exception.
	Allows web sites read existing cookies.

> In Mozilla, pretty good cookie management is built in. Access settings via Edit → Preferences → Privacy & Security → Cookies, where you can enable or disable a variety of specific cookie-handling settings (accept, flag, decline, or ask you on a per-cookie basis) based on your own privacy settings (similar to those of IE), or the originating web site's settings.

Customizing IE Cookie Handling

You're not locked into IE's preset levels of cookie handling. If you like, you can customize how it handles cookies so that you could, for example, accept or reject cookies from individual sites, or accept or reject all first-party and third-party cookies.

To accept or reject all cookies from a specific site, choose Tools → Internet Options → Privacy → Edit. You'll see the Per Site Privacy Actions dialog box, as shown in Figure 4-4. Type in the name of the site you want to accept or block cookies from, and click on either Block or Allow.

To customize how you handle first-party and third-party cookies, choose Tools → Internet Options → Privacy → Advanced. Check the "Override auto-

Figure 4-4. The Per Site Privacy Actions dialog box

matic cookie handling" box, as shown in Figure 4-5. You can accept or reject all first-party or third-party cookies, or be prompted whether to accept them. You can also decide to always allow "session cookies"—cookies that last only as long as you're on a specific web site and are deleted once you leave the site.

Export, Import, or Back Up Your Cookies

Although some cookies can be intrusive, some can also be helpful as well. They can log you into web sites automatically and customize the way you use and view the site. So, when you buy a new PC, you might want to export cookies from an older computer to it. If you have more than one PC, you might want all of them to have the same cookies. And you might want to back up your cookies for safe-keeping in case you accidentally delete the wrong ones.

To export or back up cookies from IE, choose File → Import and Export. The Import/Export Wizard will launch. Choose Export Cookies and follow

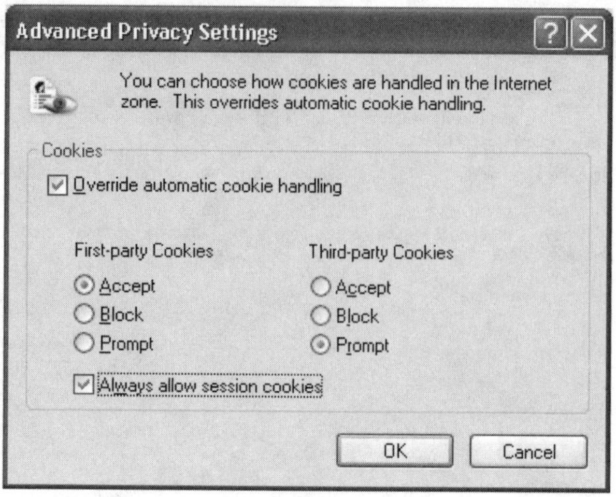

Figure 4-5. The Advanced Privacy Settings dialog box

the directions. A single text file containing all your cookies will be created in My Documents, though you can choose a different location for them. To import cookies, launch the Import/Export Wizard, choose Import Cookies, and browse to the location where the cookie file has been stored.

Examine and Delete Cookies Manually

You can't examine and delete your cookies from within Internet Explorer. However, because XP stores each IE cookie as an individual text file, you can read them and delete them just as you would any other text file. Go to *C:\Documents and Settings\Your Name\Cookies* in Windows Explorer, and you'll see a list of individual cookies in a format like this:

```
your name@abcnews.com[1].txt
```

As a general rule, the name of the web site or ad network will be after the @, but not always—sometimes it will merely be a number. Open the file as you would any other text file (in Notepad, WordPad, or another text editor). Usually, there will be a list of numbers and letters inside, though you might find other useful information in there—for example, your username and password for the web site. If you don't want the cookie on your hard disk, simply delete it as you would any other text file.

Netscape Navigator and Mozilla handle cookies differently than Internet Explorer. They store all cookies in a single file, *cookies.txt*, typically found in *C:\Documents and Settings\<Your Name>\[Application Data]\Mozilla\ Profiles\default********.slt*, where ******** is a random collection of numbers and letters. So, the directory might be *C:\Documents and Settings\Name\ Mozilla\Profiles\default\46yhu2ir.slt*. If you've set up different Netscape/ Mozilla profiles (Tools → Switch Profile → Manage Profiles → Create Profile), *cookies.txt* won't be in the *default* subfolder, but under each profile's name. You can open the file and see each individual cookie. You can't however, delete individual entries from the file by editing this file. Instead, use Netscape's built-in Cookie Manager (at Tools → Cookie Manager → Manage Stored Cookies) to read and delete cookies.

Get a Third-Party Cookie Manager

The tools built into XP for managing cookies are reasonable, but for the most flexibility in handling cookies you should get a third-party cookie manager. My favorite (and my editor's favorite) is Cookie Pal, available at *http:// www.kburra.com*. It lets you easily customize which sites you'll allow to put cookies on your PC, and it includes a cookie manager that lets you read and delete cookies. It also lets you accept or reject cookies on a case-by-case basis as you browse the Web. If you use browsers other than IE, you might be out of luck, though. As of this writing, Cookie Pal works only with Versions 3 and 4 of Netscape Navigator and Versions 4, 5, and 6 of Opera. (Mozilla and later Netscape version have similarly good managers built in, as mentioned earlier.)

Opt Out of Cookie-Based Ad Networks

Online ad networks have the potential to create in-depth, privacy-invading profiles of your web travels and personal interests, because they can place a single cookie on your hard disk that will track you across multiple sites. Normally, sites can't share cookie information with each other, but ad networks have found a way around this, so they can aggregate your behavior from many web sites.

You can fight back by opting out of some of the biggest online ad networks. You'll have them place an opt-out cookie on your hard disk that will tell the various sites not to track what you're doing; this will go a long way toward protecting your privacy.

To opt out of the DoubleClick online advertising network, go to *http://www. doubleclick.com/us/corporate/privacy/privacy/ad-cookie/* and click on the "Ad Cookie Opt-Out" button at the bottom of the page.

To see whether the opt-out worked, if you're an Internet Explorer user, go to your cookies folder, which is typically *C:\Documents and Settings\<Your Name>\Cookies*. Look for a cookie named *your name@doubleclick[1].txt—*

for example, *preston gralla@doubleclick[1].txt*. The contents of the cookie should look something like this:

```
id OPT_OUT doubleclick.net/ 1024 468938752 31583413 3447013104 29418226 *
```

In Netscape Navigator, your *cookies.txt* file is typically found in *C:\ Documents and Settings\<Your Name>\Application Data\Mozilla\Profiles\ default********.slt*, where ******** is a random collection of numbers and letters. So, the directory might be *C:\Documents and Settings\Name\Mozilla\ Profiles\default\46yhu2ir.slt*. Look in the file for an entry that looks like this:

```
.doubleclick.net    TRUE  /  FALSE 1920499138    id    OPT_OUT
```

You can instead use Netscape's built-in Cookie Manager to examine the cookie, by choosing Tools → Cookie Manager → Manage Stored Cookies.

Some other advertising networks let you opt out as well. For details, go to *http://www.networkadvertising.org/optout_nonppii.asp* and follow the instructions for opting out. To verify that you've successfully opted out of the other ad networks, click on the Verify Cookies menu item on the left part of the page.

See Also

- Stop Pop Ups, Spyware, and Web Bugs [Hack #33]
- Slam That Spam [Hack #63]

HACK #35   Read Web Pages Offline

Take the Web with you wherever you go, and put it into an easily searchable database on your PC.

One of the main problems with doing research on the Web is that there's no easy way to save all the information you find and no simple way to read web pages when you're offline. Internet Explorer includes some basic tools for saving web pages and reading through them when you're not connected to the Internet. If you need to save only occasional pages and don't need to do searches through those pages, then these tools will work reasonably well for you. But if you want to store pages in categories and folders and need to do full-text searches, then you'll need a third-party program. This hack shows you how to do both.

Reading Web Pages Offline Using IE

To save your current web page to your hard disk so you can read it again in Internet Explorer when you're not connected to the Internet, choose File → Save As. You'll be given several options for how to save it. If you're not planning to edit the HTML of the file, your best bet is to save it as a Web "Archive, single file" (*.mht*). That way, you don't clutter up your hard disk with extra folders and files stored in different locations; everything is saved to a single file. Saving it as a "Web Page, complete" stores the HTML file as well as associated graphics, in a folder structure. Saving it as a "Web Page, HTML only" saves just the HTML file itself, with no associated graphics and no folder structure. You can also save it as a text file, but if you do, expect to spend time cleaning it up, because it saves all the text on the page, often in an unstructured way. To read the page after you've saved it to your disk, choose File → Open, browse to the directory where you've saved the page, and open it.

There are times when you want to save not just the page you're on, but also the pages linked off it. To do that, you'll have to save your pages another way. First, save the page to your Favorites list by pressing Ctrl-D or choosing Favorites → Add to Favorites. Then, right-click on the page where it's listed in Favorites and choose Make Available Offline. A wizard will appear. Follow its instructions, and when you get to the screen shown in Figure 4-6, tell it how many links deep you want pages saved. Be very careful when doing this, because even choosing to keep one link level can take up a substantial amount of hard disk space.

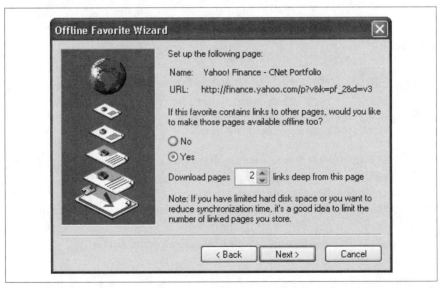

Figure 4-6. Saving web pages offline several links deep using the Offline Favorite Wizard

When you finish the wizard, you're asked how you want to synchronize the page or pages you've chosen to save to disk. When you synchronize a web page, IE grabs the latest version of the page or pages, and overwrites your existing page or pages. If you want to keep a permanent copy of the page or pages, and don't want them updated, choose "Only when I choose Synchronize from the Tools menu." Then, simply don't synchronize the page. If you instead do want to synchronize the page so that a more current version is available on your hard disk, choose "I would like to create a new schedule," and follow the instructions for creating a schedule.

Save Web Pages in an Offline Database with SurfSaver

If you need to save many web pages and want to be able to search through them by full-text or keyword searches, you'll have to use a third-party program. My favorite is SurfSaver, available from *http://www.surfsaver.com* (see Figure 4-7). It integrates directly into Internet Explorer and lets you save pages in separate folders within the program. You can add keywords and notes to each page, and then search by keyword or full text, or browse by folder.

When you visit a web page you want to save locally, right-click on the page, choose SurfSaver Save, and choose which SurfSaver folder you want to save it in. You can save the page with or without graphics. When you want to search, right-click on the page, choose SurfSaver Search, and then search by keyword, through notes, or through the full text on the page to easily find the page and information you want. SurfSaver also integrates directly with the freeform askSam database.

Better Internet Searching from Your Desktop

HACK #36 Internet Explorer's default search features are anemic at best. Do better Internet searching by installing a Google Toolbar and other specialized search toolbars and powering up the default search.

Was there ever a Web before Google? Yes, but it was a heck of a lot harder to find anything in it. Internet Explorer's default search feature leaves a lot to be desired, not the least of which is its use of MSN Search instead of Google. But there's a lot you can do to do better Internet searching from your desktop. You can get search toolbars that integrate into your browser, and you can customize the Internet Explorer search feature as well.

Google Toolbar

The best way to empower Internet searches is by installing special toolbars from two popular search engines, Google and Ask Jeeves. The Google Toolbar is the better of the two, and not only because it's a better search engine. It also has several extra features.

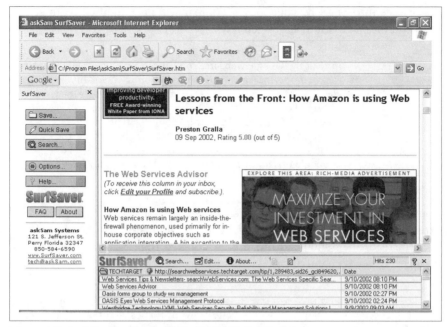

Figure 4-7. Saving web pages in a database with SurfSaver

The great thing about the Google Toolbar is, well, that it's Google. It gives you all of Google's functionality without even having to visit the site. To get the Google Toolbar for IE, go to *http://toolbar.google.com* and follow the installation instructions. It works only with Internet Explorer. Once you install it, you'll be able to search Google without having to visit the search site; just type your search term in the toolbar. In fact, you even get an extra on the toolbar that you don't get on Google itself—the PageRank feature that tells you how popular the current site you're visiting is.

> The Mozdev.org site (*http://www.mozdev.org*) has written a third-party Google Toolbar called the Googlebar (*http://googlebar.mozdev.org*) for use with Netscape 7/Mozilla browsers. It emulates most of the features of the Google Toolbar except PageRank.

The best of the Google Toolbar's best features is that it lets you do a Google search through the site you're currently on, a particularly useful tool if the site doesn't have a search box, or if the search on the site is a poor one. In fact, I rarely use sites' search boxes and prefer to use the Google Toolbar instead. Among other features, the Google Toolbar also lets you find sites related to the one you're currently visiting, and it will translate foreign-language sites into English. The Google Toolbar will also highlight your search terms on the page results if you tell it to.

> If you're at the Google web site, you can do a targeted search of only one specific site instead of the entire Web. In the Google search box, type site:www.nameofsite.com searchterm. For example, if you want to search the *www. newscientist.com* site for the word "cloning," type site:www. newscientist.com cloning. You'll get results showing all the web pages on the site containing the word "cloning". For more Google tips and tricks, see *Google Hacks* or the *Google Pocket Guide* (O'Reilly).

Using the Google Toolbar is simplicity itself: type a search term into it and press Enter. If you want to search the current site instead of the entire Web, click instead on a small button on the toolbar that pictures two pairs of googly eyes on a magnifying glass.

> If you'd prefer to search Google directly from your desktop rather than from within your browser, there's a workaround for you. Download the free program GAPIS from *http:// www.searchenginelab.com/common/products/gapis*. To use it, you'll need to get a Google developer's key. You don't actually need to be a developer to get a key, though, and it's free. To get the key, go to *http://www.google.com/apis/*. The page recommends that you download the Google developer's kit, but you don't need to do that to get your free key. Instead, click on "create a Google account" and follow the instructions. Once you have the account, you have to type the key into GAPIS the first time you use the program. After that, you'll be able to do Google searches by running GAPIS rather than using the Google Toolbar or visiting the Google site.

If you're concerned about your privacy, you should disable the PageRank option. When you enable this option, the Google Toolbar tracks the page you're on. With it disabled, it doesn't.

> Ask Jeeves has a similar toolbar, at *http://sp.ask.com/docs/ toolbar*. In addition to letting you search Ask Jeeves regardless of where you are on the Web, it includes links for weather forecasts, news, and more.

Mastering the Search Companion

If you decide to forgo the Google and Ask Jeeves search toolbars, there are still things you can do to power up Internet Explorer's Search Companion, which you get to by pressing Control-E or clicking on the Search button. You'll of course first want to get rid of the cloyingly cute animated dog that normally appears, by choosing Change Preferences when the Search Companion appears and then choosing "Without an animated screen character."

But the Search Companion has bigger problems than stray dogs. It forces you through a step-by-step search, and, worse still, it clutters up the search area with "sponsored links" from advertisers. Type in the name Preston, for example, and you'll get sponsored links such as "Hotels near Preston," "Buy Fine Wines and Beer at Libation.com" and "Preston, Idaho Travel Information." No thank you. I prefer my search results straight up.

A better bet is to use what Microsoft calls the Classic Internet Search Companion, which previous versions of Internet Explorer used. From the Search Companion choose Change Preferences → "Change Internet search behavior" → "with Classic Internet search". You'll have to close Internet Explorer and restart it for the changes to take effect. As you can see in Figure 4-8, it's simpler and allows you to perform more focused searches, specifically for web pages, addresses, business names, maps, and to perform a previous search. Click the More button to search for pictures and definitions of words.

By default, the Internet Explorer uses MSN as its search engine, but after you perform a search, if you don't find what you want, you can send the same query to other search engines by clicking "Send search to more search engines" and then picking the engine you want to use. You can also change the default search engine by opening the Search Companion, choosing Change Internet Search Behavior, scrolling down the page that appears, and choosing a new default search engine from the list of 13.

See Also

- WebFerret by Ferretsoft (*http://www.ferretsoft.com*) is free metasearch software that will send your search to multiple search engines simultaneously and display all the results in a single window, collating the results.
- Copernic Agent Basic, a metasearch tool from Copernic (*http://www. copernic.com*) lets you perform more targeted searches, by sending your search to specialized search engines in a variety of categories when you choose a targeted search.

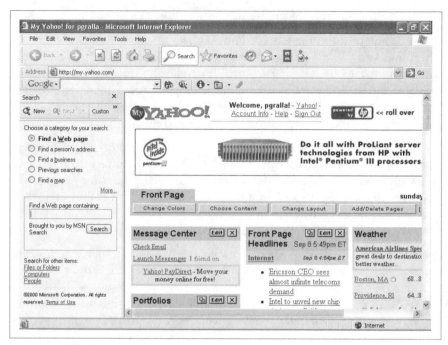

Figure 4-8. The Classic Internet Search Assistant

Hack Internet Explorer with the Group Policy Editor

XP Professional's Group Policy Editor lets you tweak Internet Explorer in countless ways—from changing its logo and background, to changing its title bar text and beyond.

XP Professional owners have a reason to feel good about spending the extra $100 or so they forked over for their version of the operating system: the Group Policy Editor, available only in Professional, can make all kinds of secret tweaks to Internet Explorer. This tool, primarily used for setting network and multiuser policies and rights, can also be used to customize the way XP and Internet Explorer look and work. It makes it easy to customize many different aspects of Internet Explorer's behavior and appearance from one central place, without having to edit the Registry or delve deep into menus, dialog boxes, and options. You can customize how Internet Explorer looks and works for each individual account on the machine, or just for a single account if there is only one.

That means that you'll be able to create customized versions of IE for a variety of different purposes. For example, you can create customized browsers for your children, or for a business if you run or administer a small business.

Run the Group Policy Editor by typing gpedit.msc at a command line or the Run box and pressing Enter. When it opens, go to User Configuration\ Windows Settings\Internet Explorer Maintenance. There are five categories of Internet Explorer settings you can modify:

- Browser User Interface
- Connection
- URLs
- Security
- Programs

To change individual settings, browse to any of the categories, then from the right pane choose the setting you want to configure—for example, to change the browser title. Double-click on the setting, then fill out the dialog box, such as the one shown in Figure 4-9, which lets you change Internet Explorer's static and animated logos.

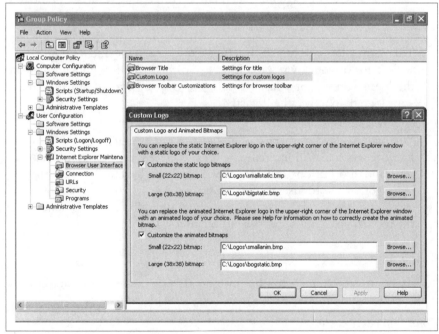

Figure 4-9. Using the Group Policy Editor to change Internet Explorer's settings

There are quite a few settings you can change with the Group Policy Editor. Next, we'll take a look at what the best of each of these categories can do.

Browser User Interface

As the name implies, this section lets you customize Internet Explorer's interface. This section, as a whole, lets you create your own customized version of Internet Explorer. For example, you can create a version of IE specifically for one of your children—take a digital photo of her and use it as the background for the toolbar, crop a headshot photo of your child and use it as the animated custom logo, and change the browser title to put her name on it. There are three types of tweaks you can make in this section:

Browser Title
> This option lets you customize Internet Explorer's titlebar text, though only to a limited degree; you can add your name or company's name to a text string of "Microsoft Internet Explorer provided by." For example, you can have the titlebar read "Microsoft Explorer provided by Preston Gralla." When you do this, Outlook Express will have the same title as well. Because you need to have that initial text string, this isn't a great hack unless you're a computer manufacturer and want to brand the browser.

Custom Logo
> This setting lets you replace Internet Explorer's static and animated logo with logos of your own. Note that to do this, you'll first have to create the logos yourself. It's easier to use the Group Policy Editor to change your logo than to use the Registry.

Browser Toolbar Customizations
> You can use your own bitmap as the background to the Internet Explorer toolbar. Additionally, you can delete the existing toolbar buttons and add buttons of your own. You don't have to worry if the bitmap you want to use is not the same size as the toolbar. XP will accommodate it—for example, by tiling a graphic that is smaller than the toolbar so that it appears multiple times.

Connection

This section lets you customize Internet Explorer's connection settings, which you would otherwise have to go to several places to set.

Connection Settings
> This lets you customize your existing Internet connection settings and import them for another use on the PC. It doesn't have any use if you're the only user of the machine; it's intended to help you set up other accounts' connection settings. If you have a network at home, for example, you could copy the settings from one machine to every other machine on the network.

Automatic Browser Configuration

This is purely an administrator's tool. It lets you automatically change browser configurations on users' machines.

Proxy Settings

This lets you tell Internet Explorer to use proxy servers. You can also set up proxy servers from within Internet Explorer. For more details on setting up proxy servers, see "Protect Your Computer with the Internet Connection Firewall" [Hack #46].

User Agent String

This lets you customize the user agent string that is sent to web sites whenever you visit them. The user agent string gives out basic information about your operating system and browser to the web site so that the site can better track usage statistics. Using this setting lets you append a specific text string to your PC's user agent string.

URLs

This section is mainly for administrators, so if you don't need administrative tools you can pretty much forgo it. If you are an administrator, it will let you specify IE settings for multiple machines, such as setting a home page for all, specifying a URL they will go to when Help is chosen, and populating their Favorites with those of your choice. If you run a small business, you can use these settings to build a business-specific browser for all of your employees. For example, set the home page to be your company's home page or populate Favorites with Intranet pages or other pages your employees need to access regularly, such as benefits information.

Favorites and Links

This lets you create a Favorites folder and links, or import them. It's primarily an administrator's tool, since it doesn't add much extra functionality to the normal way that you can manage Favorites.

Important URLs

You can specify the starting page, create your own customized Search bar, and create a Help page that will display when someone clicks on Help → Online Support. Again, this is primarily an administrator's tool.

Security

Here's where to set Internet Explorer security settings. You can change these settings from directly within Internet Explorer just as easily as changing them here, unless you need to change the settings for several accounts, in which case here's the place to go.

Security Zones and Content Rating

> You can customize both security zones and content ratings, which limit sites with objectionable content from being visited. This is primarily an administrator's tool, since these settings can be edited easily from inside Internet Explorer by choosing Tools → Internet Options → Security and Tools → Internet Options → Content. But it's ideal for parents who have networks at home and want to customize different security settings for their children's computers. You can set a higher level of security for children's computers and a lower level for parents' PCs.

Authenticode Settings

> This lets you designate specific credential agencies and software publishers as trustworthy. This is primarily an administrator's tool, since these settings can be edited easily from inside Internet Explorer by choosing Tools → Internet Options → Security and Tools → Internet Options → Content → Certificates.

Programs

Once again, this section is mainly for administrators. It lets you change default programs for multiple machines. So, for users who require only a simple email program, you can set the default to be Outlook Express. For other users, you can set it as Outlook or a third-party email program.

Programs

> This lets you change the default programs to be used for purposes such as email, HTML editing, and others. This is primarily an administrator's tool, since these settings can be edited easily by choosing Tools → Internet Options → Security and Tools → Internet Options → Programs.

H A C K   Speed Up File Downloads
#38
Don't wait any longer for slow file downloads. Use this free program to accelerate them, regardless of your connection speed.

No matter how fast your Internet connection is, it's not fast enough. Whether it's a pokey dial-up or a broadband connection, you always have complaints and you always have a greater need for speed.

This is particularly true when you're downloading files, especially large ones. While there may be no way to physically change your connection speed, you can get the free Download Accelerator Plus (DAP) program from SpeedBit (*http://www.speedbit.com*) to speed up your downloads significantly, whether via FTP or HTTP.

The program accelerates your downloads in two ways. When you start to download a file, DAP does a mirror search of all the servers that carry the same file, identifies the fastest servers closest to you, and then starts downloading from those servers instead of the one you originally chose. It also sets up a multiconnection download, downloading portions of the file from multiple fast servers simultaneously and then reassembling the file when all the pieces are on your PC. This makes the most efficient use of your available bandwidth, because normally there are pauses and hesitations when you download, and if you're downloading with multiple connections there will be fewer of those pauses.

The program also resumes broken downloads; if for some reason your connection is broken, it'll pick up where you left off when you next connect to the Internet. Also useful is the ZIP preview feature that lets you preview the contents of ZIP-compressed files before you download. And it'll schedule downloads for you as well. For example, you can schedule downloads to take place overnight, when you're away from your computer.

DAP is free, but the free version delivers ads inside the program. For $19.95 you can get a version without the ads that also includes a few minor extras, such as the ability to extract individual files from within *.zip* archives, instead of extracting the whole archive.

HACK #39 Surf Anonymously Without a Trace

Feel like someone is watching you? On the Web, they probably are. Protect your privacy by using anonymous proxy servers.

Whenever you surf the Web, you leave yourself open to being snooped upon by web sites. They can track your online travels, know what operating system and browser you're running, find out your machine name, peer into your clipboard, uncover the last sites you've visited, examine your history list, delve into your cache, examine your IP address and use that to learn basic information about you such as your geographic location, and more. To a great extent, your Internet life is an open book when you visit.

Don't believe me? Head to *http://www.anonymizer.com/snoop/test_ip.shtml*. This page, run by the Anonymizer.com web service, tells you what your IP address and machine name are. And that's just a start. Click on the links on the left side, such as "Exposed Clipboard" and "Geographical Location." You'll see just a small sampling of what web sites can learn about you. Figure 4-10 shows a web site reporting on my geographic location. It's close enough; I live in Cambridge rather than Boston, and we generally require that people turn over their passports at the border.

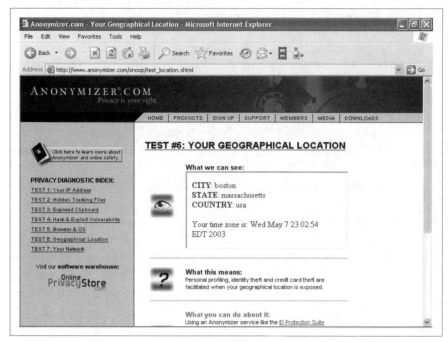

Figure 4-10. The Anonymizer.com web service, exposing my current geographic location

Much of the reason why web sites can find out this information about you is due to the trusting nature of the Internet's infrastructure and is inherent in the open client/server relationship between your web browser and the servers on the sites you visit. But a lot of it also has to do with the ability to match up information from your PC to information in publicly available databases—for example, databases that have information about IP addresses.

The best way to make sure web sites can't gather personal information about you and your computer is to surf anonymously; use an anonymous proxy server to sit between you and the web sites you visit. When you use an anonymous proxy server, your browser doesn't contact a web site directly. Instead, it tells a proxy server which web site you want to visit. The proxy server then contacts the web site, and when you get the web site's page you don't get it directly from the site. Instead, it's delivered to you by the proxy server. In that way, your browser never directly contacts the web server whose site you want to view. The web site sees the IP address of the proxy server, not your PC's IP address. It can't read your cookies, see your history list, or examine your clipboard and cache, because your PC is never in direct contact with it. You're able to surf anonymously, without a trace.

There are two primary ways to use anonymous proxy servers. You can run client software on your PC, which does the work of contacting the server for you, or you can instead visit a web site, which then does the work of contacting the server.

Web-Based Anonymizer

If you don't want to go to the hassle of installing a client—and if you don't want to pay for software—to surf anonymously, go to Anonymizer.com (*http://www.anonymizer.com*). In the box near the top of the page, type the name of the site to which you want to surf, and you'll head there anonymously. The proxy server will grab the page for you, and you'll get the page from the proxy server. You can also download a free version that runs as a toolbar in Internet Explorer. Surf as you would normally, and you'll visit those web sites directly. When you want to visit a site anonymously, click on a button and the anonymous proxy server will do the work for you.

A fuller version of the program is available on a subscription basis for $29.95 per year or $9.95 for three months. It blocks banner ads, stops pop ups, encrypts the URLs you type so that they can't be read by your ISP or network administrator, and adds a few other features as well. I don't find the extra features worth the money, but if these kinds of things are important to you, go ahead and spend the money. (To learn how to block pop-ups, turn to "Stop Pop Ups, Spyware, and Web Bugs" [Hack #33].)

 When you use this site, some sites will appear broken, with text and graphics displaying oddly. But it's a small price to pay for your privacy.

Get Software for Anonymous Surfing

If you prefer to install software, get Steganos Internet Anonym 5 (*http://www.steganos.com/en/sia*). In addition to anonymous proxy serving, it kills pop ups and manages cookies. You can try it for free, but if you want to keep it you'll have to pay $29.95.

See Also

- Take a Bite Out of Cookies [Hack #34]
- Protect Your Computer with the Internet Connection Firewall [Hack #46]
- ZoneAlarm: The World's Best Free Firewall [Hack #48]
- Go to *http://www.gilc.org/speech/anonymous/remailer.html* to send email anonymously so that it can't be traced to you as the sender. Whistleblowers might want to use this feature, but others should make sure not to abuse it.

- For shareware that cleans out your cached files, destroys your history trail, and uses a variety of other methods to clean all traces of where you've surfed, try SurfSecret Privacy Protector (*http://ww.surfsecret.com*).

HACK #40 Secrets of Web Site Hosting with Internet Information Services (IIS)

XP Professional includes a free, built-in web server. If you're planning on using it, check out these tips to improve your site's performance, cut down on bandwidth, deliver pages faster, and reduce Page Not Found errors.

If you've wanted to host a web server but don't want to go to the trouble of configuring a separate machine and server, XP Professional has help for you. Windows XP Professional comes with Internet Information Services (IIS) Version 5.1, which lets you host web sites and FTP sites and run a Simple Mail Transfer Protocol (SMTP) service for sending email. (The Home Edition doesn't include any of these capabilities.) It's not something you'll use to build a substantial web site, because it has some significant drawbacks. The web server and FTP server allow only 10 simultaneous connections, for example, and the SMTP server isn't a full-blown mail server; it can only act as a relay.

Still, if you want to host a small web site for friends, family, or only for internal use for a small business, or if you want to build a "staging server" to test out sites before publicly posting them on a different server, IIS is a good bet.

IS isn't installed by default in XP Professional. To install it, choose Control Panel → Add or Remove Programs → Add/Remove Windows Components and, from the Windows Component Wizard that appears, highlight Internet Information Services (IIS) and click on Details.

Administer your web site by using the Microsoft Management Console (MMC) IIS snap-in. Choose Control Panel → Administrative Tools and double-click on Internet Information Services. The console tree, shown in Figure 4-11, shows the structure of your web and FTP sites and also gives you control over those sites.

In this hack, I'll assume that you know the basics of building a web site with IIS, so I'll instead clue you in to secrets of IIS.

Change the Directory and Do a Redirect

residential gateways:optimizingBy default, IIS uses the *C:\Inetpub\wwwroot* directory for your web site. However, you'll most likely want to change that directory to one that better matches your own PC setup. To change it, launch the MMC snap-in as detailed earlier in this hack, then right-click on

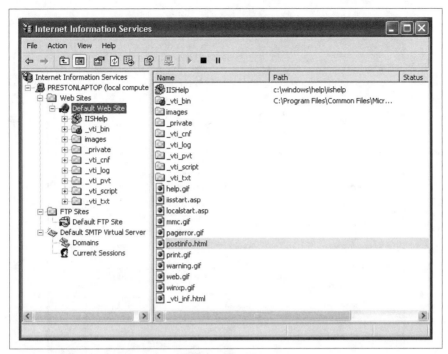

Figure 4-11. The console tree for the MMC IIS snap-in

Default Web Site and choose the Home Directory tab, shown in Figure 4-12. In the Local Path box, type in or browse to the directory you want to use.

If you want to use a directory on another computer located on the network, select "A share located on another computer." The Local Path box changes to Network Directory, and the Browse button changes to a Connect As button. Type in the directory information from the other computer, then click on Connect As to use your logon credentials to use the network share.

This tab also lets you do a redirect of your web site so that when someone visits your web site they'll be redirected to another site. That site doesn't have to be on your network; it can be any location on the Internet. This option is most useful when you move your web site to another URL but want those who use the old URL to be able to access it. To do a redirect, select "A redirection to a URL." The screen will change to the screen shown in Figure 4-13.

You have three options for your redirect:

The exact URL entered above
    This redirects all traffic to the URL you specified.

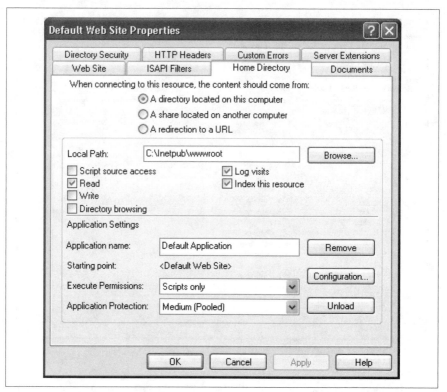

Figure 4-12. The Default Web Site Home Directory tab

A directory below this one

This lets you force a redirect of a parent directory to a child directory. For example, if someone were to type *www.mysite.com* in their browser, and you wanted them to end up at *www.mysite.com/pics*, you'd choose this option and have the location *www.mysite.com/pics* in the "Redirect to" box.

A permanent redirection for this resource

When this option is chosen, a "301 Permanent Redirect" message will be sent to the visiting browser. This can be used by some browsers to automatically update their bookmarks or Favorites list with your new site location.

Redirect Incorrect Incoming URLs

They're the bugaboo of every web site administrator—people who mistype URLs and get the dreaded "404 The page cannot be found" error. For example, if someone wanted to visit *http://www.gralla.com/mybio.htm*, but

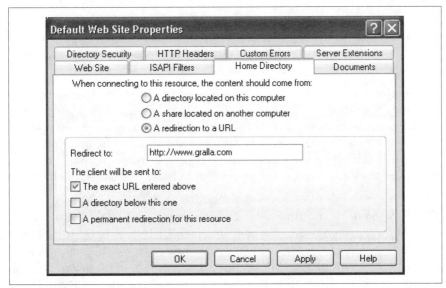

Figure 4-13. Redirecting to a URL

instead typed *http://www.gralla.com/myboi.htm* into their browser, they'd get an error message. And I'd lose a visitor.

Solve the problem with URLSpellCheck for IIS (*http://www.port80software. com/products/urlspellcheck/*). It redirects misspelled URLs to the right page, so that your visitors don't get error messages. It fixes instances in which an extra character is put into the URL, characters are transposed, a character is missing, or the wrong character is typed. It will also fix instances when the incorrect extension is typed.

> URLSpellCheck can't fix problems when someone types in the wrong domain—for example, *http://www.grala.com* rather than *http://www.gralla.com*. Domains are handled by the Domain Name System (DNS), so add-in software can't solve the problem. To solve it, you'd have to own the various misspellings of your domain and then have DNS redirect them to the proper domain.

The program runs as a snap-in to the MMC. Highlight your web site in the MMC, right-click on the Properties button, and click on the URLSpellCheck tab. From there, you'll be able to enable or disable the program.

URLSpellCheck is shareware and free to try, but if you use it for more than 30 days you're expected to pay $49.95.

Use Caching for Better Performance

When you run a web site, three issues top your list of concerns: how to pre-serve bandwidth, how to reduce the performance load on your PC, and how to make the site load faster for visitors.

Here's a three-for-one solution: use caching properly. When visitors come to your site, have them use cached images such as logos, navigation bars, and similar content from their own PC, rather than hitting your server every time. When you do this, after they retrieve the image for the first time, each subsequent time they need to get the image, it's retrieved from their own PC, rather than your server. Their pages load faster, your PC doesn't have to serve up as much content, and you don't use as much bandwidth.

To make sure your site uses caching, try CacheRight (*http://www. port80software.com/products/cacheright/*). Like URLSpellCheck, it runs as a snap-in to MMC. To use it, highlight your web site in MMC, right-click on the Properties button, and click on the CachRight tab. From there, you'll be able to enable or disable the program, as well as set options for how the cache should be used. The main option you'll set is expiration policies for the cache—in other words, at what point the visiting browser should check your web site to see whether the content the browser has cached is old and needs to be updated. You set the amount of time, such as a week, and set when that time should start, either the last time the browser visited your site or the last time you modified the cached content. I prefer to use the start time as the last time I modified the cached content; that way, browsers won't unnecessarily try to get content from my site.

CacheRight is shareware and free to try, but if you use it for more than 30 days you're expected to pay $149.95.

See Also

- The IISFAQ site (*http://www.iisfaq.com*) is a great source for tips, advice, and downloads related to IIS.

HACK #41   Run Java Applets Without Crashes or Problems

To get the most out of surfing the Web, you need the most updated version of Java. That can be harder to do than you think, but this hack will show you how.

Running a Java applet when you visit a web site should be a no-brainer; click on a link and the application should run. Unfortunately, XP users have found out that isn't always the case. You may visit Java sites only to find that you can't play games, log into interactive stock and weather sites, or do any of the other things Java can be used for.

Unfortunately, there's no single fix for all Java woes. There are many potential causes, ranging from display errors, to running an old version of Java, and more. Here, though, are the primary ways you can fix Java on your machine.

Make Sure You Have a Java Virtual Machine (JVM) Installed

In order to run Java applets, you need a Java Virtual Machine (JVM) installed on your system. Microsoft and Sun have, in the past, had competing JVMs. Applets written for one JVM may or may not work with the other JVM.

To make things more confusing, Microsoft and Sun have been locked in a bitter legal battle about Java which rivals the Jarndyce and Jarndyce court case at the center of Dickens novel *Bleak House.* To fully explain the Microsoft/Sun fight would take about as many pages as Dickens' 1,000-plus–page novel. The upshot is this, however: because of a court ruling, Microsoft will no longer distribute or support its JVM (which it calls Microsoft VM) after January 2004. And the Microsoft VM may or may not be enabled in your version of XP.

So if you're having problems with Java, the first thing to do is see whether you have a JVM installed and whether you're using the Sun version, the Microsoft version, or both versions. To see whether Microsoft VM is enabled, from Internet Explorer choose Tools → Internet Options → Security. Highlight the Internet Zone, choose Custom Level, then scroll down until you come to the Microsoft VM section, shown in Figure 4-14.

If the Disable Java button is chosen, it means the Microsoft VM is disabled on your system.

To check whether you have the Sun JVM and whether it's enabled, from Internet Explorer choose Tools → Internet Options → Advanced and scroll down. If you see a Java (Sun) entry with a checkbox next to it, as pictured in Figure 4-15, then the Sun JVM is installed.

If you don't have the Microsoft VM or the Sun JVM installed, the solution is simple: install and enable one of them. Because Microsoft will not be supporting its VM after January 2004, your best bet is to install the Sun JVM from *http://www.java.com/en/download/windows_automatic.jsp.*

If the Microsoft VM or the Sun JVM show up (as in Figure 4-14 or Figure 4-15, respectively), but they're not enabled, you'll need to enable them. To enable the Microsoft VM, in the screen pictured in Figure 4-14 choose High Safety. That will enable the VM but will take security precautions against rogue Java applets. To enable the Sun JVM, select the checkbox under Java (Sun), as shown in Figure 4-15.

Figure 4-14. Checking to see whether you're using the Microsoft VM

Uninstall Older JVM Versions

Your problem may be that you have an older JVM or Microsoft VM installed, and you need to update it. Go to *http://java.sun.com* and check the version number against the version number displayed in Figure 4-15. If your version number is older, you should install a newer JVM. Additionally, if you're using the Microsoft VM, you may instead want to install the Sun JVM in its place, since Microsoft will discontinue support for its VM.

People have reported problems when installing a newer JVM over an older one, so I suggest first uninstalling the old JVM or Microsoft VM and then installing the new one from *http://www.java.com/en/download/windows_automatic.jsp*. Unfortunately, uninstalling the Sun JVM or Microsoft VM is not a simple process and requires Registry editing as well as manually deleting files. Here's how to do each.

Uninstalling an Old Sun JVM. There's good news and bad news about uninstalling an old Sun JVM. The good news is that it might go off without a hitch and take only a single step. The bad news is that you might not be so lucky, and then it'll be time to head to the Registry.

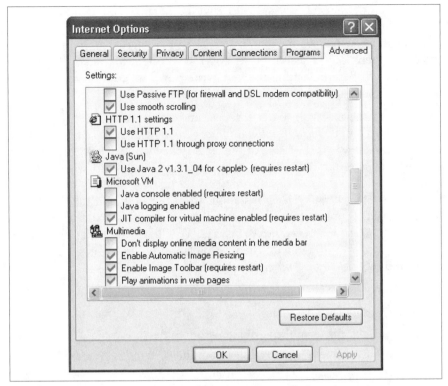

Figure 4-15. Checking to see whether the Sun JVM is installed

To uninstall an old Sun JVM, choose Control Panel → Add/Remove Programs. Select the Java Runtime Environment entry, click Change/Remove, and follow the uninstallation wizard. The JVM will be—or should be—uninstalled.

Sometimes, however, even after you do that, the Java Runtime Environment entry remains in the Add or Remove Programs screen. Theoretically, this should not cause a problem—because the underlying JVM has been uninstalled—but it's not clear whether in practice it will cause problems. So, you'll be best off to remove the entry in the Add or Remove Programs screen. You'll do it by deleting Registry entries and a folder.

Run the Registry Editor [Hack #68] and go to HKEY_LOCAL_MACHINE/Software/Microsoft/Windows/CurrentVersion/Uninstall. You'll find many keys enclosed in curly brackets, like this: {B7915B05-FC28-11D6-9D24-00010240CE95}. One of these keys is the Java uninstall Registry entry, and you need to delete it. You won't be able to know which entry to delete by the key name, because the keys aren't descriptive and each are strings of long numbers enclosed in curly brackets. To find which to delete, you need to find the one that has a `DisplayName` with a `String` value that starts with Java, such as Java 2 SDK, SE v1.4.1_02. To find out which key to delete, search for the word Java by pressing Ctrl-F in the Registry, typing the word Java, and then doing a search for it. You'll be brought to the key that needs to be deleted. Before deleting the key, write down its entire name, because you'll need it for the next step. Then you'll delete it.

Next, go to the uninstall folder for Java and delete that folder. Delete *C:\ Program Files\InstallShield Installation Information\{<Java 2 clsid key>}*, where *{<Java 2 clsid key>}* is the value of the registry key you deleted. After you do that, when you restart Add or Remove Programs, the Java entry will be gone.

Uninstalling the Microsoft VM. Uninstalling the Microsoft VM takes a bit of work as well. From the Run box, enter the command `RunDll32 advpack. dll,LaunchINFSection java.inf,UnInstall`. You'll get a warning box asking if you want to go through with the uninstallation process. Click Yes to continue, and reboot your PC when prompted.

After you reboot, delete these items:

* The *C:\Windows\java* folder
* The *java.pnf* file from the *C:\Windows\inf* folder
* The *jview.exe* and *wjview.exe* files from the *C:\Windows\system32* folder
* The Registry subkey `HKEY_LOCAL_MACHINE\SOFTWARE\Microsoft\Java VM`
* The Registry subkey `HKEY_LOCAL_MACHINE\SOFTWARE\Microsoft\Internet Explorer\AdvancedOptions\JAVA_VM`

That will completely remove the Microsoft VM. You can now install the Sun JVM from *http://www.java.com/en/download/windows_automatic.jsp*.

Change Your Display Settings

Java applets won't run unless you have a minimum color setting of 256 colors. If you don't use that minimum setting, you'll crash when you visit a web page with a Java applet. To change your display settings, right-click on the desktop, choose Properties → Settings, and in the Color Quality dropdown box choose a display setting of at least 256 colors.

If you use at least 256 colors and you still experience problems, the cause may be a buggy video driver. To help find out if this is the cause of the problem, change your current display settings to a lower resolution and color depth than you're currently using—for example, bring it from 1,024×768 to 800×600, and the colors from Highest (32bit) to 256 colors. If that solves the problem, you may have a display driver with bugs in it. Go to the manufacturer's web site and download a new driver.

CHAPTER FIVE

Networking
Hacks 42–62

XP is the most network-savvy of Microsoft's operating systems. Not only does it automatically recognize your network when you first install it, but it also includes a variety of wizards and other features that make it easy to connect to new networks and devices. Probably the biggest networking advance is built-in support for the wireless WiFi standard. Also, high on the list is a built-in firewall for protection.

In this chapter, you'll get over 20 networking hacks, including how to get the most out of wireless networking, command-line tools for troubleshooting networks, hacking firewalls, and how to optimize a home network, among many others.

HACK #42 War Driving for WiFi Access

WiFi networks are everywhere, it seems; you can get free Internet access on wireless community FreeNets armed with your laptop, a car, and software called Network Stumbler.

One of the coolest technological advances in popular use today is the wireless network. Wireless networks based on the WiFi standard (802.11x) are becoming increasingly common across the country—not only in people's homes, but also in universities, corporations, coffee shops, airports and other public places. Now you can bring your email to Starbucks.

There are frequently dozens near one another, particularly in certain urban neighborhoods and suburban office parks that house high-tech companies. Where I live—in Porter Square in Cambridge, Massachusetts—there are dozens of wireless networks in private homes, apartment buildings, and businesses within a very short walk from my home. There are at least half-a-dozen on my three-block street alone, in addition to mine. From my back porch, I get access to my own wireless network, but can also often pick up signals from four nearby WiFi networks.

The widespread availability of these inexpensive WiFi networks has led to a grassroots community wireless networking movement. The idea is simple: allow people passing by to use your WiFi network to hop onto the Internet and they in turn let you and others use their WiFi networks for Internet access when you pass near their homes or places of business. These wireless grassroots organizations are often called FreeNets. You'll find them in cities including New York, Seattle, Houston, and the San Francisco Bay area, as well as others. For more details about them and how to participate, go to Free Networks.org (*http://www.freenetworks.org*) In fact, some cities themselves are creating free wireless zones in downtown business areas to allow anyone with a wireless-enabled computer to get Internet access. Paris, for example, may soon be known for more than its beauty, culture, good food and disdain for tourists; it may turn into one giant wireless zone, allowing Internet access anywhere in the city, though for a price.

How do you find these wireless networks? The best way is by doing what has become known as *war driving*—driving through neighborhoods with your laptop, special software, and, if you want to pick up more networks, an antenna hooked up to your WiFi card.

 The extremely environmentally conscious prefer to go *war walking*, though walking around with a laptop is not particularly easy. A better way is with a WiFi-equipped PDA, like the Palm Tungsten C.

Run the software, and it not only locates the network, but also provides a variety of information about it that you can use to connect to it, such as its SSID (network name), whether it uses encryption, and the wireless channel it's on. Armed with that information, you should be able to connect to it if it's a FreeNet—for example, if it is set to allow anyone to connect to it, or if it uses a commonly agreed-upon security scheme that everyone in the FreeNet uses for their WiFi networks.

If you walk in certain urban neighborhoods, you may notice strange symbols on the sidewalk that look something like those pictured in Figure 5-1. Yes, it's a conspiracy, but in the positive sense. These are *war chalking* symbols that tell passersby that there is a nearby WiFi network. The left symbol means the wireless network is open; the middle one means it is closed; and the right one means it uses WEP encryption. There may be other information next to the symbol that gives information on how to connect to the network, such as the SSID. The symbols were inspired by the practice of hoboes, who during the Great Depression would make chalk marks near homes that were friendly to hoboes and would give them food. For more information about war chalking, go to *http://www.warchalking.org*.

Figure 5-1. War chalking symbols

To go war driving, download the free Network Stumbler program (*http://www.netstumbler.com*), which shows you detailed information about any nearby wireless network. Figure 5-2 shows what happens when I run the software on my back porch. I can detect signals from four nearby WiFi networks in addition to my own.

For each WiFi network it uncovers, Network Stumbler tells you the network's SSID, name, manufacturer, channel, type, signal strength, signal-to-noise ratio, and whether the network's encryption is enabled, among other details. Armed with that information, you can try to connect to the network.

If a network uses encryption, a small lock appears next to it; look closely at the Mookieville network in Figure 5-2 and you might be able to see it.

Once you've found a network, exit Network Stumbler. Then, to connect to the network, double-click on the small network icon in the System Tray (officially known as the XP Notification Area—the area of the Taskbar where XP corrals little icons). The Wireless Network Connection Status screen appears. (To see what it looks like, flip ahead to Figure 5-26 on page 209.) From this screen, choose Properties → Wireless Networks, and you'll see the screen shown in Figure 5-3.

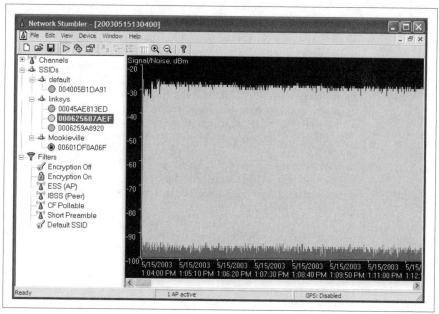

Figure 5-2. Detecting nearby wireless networks with Network Stumbler

If this screen doesn't show you the network uncovered by Network Stumbler, click Refresh. If the network still doesn't show up, that's because the signal is too weak for you to connect to it. To connect to a network shown on this screen, click Configure and fill out the information required in the screen. You'll then get into the network.

Not everyone will be able to use Network Stumbler, because it won't work with all wireless network cards. As of this writing, it worked with the following cards (and possibly some others not listed here as well): Lucent Technologies WaveLAN/IEEE (Agere ORiNOCO); Dell TrueMobile 1150 Series (PCMCIA and mini-PCI); Avaya Wireless PC Card; Toshiba Wireless LAN Card (PCMCIA and built-in); Compaq WL110; Cabletron/Enterasys Roamabout; Elsa Airlancer MC-11; ARtem ComCard 11Mbps; IBM High Rate Wireless LAN PC Card; and 1stWave 1ST-PC-DSS11IS, DSS11IG, DSS11ES, and DSS11EG. For more information, go to *C:\Program Files\ Network Stumbler\readme.html*, assuming you've installed the program in *C: \Program Files\Network Stumbler*.

Network Stumbler will find all wireless networks near you, not just those that are part of FreeNets. So, you may well find the wireless networks of people who don't realize that others outside of their homes or businesses can tap into their network. Some law enforcement officials will tell you that tapping into those people's networks is illegal, so be forewarned.

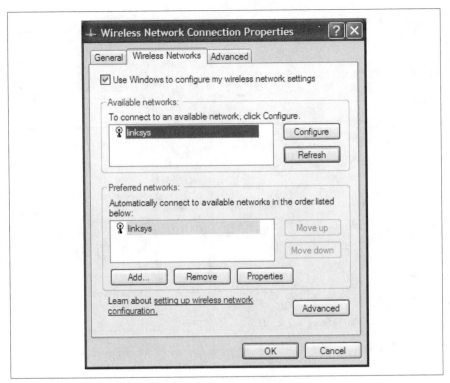

Figure 5-3. The Wireless Network Connection Properties screen

Mapping Wireless Networks

Network Stumbler lets you save your war-driving information in a file, and you can then upload that information to a web site (such as *http://wifimaps.com*) that uses your information and information provided by many other war-drivers to create maps of WiFi networks across the country. You can zoom in and out on these maps, so you can get a view of the concentration of WiFi networks in a metropolitan area, or you can see individual WiFi networks on individual streets, as shown in Figure 5-4.

Go to *http://wifimaps.com* to view the maps or to upload your Network Stumbler information. Be aware that the site is a volunteer effort, and, not uncommonly, you'll find that the maps aren't working. If that happens, check back again in a few days; it usually gets up and running after a while.

Build a Homemade Wireless Cantenna for War Driving

One way to increase the range of your war driving and the strength of the signal when you connect to WiFi networks is to build your own wireless

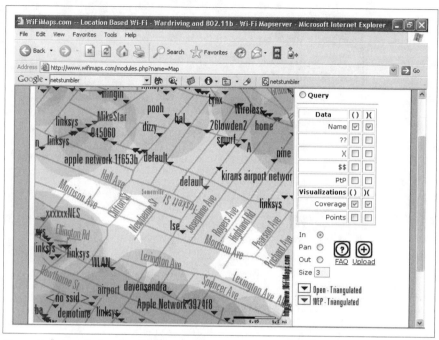

Figure 5-4. A map showing WiFi networks in my Somerville neighborhood

antenna. You can build them for a few dollars using a tin can and other stray parts, as long as you're willing to do a little bit of soldering. Because they're built out of tin cans, they're frequently called *cantennas*.

My 13-year-old son Gabe built several for his seventh-grade science fair project and compared the effectiveness of each. The results were clear: the giant 34.5–ounce coffee cans were far superior to normal-sized coffee cans and Pringle's cans.

If you haven't bought a WiFi card yet and are considering building one of these cantennas, I suggest buying an Orinoco card. It has a small connector in its side through which you connect a *pigtail connector*, which can then be hooked up to a small antenna you build out of copper wire and a small connector, which goes inside the tin can. There are a number of places you can buy a pigtail and the required connectors, including Hyperlink Technologies (*http://www.hyperlinktech.com*). If you don't have a WiFi card with a small connector, building one of these cantennas becomes much more difficult.

There are many places online where you can find good directions for making cantennas. Three good places to start are *www.oreillynet.com/cs/weblog/view/wlg/448*, *www.netscum.com/~clapp/wireless.html*, and *www.turnpoint.net/wireless/cantennahowto.html*. Just so you get the idea of what you'll do, though, you first empty and wash the can. Next, you build the small antenna that will go inside the coffee can by soldering a short piece of thick copper wire to a small piece of hardware called an *N connector*. Then, drill a hole in the can and insert the small antenna you just soldered. Attach the antenna to the can by securing it with small screws and bolts. Attach one end of the pigtail to your wireless card, attach the other end to the N connector, and voila! You have a cantenna.

See Also

- Check WiFi Network Performance with QCheck to Help Improve Throughput [Hack #57]
- Troubleshooting Network Connections with netsh, netstat, and ipconfig [Hack #53]

HACK #43 Test Your Security with Shields Up!

Head to this web site for a thorough, free check of your PC's vulnerabilities.

Do you *really* know how secure your PC is from intruders? Probably not. But there's a free online tool that will probe your PC for online security vulnerabilities and report to you on the results.

The site is run by the Gibson Research Corporation, and it tests your machine, trying to make connections to a handful of the most well-known and vulnerable Internet ports on your PC. The site runs two tests, reports to you on the results, and then explains what the reports mean—where you're vulnerable and how serious those vulnerabilities are. It also has a great deal of useful information about Internet security, as well as free and for-pay security software you can download. Visit the site at *http://www.grc.com*. You may have to do some clicking around to find the tests, but keep clicking on Shields Up! and you'll eventually get there.

The best use for the site is to test your PC's vulnerabilities, then install a firewall [Hack #46] and [Hack #48] and see the results of what you've done. It'll tell you whether there are any remaining vulnerabilities you need to fix. Figure 5-5 shows the results of a probe of a PC without a firewall. It's relatively secure, but could be more secure, because the site has found ports, even though they're closed. Figure 5-6 shows that the PC is operating in "stealth mode" after the installation of the firewall—the PC doesn't even appear to exist.

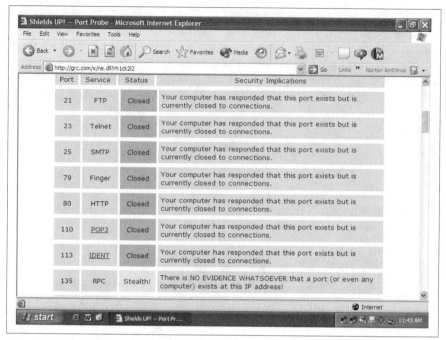

Figure 5-5. The security report on a PC before installing a firewall

HACK #44 Tweak DNS Settings for Faster Internet Access

A handful of DNS hacks for speeding up access to web sites.

You use the Web by typing in hostnames such as *www.oreilly.com*, but web servers and Internet routers can't understand plain English words, so they need those letters translated into numeric IP addresses. Whenever you type in a hostname, such as *www.oreilly.com*, it needs to be resolved to its IP address, such as 208.201.239.37. DNS servers provide that name resolution automatically and behind the scenes as you surf the Web.

There are several ways you can hack your DNS settings so that you can get faster web access.

Speed Up Web Access with a HOSTS File

It takes time to send your request to a DNS server, have the server look up the proper IP address to resolve the name, and then send the IP address back to your PC. You can eliminate that delay by creating or editing a local *HOSTS* file on your own PC that contains hostnames and their correspond-

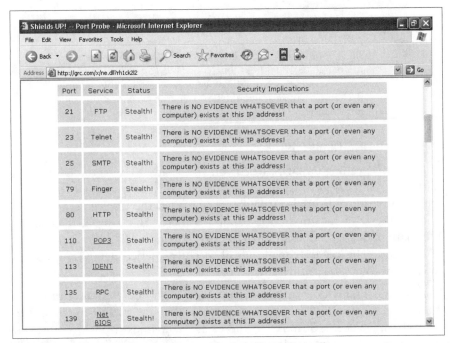

Figure 5-6. *The security report on a PC after installing a firewall*

ing IP addresses. When you create one, XP will first look into the *HOSTS* file to see if there's an entry for the hostname, and, if it finds it, it will resolve the address itself. That way, you won't have to go out to a DNS server and wait for the response before visiting a web site. The *HOSTS* file is a plain text file you can create or edit with a text editor like Notepad.

You'll find an existing *HOSTS* file in *C:\System32\Drivers\Etc\HOSTS*. The file has no extension; it is named only *HOSTS*. Open it in Notepad and enter the IP addresses and hostnames of your commonly visited web sites, like this:

```
208.201.239.37     oreilly.com
216.92131.107      simtel.net
```

Each entry in the file should be on one line. The IP address should be in the first column, and the corresponding hostname in the next column. At least one space should separate the two columns. You can add comments to the file by preceding the line with a #, in which case the entire line will be ignored by the file, or by putting a # after the hostname, in which case only the comment after will be ignored. You might want to comment on individual entries—for example:

```
130.94.155.164        gralla.com    #still in beta
```

When you're finished editing the file, save it to its existing location.

> Make sure to check your *HOSTS* file regularly and keep it up
> to date, or else you may deny yourself access to certain web
> sites. For example, if the *http://www.gralla.com* web site were
> to change its IP address, but your *HOSTS* file kept the old,
> incorrect address, your browser would not be able to find
> the site, because it would be given the wrong addressing
> information.

Adjust XP's DNS Cache Settings

As a way of speeding up DNS, when you visit a site, XP puts the DNS information into a local DNS cache on your PC. So, when you want to go to a
site, XP first looks in its local DNS cache, called the *resolve cache*, to see
whether the DNS information is contained there. That way, if it finds the
information locally, it doesn't have to query a remote DNS server to find IP
information. The cache is made up of recently queried names and entries
taken from your *HOSTS* file.

The cache contains both negative and positive entries. *Positive* entries are
those in which the DNS lookup succeeded, and you were able to connect to
the web site. When XP looks in the cache, if it finds a positive entry, it
immediately uses that DNS information and sends you to the requested web
site.

Negative entries are those in which no match was found, and you end up
getting a "Cannot find server or DNS Error" in your browser. Similarly,
when XP looks in the cache and finds a negative entry, it gives you the error
message without bothering to go out to the site.

Negative entries can lead to problems. When you try to make a connection
to a site that has a negative entry in your cache, you'll get an error message,
even if the site's problems have been resolved and it's now reachable.

You can solve this problem, though, using a Registry hack. By default, XP
caches negative entries for five minutes. After five minutes, they're cleared
from your cache. But if you'd like, you can force XP not to cache these negative entries, so that you'll never run into this problem. Run the Registry Editor [Hack #68] and go to HKEY_LOCAL_MACHINE\SYSTEM\CurrentControlSet\
Services\Dnscache\Parameters. Create a new DWORD value with the name
NegativeCacheTime and give it a value of 0. (The value may already exist. If it
does, edit its value to 0.) The DWORD determines how much time, in seconds,
to keep negative entries in the DNS cache. If you like, you can have the
entries stay alive for one second by giving it a value of 1.

After you're done editing, exit the Registry. To make the change take effect, restart your computer, or flush your cache by issuing the command `ipconfig /flushdns` at a command prompt.

> For more information about using `ipconfig`, see "Troubleshooting Network Connections with ping, tracert, and pathping" [Hack #52].

That command will flush your DNS cache—all the entries, both positive and negative, will be flushed, and it will be empty until you start visiting web sites. Negative entries, however, will not be added to the cache if you've given the `DWORD` a value of 0.

You can also use the Registry to control the amount of time that positive entries are kept in the DNS cache. By default, they are kept for 24 hours. To change the default, go to `HKEY_LOCAL_MACHINE\SYSTEM\CurrentControlSet\ Services\Dnscache\Parameters` again and create a `DWORD` value called `MaxCacheEntryTtlLimit`. (If it's already present, just edit the value.) For the value, enter the amount of time you want the entry to remain, in seconds, making sure to use Decimal as the base.

Fix DNS Problems

Sometimes when you can't connect to a web site, the cause is a DNS problem. There are things you can do to solve these problems, though. If you're having trouble connecting, to find out if DNS is a potential culprit first ping [Hack #52] the site to which you can't connect, by issuing the `ping` command like this at the command prompt or Run box, like this:

```
ping www.zdnet.com
```

If the site is live, you'll get an answer like this:

```
Pinging www.zdnet.com [206.16.6.252] with 32 bytes of data:

Reply from 206.16.6.252: bytes=32 time=119ms TTL=242
Reply from 206.16.6.252: bytes=32 time=79ms TTL=242
Reply from 206.16.6.252: bytes=32 time=80ms TTL=242
Reply from 206.16.6.252: bytes=32 time=101ms TTL=242

Ping statistics for 206.16.6.252:
    Packets: Sent = 4, Received = 4, Lost = 0 (0% loss),
Approximate round trip times in milli-seconds:
    Minimum = 79ms, Maximum = 119ms, Average = 94ms
```

If it's not, you'll get a response like this:

```
Ping request could not find host. Please check the name and try again.
```

If you ping a site and it's live, but you can't connect to it with your browser, a DNS problem might be the reason. If you suspect you're having a DNS problem, take the following actions:

Check your HOSTS file.   If your *HOSTS* file contains an incorrect or outdated listing, you won't be able to connect. Even if you don't recall adding listings to a *HOSTS* file, it still may contain listings, because some Internet accelerator utilities edit them without telling you. Open your *HOSTS* file with Notepad and see if the site you can't connect to is listed there. If it is, delete the entry, and you should be able to connect.

Check your DNS settings.   Make sure your DNS settings are correct for your ISP or network. Find out from your ISP or network administrator what yours are supposed to be. Then, to find out your current DNS settings, double-click on the problem connection in the Network Connections folder, choose Support → Details, look at the bottom of the tab to find your DNS servers. If they don't match what they're supposed to be, right-click on the problem connection and choose Properties. Then, highlight Internet Protocol (TCP/IP) and choose Properties. Change the DNS servers to the proper ones, or choose "Obtain DNS server address automatically" if your ISP or network administrator tells you to.

Flush your DNS cache.   The problem may be related to your DNS cache, so flush it out. To flush the cache, type `ipconfig /flushdns` at a command prompt.

Find out if your ISP is having DNS problems.   The cause may be your ISP. One possibility is that one of its DNS servers is down, and you're trying to access the down server. Ping each of your ISP's DNS servers and, if any of them don't respond, remove them from your DNS list, as outlined earlier in this hack.

Fix Windows Media Player's Privacy Problems
Lurking beneath Windows Media Player's slick exterior are potential invasions of your privacy. Here's how to fix them.

XP's Windows Media Player Version 8 poses potentially serious privacy problems that, theoretically, could allow Microsoft to track what DVDs you play and could allow for the creation of a *supercookie* on your PC that would let web sites exchange information about you. There are things you can do, however, to protect your privacy when you use Windows Media Player.

If you use Windows Media Player to play DVD movies, whenever a new DVD is played, Media Player contacts a Microsoft server and gets the DVD's title and chapter information. The server, in turn, identifies your specific version of Media Player, uses a cookie to identify the DVD you're watching, and then records information about the DVDs you watch on to a database on your hard disk in *C:\Documents and Settings\All Users\Application Data\ Microsoft\Media Index.*

Microsoft claims that the cookie used is an anonymous one that can't personally identify you. The company also says that it does not keep track of what DVDs individuals watch, and that the database created on your PC is never accessed from the Internet. Instead, the company says, it's used only by your own computer; the next time you put a DVD in your drive that you've played before, Media Player will get information from that database instead of getting it from a Microsoft web server.

Still, Microsoft has had its share of problems with privacy before, so you may or may not trust them to keep the information private. There are two solutions to the problem. You can change your cookie controls to the highest level [Hack #34] so that your PC will reject all cookies. That carries with it its own set of problems, however, because then you won't be able to use customization and other features of many web sites. A better solution is to open Media Player and choose File → Work Offline. That way, Media Player won't contact a Microsoft server.

As for the so-called supercookie that Windows Media Player creates, it's a unique ID number in the form of a 128-bit GUID (Globally Unique Identifier) assigned to your player and stored in the Registry. You can find it in *HKEY_CURRENT_USER\Software\Microsoft\WindowsMedia\WMSDK\General\UniqueID.* This ID number can be retrieved by any web site through the use of JavaScript. The ID number is called a supercookie because it can be retrieved by *any* web site. Normally, web sites can retrieve only cookies that they create and put on your PC, so it becomes difficult for web sites to share information about you. However, this supercookie can be retrieved by any site to track you, and web sites can share this information with each other, allowing them to create a sophisticated profile about your Internet usage. Additionally, cookie blockers can't block its use.

There's an easy way to fix the problem and protect your privacy, though. From Windows Media Player, choose Tools → Options → Player. In the "Internet settings" section, uncheck the box next to "Allow Internet sites to uniquely identify your Player." That's all it takes; the problem will be fixed.

If you download and install Windows Media Player 9, you can stop these privacy problems before they begin if you pay attention to the installation questions. During the installation, look for the screen asking you for your privacy preferences, as shown in Figure 5-7.

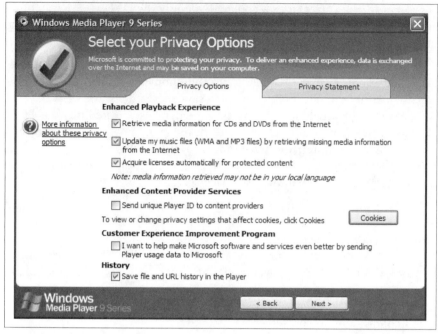

Figure 5-7. Choosing your privacy options when installing Windows Media Player 9

The Enhanced Content Provider and Customer Experience Improvement Program options are the ones that can be problematic. When you check boxes in those areas, Windows Media Player will report on your music and movie use to Microsoft and will also put the supercookie on your PC. So, if privacy is a concern of yours, just say no.

See Also

- For more information about Windows Media Player privacy issues, read articles about it by privacy expert Richard Smith at *www.computerbytesman.com/privacy/supercookie.htm* and *www.computerbytesman.com/privacy/wmp8dvd.htm.*

HACK #46 Protect Your Computer with the Internet Connection Firewall

XP's built-in firewall can do more than just provide basic protection. You can also use it to log potential attacks and send information about the intruders to your ISP.

Any time you're connected to the Internet, you're in some danger of intrusion, especially if you have a broadband connection. PCs with broadband connections are tempting targets, because their high-speed connections are ideal springboards for attacking other networks or web sites.

Whenever you're connected, your system is among many constantly being scanned for weaknesses by *crackers* (malicious hackers) and *wannabes* (often called *script kiddies*) sending automated probes looking for vulnerable PCs. In fact, these kinds of probes are so common and incessant, you can think of them as the background radiation of the Internet.

One of the best ways to protect yourself against these probes and more targeted attacks is to use a *firewall*. Firewall software sits between you and the Internet and acts as a gatekeeper of sorts, only allowing nonmalicious traffic through.

In this hack, we'll look at how to get the most out of the Internet Connection Firewall (ICF), the firewall built into XP.

> If you have a home network, your residential gateway may offer firewall protection. For details on how to optimize that protection and get the most out of other gateway features, see "Optimize Your Residential Gateway" **[Hack #49]**.

The ICF offers basic Internet security by stopping all unsolicited inbound traffic and connections to your PC and network, unless your PC or another PC on the network initially makes the request for the connection. It will not, however, block outgoing requests and connections, so you can continue to use the Internet as your normally would for browsing the Web, getting email, using FTP, or similar services.

> If you use ICF or another type of firewall, you can run into problems if you run a web server or an FTP server, or if you want to allow Telnet access to your PC. Because firewalls block unsolicited inbound communications, visitors won't be able get to your sites or get Telnet access to your PC. However, you can allow access to these resources, while still retaining firewall protection. To see how, turn to "Punch an Escape Hole Through Your Firewall" **[Hack #50]**.

If you're sharing an Internet connection through a PC, only the PC that directly accesses the Internet should run ICF. All the other PCs will be protected. Don't run the ICF on any of those other PCs, because you'll cause connection problems. And don't use the ICF with a Virtual Private Network (VPN) connection, because it will interfere with various VPN functions, including file sharing. To set up a VPN, see "Set Up a Virtual Private Network" **[Hack #62]**.

The ICF has one very serious drawback: it won't protect you against Trojans, such as the Back Orifice Trojan. Trojans let other users take complete control of your PC and its resources. For example, someone could use your PC as a launch pad for attacking web sites and it would appear you were the culprit, or he could copy all your files and find out personal information about you, such as your credit card numbers if you store them on your PC.

The ICF won't stop them, because it blocks only incoming traffic and Trojans work by making outbound connections from your PC. To stop Trojans, get a third-party firewall. The best is ZoneAlarm [Hack #48].

Turn on the ICF by right-clicking on My Network Places and choosing Properties. From the Network Connections folder that appears, right-click on the connection you want to use ICF and choose Properties → Advanced. In the Advanced tab of the Local Area Connection Properties dialog box, shown in Figure 5-8, check the box next to "Protect my computer and network by limiting and preventing access to this computer from the Internet." Click OK. The firewall is now in place.

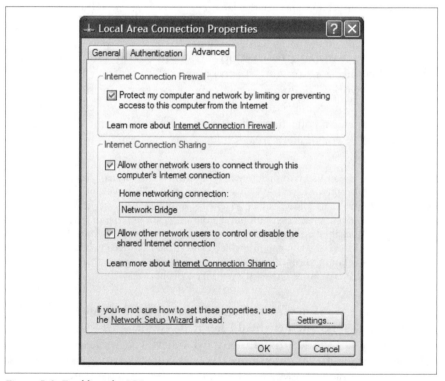

Figure 5-8. Enabling the ICF

Track Firewall Activity with an ICF Log

The ICF can do more than just protect you from intruders; it can also keep track of all intrusion attempts, so that you can know whether your PC has been targeted, and what kind of attacks the ICF has turned back. You can then send that information to your ISP, so that it can track down the intruders.

First, create a log of ICF activity. Right-click on My Network Places and choose Properties. In the Network Connections folder, right-click on the connection for which you want to set up an ICF log and choose Properties → Advanced → Settings → Security Logging. The dialog box shown in Figure 5-9 appears.

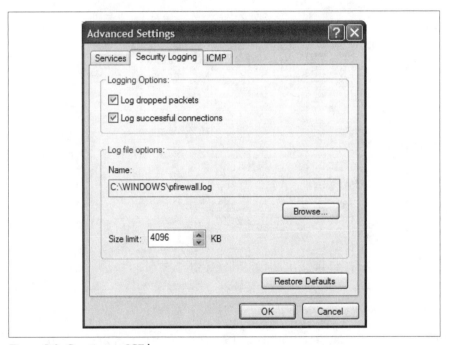

Figure 5-9. Creating an ICF log

Choose whether to log dropped packets, successful connections, or both. A *dropped packet* is a packet that the ICF has blocked. A *successful connection* doesn't mean that an intruder has successfully connected to your PC; it refers to any connection *you* have made over the Internet, such as to web sites. Because of this, there's usually no reason for you to log successful connections. If you do log them, your log will become large very quickly, and it will be more difficult to track only potentially dangerous activity. So, your best bet is to log only dropped packets.

After you've made your choices, choose a location for the log, set its maximum size, and click OK. I don't let my log get larger than 1MB, but depending on how much you care about disk space and how much you plan to use the log, you may want yours larger or smaller.

The log will be created in a W3C Extended Log format (*.log*) that you can examine with Notepad or another text editor, or using a log analysis program such as the free AWStats (*http://awstats.sourceforge.net*). Figure 5-10 shows a log generated by the ICF, examined in NotePad.

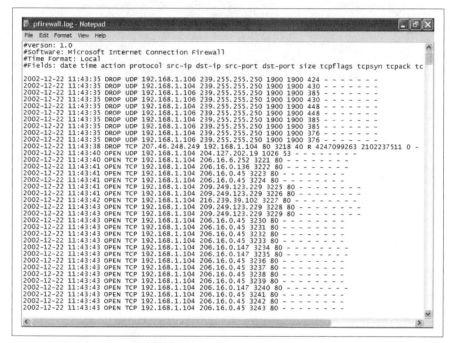

Figure 5-10. A log generated by the ICF

Each log entry has a total of up to 16 pieces of information associated with each event, but the most important columns for each entry are the first 8. (In a text editor, the names of the columns don't align over the data, but they will align in a log analyzer.) Table 5-1 describes the most important columns.

Table 5-1. The columns in the ICF log

Name	Decription
Date	Date of occurrence, in *year-month-date* format.
Time	Time of occurrence, in *hour:minute:second* format.
Action	The operation that was logged by the firewall, such as DROP for dropping a connection, OPEN for opening a connection, and CLOSE for closing a connection.

Table 5-1. The columns in the ICF log (continued)

Name	Decription
Protocol	The protocol used, such as TCP, UDP, or ICMP.
Source IP (src-ip)	The IP address of the computer that started the connection.
Destination IP (dst-ip)	The IP address of the computer to which the connection was attempted.
Source Port (src-port)	The port number on the sending computer from which the connection was attempted.
Destination Port (dst-port)	The port to which the sending computer was trying to make a connection.
size	The packet size.
tcpflags	Information about TCP control flags in TCP headers.
tcpsyn	The TCP sequence of a packet.
tcpack	The TCP acknowledgement number in the packet.
tcpwin	The TCP window size of the packet.
icmtype	Information about the ICMP messages.
icmcode	Information about ICMP messages.
info	Information about an entry in the log.

The source IP address is the source of the attack. You may notice the same source IP address continually cropping up; if so, you may be targeted by an intruder. It's also possible that the intruder is sending out automated probes to thousands of PCs across the Internet and your PC is not under direct attack. In either case, you can send the log information to your ISP and ask them to follow up by tracking down the source of the attempts. Either forward the entire log or cut and paste the relevant sections to a new file.

Watch Out for Problems with Email and the ICF

Depending on the email program you use and how it gets notification of new email, the ICF could interfere with the way you retrieve your email. It won't stop you from getting your email, but it could disable your email program's notification feature.

The ICF won't interfere with the normal notification feature of Outlook Express, because the initial request asking for notification of new email comes from Outlook Express, inside the firewall. When the server responds to the request, the firewall recognizes that the server is responding to the request from Outlook Express, so it lets the communication pass through.

However, if you use Outlook and connect to a Microsoft Exchange server using a remote procedure call (RPC) to send email notifications (which is usually the case with Exchange), you'll run into problems. That's because the RPC initially comes from the server, not from Outlook, so the firewall doesn't allow the notification to pass to you. In this case, you can still retrieve your email, but you'll have to check for new email manually; you won't be able to get automatic notification from the server. So, if you don't get new mail notifications after you install the ICF, it's not that coworkers, friends, and spammers are suddenly ignoring you; you'll just have to check for new mail manually.

See Also

- Close Down Open Ports and Block Protocols [Hack #51]
- Test Your Security with Shields Up! [Hack #43]

HACK #47 Use a Proxy Server to Protect Your PC

Many private businesses protect their networks with proxy servers. But you can get the same kind of protection at home—for free—without buying any new hardware.

Proxy servers protect your PC by offering a kind of relay protection. When you use a proxy server, Internet Explorer contacts the proxy instead of the Web site. The proxy delivers the page to you if the page is in its cache. If the page is not in its cache, it contacts the site, grabs the page, and then delivers the page to you. In this way, you never directly contact a web site or other Internet location; instead, the proxy server does, so it, rather than you, will be the target of attack or privacy invasion by the site. Proxy servers can be configured for any kind of Internet access, not just web browsing.

Some businesses use proxy servers as part of corporate-wide security precautions, and if you work at such a business your work PC has been specifically set up to use those servers. But even if you are not at a business with a proxy server you can still use one to protect your PC. You won't have to set up and run the proxy server yourself; instead, you can use one of the many free ones available on the Internet.

Setting up a proxy server in this way is a two-step process. First, find a free, public proxy server. Then, set up your PC to use it. To find a free, public proxy server, go to Stay Invisible (*http://www.stayinvisible.com*) and click on View Proxies. The site lists hundreds of free, public proxies from around the world and updates the list daily, as shown in Figure 5-11.

Choose a proxy server from the list, and copy down its IP address and port number. If you want to double-check that the server is functioning, go to the Check Your Proxy section on the left side of the web page, type its IP address and port number, and click on Check. If the server is functioning, a

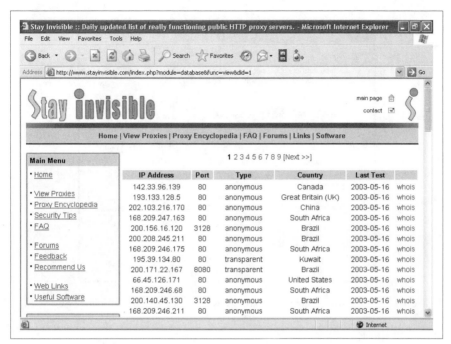

Figure 5-11. Stay Invisible's list of free public proxy servers around the world

page will pop up with the server's IP address and name (often, the name is the same as the IP address). If the server is not functioning, you'll get a message telling you the connection can't be made.

Once you've confirmed a working proxy server and copied down its IP address and port number, it's time to configure Internet Explorer to use it. Open Internet Explorer, choose Tools → Internet Options → Connections, and click on Settings if you use a dial-up connection and LAN Settings if you access the Internet using an always-on connection, such as over a LAN or via a cable modem or DSL modem. The options will be the same for both ways of access. Figure 5-12 shows the LAN Settings dialog box for configuring a proxy server.

Type in the address of the proxy server and its port number. For local domains, you need to use a proxy server because they will be secure. Check the "Bypass proxy server for local addresses" box if you know your local domain is secure.

If you're at work and the company uses separate proxy servers for different Internet services, such as FTP and Gopher, click on the Advanced button. From there, you'll be able to fill in the specific information about proxy servers for each Internet service.

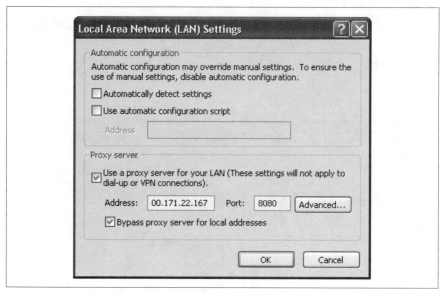

Figure 5-12. Configuring your proxy settings using the LAN Settings dialog box

Hacking the Hack

If you have a reason for wanting to limit your PC to visiting only certain web sites and banning it from visiting any others—such as for a child's computer, which you want to have only very limited Internet access—you can hack the proxy server settings to accomplish that.

Go to the LAN Settings dialog box (shown in Figure 5-12), and enable use of a proxy server. Then, click on the Advanced button and the Proxy Settings dialog screen appears, as shown in Figure 5-13.

For the HTTP: entry, type in a word, such as nowhere, or type in an Internet address that doesn't exist. When you do this, you're telling Internet Explorer to use a proxy server that isn't there. This effectively blocks access to the Internet, because instead of going to a web site, Internet Explorer will go to a proxy server. But because the proxy server doesn't exist, your browser won't be able to visit any site.

Next, check the box next to "Use the same proxy server for all protocols." This will ensure that you're blocking Internet access for other services, such as FTP, not just for the Web.

You've now effectively blocked access to the Internet for the PC. Now you can enable a setting that will let the PC visit only specific web sites. In the Exceptions section, type the locations of the web sites you want to allow to be visited, separated by a semicolon. This Exceptions box tells Internet

Figure 5-13. Use the Proxy Setting dialog box to limit the Web sites your PC can visit

Explorer to bypass the proxy server for the listed sites, so it will go straight to those sites, bypassing the not-there proxy.

Once you put those settings into effect, whenever your PC tries to access the Web it will look for a proxy server that doesn't exist, so it won't be able to get onto the Internet. However, it will let you go to the web sites that you've put in the Exceptions section.

See Also

- Close Down Open Ports and Block Protocols **[Hack #51]**
- Test Your Security with Shields Up! **[Hack #43]**
- Surf Anonymously Without a Trace **[Hack #39]**

HACK #48 ZoneAlarm: The World's Best Free Firewall

For the best protection, get this firewall that's far superior to XP's Internet Connection Firewall, and keeps you safe from Trojan horses and other dangers.

The Internet Connection Firewall (ICF) that ships with XP has one very serious deficiency: it can't monitor and block outbound traffic from your PC to the Internet. Many Trojan horses do their damage by installing themselves on your system and then allowing others to take control of your PC, or using your PC to attack web sites, servers, and other computers. The ICF won't offer you protection against these types of Trojans; it won't be able to tell when a Trojan is making an outbound connection, so the Trojan will be able to do its damage without your knowledge.

Other firewalls, however, will offer that protection. The best of them is ZoneAlarm (*http://www.zonealarm.com*). There are three versions of the program, a free version and two for-pay versions with differing levels of protection. The free version offers excellent protection against inbound threats as well as against Trojans. It also tells you whenever someone is probing your computer for security holes and gives information about the prober, often including his IP address, and the nature of the probe.

ZoneAlarm Plus, which sells for $39.95, also protects you against email-borne worms and viruses and does better tracking and reporting about those who may have tried to attack your PC. ZoneAlarm Pro, which sells for $49. 95, does all that and gives you control over cookies, stops pop-up ads, and controls rogue ActiveX Controls and JavaScript applets. At a minimum, try ZoneAlarm, because, well, because it's free. If you feel you need more protection, you can go with a for-pay version. I've been using the free version for several years and have never felt the need to go to the paid version. Figure 5-14 shows a record of activity that ZoneAlarm Pro has monitored and blocked.

Configuring ZoneAlarm to Block Trojans

The most important feature of ZoneAlarm is its ability to block outgoing traffic from your PC. That way, you can be sure that a Trojan hasn't infected your PC and can't "call out" to make contact with someone malicious, or be used to attack others from your PC. All versions of ZoneAlarm, the free as well as the for-pay, offer this protection. Since that's the most important feature, that's what's covered in most of this hack.

After you install ZoneAlarm, click on Firewall in the left panel, and you'll get to choose the level of protection (from Low to High) you want for the Internet Zone and the Trusted Security Zone (for computers on your network, or that you trust for some other reason). The settings are self-explanatory.

When you start using ZoneAlarm, alerts (such as the one shown in Figure 5-15) will start popping up every time a program attempts to make a connection to the Internet. It will most likely be a program you are familiar with, such as Internet Explorer, Outlook Express, or a similar program. If

Figure 5-14. Activity that ZoneAlarm has monitored and blocked

it's a program you're familiar with and you want the program to always be able to access the Internet, click on the box that reads "Remember this answer the next time I use this program," and then click Yes to let the program access the Internet.

If it's a program you're unfamiliar with or a program that you don't know why it would be connecting to the Internet, click on More Info. You may be asked whether to allow your browser to access the Internet. Click Yes, and you'll be sent to ZoneAlarm's site, which will offer some basic information about the alert. The general rule, though, is to allow only programs you are familiar with to access the Internet. If you've just launched a program that requires Internet access and you get the alert, let the program access the Internet. Or, you might want to let a program you've just installed contact the maker's web site for automatic updates and patches, if you like that sort of thing. But if the alert pops up for no reason at a random time and you're unfamiliar with the program, you should deny it access. You should also immediately run an antivirus program to see whether it can detect a Trojan.

If you allow the program to access the Internet, and check the box so that you're not alerted next time, it will always be able to access the Internet. If you want to always be alerted when the program tries to access the Internet, don't check the box.

Figure 5-15. A ZoneAlarm warning

After you designate a program as always being allowed to access the Internet, it will be put into a list that ZoneAlarm maintains about trusted programs. You can customize any program on that list, take programs off the list, or customize their security settings: click on Program Control in ZoneAlarm's left panel, and click on the Programs tab. You'll see a screen similar to Figure 5-16.

Use this screen to customize how you'll allow each program to access the Internet. By inserting a check mark in the appropriate column, you can choose whether to allow the program to access the Internet or Trusted Zone, whether you want it to act as a server in the Internet or Trusted Zone, and similar features. A check mark means that the program is allowed to access the Internet; an X means that it's not allowed to access the Internet; and a ? means that it should ask before being allowed to access the Internet.

See Also

- Stop Pop Ups, Spyware, and Web Bugs [Hack #33]
- Take a Bite Out of Cookies [Hack #34]
- Surf Anonymously Without a Trace [Hack #39]
- Punch an Escape Hole Through Your Firewall [Hack #50]

Figure 5-16. Customizing the way a program can access the Internet

 ## Optimize Your Residential Gateway

HACK #49

Residential gateways let you share broadband Internet access and build a home network. Here's how to get the most out of your residential gateway.

Encrypting File SystemIt's quite easy to set up inexpensive hubs/routers, usually called *residential gateways*, for setting up a network at home and sharing Internet access. But the default settings aren't always optimal, because no network is one-size-fits-all. And, frequently, the documentation for the gateways is so poor that it's hard to tell even what the settings are and what options you have.

Residential gateway options differ somewhat from model to model. Here's advice for how to customize the most common and most important settings:

Connect on Demand and Maximum Idle Time settings

Depending on your Internet service provider (ISP), you may become disconnected from the Net after a certain amount of time of not using the Internet. To solve the problem, if your residential gateway has a Connect on Demand setting, enable it; that will automatically re-establish your Internet connection when you use an Internet service, even if your ISP has cut you off. If there is a Maximum Idle Time setting, set it to 0 so that your gateway will always maintain an Internet connection, no matter how long you haven't used the Internet. As a practical matter, you should need to use only one of these two settings; either one will maintain a constant Internet connection for you.

Keep Alive setting

Use this setting to maintain a constant Internet connection, even if your PC is idle. It's similar to Connect on Demand and Maximum Idle Time settings, except that it doesn't let your connection disconnect, so it is an even better setting to enable, if your gateway has it.

Router Password

Your router requires a password for you to use its administrator account. It comes with a default password. For example, Linksys routers come with a default password of admin. Change the password for maximum security.

Enable Logging

For security reasons, it's a good idea to enable logging so that you can view logs of all outgoing and incoming traffic. Depending on your gateway, it may save permanent logs to your hard disk or allow only the viewing of temporary logs. You may also be able to download extra software from the manufacturer to help keep logs. For example, Linksys routers use temporary logs, but if you want to save permanent logs, you can download the Linksys Logviewer software from *http://www.linksys.com*. You can view logs using a text editor, like Notepad, or a log analysis program, such as the free AWStats (*http://awstats.sourceforge.net*).

Special Hub/Router Settings for DSL Access

If you have DSL access, you may need to customize your gateway's settings in order to provide your network with Internet access; sometimes the gateway's settings block Internet access. Here are the settings you'll need to change so you can get onto the Internet:

PPPoE (Point to Point Protocol over Ethernet)

Some DSL ISPs use this protocol when offering Internet access. By default, this protocol is disabled on gateways, because it's normally not required for Internet access. However, if you have DSL access, you may need to enable it in your gateway.

Keep Alive setting

Some DSL ISPs will automatically disconnect your connection if you haven't used it for a certain amount of time. If your gateway has a Keep Alive setting, enable it by clicking on the radio button next to it; this will ensure that you are never disconnected.

MTU (Maximum Transmission Unit)

As a general rule, DSL users should use a value of 1492 for their MTU. The MTU sets the maximum size of packets that a network can transmit. Any packets larger than the MTU setting will be broken into smaller packets. DSL ISPs often set the MTU to 1492, so if you set a packet size larger or smaller than that, you may slow down Internet access.

 You should also check with your DSL provider, because these settings may vary somewhat from provider to provider.

Settings for Using a VPN

If you use a Virtual Private Network (VPN) **[Hack #62]** to connect to your corporate network from home and you use a residential gateway, you may run into difficulties and not be able to connect to the VPN. Some gateways, such as those from Linksys, are specifically designed to work with VPNs and have specific setup screens for them; if you have one of those, you shouldn't have any problems. Make sure to get the proper encryption, authentication, and similar information about the VPN from your network administrator, and then use those settings for the VPN setup screen in your gateway.

However, you may run into problems running a VPN with a gateway that doesn't have specific VPN settings, even if the device claims that it will work with VPNs. In particular, one default setting, hidden fairly deeply in most gateway setup screens, may disable VPN access; some gateways, such as those made by Linksys, include an option called *Block WAN Request*. By default, this option is enabled and blocks requests into the network from the Internet; for example, it stops ping requests into the network. However, enabling this option also blocks VPN access. VPN access requires that requests get into the network from the Internet, so if you block those requests the VPN won't work. If you have a Linksys router, disable this setting by logging into your administrator's screen, choosing Advanced → Filters, selecting Disable Block WAN Request, and clicking Apply. For other routers, check the documentation.

VPNs use a variety of protocols for tunneling through the Internet, such as IPSec and the Point-to-Point Tunneling Protocol (PPTP). Make sure that these settings are enabled on your gateway if you want to use it in concert with a VPN.

Enable Specific Internet Services: Port Forwarding

Residential gateways often use Network Address Translation (NAT), in which the gateway's single, external IP address is shared among all the computers on the network, but each computer has its own internal IP address, invisible to the Internet. For example, to the Internet each computer looks as if it has the address of 66.32.43.98, but internally they have different addresses, such as 192.168.1.100, 192.168.1.101, and so on. The gateways have built-in DHCP servers that assign the internal IP address. These internal IP addresses allow each PC to communicate with each other and to connect to the Internet, and they also offer protection to PCs on the network. To the rest of the Internet, each PC has the IP address of the gateway, so each PC's resources can't be attacked or hijacked—they're invisible. The gateway itself doesn't have resources that can be used to attack you PCs, so you're safe.

But if you have servers on your network that need to provide Internet-related services (perhaps you have an FTP or web server), or if you need to allow certain PCs to be connected to from the Internet for specific purposes (such as for playing multiplayer games), you'll run into trouble because they don't have IP addresses that can be seen by the rest of the Internet.

However, with this trick, you can use your router to forward incoming requests to the right device on your network. For example, if you have a web server, FTP server, or mail server and want people to be able to connect to them, you'll be able to route incoming requests directly to those servers. PCs on the Internet will use your gateway's IP address, and your gateway will then route the requests to the proper device on your network. Normally, the devices would not be able to be connected to, because the IP addresses they are assigned by the gateway are internal LAN addresses, unreachable from the Internet.

Not all gateways include this capability. To use this feature in a Linksys gateway, log into to your administrator's screen and choose Advanced → Forwarding to get to the screen shown in Figure 5-17.

When this feature is enabled, the gateway examines incoming requests, sees what port they're directed to (for example, port 80 for HTTP), and then routes the request to the proper device.

Fill in each device's IP address, the protocol used to connect to it, and the port or port range that you want forwarded to it. It's also a good idea to disable DHCP (Dynamic Host Configuration Protocol) on each device to which you want to forward requests, and instead give them static internal IP addresses. If you continue to use DHCP instead of assigning them a static IP

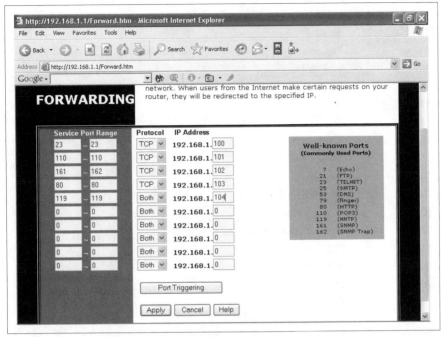

Figure 5-17. Forwarding incoming requests to the proper server or device

address, the IP addresses of the servers or devices may change and would therefore become unreachable. Check your gateway's documentation on how to force it to assign static IP addresses to specific devices.

Table 5-2 lists port addresses for common Internet services. For a complete list of ports, go to *http://www.iana.org/assignments/port-numbers*.

Table 5-2. Common Internet TCP ports

Port number	Service
7	Echo
21	FTP
22	PCAnywhere
23	Telnet
25	SMTP
42	Nameserv, WINS
43	Whois, nickname
53	DNS
70	Gopher
79	Finger
80	HTTP

Table 5-2. Common Internet TCP ports (continued)

Port number	Service
81	Kerberos
101	HOSTNAME
110	POP3
119	NNTP
143	IMAP
161	SNMP
162	SNMP trap
1352	Lotus Notes
3389	XP's Remote Desktop
5010	Yahoo! Messenger
5190	America Online Instant Messenger (AIM)
5631	PCAnywhere data
5632	PCAnywhere
7648	CU-SeeMe
7649	CU-SeeMe

Cloning a MAC Address for Your Gateway

This hack can help you avoid an extra charge from the cable company for your broadband service, or at least avoid having to call them with new information. Many broadband ISPs—cable modem ISPs in particular—require that you provide them with the MAC (Media Access Control) address of your network adapter in order for your connection to work. If when you began your broadband service you had a single PC, but you've since installed a gateway at home in order to set up a network and share Internet access among several PCs, you'll have to provide the ISP with your new gateway's MAC address.

Some ISPs might charge you a higher rate for cable access if you're sharing several PCs in this way. (Because of increasing competition among broadband providers, though, this has become far less common than it was previously.) There is a way, however, to use your existing MAC address with your new gateway by cloning the address. To your ISP, it looks as if your MAC address hasn't changed. You might want to do this even if your cable provider doesn't charge extra for several PCs, because it will save you having to call up the cable company's tech support line to provide a new MAC address.

Note that not all gateways have this capability, so yours may not be able to do it. Most Linksys gateways let you do this, so if you have a Linksys, do the following to clone your MAC address. Depending on your model, the exact steps may vary:

1. Find out your current network adapter's MAC address (the MAC address your broadband provider already has) by opening a command prompt, typing `ipconfig /all`, and looking under the entry for Ethernet adapter Local Area Connection. You'll see an entry like this:

   ```
   Physical Address. . . . . . . . . : 00-08-A1-00-9F-32
   ```

   That's your MAC address.

2. Log into your administrator's screen for the Linksys router and choose Advanced → MAC Addr. Clone. A screen similar to Figure 5-18 appears.

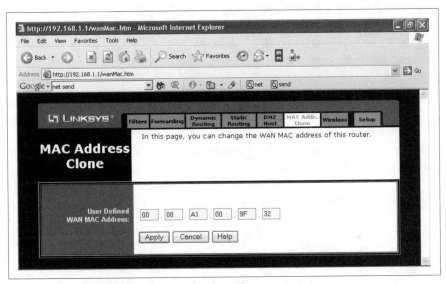

Figure 5-18. Cloning an existing MAC address

3. Type in the name of the MAC address you've obtained from your network adapter and click Apply. Your gateway will now be recognized by your ISP. Note that you may have to power down and power back up your cable modem in order for the gateway to be recognized.

> If your ISP requires a MAC address and you don't clone an existing one, you'll have to provide your ISP with your gateway's address. Make sure that you give them the right one. Your gateway typically has two MAC addresses, a LAN MAC address and a WAN MAC address. The LAN address is used only for the internal network, so make sure to provide your ISP with the device's WAN MAC address. If you give the LAN address, you won't be able to access the Internet.

Punch an Escape Hole Through Your Firewall

HACK
#50

Sometimes firewalls offer too much protection; they block unsolicited incoming traffic that you want to receive, such as if you're hosting a web site. Here's how to open a hole in your firewall to let only specific incoming traffic through.

Most firewalls block all unsolicited inbound traffic and connections, which can be a problem if you're running a web site, email or FTP server, or other service that requires you to accept unsolicited inbound packets. But you can punch a hole through your firewall, to let only that traffic in, while still keeping potentially dangerous intruders out.

First, decide what kind of unsolicited inbound traffic and connections you want to let through, and then find out which ports they use. For example, if you have a web server, you'll have to allow traffic through that's bound for port 80. Table 5-2 [Hack #49] lists common ports; for a complete list, go to *http://www.iana.org/assignments/port-numbers*.

How you allow traffic through a firewall varies from firewall to firewall. To do it for XP's built-in Internet Connection Firewall (ICF), first right-click on My Network Places to open the Network Connections folder. Then, right-click on the connection for which you want to enable the incoming services and choose Properties → Advanced → Settings. The Advanced Settings dialog box appears, as shown in Figure 5-19. To enable a service and allow its incoming traffic through the firewall, put a check next to it and click OK.

> If you haven't enabled ICF, the Settings button will be grayed out, and you won't be able to get to this screen. To find out how to enable ICF, see "Protect Your Computer with the Internet Connection Firewall" [Hack #46].

For this screen, you won't have to know the port numbers for the services whose incoming traffic you want to let through; you just need to know which service you want to allow. XP will know to block or unblock the proper port.

If the default settings for the service you want to allow don't work properly, you can edit them. Depending on the service, you can change the service's name or IP address, its description, the internal and external port numbers the service uses, and whether it uses the TCP or UDP protocol. For example, if your business uses a VPN [Hack #62] with a different port number than the one used by ICF, you can change the port number ICF uses, so that your VPN will work. Some services include hardcoded properties that you can't

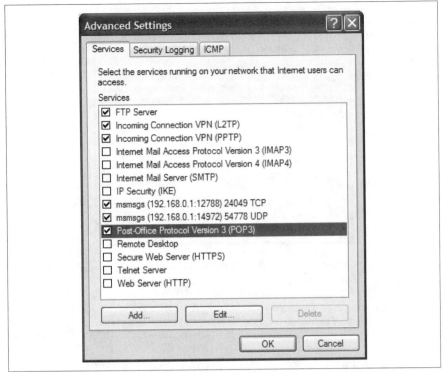

Figure 5-19. Enabling specific incoming services and traffic to bypass XP's ICF

change, while others will let you edit them. For example the Remote Desktop [Hack #58] can use only 3389 for external and internal ports and TCP as its protocol, and those can't be edited. But a few of the services, notably the VPN connections, let you edit the ports and protocol.

To edit the properties for one of the services, select it, choose Edit, and you'll see the Service Settings screen, as shown in Figure 5-20.

ICF allows you to let in about half-a-dozen services. Table 5-3 describes what each of the default services does. Note that the entry msmsgs might or might not show up in your system; Windows Messenger appears if you've used Windows Messenger or Outlook Express (which uses some Messenger components). Unlike all the other services listed, it is enabled by default, so it can already bypass the ICF. By default, though, all the other services listed in Table 5-3 are disabled.

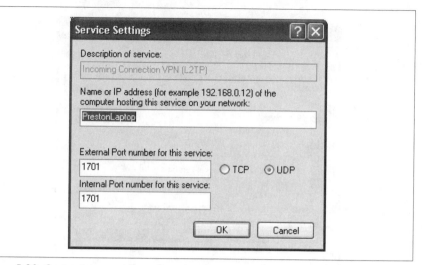

Figure 5-20. Customizing an inbound service that you want to pass through the ICF

Table 5-3. Services that can be allowed to bypass the ICF

Service	What it does
FTP Server	Allows others to connect to an FTP server on your PC.
Incoming Connection VPN (L2TP)	Allows for the use of a Virtual Private Network using the L2TP tunneling technology.
Incoming Connection VPN (PPTP)	Allows for the use of a Virtual Private Network using the PPTP tunneling technology.
Internet Mail Access Protocol Version 3 (IMAP3)	Allows others to connect to an IMAP3 email server on your PC to retrieve email.
Internet Mail Access Protocol Version 3 (IMAP4)	Allows others to connect to an IMAP4 email server on your PC to retrieve email.
Internet Mail Server (SMTP)	Allows others to use a Simple Mail Transfer Protocol (SMTP) server on your PC for sending email.
IP Security (IKE)	Allows for the use of the Internet Key Exchange (IKE) security technology.
msmsgs	Allows for the use of Windows Messenger, plus any software that uses its components, such as Outlook Express.
Post-Office Protocol Version 3 (POP3)	Allows others to connect to a POP3 email server on your PC to retrieve email.
Remote Desktop	Allows others to connect to your PC and take control of your desktop using XP Professional's Remote Desktop feature. (Available in XP Professional only.)

Table 5-3. Services that can be allowed to bypass the ICF (continued)

Service	What it does
Secure Web Server (HTTPS)	Allows other to connect to a web server on your PC that uses the HTTPS security protocol
Telnet Server	Allows others to use a Telnet server on your PC to use your PC's resources.
Web Server (HTTP)	Allows other to connect to a Web server on your PC.

Just because a service isn't listed in Table 5-3 doesn't mean that you can't allow its incoming traffic to bypass the ICF. You can add any service if you know its port information and the name or IP address of the PC on your network where you want the traffic routed. For example, to play some instant messenger games you'll need to allow port 1077 to get through. To add a new service, get to the Advanced Settings dialog box shown in Figure 5-19. Then click on the Add button and fill out the dialog box shown in Figure 5-21.

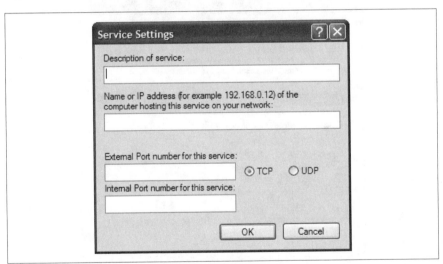

Figure 5-21. Adding a new service that can bypass the ICF

Fix ICF's Disabling of File Sharing

When you use the ICF and try to browse to another computer on your network to share its files, you may get an error message and you won't be able to connect to those files. That's because the ICF closes the ports used for file sharing and server message block (SMB) communications. (SMB is used by the network to allow file and printer access.) You also may not be able to browse the Internet through My Network Places.

To allow file sharing to work across the network and to allow browsing the Internet through My Network Places, open UDP ports 135 through 139, TCP ports 135 through 139, and TCP and UDP port 445 in the ICF.

Allow Diagnostic Services to Bypass the Firewall

The Internet Control Message Protocol (ICMP) enables troubleshooting and diagnostic services, such as ping [Hack #52]. By default, though, the ICF won't allow incoming ICMP traffic. You can allow various ICMP-enabled services to pass through your firewall by clicking on the ICMP tab on the Advanced Settings dialog box shown in Figure 5-19. From the screen that appears, shown in Figure 5-22, check the boxes next to the services you want to allow. To get a description of each service, highlight it and read about it in the Description area.

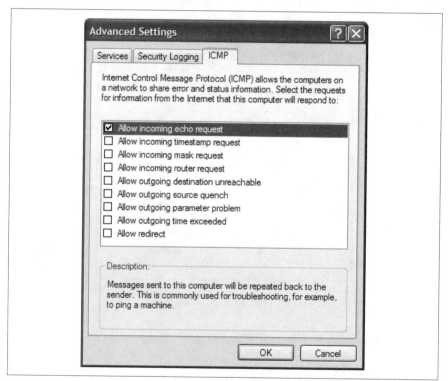

Figure 5-22. Using the ICMP tab to allow diagnostic services to bypass the ICF

Punch a Hole Through ZoneAlarm

If you use the ZoneAlarm firewall [Hack #48], you can also allow specific unsolicited incoming traffic through. Click on the Firewall button on the left side of the screen, and then click on Custom for each of your security zones. The Custom Firewall Settings dialog box appears, as shown in Figure 5-23. Click on the service you want to allow through, click OK, and you'll be done.

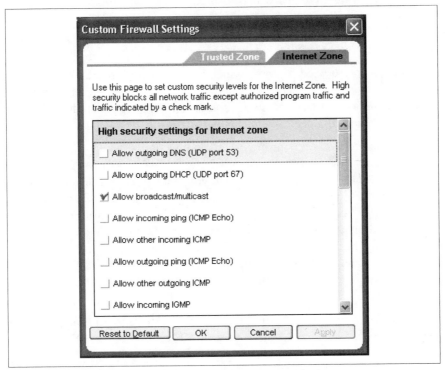

Figure 5-23. Allowing specific incoming traffic to bypass ZoneAlarm

See Also

- ZoneAlarm: The World's Best Free Firewall [Hack #48]
- Protect Your Computer with the Internet Connection Firewall [Hack #46]

HACK #51 Close Down Open Ports and Block Protocols

You don't need a firewall to protect your PC; you can manually close down ports and block certain protocols.

As noted in "Protect Your Computer with the Internet Connection Firewall" [Hack #46]] and "ZoneAlarm: The World's Best Free Firewall" [Hack #48], firewalls can protect your PC and your network from intruders. But if you don't want to install a firewall and you still want protection, you can manually close down ports and block protocols.

Some of these ports and protocols are more dangerous than others. For example, leaving open the port commonly used by Telnet (port 23) means that someone could use that service to take control of your PC. And the infamous Back Orifice Trojan, which also can give malicious users complete control of your PC, uses a variety of ports, including 31337 and 31338 among others. For a list of which ports are used by Trojans, go to *http://www.sans.org/resources/idfaq/oddports.php*.

In this hack, you'll need to know which ports you want to be open on your PC, such as port 80 for web browsing, and you'll close down all others. For a list of common ports, see Table 5-2 [Hack #49]. For a complete list of ports, go to *http://www.iana.org/assignments/port-numbers*.

To close down ports and protocols manually, right-click on My Network Places and choose Properties to open the Network Connections folder. Right-click on the connection for which you want to close ports and choose Properties. Highlight the Internet Protocol (TCP/IP) listing and choose Properties. On the General tab, click the Advanced button. From the Advanced TCP/IP Settings dialog box that appears, choose Options, highlight TCP/IP filtering, and choose Properties. The TCP/IP filtering dialog box appears. To block TCP ports, UDP ports, and IP protocols, choose the Permit Only option for each. Doing this will effectively block all TCP ports, UDP ports, and IP protocols.

You don't want to block all ports, though, so you have to add the ports that you want to allow to pass—such as port 80 for web access. You need to keep port 80 open if you want to browse the web. Click Add to add the ports or protocols that you will allow to be used, as shown in Figure 5-24. Keep adding as many ports and protocols as you wish to be enabled, and click OK when you're done. Only the ports and protocols that are listed will be allowed to be used.

Keep in mind that there are many hundreds of TCP and UDP ports used by Internet applications and services. If, for example, you enable only web access, you won't be able to use all other Internet resources, such as FTP, email, file sharing, listening to streaming audio and video, and so on. So, use this hack only if you want a very limited number of Internet services and applications to be used by your PC.

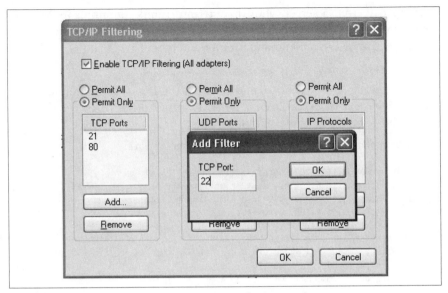

Figure 5-24. Blocking TCP ports, UDP ports, and IP protocols

Troubleshooting Network Connections with ping, tracert, and pathping

HACK #52

When you need help tracking down network connection problems, the command line is the place to go.

If you're having problems with your network and network connections and you need troubleshooting help, forget XP's GUI; it doesn't offer you enough help. To get to the root of the problems, you're going to have to get down and dirty with command-line tools. ping and tracert are familiar tools that you might have used on occasion, but you might not know the depth of their power or the switches available to use with them. And you probably haven't heard of pathping, a kind of combination of the two commands.

Troubleshoot TCP/IP Problems with ping

The quickest, most commonly used, and, frequently most helpful TCP/IP troubleshooting tool is the command-line tool ping. Use ping to find out whether the resource or server you're trying to connect to on your network or the Internet is active, and to see if there are any problems with the hops along the way to that resource or server. ping sends Internet Control Message Protocol (ICMP) Echo Request messages to the destination you're checking on, receives responses in return, and reports to you information about the connection path between you and the destination and how quickly the packets made their trip. For example, if you are having trouble getting email from a server, your first step in troubleshooting should be to ping the server to see whether the server is live, and to see how responsive it is. To use ping, get to a command prompt and type:

```
ping target
```

where *target* is either a hostname or an IP address—for example, *pop3. catalog.com*, *zdnet.com*, or *209.217.46.121*. In response, you'll get information in this format:

```
Pinging zdnet.com [206.16.6.208] with 32 bytes of data:

Reply from 206.16.6.208: bytes=32 time=83ms TTL=242
Reply from 206.16.6.208: bytes=32 time=73ms TTL=242
Reply from 206.16.6.208: bytes=32 time=91ms TTL=242
Reply from 206.16.6.208: bytes=32 time=72ms TTL=242

Ping statistics for 206.16.6.208:
    Packets: Sent = 4, Received = 4, Lost = 0 (0% loss),
Approximate round trip times in milli-seconds:
    Minimum = 72ms, Maximum = 91ms, Average = 79ms
```

If the host isn't active, instead of getting this report, you'll get the message "Request timed out."

If you enter a hostname, ping reports back with its IP address and then gives details about its four attempts to contact the host, a measurement of how long (in milliseconds) the packet took to make the round trip between your PC and the host, the Time To Live (TTL) information about each packet, and a summary of its findings.

The TTL field can tell you how many hops the packets took to get from your PC to its destination. TTL initially specified the amount of time a packet could live, in seconds, before it expires, as a way to make sure that packets didn't simply bounce around the Internet forever and create traffic jams. However, it has been reinterpreted to mean the maximum number of hops that a packet will be allowed to take before its destination. The default number is 255. Each time a packet takes another hop, its TTL is reduced by one. The TTL number that ping reports is the packet's final TTL when it reaches its destination. To find out the number of hops a packet takes, subtract its initial TTL (by default 255) from the TTL reported by ping. In our example, the packets took 13 hops to get to their destination.

You can use ping with switches, like so:

```
ping -a -l 45 208.201.239.237
```

This command changes the packet size sent from its default size of 32 bytes to 45 bites, and resolves the IP address to a hostname—in other words, it lists the IP address's hostname.

ping has a wide variety of useful switches that you can use for all kinds of troubleshooting. You use the basic ping command to check whether an Internet or network resource is live and to see if there are any delays in reaching it. But, as Table 5-4 shows, you can use ping and its switches for many other purposes as well—for example, to find out the IP address of a hostname and vice versa.

Table 5-4. Useful ping switches

Switch	What it does
-a	Resolves an IP address to a hostname.
-f	Turns on the "Don't Fragment" flag for a packet. This lets you send packets that don't get broken up and can be useful for when you want to test whether packets of a certain size are getting through.
-i *value*	Sets the value of the TTL field, using a number from 0 to 255. When you use this field, even though the field will be set to the number you specify, note that the ping report will report back as if it were set to 255. For example, if you set a TTL of 20 and the packet takes 15 hops, the TTL value that ping reports will be 240.
-l *value*	Pings using the value specified, in number of bytes.
-n *count*	Specifies the number of ICMP Echo Request messages sent, instead of the default number of 4.
-r *count*	Displays the IP addresses of the hops taken along the route to the destination. Specify a number between 1 and 9. If the number of actual hops exceeds the number you specify, you will get a "Request timed out" message.
-s *count*	Displays a timestamp for the Echo Request and the Echo Reply Request for hops along the route. Specify a number between 1 and 4. If the number of actual hops exceeds the number you specify, you will get a "Request timed out" message.
-t	Keeps sending the Echo Request message continually until stopped by pressing Ctrl-Break, Pause, or Ctrl-C.
-w *value*	The maximum amount of time (in milliseconds) to wait for an Echo Reply message for each Echo Request message before issuing a timeout message. The default is 4,000 (4 seconds).

Trace Your Network and Internet Data Path with tracert

Frequently, you have a connection problem over your network or the Internet not because your final destination is down, but because there's a problem with a router somewhere between you and your final destination. For troubleshooting those kinds of problems, use tracert. It displays the path that data takes en route to the server or service that you're trying to reach, either on your network or across the Internet. As with ping, it does this by sending ICMP Echo Request messages to the destination you're checking on. To use it, type tracert *destination* at a command prompt, where *destination* can be either an IP address or a hostname. Following is a typical response from a tracert command:

```
Tracing route to redir-zdnet.zdnet.com [206.16.6.208]
over a maximum of 30 hops:

 1     9 ms   11 ms     10 ms   10.208.128.1
 2     8 ms    8 ms      7 ms   bar02-p0-1.cmbrhe1.ma.attbb.net [24.128.8.53]
 3     9 ms    *        32 ms   bar03-p7-0.wobnhe1.ma.attbb.net [24.147.0.193]
 4     8 ms   14 ms      9 ms   12.125.39.213
 5    12 ms   10 ms      9 ms   gbr2-p70.cb1ma.ip.att.net [12.123.40.102]
 6    25 ms   26 ms     24 ms   gbr4-p80.cb1ma.ip.att.net [12.122.5.65]
 7    36 ms   39 ms     64 ms   gbr4-p40.cgcil.ip.att.net [12.122.2.49]
 8    33 ms   33 ms     48 ms   gbr3-p60.cgcil.ip.att.net [12.122.1.125]
 9    72 ms   80 ms     78 ms   gbr3-p30.sffca.ip.att.net [12.122.2.150]
10    72 ms   77 ms     73 ms   idf26-gsr12-1-pos-6-0.rwc1.attens.net [12.122.
255.222]
11    76 ms   78 ms     79 ms   mdf3-bi4k-2-eth-1-1.rwc1.attens.net [216.148.
209.66]
12    73 ms   72 ms     74 ms   63.241.72.150
13    72 ms   74 ms     71 ms   redir-zdnet.zdnet.com [206.16.6.208]
```

If the destination can't be reached, you will get the message "Destination unreachable."

As you can see, tracert shows the IP address and hostname address of each hop, along with timing data for each hop. If you're having problems on your network, this can help you locate the source of the problem; if a hop has a particularly long delay, you know that's the cause.

You can use several switches with tracert, like this:

```
Tracert -d -h 45 zdnet.com
```

This command traces to *zdnet.com*, displaying only the IP addresses of each router and specifying a maximum number of 45 hops en route to the destination. Table 5-5 shows the most useful tracert switches.

Table 5-5. Useful tracert switches

Switch	What it does
-d	Does not display the hostname of each router.
-h *value*	Sets a maximum number of hops for the trace to the destination.
-w *value*	Sets the maximum amount of time in milliseconds to wait for a reply.

Troubleshoot Network Problems with pathping

The pathping command works like a combination of ping and tracert. Type pathping from the command line, like this:

```
pathping target
```

where *target* is either a hostname or an IP address—*pop3.catalog.com* or *209.217.46.121*, for example. You then get a two-part report: first a list of every hop along the route to the destination, and then statistics about each hop, including the number of packets lost at each hop. It uses switches—for example:

```
pathping -n -w 1000 oreilly.com
```

This command tells pathping not to resolve the IP addresses of routers, and to wait one second (1,000 milliseconds) for an Echo Replay message. Table 5-6 lists the most important pathping switches.

Table 5-6. Useful pathping switches

Switch	What it does
-n	Does not display the hostname of each router.
-h *value*	Sets a maximum number of hops for the trace to the destination. The default is 30 hops.
-w *value*	Sets the maximum amount of time (in milliseconds) to wait for a reply.
-p	Sets the amount of time (in milliseconds) to wait before a new ping is issued. The default is 250.
-q *value*	Sets the number of ICMP Echo Request messages to transmit. The default is 100.

See Also

- Troubleshooting Network Connections with netsh, netstat, and ipconfig [Hack #53]

HACK #53 Troubleshooting Network Connections with netsh, netstat, and ipconfig

More command-line tools for tracking down problems with your network connection.

In addition to well-known command-line network utilities such as ping, tracert, and pathping, there are several other all-purpose utilities that can help you troubleshoot network connections: netsh, netstat, and ipconfig.

Use netsh to Troubleshoot Network and Internet Connections

netsh is a wide-ranging command-line diagnostic tool that has an exceedingly large number of commands available. (For a complete list of available commands, use Windows XP Help and Support and search for netsh.) Here you'll learn the most interesting.

Perhaps the most useful of the netsh commands are the netsh diag commands. Use them to find out information about your PC's network setup, such as finding the IP address of its mail server, newsgroup server, DNS server, and similar resources.

There are two ways to use netsh: directly from the command line with all its switches, or first getting to the netsh console by typing netsh at the command line and then typing the command from the netsh> prompt that appears. For example, you could type netsh diag show adapter at the command line, which lists every network adapter on your PC, or you could get to the netsh> prompt and type diag show adapter.

Use the netsh command to connect to the resources and then get information about them. For example, to find out the IP address of your DNS servers, type netsh diag show dns; to find out the IP address of your mail server, type netsh diag connect mail.

Table 5-7 list the most useful of the netsh diag commands. Precede each of them with netsh diag. Note that they each have many switches associated with them. For more details, use Windows XP Help and Support and search for netsh.

Table 5-7. Useful netsh diag commands

Command	What it does
connect ieproxy	Establishes a connection to Internet Explorer's proxy server, if one exists.
connect mail	Establishes a connection to the default Outlook Express mail server.
connect news	Establishes a connection to the default Outlook Express newsgroup server.
ping adapter	Establishes a connection with the named adapter.
ping dhcp	Establishes a connection with a DHCP server.
show adapter	Lists all the adapters on the PC.
show all	Lists all the network objects defined for the local PC, such as adapters, network clients, servers, modems, and other objects.
show dhcp	Lists all the DHCP servers for the specified adapter.
show dns	Lists all the DNS servers for the specified adapter.
show gateway	Lists all the gateways for the specified adapter.

Use netstat to Get Information About Open Network Connections

If you want to get a snapshot of all incoming and outgoing network connections, use the netstat command. At a command prompt, type netstat. It lists all connections, including the protocol being used, the local and Internet addresses, and the current state of the connection, like this:

```
Active Connections
  Proto  Local Address        Foreign Address           State
  TCP    PrestonGralla:1031   localhost:2929            ESTABLISHED
  TCP    PrestonGralla:2887   192.168.1.103:netbios-ssn TIME_WAIT
  TCP    PrestonGralla:2899   www.oreillynet.com:http   ESTABLISHED
  TCP    PrestonGralla:2900   www.oreillynet.com:http   ESTABLISHED
  TCP    PrestonGralla:2932   mail.attbi.com:pop3       ESTABLISHED
  TCP    PrestonGralla:2936   vmms2.verisignmail.com:pop3 ESTABLISHED
```

It will help you know whether connections are live, the network or Internet device to which they're connected, and which local resource is making the connection. It's best suited for when you're troubleshooting network problems and want to find out whether certain ports are open, why certain computers on the network are having connection problems, and similar issues. You can use command-line switches with netstat. For example, display open ports and open connections with this syntax: netstat -a. Table 5-8 lists netstat switches.

Table 5-8. Netstat switches

Switch	What it does
-a	Displays all open connections and ports.
-e	Displays Ethernet statistics about packets transmitted and received. Can be combined with the -s switch.
-n	Displays the addresses and ports in numeric, IP address form.
-o	Displays the process identifier (PID) that owns each connection.
-p *proto*	Displays the connections used by the protocol, which can be IP, IPv6, ICMP, ICMPv6, TCP, TCPv6, UDP, or UDPv6.
-r	Displays the network's routing table.
-s	Displays statistics for each protocol. It lists all statistics for all protocols, but you can list only those for a specified protocol if you combine it with the -p switch.
interval *value*	Run netstat repeatedly, pausing *value* seconds between each new display. To stop the display, press Ctrl-C.

Use IPConfig to Troubleshoot TCP/IP

One of the most powerful tools for analyzing and troubleshooting TCP/IP problems is the ipconfig command-line utility. It provides information about each of your adapters, including the assigned IP address, subnet mask, default gateway, MAC address, DNS servers, whether DHCP is enabled, and a variety of other data. To see basic information about your adapters, type ipconfig at a command prompt, and you'll see information like this:

```
Windows IP Configuration
Ethernet adapter Local Area Connection:
```

```
           Connection-specific DNS Suffix  . : ne1.client2.attbi.com
           IP Address. . . . . . . . . . . : 192.168.1.100
           Subnet Mask . . . . . . . . . . : 255.255.255.0
           Default Gateway . . . . . . . . : 192.168.1.1
PPP adapter {6A724E76-AB59-4ABC-BBF5-41CA4410EB8D}:
           Connection-specific DNS Suffix  . :
           IP Address. . . . . . . . . . . : 172.165.155.106
           Subnet Mask . . . . . . . . . . : 255.255.255.255
           Default Gateway . . . . . . . . :
```

As you can see, ipconfig provides basic information about your IP address, subnet mask, default gateway, and a connection-specific DNS suffix, if any. However, you can get much more detailed information by using the /all switch, like this: ipconfig /all. For most troubleshooting purposes, use the /all switch. You get a much more comprehensive listing, as shown here:

```
Windows IP Configuration
           Host Name . . . . . . . . . . . : PrestonGralla
           Primary Dns Suffix  . . . . . . :
           Node Type . . . . . . . . . . . : Hybrid
           IP Routing Enabled. . . . . . . : No
           WINS Proxy Enabled. . . . . . . : No
Ethernet adapter Local Area Connection:
           Connection-specific DNS Suffix  . : ne1.client2.attbi.com
           Description . . . . . . . . . . : CNet PRO200WL PCI Fast Ethernet
Adapter
           Physical Address. . . . . . . . : 00-08-A1-00-9F-32
           Dhcp Enabled. . . . . . . . . . : Yes
           Autoconfiguration Enabled . . . : Yes
           IP Address. . . . . . . . . . . : 192.168.1.100
           Subnet Mask . . . . . . . . . . : 255.255.255.0
           Default Gateway . . . . . . . . : 192.168.1.1
           DHCP Server . . . . . . . . . . : 192.168.1.1
           DNS Servers . . . . . . . . . . : 204.127.202.19
                                             216.148.227.79
           Lease Obtained. . . . . . . . . : Saturday, December 28, 2002 8:
53:40 AM
           Lease Expires . . . . . . . . . : Sunday, December 29, 2002 8:53:
40 AM

PPP adapter {6A724E76-AB59-4ABC-BBF5-41CA4410EB8D}:
           Connection-specific DNS Suffix  . :
           Description . . . . . . . . . . : WAN (PPP/SLIP) Interface
           Physical Address. . . . . . . . : 00-53-45-00-00-00
           Dhcp Enabled. . . . . . . . . . : No
           IP Address. . . . . . . . . . . : 172.165.155.106
           Subnet Mask . . . . . . . . . . : 255.255.255.255
           Default Gateway . . . . . . . . :
           DNS Servers . . . . . . . . . . : 64.12.104.134
           NetBIOS over Tcpip. . . . . . . : Disabled
```

You can also use `ipconfig` to release and renew IP addresses, and perform other troubleshooting functions as well. For example, to renew an adapter's IP address, use this command:

```
ipconfig /renew "adapter name"
```

where *adapter name* is the name of the adapter whose IP address you want to renew. Make sure to put quotes around the adapter name and use spaces if there is more than one word in the adapter name. Table 5-9 lists other switches you can use with `ipconfig`.

Table 5-9. Command-line switches for ipconfig

Switch	What it does
/all	Displays complete TCP/IP configuration information.
/displaydns	Displays information from the DNS resolver cache (for more information [Hack #44]
/flushdns	Clears the DNS resolver cache [Hack #44]
/registerdns	Refreshes all DHCP leases and reregisters DNS names.
/release "*adapter*"	Released the IP address for the specified adapter.
/renew "adapter"	Renews the IP address for the specified adapter.
/setclassid "adapter" newclassid	Resets the DHCP Class ID for the specified adapter.
/showclassid "*adapter*"	Displays the DHCP Class ID for the specified adapter.

HACK #54 Speed Up Network Browsing

Speed up your network browsing by tweaking your registry.

When you use My Network Places to browse for other machines on your network, it usually takes a long time to display the list of shared resources for the target machine. This is because Windows XP first checks for the scheduled tasks on the target machine before listing the shared resources present on the computer.

> To schedule a task using Windows XP's Scheduled Tasks, choose Start → Programs → Accessories → System Tools → Scheduled Tasks.

This unnecessary checking can easily add 30 seconds of delay. You can decrease the time browsing takes by modifying the Registry to turn off this checking:

1. Invoke the Registry Editor by typing `regedit` [Hack #68] at the command line.

2. Open the Registry key:

```
HKEY_LOCAL_MACHINE\SOFTWARE\Microsoft\Windows\CurrentVersion\Explorer\
Remote Computer\NameSpace
```

3. Delete the following key (the value for it is the Scheduled Tasks, as shown in Figure 5-25):

```
{D6277990-4C6A-11CF-8D87-00AA0060F5BF}
```

4. Close the Registry and reboot.

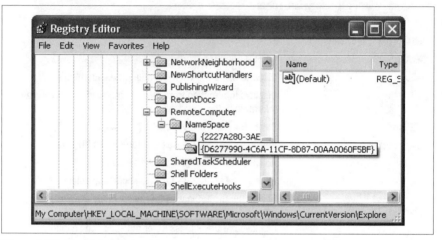

Figure 5-25. Modifying the registry

That's it! You should now be able to browse to another computer on the network without much delay.

—Wei-Meng Lee

Extend the Range of Your Wireless Network

HACK #55

The efficiency and throughput of WiFi networks can vary dramatically. Make sure you get maximum throughput from your wireless network.

If you have more than one PC at home, the best way to hook them together and share a high-speed Internet connection is via a wireless network—in particular, one based on the WiFi standard, which is actually a family of standards known under the umbrella term of 802.11x.

The biggest problem in setting up a home network usually involves running the wires between PCs and a residential gateway. If your PCs are on different floors of the house, you may have to drill holes in your walls, ceiling, and floors and run wire through. Even when PCs are on the same floor, you have to deal with the problem of wires snaking along the floor.

That's the problem I've had in my 150-year-old home in Cambridge. Drill through a wall, ceiling, or floor here, and you never know what you'll find (horsehair insulation was only one of our many surprises). Even my electrician shudders when he has to take out the drill.

So, for me, a wireless network was a no-brainer. I now have got half-a-dozen PCs and laptops and three printers in remote parts of the house from each other, all connected via a combination wired/wireless network and sharing a single broadband Internet connection. And when the weather is nice here (twice a year, by my last calculation), I take my laptop out on my back porch and work from there while still connected to the Internet and other PCs and printers in the house.

But there's a catch with all wireless networks, including mine. Wireless networks rarely deliver data at their rated bandwidth speed. One factor affecting bandwidth speed is the distance between the access point and the wirelessly equipped PC. Compaq, for example, notes that at a distance of 150 feet the throughput of its wireless access point drops from 11 Mbps to 5.5 Mbps, and at a distance of 300 feet it drops to 2 Mbps. Even that significantly understates the drop-off in speed, and most people find that the drop-off is much more dramatic than that, most commonly by a factor of two.

Distance is only one factor affecting performance. Interference from other devices and the exact layout of the house or office can also affect it dramatically. However, there are things you can do to extend the range of your network and get more throughput throughout your home:

Centrally locate your wireless access point. This way, it's most likely that all of your wirelessly equipped PCs will get reasonable throughput. If you put it in one corner of the house, nearby PCs may get high throughput, but throughput for others may drop significantly.

Orient your access point's antennas vertically. As a general rule, transmission will be better when antennas are vertical rather than horizontal. Keep in mind, though, that this is only a starting point for positioning its antenna. The exact layout of your house may alter the best positioning of the antenna.

Point the antennas of your wireless PCs toward the access point. Although 802.11 technology does not require a direct line of sight, pointing them in this way tends to increase signal strength. USB wireless cards generally have small antennas that can be positioned, but frequently wireless PC cards don't, so you may have trouble figuring out the antenna orientation in a wireless PC card. If you have a wireless PC card that doesn't

WiFi and Buying New Equipment

There are several versions of the 802.11x WiFi standard, and unfortunately, they don't all work with one another. So, when you're buying WiFi equipment such as hubs/routers, make sure they're compatible. The 802.11b standard was the first one to be ratified, is the most common type of WiFi network, and its equipment is the least expensive. (This is the standard commonly used by public wireless "hot spots" in coffee shops, airports, hotels, and other locations.) It operates in the 2.4 GHz part of the spectrum and its maximum throughput is 11 Mbps.

Increasingly popular, though, is the 802.11g standard, which also operates in the 2.4 GHz part of the spectrum but has a much higher maximum throughput: 54 Mpbs. 802.11b cards will connect to a 802.11g access point, but only at a maximum of 11 Mpbs. However, 802.11g cards can't connect to an 802.11b access point. As of this writing, problems have been reported using 802.11b hardware on an 802.11g network, however. There have been reports of incompatibilities and of the 802.11b hardware slowing the entire 802.11g network down to its slower speed. However, that's because the 802.11g hardware was built when the standard was only a draft and not a final standard. The standard has since been finalized, so if you buy new equipment, you should be safe. Be wary of buying older, used equipment, though.

have what appears to be an antenna, the antenna is generally located at the periphery of the card itself, so point that at the access point.

Don't place your access point next to an outside wall. If you do that, you'll be broadcasting signals to the outside, not the inside, of the house. That's nice if you want to give your neighbors access to your network, but not great if you want to reach all the PCs in your house.

Avoid putting your access point or PCs near microwave ovens or cordless phones. Many microwave ovens and cordless phones operate in the same 2.4 GHz part of the spectrum as 802.11b WiFi equipment. So, microwave ovens and cordless phones can cause significant interference. Cordless phones tend to be the bigger problem.

Avoid placing the antennas of access points or PCs near filing cabinets and other large metal objects. They can both cause significant interference and dramatically reduce throughput.

Consider using external and booster antennas. Some PC cards, notably Orinoco cards, will accept external antennas that you can buy or build on your own. They have a small connector to which you attach a *pigtail* and wire and then attach that wire to an antenna. (For information about building your own antenna, see "War Driving for WiFi Access" [Hack #42]). Some access points often accept booster antennas that you can buy as well.

> If you have a Linksys wireless network and are looking to improve its signal strength, you can buy a $99 add-in that promises to extend its range and strengthen its signal. The WSB24 Wireless Signal Booster sits on top of your existing wireless router. You take the antennas off your router, attach them to the booster, then attach the booster to the router via cables. I haven't tried it myself, so I can't personally vouch for it, but those who have tried claim it works.

Try and try again. The ultimate way to find the best placement for your access point and wireless PCs is to continuously experiment and see what kind of throughput you get. Each house and office is so different that no single configuration can suit them all.

Carefully monitor your throughput as you make these changes, so that you determine the best positioning for your access point and PCs. To determine your true throughput, use the free network analysis program QCheck [Hack #57].

See Also

- War Driving for WiFi Access [Hack #42]
- Check WiFi Network Performance with QCheck to Help Improve Throughput [Hack #57]

HACK #56 Install NetBEUI for Better Peer-to-Peer Networking

If you run into problems when networking PCs with different versions of Windows, the NetBEUI protocol should solve your problems. But beware: don't use the XP-specific version. Instead, follow this hack.

The Holy Grail of Windows peer-to-peer networking is the absolute reliability of network connections between computers. When you open My Network Places and try to access the shared resources of any other computer on your network, you shouldn't have to wait a long time or be faced with mysterious error messages.

Unfortunately, Windows XP is surprisingly prone to these sorts of peer network problems in mixed-Windows-version networks, especially when you network NT/2000/XP with 9x/Me computers. Most experienced Windows network administrators believe you get the best network browsing reliability by using Microsoft's NetBEUI network transport protocol and TCP/IP. But there's a problem. With the release of Windows XP, Microsoft officially stopped supporting NetBEUI. The network protocol is included in a *legacy* folder on the Windows XP CD. But the XP version of NetBEUI is considered to be inferior to the Windows 2000 version, and Microsoft has even admitted that possibility.

The solution is fairly simple, then. Install the Windows 2000 version of NetBEUI on your XP PCs instead of using the XP version. Caveats? Yes, two. Some people have problems with NetBEUI in wireless networking environments (my belief is that this is a broadband-router-specific issue). The second caveat is that NetBEUI does not support hibernation or standby power-management operations properly. (For more details on why, as well as alternatives to NetBEUI—such as IPX/SPX with NetBIOS—please see "NetBEUI Power Down" from Scot's Newsletter: *http://www.scotsnewsletter.com/ 42.htm#pwrprob*.)

> Installation of any version of NetBEUI on Windows XP is trickier than most people realize. It's very easy to wind up with an improperly installed protocol without even realizing that you have done so. The symptoms consist of intermittent network-connection problems (exactly what you're trying to avoid). The instructions that follow represent hours of research that literally scores of Scot's Newsletter readers confirmed with their own networks. Bottom line: follow the directions exactly; don't take shortcuts; it'll work for you too. End warning.

First, get a copy of the Windows 2000 version of NetBEUI. It consists of two files, *Nbf.sys* and *Netnbf.inf*. If you don't have the Windows 2000 CD, you can download the files from a more detailed and periodically updated website version of this hack, which originally appeared in Scot's Newsletter in January 2003 under the title "How to Install Win2K's NetBEUI in XP" (*http:// www.scotsnewsletter.com/38.htm#tipadaweek*).

If you have the Windows 2000 CD, go to the CD's \i386 directory and find the compressed files *Nbf.sy_* and *Netnbf.in_*. Use WinZip to open and extract them to a folder called something like *NetBEUI for Win2K*. Once the files are extracted, copy your destination folder to all XP computers on your network. Detailed extraction instructions are available at *http://www. scotsnewsletter.com/38.htm#tipadaweek* (including how to do this without WinZip).

Once you have the files, begin the NetBEUI installation by copying *Nbf.sys* to *C:\Windows\System32\Drivers*, and *Netnbf.inf* to *C:\Windows\Inf*. Then restart Windows XP.

> If you have ever installed or tried to install any version of NetBEUI on any Windows XP PC on your network, you must take an additional step before installing NetBEUI; remove the protocol from the PC's network configuration and then manually delete the two NetBEUI files. Failure to do this before installing NetBEUI again will almost certainly wind up in a botched installation. For step-by-step instructions on how to fully uninstall NetBEUI from Win XP, see *http://www.scotsnewsletter.com/38.htm#tipadaweek*.

After you've restarted, open the Network Connections folder by choosing Control Panel → Network Connections. Right-click the network connection icon to which you want to add NetBEUI (the default name of the primary connection is Local Area Connection) and choose Properties → General → Install → Protocol → Add. Select the NetBEUI protocol from the list and click OK. Restart your computer if you receive a prompt to complete the installation.

Next, unbind TCP/IP from sharing. For security reasons, TCP/IP file and printer sharing should be disabled on all computers on your network to separate the Internet from the LAN. Open the Control Panel called Network Connections. There are several ways to do that, only some of which may apply to you, depending on interface settings you chose in past. You can right-click either My Network Places (if it's visible on your desktop) or the Network icon (if it's visible on the system tray) and then choose Properties. If neither of those methods work, click Start and open the Control Panel. Find and double-click the Network Connections or Network and Dial-Up Connections icon.

Once Network Connections is open, choose the Advanced menu and select Advanced Settings. On the Adapters and Bindings tab, under "Bindings for [your network connection name]," remove the check mark beside Internet Protocol (TCP/IP) and click OK.

Finally, test your NetBEUI installation. Reboot all your PCs and check that they're able to connect to all shared drives, folders, and other resources. Either the Guest account will need to be turned on or the workstation names of the other PCs on your network must be added to Users and Groups. In tests, I've found freshly installed NetBEUI to be a little sticky (and this may affect any computer on your network). After opening My Network Places, you'll sometimes see an error message the first two or three times you attempt to connect to another PC. Once it connects the first time, it usually connects reliably after that.

See Also

- Speed Up Network Browsing [Hack #54]

—Scot Finnie

HACK #57 Check WiFi Network Performance with QCheck to Help Improve Throughput

XP can't tell you the true throughput or your wired or wireless network. For that, you'll need free, third-party software that can help you improve throughput.

When you buy network hardware, including a hub/router and network cards, you're told that hardware's rated speed—for example, 100 Mbps for an Ethernet network, or 11 Mpbs for a an 802.11b WiFi network.

But those numbers only tell you how your network may perform in ideal conditions; as the saying goes, "your mileage may vary," and usually does. WiFi networks are particularly finicky and are especially prone to being affected by interference and other factors. Where you place your wireless access point and PCs and how you position their antennas [Hack #55] can make a dramatic difference in the actual speed of your network. So, you'll want to know the true connection speed of your network, WiFi networks in particular, so that you can optimize their performance when you troubleshoot them.

But how can you find out your true network performance? If you have a WiFi card, you can find information about your connection by double-clicking on the small network icon in the Notification Area (also called the *system tray*). When you do that, the Wireless Network Connection Status screen appears, as shown in Figure 5-26.

There's only one problem with that screen: it's highly inaccurate. True, its little green bars and Signal Strength indication give you a broad picture of the relative strength of your network connection. But the Speed indication isn't an actual measurement as far as I can tell; it appears to tell you only your maximum theoretical connection speed, given the nature of your hardware, and doesn't reflect your true current connection speed. When I use my WiFi network, it always tells me the speed is 11 Mbps, even when actual, real-time measurement shows my true throughput is less than half of that.

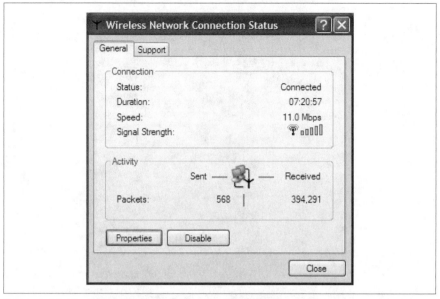

Figure 5-26. The Wireless Network Connection Status screen

So, how do you measure the true speed of a network in your real-world conditions? Get NetIQ's free QCheck (*http://www.netiq.com/qcheck/*). It performs a series of tests, including throughput and response time, and gives you a good snapshot of your network's real performance. When trying to optimize a WiFi network, run QCheck on each PC on the network to get baseline performance results for each. Then run the test for each PC after you move the base station and PCs, change the positioning of the antennas, and so forth, as outlined in [Hack #55]. That way, you'll be able to fine-tune your network for optimum efficiency.

Once installed on every machine in your network, QCheck measures the performance of the network between any two of your PCs. QCheck is made up of two components: the console where you run your tests, shown in Figure 5-27, and an endpoint, which runs invisibly in the background on each PC on which you've installed QCheck. While the exact metrics vary from test to test, the program works by sending data from one PC to another on your network. The data is then sent from the receiving PC back to the originating PC, and QCheck measures the round-trip time, calculates throughput, and displays the results.

Note the throughput in Figure 5-27; it's 5.128 Mbps. I was measuring the speed of my WiFi network whie seated on my backyard porch, which is about 30 feet and a wall away from my access point. Just to show you how much more accurate QCheck is, the Wireless Network Connection Status

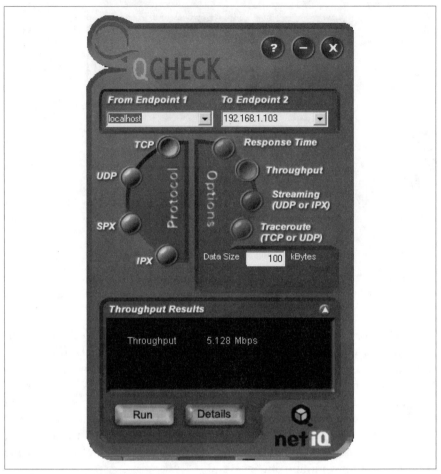

Figure 5-27. The QCheck console

screen reported my speed as 11 Mbps—the exact connection speed my laptop would have if I were inches away from the wireless access point. (And in actuality, the connection speed of a WiFi network, even when devices are next to one another, is well under 11 Mbps.)

To run the QCheck tests, run the console and then choose the two PCs between which you want to measure speed on your network. Only one must be the PC with the console on it, but each PC does have to have QCheck on it. You don't need to run the console on each machine, because the endpoints are running on them invisibly in the background; during QCheck's installation the endpoints launch on startup.

You'll need to know the IP addresses of the PCs you want to test. If one of the PCs you're testing is the one running the console, choose *localhost* for that endpoint. To find the IP address of other PCs on your network, first go to that PC, right-click on My Network places, then double-click on your network connection (it might read Local Area Connection, for example, or Wireless Network Connection). Click on the Support tab, and you'll see your IP address.

Once you choose the PCs you want to test, choose the specific test to run. The best overall benchmark will be the Throughput test using either the TCP or UDP protocols. If you happen to use IPX or SPX on your network (some people still use these older protocols rather than TCP/IP), you can do benchmark throughput tests using them as well, though few home networks use those protocols. If you run any kind of streaming media across your network—for example, if you will be using your network to play MP3 files or other digital music on a PC and then stream it to another location in your house—choose the UDP streaming test. Streaming media use the UDP protocol, so the only way to test how they will perform on your network is to use the test for that protocol.

Make sure to run your test multiple times, and, to be safe, run them a half-hour or more apart. Because of the fickle nature of wireless transmissions, you can find dramatic differences in throughput from one moment to the next. For example, a few minutes after running the throughput test shown in Figure 5-27, I ran it again and was shown a throughput of 1.602 Mbps. That one test was an anomaly, and other tests were more in keeping with my initial ones.

See Also

- War Driving for WiFi Access [Hack #42]

Control Another PC with Remote Access

#58   You can control a computer—virtually moving its mouse and typing on its keyboard—over the Internet, using either Windows XP's built-in features or a third-party program.

When you are at work, wouldn't it be nice if you could log onto your home computer to check your email or find a file you took home? How about using your home or office desktop computer from your laptop on the road? You can use a remote control program to use another computer over the Internet, viewing its screen on your screen and giving commands via your mouse and keyboard. Windows XP comes with a feature called Remote Desktop, or you can use a third-party program. Windows Messenger [Hack #78] also enables people who are chatting to share control of each other's computers.

The computer you will control is called the *remote server*, and the computer you are actually sitting in front of is the *remote client*. Windows XP comes with a remote client program (Remote Desktop Connection), and Windows XP Professional comes with a remote server (Remote Desktop) that works with one client at a time—that is, one computer can "take over" your computer remotely (with luck, it'll be you doing the takeover!).

> Remote Access Server (RAS) on Windows NT or 2000 servers and the Routing and Remote Access utility on Windows Server 2003 both act as remote servers that allow multiple remote clients to connect.

Windows XP Home Edition can't act as a remote server; if you need to be able to access a Home Edition system remotely, you need to upgrade to Windows XP Professional or use a third-party program. We recommend VNC, the small, free, open source program from the University of Cambridge Department of Engineering (information and free downloads are available at *http://www.uk.research.att.com/vnc*).

Configuring the Windows XP Remote Server

If you want to be able to control your Windows XP Professional system remotely, set it up as a remote server. Using an administrator user account, choose Start → Control Panel → Performance and Maintenance → System (or press the Windows-Break key), click the Remote tab, select the checkbox in the Remote Desktop section of the tab to enable incoming connections ("Allow users to connect remotely to this computer"), and click the Select Remote Users if you want to control which user accounts can be used by remote clients. (Windows automatically allows connections from the current user, along with all user accounts in the local Administrators and Remote Desktop Users groups.)

Normally, remote clients connect to the server via a local area network or a permanent Internet connection. However, you can also configure the remote server to accept incoming phone calls if you have a dial-up modem. Create a dial-up connection that accepts incoming calls by running the New Connection Wizard (click "Create a new connection" from the task pane in the Network Connections window). Choose "Set up an advanced connection" as the Network Connection Type, choose "Accept incoming connections," choose your modem, choose whether to accept VPN connections [Hack #49], and choose which user accounts the incoming connection can connect to.

Firewalls usually refuse remote access connections [Hack #46] and [Hack #48], so if you want your remote server to be accessible from the Internet, you need to open a port in your computer's firewall [Hack #50]. Remote Desktop uses port 3389. If you use Windows XP's built-in firewall, display the Network Connections window, right-click the Internet connection, choose properties from the shortcut menu, click the Advanced tab, and click Settings to display the Advanced Settings dialog box. Click the Remote Desktop checkbox; if the Service Settings dialog box appears, just click OK.

> If you want to change the Remote Desktop server port to a number other than 3389 (perhaps to decrease the likelihood of hackers breaking through it), see the Microsoft Knowledge Base article Q187623 (at *http://support.microsoft.com*, type the article number in the "Search the Knowledge Base" box).

When you connect from your remote client (described later in this hack), you need to provide a domain name or IP address. If your computer connects via a dial-up, DSL, or cable connection, its IP address changes each time you connect, and the computer doesn't have a domain name. One solution is to have someone at the remote server display the Network Connections window, right-click the Internet connection, choose Status from the shortcut menu, click the Support tab, and call, IM, or email you with the IP address that appears. However, this solution is no good if no one is available to do this. Instead, you can sign up for a dynamic DNS service [Hack #59] at *http://www.dyndns.org* or *http://www.tzo.com*. The dynamic DNS service at DynDNS.org gives you a free domain name in the form *<yourname>.dyndns.org* (they offer several dozen domain names to which you can add your name). TZO.com provides a subdomain at *<yourname>.tzo.com* for $25 per year. You install a small utility on your computer that automatically tells the dynamic DNS whenever your computer's IP address changes.

One final configuration note: when a client connects to your server via Remote Desktop, the user logs into one of the Windows XP user accounts. You can't log into accounts that have no password. Choose which account you plan for remote user(s) to log in with, and give it a password.

Setting Up the Remote Client

To set up the remote client software that comes with Windows XP, connect to the Internet and then choose Start → All Programs → Accessories → Communications → Remote Desktop Connection. (If it's not there, you need to install it from your Windows CD.) In the Remote Desktop Connection window, type the domain name or IP address of the server computer and click Connect. Log on with the Windows XP user account and password for the remote server. Your computer screen now shows what's on the screen of the server computer. A connection bar appears as a button on the screen, showing the IP address of the remote server, along with Minimize, Restore, and Maximize buttons you can use to resize the remote client window.

Once you're connected, you can cut and paste information from the remote client window to other windows. You can also use local files in your remote session; your local disk drives appear in My Computer (Windows Explorer). When you print from the remote client, the print job goes to your default local printer, not the printer on the server.

—Margaret Levine Young

HACK #59 Make Servers Always Available by Mapping a Hostname to a Dynamic IP Address

Make sure that the web site or other kind of Internet server you run at home is always available to the world.

If you run your own web server, mail server, or other kind of server at home and are connected to the Internet via a cable modem or DSL modem, people frequently may not be able to connect to your server. That's because, typically, broadband ISPs assign you a dynamic IP address that changes regularly, even if you don't turn off your PC. Because your IP address constantly changes, there is no way for people to connect to you. One day its IP address might be 66.31.42.96, the next it might be 66.41.42.136, and if people don't know your server's current IP address they won't be able to find it. You won't be able to solve the problem by getting your own domain (such as *www.gralla.com*) and publishing that, because DNS servers won't be able to keep track of your changing IP address either. If people type in your domain name, the servers won't be able to report on your IP address—and again, your server won't be able to be reached.

There is a way to solve the problem, however: you can map your server's hostname to a dynamic IP address. When you do this, it doesn't matter that your IP address changes; when people type in your web site's URL, they will be forwarded to your new IP address automatically.

You can do this for free by signing up with a service that provides automatic mapping. A number of services will do it for free, such as No-IP.com (*http://www.no-ip.com*). When you sign up for the service, you choose a hostname for your server and give that hostname out to people who want to connect to the server. Whatever name you choose will end in *.no-ip.com*—for example, *grallasite.no-ip.com*.

After you get your hostname, you download client software that continually monitors your IP address. It reports on your server's current IP address to the No-IP.com site. Whenever the IP address changes, it reports that new IP address to the site. The client checks your IP address every three seconds.

Whenever a PC tries to connect to your server, it first goes to a No-IP.com server, which looks up your server's current address and then redirects the PC to your server, based on your current IP address. The person contacting your site will not have to do anything different than he normally does; he just types in your URL and is connected to your site.

If you own a domain and want to map that hostname to a dynamic IP address instead of using a No-IP.com address, you'll have to sign up for No-IP.com's No-IP Plus service for $24.95 a month.

If you're using a residential gateway at home to share Internet access among several PCs, you may run into problems using the service. Many gateways use Network Address Translation (NAT), in which all PCs on the network share a single external Internet address but are assigned internal network addresses. The No-IP.com client will track your external address, but because that single address is used by all PCs on the network, not just the server, incoming traffic won't be routed to your server. You can fix the problem by using the port forwarding feature of your route to send the incoming traffic to the server [Hack #49].

You may run into another problem as well: when you try to test your server by connecting to it from a PC inside your network, you might not be able to connect to it. That's because you might not be able to connect to the external IP address from inside the network. If this happens, the only solution is to connect to the site from a PC outside of your network or ask a friend to connect to it.

One more thing to watch out for: if you're behind a firewall, the No-IP.com client may have trouble connecting back to the No-IP.com site to report on your changing IP address. If you're using a firewall like ZoneAlarm [Hack #48] or a similar one that blocks outbound connections, tell it to allow the client to make outbound connections. Also, depending on the firewall you use, you may need to configure it to open TCP port 8245, because that's the port the client uses to contact No-IP.com with your new IP address.

See Also

- Secrets of Web Site Hosting with Internet Information Services (IIS) [Hack #40]

Renewing Your DHCP-Assigned IP Address

H A C K
#60

Sometimes, while assigned an IP address by a DHCP server, your PC doesn't appear to be on the network and you can't get Internet or network access. Renewing your IP address often solves the problem.

If you're on a network but you can't send or receive data, use any network resources, or visit the Internet, the culprit may be a problem with your DHCP-assigned IP address. The simplest way to fix it is to renew the IP address—get rid of the old one, and ask the DHCP server to send along a new one.

Before trying this, first make sure you're using a DHCP-assigned IP address rather than a static one. Right-click on My Network places and choose Properties to get to the Network Connections folder. Right-click on your current network connection and choose Properties. On the General tab, select Internet Protocol (TCP/IP) and choose Properties. On the General tab, the radio button next to "Obtain an IP address automatically" will be selected if you're using DHCP.

After you've confirmed you're using DHCP, release your current IP address by typing `ipconfig /release` at a command prompt. The `ipconfig` command is an all-purpose command that lets you solve many network-related problems, as detailed in "Troubleshooting Network Connections with netsh, netstat, and ipconfig" [Hack #53]. To renew the address and get a new IP address from the DHCP server, type `ipconfig /renew` at a command prompt. Your new IP address should fix the problem.

To find your new IP address, type `ipconfig` at a command prompt. You can also select your connection in the Network Connections folder, click on "View status of this connection," and click on the Support tab. You'll see the screen shown in Figure 5-28, which shows your new IP address and confirms that it was assigned by a DHCP server.

Repair a Broken TCP/IP Connection

H A C K
#61

Get back onto the Internet fast if you have TCP/IP woes.

TCP/IP problems can be exceedingly difficult to troubleshoot, and at times they appear to break for no apparent reason. Everything looks like it should be working, but you're not able to connect using the protocols. If you have a broken connection, try the following:

Try automated repair.   Right-click on the broken connection in the Network Connections folder and choose Repair.

Figure 5-28. Confirming that you've gotten a new IP address

Run the Network Setup Wizard.   It walks you step by step through TCP/IP and network configuration and will correct any errors you may have introduced inadvertently.

Reset your router.   If you have a home network, the problem may lie with the router or in the connection between the router and your broadband provider. Follow the directions for resetting the router.

Reset your cable modem or DSL modem.   If you have a broadband connection, the problem may lie in the assignment of your IP address by your ISP. Power off your cable modem or DSL modem, unplug its Ethernet cable, and leave it powered off for five minutes. Then restart it. This is also a good time to reset your router. You can also try releasing and renewing after you've turned the connection back on.

Reset TCP/IP to its original configuration.   If all else fails, you can try to reset your TCP/IP stack to the same state that it was in when XP was first installed on the computer. Use the NetShell utility [Hack #53]. Issue this command: netsh int ip reset [*log_file_name*], where *log_file_name* is the name of a file where the actions taken by NetShell will be recorded.

HACK #62 Set Up a Virtual Private Network

Sometimes you would like to connect to your home machine from work or while traveling. Making your home machine a virtual private network (VPN) server is a secure way to accomplish this.

If you've ever taken files home to work on your personal computer you've probably had the experience of arriving to work the next day only to realize you've forgotten to bring the files back with you. If the work was important enough, you probably had to drive all the way back home get it or make a lame excuse to your boss as to why you don't have the TPS report ready yet. Perhaps you're a road warrior who has found himself stranded in a hotel room on a Monday morning, just hours before a big meeting without that copy of the presentation you thought you had copied from your home machine. If either of these sound like a situation you've been in, this is the hack for you.

It is well known that Windows XP has a VPN client built into it, which allows you to make secure connections to your company's network. Less well known is that Windows XP also has the ability to act as a VPN server, allowing you, or others you designate, to make secure connections into your home network. While you have an established VPN session with your home machine, you can access files from its hard drive or other machines on the network that have file sharing enabled. All you need is a local Internet connection and a VPN client that supports the Point to Point Tunneling Protocol (PPTP), which the client for all versions of Windows does.

Preparing your home machine to accept VPN connections is fairly straightforward. Click Start → Settings → Control Panel → Network and Internet Connections → Network Connections → Create a New Connection. This will launch the New Connection Wizard. While advancing through this wizard, the options you want to enable are "Set up an advanced connection," "Accept Incoming Connections," and "Allow virtual private connections." The sixth screen of the wizard allows you to specify the users that can use the VPN; make sure you enable at least one account. If you haven't created a password for your user, now is the time to do so. You are essentially opening up a part of your machine to the Internet, so make sure you choose a good password. After the wizard is complete, nothing further needs to be done; the VPN is ready to accept incoming connections. You can test this by using a VPN client to connect to the IP address of the VPN server machine.

Most home users use a router that provides Network Address Translation (NAT), which obscures the actual IP address of the machine they want to make a VPN connection to. This means you won't be able to make a VPN connection to your machine until you configure your router to allow the VPN traffic to pass through to your VPN server. See "Enable Specific Internet Services: Port Forwarding" in [Hack #47].

CHAPTER SIX

Email

Hacks 63–67

If you're like a lot of people, email is a big part of your life. For many, it's replaced the telephone for keeping in touch with friends and family—and, of course, it's absolutely vital for work as well.

But the odds are, you're not getting the most out of your email. You may be bedeviled by spam, you may be blocked from opening specific files sent to you via email, and you may not know how to back up your mail programs. In this chapter, you'll find hacks for all that and more, including great Registry hacks for getting the most out of Outlook and Outlook Express, as well as Outlook alternatives.

HACK #63 Slam That Spam

You don't have to be bedeviled by unwanted mail. Use this hack to kill as much as 90% (or much more, in my case) of your spam.

If you have certain body parts that you'd like enlarged, expect Nigerian strangers to shower several million dollars upon you, favor spending boatloads of money for semiworthless goods, and enjoy vile, pornographic come-ons littering your email box, then you're a spam lover.

Everyone else, like you and me, hates the stuff.

While there's no foolproof way of stopping all the spam that makes its way into your mailbox, I've found ways to block at least 90% of what I don't want headed my way. To get that effective a blocking rate, you'll need to use downloadable software; the antispam features built into Outlook and Outlook Express simply don't cut it. (However, if you're bent on trying to use Outlook and Outlook Express's antispam features, head to the end of this hack to learn how.)

There are two primary kinds of software you can use to block spam. One type sits between your email program and the mail servers where you pick up your email. It checks your mail, marks email that it considers spam, and then (depending on the program) lets you handle that spam in a variety of ways, such as automatically deleting it, letting you manually delete it, or marking it in a way that will alert your normal email program that it's spam—and letting the email program filter or kill the spam. In all cases, you'll be able to read the messages before they're deleted, if you want.

The other type of software integrates directly into Outlook or another email program and kills spam from directly within the program. I favor this kind, because it's a simpler, one-step process. But I've used both types, and both work well.

For the kind of spam killer that sits between your email program and your mail server, I suggest the free program MailWasher (*http://www.mailwasher.net*). It imports your existing email server account settings so that you don't have to set them up from scratch, and it lets you read and preview messages before deleting spam. I especially like its bounced mail feature; it will send a false "address not found" address to the sender so that it will appear your email doesn't exist. While not all spammers bother to clean up their list of addresses, there's at least the possibility this could lead to less spam ultimately coming into your mailbox. As with most spam killers, you can add addresses to a list of known spammers, though spammers so frequently spoof their addresses, this may or may not be of much help. You can also create filters with specified words or groups of words that MailWasher will look for in email, and if it finds them it will consider the message spam.

A more powerful, for-pay version of the program is available for $29.95. Its primary benefit is that it will check multiple email accounts for spam; the free version will check only one. If you need to check only a single account, stay with the free version.

One of the tricks that spammers use is to target a site and send a *dictionary attack* to many potential email accounts on a server. They will send to "bob", "nancy", etc., as well as "asmith", "bsmith", "csmith", etc. Most of the emails will bounce, but the spammer doesn't care. They encode the email in HTML with an embedded <IMG> tag. The tag has information encoded within it to uniquely identify the valid email addresses. For example, say *cjones@mycompany.com* gets an email in HTML format. Inside the email is:

```
<img src=83.48.123.74/img/jojo_jpg_cjones_mycompany_com.jpg>
```

The web server at 83.48.123.74 will load the image named *jojo.jpg* to an email in cjones' email program. When the user sees the advertisement for herbal Viagra or whatever, she will delete it. However, the damage has already been done. The spammer knows that *cjones@mycompany.com* exists because they know the image was downloaded. The user cjones will soon be getting more than just offers for herbal Viagra.

One way to prevent this type of attack is to turn off displaying HTML in emails. Unfortunately, there's no direct way to do this in Outlook, but there's a hack that will do the trick for you. When you're in your inbox, turn off Outlook's Preview Pane by choosing View → Preview Pane. (To restore the pane, choose View → Preview Pane again.) HTML email will grab pictures from web servers only when you've opened the mail or viewed it in the Preview Pane, so all you have to do is delete spam without opening it—by using spam killers as outlined earlier in this hack—and you'll be safe. In Outlook Express, you can do the same thing by choosing View → Layout and unchecking the box next to "show preview pane." You can also download a handy plugin for Outlook that will turn off HTML email, called NoHTML, at *http://ntbugtraq.ntadvice.com/default.asp?pid=55&did=38.*

> In Eudora, this is done via Tools → Options → Display → uncheck "Automatically download HTML graphics" (this turns off the display of HTML email), Tools → Options → Display → uncheck "Allow executables in HTML content," and Tools → Options → Styled Text → check "Send plain text only" (this turns off the sending of HTML email, which is just a polite thing to do).

Peer-to-Peer Technology Fights Spam

I've tried quite a few Outlook add-in spam killers, and my favorite is Spam-Net (*http://www.cloudmark.com*). I've found that it blocks well over 90% of the spam that I receive. It uses peer-to-peer technology to gather the collective intelligence of thousands of other email users in order to fight spam. When you install it, it creates a Spam folder in Outlook and routes any spam into that folder, where you can review it and then delete it. If you get spam that isn't automatically routed to the folder, you can mark it as spam. Not only is the mail then sent to the Spam folder, but SpamNet servers are also told that you consider that piece of mail spam. That information goes into a database, along with similar information from hundreds of thousands of other people who use the program. A variety of algorithms are used to determine what is spam and what isn't, and that's what ultimately blocks spam on everyone's system. It uses collective intelligence, which may be the ultimate spam killer.

You can also block and unblock messages as spam, so if mail is accidentally marked as spam it won't be blocked in the future. I've used the program for well over six months, and I've found that it increases in effectiveness over time. By now, I estimate that it blocks about 95% of spam, though that changes on a daily basis.

SpamNet runs as a small toolbar in Outlook, as shown in Figure 6-1. A nice little touch is the message bar that tells you how much spam the program has blocked, how much time it's saved you, or how much spam it's blocked in a day. Depending on my mood, when I see the total amount of spam it's blocked, I'm either depressed that there's so much spam in the world or pleased at how much spam I've been able to avoid.

Figure 6-1. SpamNet running on the Outlook toolbar

When SpamNet was in its extended beta period, it was free, and beta users can continue to use the beta for free. But for Version 1.0 and above you'll have to pay $4.99 a month. That's admittedly a hefty price for a spam killer, considering that others are available for free. But if you get enough spam, you may consider it worth the money.

Slam Spam Before It Starts

The best way to fight spam is to make sure it never gets sent to your email box in the first place. So, how do you end up on spam lists? There are many ways, but the most common, according to a comprehensive study done by the Center for Democracy & Technology, is that your email address is harvested by spammers who use programs to automatically scan web pages and gather email addresses from them. Those addresses are then sold to other spammers, so you could end up on dozens of lists.

There might be many reasons why you need to have your email address on a public web site, so removing your address from sites might not be an option. However, there are ways to hide your address from spammers, even when it's in plain view.

One way used to be to spell out your email address—for example, post "preston at gralla dot com" instead of *preston@gralla.com*. Automated harvesting programs won't be able to grab your address that way.

At least you used to be able to use that trick. Some spammers have figured it out by now. My new favorite trick is to use a bit of inline JavaScript to generate your email address at page load time. Harvester bots see a <script> tag, but users see *bob@bob.com*.

```
<script type="text/javascript" language="javascript">
<!--
    {    document.write(String.
fromCharCode(60,97,32,104,114,101,102,61,34,109,97,105,108,116,111,58,98,111
,98,64,98,111,98,46,99,111,109,34,62,98,111,98,64,98,111,98,46,99,111,109,60
,47,97,62))
    }
//-->
</script>
<noscript>
<a href = "mailto:%62%6F%62%40%62%6F%62%2E%63%6F%6D">email me</a>
</noscript>
```

I got the JavaScript generator from *http://www.u.arizona.edu/~trw/spam/spam.htm*. You feed it your email address, and it generates the javascript.

Another solution is to use HTML characters for your address rather than plain text characters. That way, a person who visits the page can see the email address, since HTML translates the underlying code into a readable address, but an automated harvester won't be able to read it. To use HTML characters, you need to use the ANSI characters and precede each character with &#. Separate each HTML character by a ; and leave no spaces between characters. For example, in HTML, the *preston@gralla.com* address is:

```
&#112;&#114;&#101;&#115;&#116;&#111;&#110;&#64;&#103;&#114;&#97;&#108;&#108;
&#97;&#46;&#099;&#111;&#109;
```

Keep in mind, though, that if you use HTML characters to spell out your email address, you won't be able to put automated HTML "MailTo" links; that requires the text to actually be spelled out rather than using HTML characters.

Table 6-1 lists the common ANSI codes you'll need for most email addresses.

Table 6-1. Common ANSI codes

A	65	J	74	S	83	b	98
B	66	K	75	T	84	c	99
C	67	L	76	U	85	d	100
D	68	M	77	V	86	e	101
E	69	N	78	W	87	f	102
F	70	O	79	X	88	g	103
G	71	P	80	Y	89	h	104
H	72	Q	81	Z	90	i	105
I	73	R	82	a	97	j	106

Table 6-1. Common ANSI codes (continued)

k	107	r	114	y	121	3	51
l	108	s	115	z	122	4	52
m	109	t	116	@	64	5	53
n	110	u	117	.	46	6	54
o	111	v	118	0	48	7	55
p	112	w	119	1	49	8	56
q	113	x	120	2	50	9	57

For a more comprehensive list of ANSI codes and special HTML characters, go to *http://www.alanwood.net/demos/ansi.html*.

There are several other things you can do to keep your address out of spammer's hands. When registering at a site, always read the fine print to see whether you're also signing up to get unsolicited mail. I also suggest using multiple email addresses, including those from free mail services like Hot-Mail and Yahoo, and to use those addresses when registering at sites. That way, any spam will be sent to them rather than your normal mail address.

Viewing Mail Header Information in Outlook and Outlook Express

As a general rule, spammers spoof their email addresses so that you won't be able to find them. However, not all do, and if you examine email header information you may be able to trace spam to its source. Once you find the originating mail server, you can send a message to the ISP's administrator, asking to block mail from the sender. It might not always work, but it's worth a try.

The problem for Outlook and Outlook Express users is that those programs don't show mail header information—information such as the original sender of the message, the original mail server, and relay information in your messages. However, there is a way to view it.

In Outlook, right-click on the message whose header you want to view, and choose Options. Header information appears at the bottom of the screen, as shown in Figure 6-2. You can scroll through it and copy and paste from it. You can also view this information if you're reading a message, by choosing View → Options.

Note that if you use logic when trying to view header information in Outlook, it won't work. If you choose View → Message Header, for example, you won't see your header information. Instead, that option toggles the To:, cc:, and Subject: lines on and off.

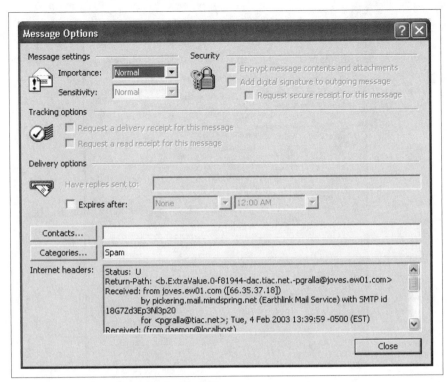

Figure 6-2. Header information in Outlook

In Outlook Express, right-click on a message, choose Properties → Details, and you'll see header information, as shown in Figure 6-3.

Handling Spam in Outlook Express

Both Outlook and Outlook Express include ways to handle spam, though neither does a particularly effective job because they require that you manually determine what spam is and then block future spam based on that. Because spam comes in from so many different email addresses and includes so many different subject lines, it's difficult to control spam this way. However, you can give it a try. Here's how to do it in Outlook Express.

Outlook Express handles spam by letting you add email addresses and domains to a Blocked Senders List. Then, every time a message comes in from the address or domain, the mail is automatically sent to the Deleted Items folder. To add an address or domain to the list, choose Tools → Message Rules → Blocked Senders List. The Blocked Senders tab of the Message Rules dialog box appears. Click Add, and you'll see the screen pictured in

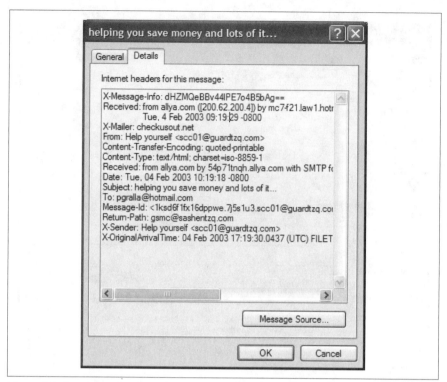

Figure 6-3. Displaying header information in Outlook Express

Figure 6-4. Type in the email address or domain you want to block. You can block mail, newsgroup messages, or both. Click OK when you're done.

Handling Spam in Outlook

Outlook handles spam differently than Outlook Express; it won't automatically send spam to the Deleted Items folder. Instead, it will color junk mail gray and color messages with adult content maroon. You can then scan your inbox for messages with those colors and delete them manually.

When you receive a message that you consider spam or that contains adult content, right-click on it and choose Junk Email. From the flyaway menu, choose "Add to Junk Senders list" or "Add to Adult Content Senders list." You can also manually add senders to either list by clicking the Organize button on the Outlook toolbar and then choosing Junk E-Mail. The screen shown in Figure 6-5 appears. From here, you can turn on and off the Junk Senders list and the Adult Content Senders list. To add to either list, click on the "click here" link, then click on Edit Junk Senders or Edit Adult Content Senders, and add addresses to either list.

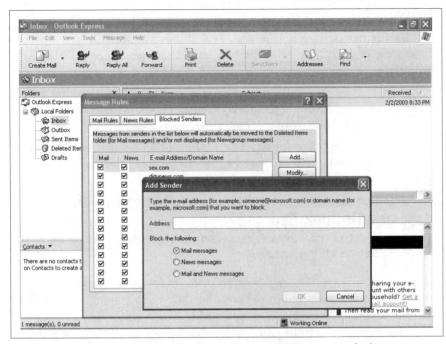

Figure 6-4. Blocking spam in email and newsgroup messages using Outlook Express

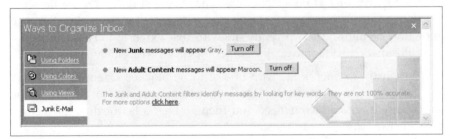

Figure 6-5. Turning spam filters on and off and adding new senders to the spam lists

You can also use Outlook's normal filters to handle spam. You can define a rule that will route messages from certain senders, or that contains certain content, to folders that you define, or to the Deleted Items folder. To create rules for doing this, choose Tools → Rules Wizard and follow the instructions. Keep in mind, though, that because spammers use different email addresses constantly, this won't help you a great deal.

See Also

- The Center for Democracy and Technology's report on how spam is generated and how to avoid it, at *http://www.cdt.org/speech/spam/030319spamreport.shtml*.

- SpamPal (*http://www.spampal.org*) is a free spam fighter that marks email as spam before it gets to your email program. You then use your email program's filters to filter out the resulting spam.

- An excellent resource for news and information about spam, and what you can do to stamp it out, can be found at *http://spam.abuse.net*.

HACK #64   Open Blocked File Attachments in Outlook and Outlook Express

Force Outlook and Outlook Express to let you open a wide variety of file attachments that they normally block.

The world is full of nasty email-borne worms and viruses, and everyone certainly needs to be protected from them. But Microsoft, in the latest versions of Outlook and Outlook Express, takes a Big Nurse, draconian approach to the problem; it refuses to let you open a wide variety of file attachments sent to you via email, including those ending in *.exe*, *.bat*, and many other common file extensions. (Eudora doesn't!) The theory is that there's a possibility that a file with one of those extensions may be dangerous, so you shouldn't be allowed to open *any* file with that extension. That's like banning all cars because some people sometimes get into accidents.

When you try to open a file with one of those blocked extensions, you get the following error message: "Outlook blocked access to the following potentially unsafe attachments," and then you get a list of the attachments in your email that you can't open.

Depending on your version of Outlook, Outlook Express and whether you've applied a Service Pack update to either of them, your version may or may not exhibit this behavior. Some older versions don't act this way; all newer versions do.

The simplest way to know whether your version acts this way is to see what happens when you get one of the blocked file attachments. If it's allowed to go through, there's no need to use this hack. If it's blocked, get thee to the keyboard. Outlook and Outlook Express handle the problem differently, so we'll take a look at each.

Force Outlook to Let You Open Blocked File Attachments

Outlook assigns a level of risk to every file attachment sent to you. Level 1 is considered unsafe, so Outlook blocks your access to them; you won't be able to open the files. Level 2 is considered a moderate risk, and you won't be able to open those files directly. Instead, you have to save the files to disk, and then you'll be able to open them. I'm not clear on how that increases security, but that's what Microsoft has done. Oh, and there's another odd-ball fact about Level 2: no file types are considered Level 2 risks. The only way for a file to be considered at that risk level is if you use Outlook in concert with a Microsoft Exchange Server and the administrator uses his administration tools to put file extensions into that risk category. The administrator is also the only person who can take file extensions out of the category. So, you can pretty much ignore that category, unless you have some convincing official reason for changing your company's policy. Any file types not in Levels 1 and 2 are considered "other" and you can open them normally.

To force Outlook to let you open blocked file attachments, use this Registry hack. Before starting, you need to know the list of Level 1 file attachments that Outlook blocks. They're listed in Table 6-2. Just to make things more confusing, depending on your version of Office and what Service Pack you've installed, not all of these extensions may be blocked.

Table 6-2. Blocked file extensions in Outlook

Extension	File type
.ade	Microsoft Access project extension
.adp	Microsoft Access project
.app	Visual FoxPro Application
.asx	Windows Media audio/video
.bas	Microsoft Visual Basic class module
.bat	Batch file
.chm	Compiled HTML Help file
.cmd	Microsoft Windows NT Command script
.com	MS-DOS program
.cpl	Control Panel extension
.crt	Security certificate
.csh	Unix shell extension
.exe	Executable program
.fxp	Visual FoxPro Compiled Program
.hlp	Help file
.hta	HTML program

Table 6-2. Blocked file extensions in Outlook (continued)

Extension	File type
.inf	Setup information
.ins	Internet Naming Service
.isp	Internet Communications settings
.js	Jscript file
.jse	Jscript Encoded Script file
.ksh	Unix shell extension
.lnk	Shortcut
.mda	Microsoft Access add-in program
.mdb	Microsoft Access program
.mde	Microsoft Access MDE database
.mdt	Microsoft Access workgroup information
.mdw	Microsoft Access workgroup information
.mdz	Microsoft Access wizard program
.msc	Microsoft Common Console document
.msi	Microsoft Windows Installer package
.msp	Microsoft Windows Installer patch
.mst	Microsoft Windows Installer transform; Microsoft Visual Test source file
.ops	Office XP settings
.pcd	Photo CD image; Microsoft Visual compiled script
.pif	Shortcut to MS-DOS program
.prf	Microsoft Outlook profile settings
.prg	Visual FoxPro Program
.reg	Registry entries
.scf	Windows Explorer command
.scr	Screen saver
.shb	Shell Scrap object
.shs	Shell Scrap object
.url	Internet shortcut
.vb	VBScript file
.vbe	VBScript Encoded script file
.vbs	VBScript file
.wsc	Windows Script Component
.wsf	Windows Script file
.wsh	Windows Script Host Setting file

Decide which of the file extensions you want to be able to open from within Outlook, and close down Outlook if it's running. Then run the

Registry Editor [Hack #68] and go to HKEY_CURRENT_USER\Software\Microsoft\
Office\10.0\Outlook\Security, which, as its name implies, handles Outlook security. Create a new String value called Level1Remove. In the Value
Data field, type the name of the file extension that you want to be able to
open—for example, *.exe*. You can add multiple file extensions. If you do,
separate them with semicolons, but no spaces, like this: .exe;.bat;.pif.
Use Table 6-2 as a guide for which blocked file extensions you want to be
able to open.

When you're done, exit the Registry and reboot. You'll now be able to open
the file extensions you specified.

There's also an Outlook add-in that will let you open blocked email attachments without having to edit the Registry. The Attachment Options add-in,
available from *http://www.slovaktech.com/attachmentoptions.htm*, lets you
visually change which attachments you can open, and it also lets you set an
additional option—having Outlook ask you whether you want to open certain file extensions on a case-by-case basis, rather than blocking them or
automatically opening them. The author asks that you send a $10 donation
if you use the add-in.

> If you know who's sending you a certain attachment, you
> can also have them zip the file and resend it to you. That
> way, you're getting a file with a *.zip* file extension, which will
> get through.

Force Outlook Express to Let you Open Blocked File Attachments

Depending on your version of Outlook Express, it may prevent you from
opening certain email file attachments, in the same way that Outlook blocks
certain files.

> If you have installed Windows XP Service Pack 1, Outlook
> Express Service Pack 1, or Internet Explorer 6 Service Pack 1,
> you'll be blocked from opening certain email file attach-
> ments. Also, if you have a newer version of XP, you may also
> be blocked.

With Outlook Express, unlike with Outlook, you won't be able to determine on an extension-by-extension basis which attachments you can open.
Instead, you can tell the program to let you open all blocked extensions or
you can tell it to stop you from opening any blocked extensions.

To tell Outlook Express to let you open blocked attachments, choose Tools
→ Options → Security and clear the box next to "Do not allow attachments

to be saved or opened that could potentially be a virus," as shown in Figure 6-6. You may have to close Outlook Express and restart it in order for the settings to take effect.

Figure 6-6. Forcing Outlook Express to let you open all email attachments

HACK #65 Back Up and Restore Outlook and Outlook Express Data Files

If email and contact lists are your lifeblood, you need to back them up regularly, but there's no easy way to do that using Outlook or Outlook Express. This hack tells you how to do it in each program.

There are two ways to back up and restore Outlook and Outlook Express data files: the easy way and the hard way. In the hard way, you manually back up all the data files, which can be a long and laborious process because those files are kept in so many different places. Do it once, and you may not do it again. In the easy way, you get an add-in that does the backup for you.

Backing Up Outlook Manually

If all you want to do is back up your Outlook messages and contacts, then it's a breeze. Outlook keeps all messages, contacts, and your calendar in a single file that ends in a *.pst* extension, typically *Outlook.pst* in the *C:\Documents and Settings\<Your Name>\Local Settings\Application Data\Microsoft\ Outlook* folder. If it's not there, you can locate them by right-clicking on the Outlook Today icon in Outlook, choosing Properties → Advanced, and looking in the Filename box. If you archive your old email messages, there will also be a file named *Archive.pst* in the same folder as your *Outlook.pst* file. To back up Outlook, just back up these files to a disk or another computer. To restore them, copy them back to their original locations.

If you don't use Outlook for your contacts, and instead use the Windows Address Book, then your contact information will be kept in a file with the extension *.pab*. So, you'll need to back up that file along with your *.pst* file to have a backup of your contact list.

> If you use Outlook on an Exchange Server, there may not be any *.pst* files on your system. You won't be able to back up your messages, contacts, and calendar yourself. Your Exchange administrator should be doing it for you.

That's fine if you want to back up only your email, calendar, and messages. But there is also a whole host of other Outlook information you might want to back up, including your Outlook bar shortcuts; the mail rules you've created; your customized toolbar settings; your stationery, signatures, and templates; and other customizations and files. These files may be in the same folder as *Outlook.pst*, in *C:\Documents and Settings\<Your Name>\Application Data\Microsoft\ Outlook*, or in another folder. Various flavors and versions of Outlook are notorious for keeping their files in different locations. Back these files up as you do your *Outlook.pst* file, to a disk or another computer, and restore them by copying them back into their original folder.

Table 6-3 describes what each of Outlook's files does. Depending on how you use Outlook, not all these files may be present on your system.

Table 6-3. Outlook files and their extensions

Type of file	Extension
Personal Folders	.pst
Personal Address Book	.pab
Outlook Bar shortcuts	.fav
Rules Wizard rules (Outlook 2000 and earlier versions)	.rwz

Table 6-3. Outlook files and their extensions (continued)

Type of file	Extension
Nicknames for AutoResolution	.nick
Nicknames for AutoComplete (Outlook 2002)	.nk2
Customized print settings	OutlPrnt
Customized toolbar settings	Outcmd.dat
Customized system folder views	Views.dat
Macros and VBA programs	VbaProject.otm
Send/Receive group settings (Outlook 2002)	.srs
Stationery	.htm files
Templates	.oft files
Dictionary	.dic files
Junk Senders lists	Junk Senders.txt
Adult Senders list	Adult Senders.txt

If you have a laptop and a desktop PC, you've already found that you apparently can't synchronize Outlook between them; they each have different data stores of your email messages. To keep them in synch, simply copy the *Outlook.pst* file from one to the other. For example, when you're working normally at home or the office, your desktop PC should have the complete, current version of the *Outlook.pst* file. When you travel with your laptop, copy the file over to it, and your laptop will have the current version of your files. When you return home or to the office, copy the file back to your desktop PC.

Backing Up Outlook Express Manually

Outlook Express has a different data structure than Outlook, so you'll need to back up different files than with Outlook. Express is messier than Outlook; it stores your email in multiple files, and you'll have to back up them all, instead of a single file as you do with Outlook. And you'll back up Registry keys as a way to save your personal settings.

Mail messages in Outlook Express are kept in files with *.dbx* extensions. To find out their locations, open Outlook Express and chose Tools → Options → Maintenance → StoreFolder. You'll see a dialog box (shown in Figure 6-7) that will tell you the location of the *.dbx* files. Go to that folder and back up all the *.dbx* files. Expect to see a lot of them; two dozen or more are not that uncommon, depending on how many mail folders you have. Then, to restore them, just copy them back to their original folder.

Figure 6-7. Finding the location of Outlook Express's .dbx files so you can back them up

The information about your mail settings, accounts, and preferences is stored on a single Registry key, HKEY_CURRENT_USER\Software\Microsoft\ Internet Account Manager. Back up the entire key and its subkeys to a single *.reg* file. When you want to restore them, restore the key as you would using any other *.reg* file.

> For information on backing up to *.reg* keys, restoring using *.reg* keys, and other ways to back up the Registry, see "Safely Edit the Registry Using .reg Files" **[Hack #70]** and "Better Registry Backups" **[Hack #71]**.

Outlook Express uses the Windows Address Book for contact information, so you need to back up the *.dbx* file or files. Typically, *.dbx* files are stored in *C:\Documents and Settings\<Your Name>\Application Data\Microsoft\ Address Book*, but you might have to look elsewhere. Restore the *.dbx* file by copying it back to its original location.

Mail rules are stored in the Registry, in the HKEY_CURRENT_USER\Identities key and its subkeys. As outlined in "Backing Up Outlook Manually" earlier in this hack, back this key and its subkeys up to a *.reg* file, and restore back to the Registry if you need to.

Backing Up Outlook and Outlook Express Using Add-In Software

If you don't want to go through the trouble of manual backups and restores, you can try out Outlook Express Backup and Outlook 2000/XP Backup from Genie-Soft (*http://www.genie-soft.com*), which will automate your backups for you. You get a wide variety of backup options, including backing up multiple identities and information, viewing emails from inside the backup and copying text from them, using an automated backup scheduler, encrypting your backups, spanning multiple disks when you backup, and compressing your backups. Both are shareware and free to try, but if you continue to use either of them, you are expected to pay $29.95.

See Also

- Microsoft has a free add-in for Outlook 2000/2002 that will automatically backup and restore your *.pst* files. It won't, however, backup any other Outlook settings. Get it at *http://office.microsoft.com/downloads/2002/pfbackup.aspx*.

Fire Outlook and Outlook Express

Contrary to popular belief, Microsoft doesn't make the only two email programs on the planet. Eudora and Pegasus are great, free alternatives.

Strange, but true: before Outlook and Outlook Express, there was email software. I know it, because I used it all the time. That email software is still around, and some believe it is superior to Outlook and Outlook Express in some ways. While there are many alternative email programs out there, my two favorites, Eudora and Pegasus, have both been around a very long time. While both have some drawbacks, they each have enough unique features that they may make you want to throw away Outlook and Outlook Express.

Check Your Mood with Eudora

Once upon a time, Eudora ruled the roost. In the pre-Outlook and pre-Outlook Express days, you'd find it on the desktops of power users everywhere. Although it's not nearly as popular today, it has its fans, and with good reason, because it has some unique features you won't find in any other email software.

Foremost is one of the all-time great features in an email program, a feature that will be welcomed gladly by anyone who has ever blasted out a red-hot email in a fit of anger. As you type, MoodWatch analyzes your messages for their degree of aggressiveness and rates them on a scale of ice cube all the way up to three chili peppers. You see the rating as you write and you get a warning before sending the message if it might be offensive.

Another goody is the ability to share files on a peer-to-peer basis with other Eudora users, through the Eudora Sharing Protocol (ESP). You define groups of people with whom you want to share files, and they're the only ones who can access those files. In turn, you can can share files with people who give you access to files on their computers. The New ESP Share Group Wizard walks you through setting up a share group. Choose Tools → ESP Groups → New... → "Create a brand new share group" → Next. You can customize many features of this tool, including the ability to set up a new mailbox just for users in this group, so that the messages from users in your new group will be filtered automatically into the appropriate mailbox. The wizard prompts you for this and other options, including share group name, share group description, transfer to new or existing mailbox, share group folder (choose where the files to be shared with the group will live), and even the choice of which Eudora personality—Dominant or otherwise— should be associated with the file share group. You can also set all Eudora preferences for each file share group (right-click on the group's name and choose Options) and set filtering options for messages from the file share group (should messages go through the normal filters or not?) with the ESP Settings button. For each user, you can specify their role within the group (can they send updates, only receive updates, or both?). Then, you can share files across machines and collaborate on any sort of document. It's pretty amazing and might even convince non-Eudora users to make the switch (see Figure 6-8).

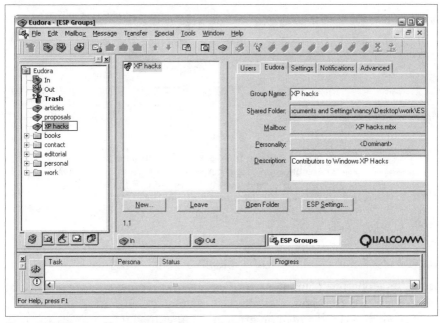

Figure 6-8. Sharing files with others in your invited group

Also included is a way to send voice messages via email, and very powerful filtering and searching. If you're a statistics hound, you'll find a usage stats area (Tools → Statistics) that analyzes that displays statistics, such as how much time you've spent using the program and the time of day you send and receive the most messages. Email addicts will love it (see Figure 6-9).

An ad-supported version of Eudora is available for free from *http://www. eudora.com*. If you want to do away with the ads, you can either pay $49.95 or switch to the "light" version, which lacks some of the program's features.

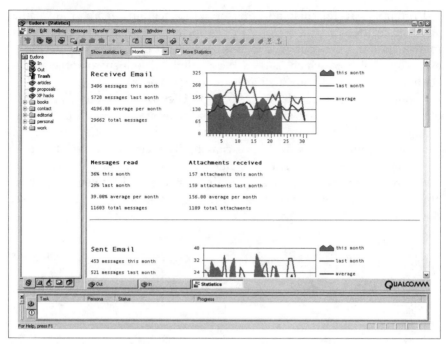

Figure 6-9. Email usage statistics

If you want to amaze friends and acquaintances with little-known technology facts, here's one for you. Eudora was named after the well-known fiction writer Eudora Welty, because of a short story she wrote in 1941, "Why I Live at the P.O.," about a woman who moves to live in her post office.

Move Forward to the Past with Pegasus

If you're a longtime computer user, Pegasus may remind you of your youth, when there were no common interface standards and a program reflected the personality of individual programmers rather than focus groups and user interface whizzes. In part, that's because this program was first released in 1990, in the days of Windows 3.0. Its eccentric layout and tiny icons will whisk you back in the Wayback Machine to those days gone by.

That is this program's strength and its weakness. Good luck trying to figure out this program when you first install it; it's bristling with often-undecipherable icons. Even the tooltips that appear when you hold your mouse over these icons don't necessarily help. For example, can anyone explain to me what "Open a list of local people on your system" means?

However, the strength is that these eccentricities carry over into the list of the program's features, and it's a very powerful program. The ways it handles rules for how to automatically process incoming messages are extremely sophisticated. For example, you can to use it to create a set of rules that would allow you to automatically allow people to subscribe to listserv email discussion groups that you run using Pegasus.

Its message-viewing capabilities are also exceptional. You can choose a view that lets you quickly switch between displaying an HTML message either as plain text or as full-blown HTML, and in the "Raw view" you can see the entire message, including all the header information showing you the path the email took to reach you.

There are also some decidedly odd features buried deep in this program. For example, one feature lets you send an email that includes preformatted text telling someone they've received a phone call. Somehow, I don't think that one came out of a focus group.

Pegasus is free and available from *http://www.pmail.com*. If you want manuals and support, you can pay $29.95.

See Also

- If you decide to stick with Outlook but want a way to improve it, try Nelson's Email Organizer (*http://www.caelo.com*). It offers ways to manage your email overload better, automatically sorts your email by putting it into a variety of easy-to-use folders, does lightning-quick searches on your mail, notifies you when new email arrives, and lets you view your email with many different views. It's shareware and free to try, but if you continue to use it, you are expected to pay $39.95.

- Annotis Mail is another Outlook or Outlook Express add-in (*http://www.annotis.com*). It lets you embed pictures, markers, rubber stamps, sticky notes, sounds, and videos in your email using either Outlook or Outlook Express. It's shareware and free to try, but if you continue to use it, you are expected to pay $24.95.

HACK #67 Retrieve Web-Based Email with Your Email Software

There's no longer a need for Hotmail and Yahoo! mail users to be forced to abandon their email software when checking their email. This hack lets you use your email client to gather web-based email from them.

I have more email accounts than any person has any right to. In addition to my normal POP3-based email accounts, I have web-based accounts on

Yahoo! and Hotmail. This means that there's no apparent way to get all my email in one location; I use Outlook for POP3-based email and the Web for Yahoo! and Hotmail. It also means that I can never have all my email on my hard disk, because Yahoo! and Hotmail store it on the Web. But I like to keep all my outgoing and incoming email in one location. What to do?

I've found two free add-ins that let you use your normal email program with Yahoo! mail and HotMail, whether it's Outlook, Outlook Express, Eudora, or any other. YahooPOPs! lets you send and receive Yahoo! email, and Hotmail Popper does the same for Hotmail.

Getting Yahoo! Mail with YahooPOPs!

Several years ago, you had the free option of getting your Yahoo! mail using Yahoo! POP mail server. No longer. Today, if you want to do that directly from Yahoo!, you'll have to pay a fee.

But with the simple-to-set-up YahooPOPs! (*http://yahoopops.sourceforge.net*), you can treat Yahoo! like any other mail server and get email from it without having to pay. It's open source software that has a POP3 interface on one end to talk to your email client, and on the other end it uses an HTTP interface to talk to Yahoo! and get your mail.

 If you use Linux or Mac OS X on another computer, you can use Linux- and Mac-specific versions of YahooPOPs! on those computers and get your Yahoo! mail on them as well.

There are two steps to getting it working. First, configure the program itself; then, configure your email client to work with it. If you like, you don't have to configure the program itself; you can leave its defaults, but I recommend making a few changes to the defaults before using it.

After you install the program and run it, it sits in your system tray. To configure it, double-click on its icon. While there's a good deal you can configure, I recommend leaving most defaults. However, in Receiving Email under Email Preferences, uncheck "Download emails from the Bulk Mail folder," as shown in Figure 6-10. If you leave that box checked, you'll receive all the spam that Yahoo! has filtered into your Bulk Mail folder.

As you can see in Figure 6-10, you can configure other preferences here as well, such as whether to download all email or only flagged or unread emails. I stay with the defaults, but you can change them if you wish.

Now it's time to configure your email program to work with it. How you do that varies from program to program, so check the program's documenta-

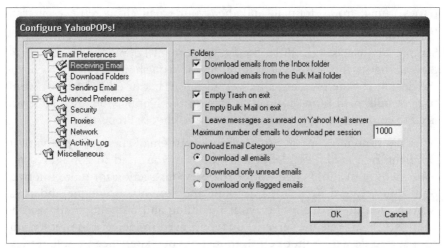

Figure 6-10. Making sure you don't download email from your Bulk Mail folder

tion on the Web for how to do it for individual mail clients. Essentially, though, you create a new mail account in your mail client and call both the incoming mail server and outgoing mail server "localhost." That configures your client to get the mail from YahooPOPs!. So, the client doesn't contact Yahoo! directly. Instead, YahooPOPs! does that; then your client gets the email from YahooPOPs!.

To configure Outlook to work with YahooPOPs!, select Tools → Email accounts → "Add a new email account" → Next. Then Select POP3 as the Server Type. Click Next and enter your username and Yahoo! email address under User Information. Under Logon Information, enter your Yahoo! login ID and password. Select "localhost" as your Incoming mail server and "localhost" as the SMTP server as your outgoing mail server. Then, select More Settings → Advanced and increase the Server Timeout to 10 minutes. Select the Outgoing Server tab and enable "My outgoing server (SMTP) requires authentication." Then, select "Log on using" and enter your Yahoo! Mail address as the username and your Yahoo! Mail password as the password. Click OK to close the More Settings dialog box. Click Next and then click Finish.

Once you do that, all your outgoing and incoming Yahoo! email will show up in Outlook, just as if the mail were being delivered by any POP3 mail server.

Getting Hotmail Mail with Hotmail Popper

Hotmail Popper (*http://www.boolean.ca/hotpop/*) works in the same way as YahooPOPs! to let you retrieve and send mail via your Hotmail account. It retrieves mail from Hotmail, and then your email client retrieves it from from Hotmail Popper.

Setup is similar as well. First, configure Hotmail Popper to get your mail; then configure your email client to retrieve it. You shouldn't need to change the defaults of the program after you install it, because by default it won't retrieve bulk mail from Hotmail. It runs in the Notification area, so if you need to configure it right-click on its icon and choose Properties.

Once it's running, you have to configure your email client to work with it. Configuration is almost identical to the way you need to configure your mail client for YahooPOPs!, so see the previous section for more information. You create a new POP3 account and set your username and password as you do normally. For your incoming and outgoing mail, use the address 127.0.0.1 as the server. You won't need to increase the server timeout as you do with YahooPOPs!, though if you experience trouble retrieving mail from the server you can try doing that as a way to solve the problem.

Once you've configured it, use it as you would any other POP3 mail account.

The Registry
Hacks 68–72

When it comes to hacking XP, no other tool comes close to the Registry. It contains the underlying organization of the entire operating system, and its often-incomprehensible settings hold the key to countless hacks. In simpler days, one could hack Windows without bothering with the Registry; a solid knowledge of things like *.ini* files would suffice. But no longer. If you want to get hacking, the Registry holds the key—literally, since it's organized by way of keys.

Even if you've edited the Registry before, you'll find a lot in this chapter to help. It teaches not just the mechanics of using the Registry, but also explains its underlying organization. You'll find ways to keep your Registry safe, learn how to back it up, and find downloadable tools to make the most of the Registry. As a bonus, I've thrown in a grab-bag of other great hacks.

HACK #68 Don't Fear the Registry

The Registry is the single best tool available for hacking XP. Here's an introduction to how it's organized and how to use it.

If you haven't spent much time in the Registry, you can easily be cowed by it. At first glance, it's a maze of apparently incomprehensible settings. In fact, though, there's a method to the madness. The Registry is a hierarchical database of information that defines exactly how your system works, including virtually every part of XP and its applications. Editing the Registry database is often the best way to hack XP. In fact, there are many changes to the operating system that you can make in no other way.

Even if you've never used the Registry directly before, you've changed it without realizing it. Whenever you change a setting using the Control Panel, for example, behind the scenes a Registry change is made that puts that new setting into effect. The menus and dialog boxes you see in XP are often little more than a visual front-end to the Registry.

If you want to optimize XP and master every part of it, you'll have to use the Registry. XP contains so many different settings and customizations that it simply wasn't possible for Microsoft to build a graphical interface for every conceivable possibility. And there are many times when it's easier and you get more options when you edit the Registry rather than using the graphical XP interface. You can use Windows XP without ever editing the Registry—many users do—but advanced users understand its power tool status.

The way to edit the Registry is by using the *Registry Editor*, also called Reg-Edit, which is shown in Figure 7-1. To run it, type `regedit` at the Run box or command line and press Enter.

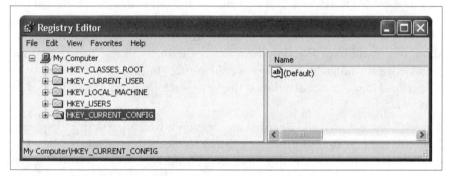

Figure 7-1. Controlling Registry settings by using the Registry Editor

Before you edit the Registry, though, you should first get a basic understanding of its structure.

 Sometimes, we power users like to jump in without reading the manual. The Registry is not the best place to experiment and learn as you go, until you understand at least a little what's going on. You could render your system useless and unrecoverable with just a few changes. So, we recommend making a backup **[Hack #71]** and reading at least most of this chapter first. You'll be glad later if you do this now.

The Five Logical Registry Hives

The Registry has many thousands of settings; in fact, it often has tens of thousands of them. They are organized into five main Registry sections, called *Registry hives*. Think of each hive as a root directory. Each of the hives has a different purpose. When you start to delve into the Registry, you may notice that many of the settings seem to be exact duplicates of one another—in other words, settings in one hive mirror the settings in another hive. In fact, frequently one set of settings is merely an alias (called a *symbolic link*) of another, so that when you change those settings in one place, the changes are made in both hives.

> The hives themselves are stored in the *C:\Windows\system32\config* and *C:\Documents and Settings\{username}* files.

Following are the five hives and what each does:

HKEY_CLASSES_ROOT
> This hive contains information about file types, filename extensions, and similar information. It instructs XP how to handle every different file type and controls basic user interface options, such as double-clicking and context menus. This hive also includes class definitions (hence the word "CLASSES" in its name) of unique objects, such as file types or OLE objects. Frequently, classes associated with file types contain the Shell subkey, which defines actions, such as opening and printing, that can be taken with that file type.

HKEY_CURRENT_USER
> This hive contains configuration information about the system setup of the user that is currently logged into XP. It controls the current user's Desktop, as well as XP's specific appearance and behavior for the current user. This hive also manages network connections and connections to devices such as printers, personal preferences such as screen colors, as well as security rights. Also included in this hive are Security Identifiers (SIDs), which uniquely identify users of the PC and which have information about each user's rights, settings, and preferences.

HKEY_LOCAL_MACHINE
> This hive contains information about the computer itself, as well as about the operating system. It includes specific details about all hardware, including keyboard, printer ports, storage—the entire hardware setup. In addition, it has information about security, installed software, system startup, drivers, services, and the machine's specific XP configuration.

HKEY_USERS
> This hive contains information about every user profile on the system.

HKEY_CURRENT_CONFIG
> This hive contains information about the current hardware configuration of the system, in the same way that HKEY_CURRENT_USER contains information about the current user of the system.

Using Keys and Values

Each hive is at the top of the hierarchy, and underneath each hive are keys, which can in turn contain subkeys, and those subkeys can contain subkeys, and so on, organized in folder-like fashion, much like a hard drive.

Keys and subkeys contain a value, which controls a particular setting. For example, this key:

```
HKEY_CURRENT_USER\Control Panel\Mouse\DoubleClickSpeed
```

determines the amount of time between mouse clicks that must elapse before Windows won't consider it to be a double-click. To set the amount of time, you change the key's value. In this case, the default value is 500, measured in milliseconds, and you can edit the Registry to change it to whatever value you want, as shown in Figure 7-2. You can also make the changes using the Mouse Properties dialog box (Start → Control Panel → Printers and Other Hardware → Mouse). When you make changes to that dialog box, the changes are in turn made in the Registry, which ultimately controls the setting. In essence, the dialog box is merely a convenient front-end to the Registry.

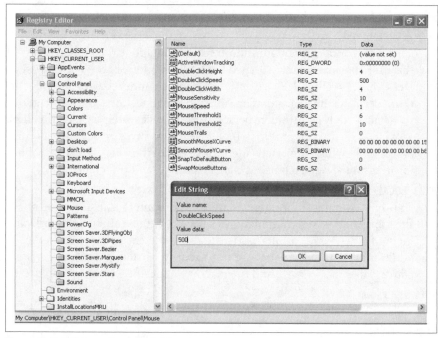

Figure 7-2. Editing a Registry key's value

A key can contain one or more values. Following are the five primary data types of values in the Registry:

REG_SZ *(String value)*

This data type is easy to understand and edit because it is made up of plain text and numbers. It is one of the most common data types in the Registry. The value for DoubleClickSpeed, mentioned earlier in this hack, is of this type.

REG_MULTI_SZ *(String array value)*

This data type contains several strings of plain text and numbers. The Registry Editor will let you edit these values, but it won't let you create them.

REG_EXPAND_SZ *(Expanded string value)*

This data type contains variables that Windows uses to point to the location of files. For example, to point to the location of the Luna theme file, the expanded string value in the Registry is %SystemRoot%\ resources\Themes\Luna.theme.

REG_BINARY *(Binary values)*

This data type is made up of binary data: 0s and 1s. Figure 7-3 shows a typical example of a binary value. As a general rule, you won't edit binary values—instead you'll edit string values because they're made up of text and numbers, as shown in Figure 7-4.

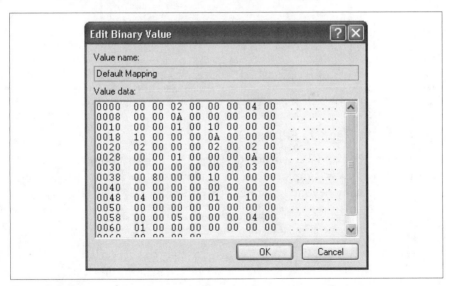

Figure 7-3. Binary values

REG_DWORD *(DWORD values)*

This data type is represented as a number. Sometimes a 0 turns on the key or 1 turns off the key, though it can use other numbers as well.

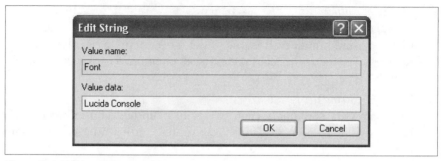

Figure 7-4. Editing String values

While you see and edit the value as a number, such as 456, the Registry itself views the number as a hexadecimal number, 1C8. Figure 7-5 shows a DWORD value being edited.

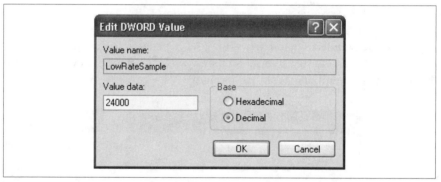

Figure 7-5. Editing DWORD values

Launching the Registry Editor

There's an upside and a downside to using XP's Registry Editor. The upside is that it's relatively simple to use. The downside is that it doesn't offer much functionality beyond basic Registry editing.

> In some instances, when you make changes using the Registry the changes take effect as soon as you exit the Registry. In other instances, they'll take effect only after you log out and then log back in. And, in yet other instances, they'll take effect only after you restart Windows.

To run the Registry Editor, type regedit in the Run box or a command prompt and press Enter. If this is the first time you've run the Registry Editor, it will open highlighting the HKEY_CURRENT_USER hive, as shown in

Figure 7-6. If you've previously used the Registry Editor, it will open high-lighting the last key you edited or the last place you were in the Registry.

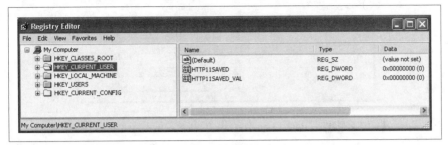

Figure 7-6. Using the Registry Editor for the first time

You can browse through the Registry with the Registry Editor in the same way you browse through a hard disk using Windows Explorer. Clicking a + sign opens a key to reveal the next level down of the hierarchy. Clicking a − sign closes the key.

The Registry can be several levels deep in keys and subkeys, so navigating it using a mouse can take a substantial amount of time. (Every time you open it, it jumps to the last-used key.) You can use shortcut keys, though, to more easily navigate through the Registry. The right arrow key opens a key to reveal subkeys; the left arrow key closes a key and moves one level up in the key hierarchy. To jump to the next subkey that begins with a specific letter, press that letter on the keyboard.

You use the Registry Editor to edit existing keys and values, create new keys and values, or delete existing keys and values. Sometimes, the changes take effect as soon as you make the change and exit the Registry Editor; other times, you'll have to reboot for them to take effect. Keep in mind that there is no "Save" button. When you modify a value, it changes right then and there. There is also no Undo button, so make your changes carefully.

If there's a particular key that you want to edit, an even faster way to navigate is to use the Find command from the Edit menu. (You can also use the Find command by pressing Ctrl-F.) To find successive keys with the same value, press the F3 key.

To edit the data associated with a value, double-click on the value in the right pane of the Registry Editor; a box appears that lets you edit the value, as shown in Figure 7-7.

When you're editing the Registry, it's often hard to tell what key you're editing, because the Registry Editor doesn't highlight that key. Instead, it shows only an open folder icon next to it, but it's easy to miss that icon. Check the

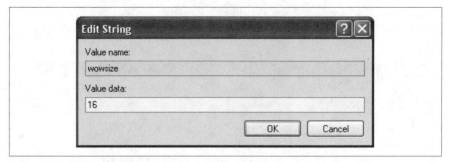

Figure 7-7. Editing a value

status bar at the bottom of the Registry Editor; it should display the key you're editing. If it doesn't, choose View → Status Bar from the Registry Editor menu.

To rename a key, select it and choose Edit → Rename from the menu. You can also right-click on the key and choose Edit → Rename.

Adding and Deleting Keys and Values

Editing the Registry often requires that you add and delete keys and values To add a new key, select the new key's parent key in the left pane. Then, choose Edit → New → Key from the menu. Type in the new key's name. You can also right-click on the new key's parent key and choose Edit → New → Key. To delete a key, select it and press the Delete key.

Very often, you need to add values to a key in order for its changes to take effect. To add a value to a key, select the new key's parent key in the left pane. From the menu, choose Edit → New, and from the submenu, select the type of value you want to create. We've already covered the five types of values you can create; as a reminder, they're detailed in Table 7-1.

To create a new value, type in the name of the new value and press Enter. Press Enter again. The Edit Value dialog box appears, as shown in Figure 7-7. Enter your data and press Enter.

Table 7-1. Values you'll encounter in the Registry

Value name	Registry data type
String value	REG_SZ
Binary value	REG_BINARY
DWORD value	REG_DWORD
String array value	REG_MULTI_SZ
Expanded string value	REG_EXPAND_SZ

See Also

- For an excellent collection of Registry hacks, go to the Registry Guide for Windows at *http://www.winguides.com/registry*. Make sure to sign up for the newsletter that offers Registry advice and hacks.

Hacking Away at the Registry

Nine great hacks that use the Registry to do their magic.

You'll find many dozens of Registry hacks sprinkled throughout this book, but to give you a sense of the breadth of the kinds of hacks that you can accomplish using the Registry, I've put a wide-ranging sample of Registry hacks here as well.

Automatically Close Programs at Shutdown

When you shut down Windows, if you have any programs running you'll get a message box warning you that a program is still running. You then have to close the program and tell XP again to shut down. It's a fairly point-less warning—better yet would be if XP automatically killed the programs without issuing the warning. That way, you wouldn't get error messages and wouldn't have to close each individual application before shutting down your computer.

To have XP automatically close programs at shutdown, run the Registry Edi-tor and go to `HKEY_CURRENT_USER\Control Panel\Desktop`. Edit the `AutoEndTasks` key so that is has a value of 1. If the key doesn't exist, create it as a `DWORD` value and give it the value of 1. To disable it, either delete the key, or set the value to 0.

Disable XP Shutdown

There may be times when you want to make sure that XP can't be inadvert-ently shut down. You can use a Registry hack to disable the normal Shut Down. Run the Registry Editor and go to `HKEY_CURRENT_USER\Software\ Microsoft\Windows\CurrentVersion\Policies\Explorer`. Create a new `DWORD` value named `NoClose` with a data value of 1. Exit the Registry and reboot in order for the change to take effect. You won't be able to shut down Win-dows in the normal manner from now on; you'll have to run Task Manager by pressing Ctrl-Alt-Delete or right-clicking on the Toolbar, choosing Task Manager, and then using the Task Manager's Shut Down menu to close Windows. If you want to reenable normal shutdowns, delete the `NoClose` value.

Change the Names of the Registered User and Company

When you install XP or when it comes factory-fresh on a PC, a username and company name are entered as the owner of the system. And that's the way it stays, like it or not. But a Registry hack will let you change both. Run the Registry Editor, go to HKEY_LOCAL_MACHINE\SOFTWARE\Microsoft\Windows NT\CurrentVersion, and look for the values RegisteredOwner and RegisteredOrganization. Edit their value data to whatever username and company name you want.

Change the Amount of Time Before Programs Time Out

When an application hangs and no longer responds, XP displays a dialog box that prompts you to kill the application or wait a while longer. By default, the dialog box appears after the application hasn't responded for five seconds.

This can cause problems. For example, if a program is doing heavy-duty calculations in the background, it won't respond until the calculation is done, so the operating system will report that the application is hung, even though it isn't. You can use a Registry hack to increase or decrease the amount of time it takes before XP reports that the program has hung.

Run the Registry Editor and go to HKEY_CURRENT_USER\Control Panel\Desktop. Select the HungAppTimeout entry and edit it to input a new value, in milliseconds. The default is 5000. Exit the Registry. You may need to reboot for the new setting to take effect. Try increasing the number in increments of 1,000 until you find a number that works.

Disable the Disk Cleanup Warning

If your hard disk has what XP decides is too little space left on it, the operating system will pop up a warning and recommend that you run Disk Cleanup. But you may be like me and not want a virtual nanny nagging you to clean up your mess. You can turn off the warning with a Registry hack. Run the Registry Editor and go to HKEY_CURRENT_USER\Software\Microsoft\Windows\CurrentVersion\Policies\Explorer. Create a DWORD value called NoLowDiskSpaceChecks and give it a value of 1. Exit the Registry and reboot. You can also do this by using TweakUI [Hack #8].

Change the Default Location for Installing Programs

XP uses the *C:\Program Files* directory as the default base directory into which new programs are installed. However, you can change the default installation drive and/or directory by using a Registry hack. Run the Registry Editor and go to HKEY_LOCAL_MACHINE\SOFTWARE\Microsoft\Windows\ CurrentVersion. Look for the value named ProgramFilesDir. By default, the value will be C:\Program Files. Edit the value to any valid drive or folder; XP will use that new location as the default installation directory for new programs.

Allow Laptops to Enter Power-Saving State (Increase the USB Polling Interval)

Some laptops' processors may not be able to enter their power-saving state, even when they're idle, because USB polling fools the processor into thinking that the laptop is active. Your system polls your USB ports once every millisecond to see whether a device is present. So, even if a device isn't present, it continues that polling. The problem is that some laptop processors won't go into their power-saving state because the constant polling makes it think that the laptop is active.

With a Registry hack, you can increase the polling interval from the default of one millisecond, letting the processor enter its power-saving state. Run the Registry Editor and go to HKEY_LOCAL_MACHINE\System\CurrentControlSet\ Control\Class\{36FC9E60-C465-11CF-8056-444553540000}\0000. Create the new DWORD value IdleEnable and set the data value to a number between 2 and 5. This will set the polling interval, in milliseconds. If there are additional subkeys for HKEY_LOCAL_MACHINE\System\CurrentControlSet\Control\ Class\{36FC9E60-C465-11CF-8056-444553540000} (such as 0001, 0002, etc.), repeat the procedure and create the IdleEnable DWORD in each of them. Exit the Registry. You may need to reboot for the new setting to go into effect. You also may need to try several different values until you find one that works.

Change the Size of Your Mouse and Keyboard Buffer

You sometimes may get an error message telling you that you have an overflow in your mouse buffer or keyboard buffer. When that happens, it means the buffer isn't large enough and you need to increase its size. To increase your mouse buffer, run the Registry Editor, go to HKEY_LOCAL_MACHINE\ SYSTEM\CurrentControlSet\Services\Mouclass\Parameters, and find the MouseDataQueueSize subkey. The default setting is 100 (64 hex). Increase the decimal number to increase the size of the buffer; then exit the Registry and reboot. You may need to try several different settings until you find the right one.

To increase the keyboard buffer, look for the KeyboardDataQueueSize subkey in HKEY_LOCAL_MACHINE\SYSTEM\CurrentControlSet\Services\Kbdclass\ Parameters. The default setting is 100 (64 hex). Increase the number to increase the size of the buffer; then exit the Registry and reboot. Again, you may need to try several different settings until you find the right one.

Safely Edit the Registry Using .reg Files

HACK
#70

Forgo the dangers and inconvenience of editing the Registry directly. Instead, use plain-text *.reg* files.

When you're editing the Registry, it's easy to make small errors that cause major repercussions. You may inadvertently edit the wrong key, put in a wrong value, or—given how confusing the Registry is—even make changes without realizing it. The Registry is unforgiving when this happens. It doesn't keep a backup, so you're stuck with the new setting unless you've made backups yourself, as outlined in "Better Registry Backups" [Hack #71].

When you edit the Registry directly, you're also apt to make errors if you're making multiple changes, because you have no chance to look at all the changes you're making at once.

There's a way to solve both problems: use *.reg* files to edit the Registry. These are plain ASCII text files that you can create or read with Notepad or any text editor and that you merge into the Registry to make changes. You can create a *.reg* file from scratch, or you can export it from a portion of the Registry, edit it with Notepad or another text editor, and then merge it back into the Registry. You'll find that *.reg* files are particularly useful if you're going to make changes to the Registry of several computers or if you are leery about editing the Registry directly.

You should also consider creating *.reg* files to copy the parts of the Registry that you're about to edit using the Registry Editor. Then, if you make a mistake with the Registry Editor, you can revert to the previous version of the Registry by merging the *.reg* file into the Registry. They're also useful if you need to do search-and-replace operations on parts of the Registry, because the Registry Editor doesn't include search-and-replace functionality. You can do the search-and-replace operation in your text editor and then merge the edited file back into the Registry.

To create a *.reg* file from an existing portion of the Registry, run the Registry Editor, highlight the key or portion of the Registry that you want to export, and choose File-> Export. Choose a name and location for the file. You can export an individual key, a branch of the Registry, a hive, or the entire Registry. Following is an example a *.reg* file exported from the HKEY_CURRENT_USER\Control Panel\Accessibility branch:

```
Windows Registry Editor Version 5.00
[HKEY_CURRENT_USER\Control Panel\Accessibility]
[HKEY_CURRENT_USER\Control Panel\Accessibility\Blind Access]
```

```
"On"="0"
[HKEY_CURRENT_USER\Control Panel\Accessibility\HighContrast]
"Flags"="126"
"High Contrast Scheme"="High Contrast Black (large)"
[HKEY_CURRENT_USER\Control Panel\Accessibility\Keyboard Preference]
"On"="0"
[HKEY_CURRENT_USER\Control Panel\Accessibility\Keyboard Response]
"AutoRepeatDelay"="1000"
"AutoRepeatRate"="500"
"BounceTime"="0"
"DelayBeforeAcceptance"="1000"
"Flags"="126"
[HKEY_CURRENT_USER\Control Panel\Accessibility\MouseKeys]
"Flags"="62"
"MaximumSpeed"="80"
"TimeToMaximumSpeed"="3000"
[HKEY_CURRENT_USER\Control Panel\Accessibility\SerialKeys]
[HKEY_CURRENT_USER\Control Panel\Accessibility\ShowSounds]
"On"="0"
[HKEY_CURRENT_USER\Control Panel\Accessibility\SoundSentry]
"Flags"="2"
"FSTextEffect"="0"
"WindowsEffect"="1"
[HKEY_CURRENT_USER\Control Panel\Accessibility\StickyKeys]
"Flags"="510"
[HKEY_CURRENT_USER\Control Panel\Accessibility\TimeOut]
"Flags"="2"
"TimeToWait"="300000"
[HKEY_CURRENT_USER\Control Panel\Accessibility\ToggleKeys]
"Flags"="62"
```

Edit a *.reg* file as you would any other text file. As you can see, the first line of the *.reg* file starts with Windows Registry Editor Version 5.00. Don't change this; Windows XP uses it to confirm that the file does in fact contain Registry information. Previous versions of Windows have a different first line; for Windows 95/98/Me and Windows NT 4, the first line reads either REGEDIT4 or Registry Editor 4.

The names of Registry subkeys are surrounded by brackets, and they include the full pathname to the subkey, such as [HKEY_CURRENT_USER\Control Panel\ Accessibility\Keyboard Response] in our example. Following each subkey are the subkey values and data. Values and data are both surrounded by quotation marks. Here is the full section of a subkey, along with its associated values and data:

```
[HKEY_LOCAL_MACHINE\SYSTEM\CurrentControlSet\Services\Mouclass]
"ErrorControl"=dword:00000001
"Group"="Pointer Class"
"Start"=dword:00000001
"Tag"=dword:00000001
"Type"=dword:00000001
"DisplayName"="Mouse Class Driver"
```

As you can see, quotes surround data for String values. DWORD values, however, are preceded by dword: and don't have quotes surrounding them. Similarly, binary values are preceded by hex: and don't have quotes surrounding them.

Edit the value and data and save the file. When you've made your changes, import the file back into the Registry by choosing File → Import in the Registry Editor and opening the file. An even easier way to import it is to double-click on the file. XP will ask whether you want to import it; when you answer yes, XP will import it and make the changes to the Registry. This is somewhat counterintuitive and can be confusing; you may at first think that double-clicking on a *.reg* file will open it for editing. But it won't; it will merge it into the Registry. To open a *.reg* file, open Notepad or another text editor and then open the *.reg* file. Alternatively, you can right-click on the *.reg* file and choose Edit.

> Because double-clicking on a file merges it back into the Registry, it's easy to mistakenly make Registry changes when you really just want to edit a *.reg* file. To protect yourself against this kind of mistake see later in this hack.

Delete Registry Keys and Values Using .reg Files

You can use a *.reg* file not just to create new keys or values or modify existing ones, but to also delete keys and values. To delete a key with a *.reg* file, put a minus sign in front of the key name, like this:

```
-[HKEY_CURRENT_USER\Control Panel\Accessibility\Keyboard Response]
```

When you import the *.reg* file, that key will be deleted. Keep in mind that you won't be able to delete a key this way unless all of its subkeys have first been deleted, so you'll have to delete them first.

You can also delete a key's value using a *.reg* file, by putting a minus sign after the equals sign in a *.reg* file, like this:

```
"BounceTime"=-
```

When you import this into the Registry, the value will be deleted but the key will still stay intact.

Protect the Registry by Changing the Default Action for Double-Clicking a .reg File

As I mentioned earlier in this hack, when you double-click on a *.reg* file, the file doesn't open for editing; instead, it gets merged directly into the Registry. This can easily cause serious problems, because you might want to edit the file, and so end up double-clicking on it, the way you normally open files in XP. But the file will end up merging it into the Registry and making Registry changes you didn't want to make.

To solve the problem, you can change the default action so that a *.reg* file is opened for editing in Notepad rather than merged when you double-click on it. In Windows Explorer, choose Tools → Folder Options → File Types to open the File Types dialog box. Highlight the REG entry and click Advanced. Highlight the Edit action and click Set Default. The Edit action should turn bold. Click OK.

Change the Default Editor for .reg Files

Notepad is the default editor for editing *.reg* files, but if you have another text editor you'd rather use you can force that to be the default instead. First, follow the directions from the previous section to open the File Types dialog box and highlight the REG entry's Edit action. Then, click on the Edit button and type in the full path and filename of the text editor you want to use to edit *.reg* files, followed by %1—for example:

```
C:\Program Files\TextPad 4\TextPad.exe %1
```

Then click OK twice.

> Never use a word processor such as Word to edit *.reg* files (unless you *make sure* to save it as a plain text file from within the word processor!). Word processors add extra codes that the Registry can't understand. Always use a text editor such as Notepad or WordPad.

HACK #71 Better Registry Backups

Avert disaster by backing up the Registry so that you'll always be able to revert to a clean copy.

The Registry is unforgiving; once you make a change to it, that change is permanent. There is no undo function. To get the Registry back to the way you want it, you'll have to reedit it and remember the often arcane and complicated changes that you made—if you can. And, unlike most other Windows applications, the Registry Editor doesn't ask you whether you want to save your changes. Make the change, and it's done. To paraphrase F. Scott Fitzgerald, there are no second acts when you edit the Registry.

Because of this, you should take precautions to keep your Registry safe and ensure that you can restore it to its previous safe settings whenever you want to. The best way to do that is to back up your Registry before you edit it.

You should make copies of your Registry not only to protect against accidentally doing damage while you're editing it, but also to ensure that you can restore your system in the event of a system crash.

Here are the best ways to back up your Registry:

System Restore

One of the simplest ways to back up and restore the Registry is by using System Restore. System Restore creates a snapshot of your entire system, including the Registry, and lets you revert your system to that snapshot. To use System Restore, before editing the Registry choose Start → Control Panel → Performance and Maintenance → System Restore and then follow the wizard to create a restore point. If after you edit the Registry you want to restore it to its preedited state, use the same wizard to do so.

Backup utility

You can also use Windows Backup utility to back up and restore the Registry.

> By default, the Backup program is installed in XP Professional, but not XP Home Edition. If you have the Home Edition, you must install Backup manually. For more on backup strategies, see "Build a Better Backup Strategy" [Hack #75].

Run the Backup utility by choosing Start → All Programs → Accessories → System Tools → Backup. If you use the Backup Wizard, when you get to the "What to Back Up" screen, choose "Only back up the System State data." Then, follow the Wizard's directions. It will back up the Registry as well as other system files, including boot files used to boot XP.

If you don't use the Backup Wizard, click on the Backup tab in the Backup utility, check the box next to System State, and then click on Start Backup. When you want to restore your system, run the Backup utility. Click Restore and Manage Media → Start Restore.

Registry Editor

You can also use the Registry Editor to back up the Registry. This is probably the easiest way to back up the Registry, but it won't back up two Registry keys: the SAM and Security keys that control password policies, user rights, and related information. Unless you have a complex system with many users, though, these keys are not absolutely vital.

Run the Registry Editor by typing Regedit in the Run box or a command prompt and pressing Enter. Highlight My Computer. If you highlight an individual Registry hive instead, only that hive will be backed up. Next, choose File → Export. The Export Registry File dialog box appears, as shown in Figure 7-8. Give the file a name, choose a location, and save it. For safety's sake, also make backups to another machine and to a CD.

To restore the Registry, run the Registry Editor, choose File → Import, and then import the file.

Figure 7-8. Using the Export Registry File screen to back up the Registry

Track and Restore Registry Changes with RegSpy

Protect your Registry and track changes to it made by programs with this downloadable goodie.

An excellent way to keep your Registry safe is with RegSpy, which watches the changes programs make to the Registry, tracks and reports on those changes, and then lets you restore your Registry or use your knowledge about the changes the program makes to fine-tune the way the program runs. One of the program's more useful features is the way it lets you undo changes on a program-by-program basis by building a RollBack script for that program. When you roll back the Registry, you'll roll back only changes made by that one program, not by any others. This is far superior to XP's System Restore, because System Restore makes changes en masse; there's no way to use it to save some changes and delete others.

My favorite RegSpy feature is its SnapShots, which creates files in JavaScript or Visual Basic format and lets you review all the Registry changes and repeat all the Registry changes that took place, step by step. That way, you can get a better understanding of the changes programs make during the installation process, and you can better undo or customize any changes made. It's also a great way to learn more about the Registry; watching the changes made by several different programs gives you insight into its inner workings.

RegSpy is shareware and free to try, but it costs $19.95 if you continue to use it. It's available from *http://www.utils32.com/regspy.htm*.

See Also

- RegCleaner and Registry First Aid (shareware from *http://www. rosecitysoftware.com*), both will clean up your Registry by deleting old and unneeded Registry entries that clog up your system.

- Registry Commander is a free utility that gives you a host of features that the Windows Registry Editor leaves out, such as a history list that lets you jump to recently edited keys, the ability to copy and paste entire keys and bookmark keys, and advanced search tools. Get it from *http:// www.aezay.dk/aezay/regcmd*.

- Resplendent Registrar is shareware that includes even more tools that the Registry Editor leaves out, such as search-and-replace, a Registry defragmenter to reclaim wasted disk space, an activity monitor that tracks all Registry activity, and a tool that lets you compare the contents of two Registry keys, among other features. Get it from *http:// www.resplendence.com*.

Basic Utilities
Hacks 73–79

XP comes with a suite of basic utilities, such as the Clipboard, a disk defragmenter, instant messenger, backup software, and more. For what they do, these utilities work reasonably well. But if you're dedicated to optimizing your computer, reasonably well isn't good enough.

In this chapter, we'll look at hacks that will give you a better Clipboard, do defragmenting and backup better, make Windows Messenger do tricks you never thought possible, and more. There's even advice on universal messaging software.

HACK #73 Store Multiple Clips and Boilerplate Text with a Better Clipboard

If you need to store clipboard text and images (or "clips") permanently and call them back whenever you need them, use this XP clipboard enhancer.

I make my living as a writer (or at least, I try to), and because of that I need to store text, articles, and graphics all day. When gathering research, I need to keep copies of what I find, so that I can paste them into documents for easy access. When writing books, I need to store special coding that I have to insert into my manuscript so that the typesetting comes out right. And I also have email signatures I like to pop into certain emails. In fact, like most people, I have a need for storing reusable boilerplate text of all kinds.

I can't use the XP Clipboard to do any of that for me, though. As far as it goes, the Clipboard is fine—a kind of waystation where you can store a single clip at a time before you pop the clip into another application. But it doesn't store more than a single clip at a time, so it isn't suitable for my needs.

Instead of the Clipboard, I use ClipCache Plus (*http://www.clipcache.com*), which is shareware and free to try, and $19.95 if you decide to keep using it.

It captures all clips and lets me organize them into folders and then reuse any clip when I need it, as shown in Figure 8-1. As you can see, it retains all formatting of the original clip. It captures files of any kind—including graphics, spreadsheets, and word processing files, as well as others—and gives you details about all your saved clips, including their date and time of capture, size, format, and application from which they were captured.

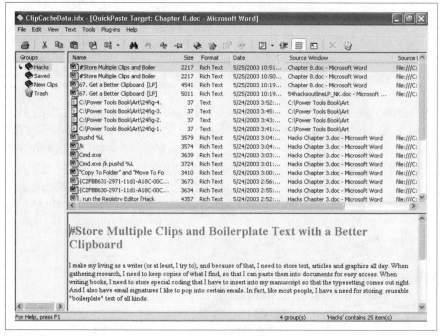

Figure 8-1. Storing and reusing multiple clips with ClipCache Plus

ClipCache is far more useful than the Office clipboard, which also stores multiple clips. The Office clipboard stores only a dozen clips at a time, while ClipCache lets you store as many as you want. ClipCache lets you organize your clips into folders, which the Office clipboard doesn't do. The Office clipboard captures clips only when you're working with Office, while ClipCache captures clips from any application. And the Office clipboard doesn't have a variety of other ClipCache features, such as the ability to clean up clips by removing line breaks.

You don't need to do anything to start storing clips with the program. Just install it and it starts saving them for you automatically. But you'll want to organize your clips into folders (which the program calls *groups*), by right-clicking on the small book symbol in the Groups pane and choosing New Group. Once you've created a new group, if you want to put new clips into it, right-click on the group and choose Activate Group. From now on, new clips will be saved into the group. That's what I did when I started writing this book; I created a group called Hacks and started collecting my favorite hacks there.

To paste a clip into an application, run ClipCache—either by double-clicking on its icon in the Notification Area, or by pressing the hot-key you've defined for it (for example, Ctrl-Shift-C)—then double-clicking on the clip you want to paste. You can then paste it as you would any other clip, by using Ctrl-V or Shift-Insert. For a quick shortcut, right-click on ClipCache's icon, then clip within a group you want to paste, as shown in Figure 8-2.

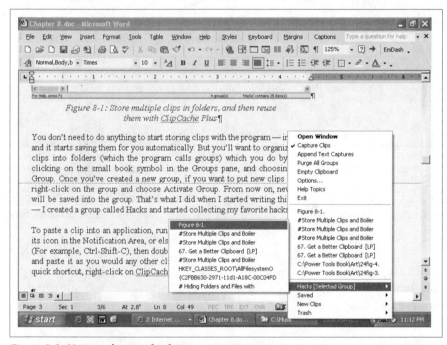

Figure 8-2. Using a shortcut for faster pasting

There's one more feature that I use all the time and that by itself is worth the price of the program—the ability to clean up text by taking out linebreaks, extra spaces, and indentations. This is particularly useful if you want to clean up email and reuse the text in it, especially if the email is part of a chain in which there are extra spaces and line breaks added and in which the > symbol is used to precede text quoted from a previous email. For example, look at the text at the bottom of the screen in Figure 8-3. It's part of an email I received, and it is full of extra spaces and > symbols because it was quoted from a previous email.

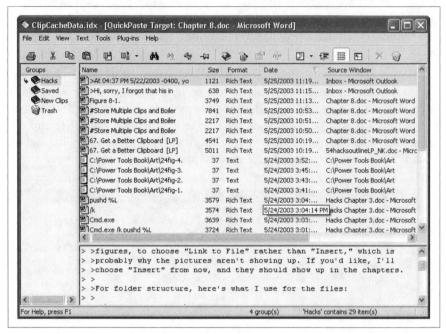

Figure 8-3. Text from an email, filled with indents and extra > characters

To clean it up, I choose Text → Cleanup Text and tell it to remove email indents and the > symbols. As you can see in Figure 8-4, ClipCache cleans out all extraneous characters and indents.

There's a lot more to this program as well, such as the ability to drag and drop clips between groups, edit clips, merge clips, and more. But for me, the simple ability to organize clips, save them in groups, and clean up emails is its strength.

One limitation is that ClipCache won't copy HTML-formatted text across <table> boundaries.

See Also

- ClipMate (*http://www.thornsoft.com*) is another excellent clipboard program.

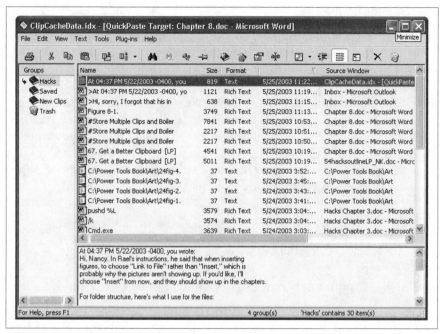

Figure 8-4. The cleaned-up clip

Speed Up Your Hard Disk by Improving Defragging

HACK
#74

One of the simplest ways to speed up your PC is by defragmenting your hard disk. Here's how to get the most out of XP's built-in defragmenter and a third-party program that should speed up your hard disk even more.

Perhaps the simplest way to speed up your PC is to use a disk defragmenter, which will help you open applications and files more quickly. As you use applications and files, they get spread out in fragments across your hard disk. The next time you go to use them, they take longer to open because your hard disk has to find each of those disparate fragments so they can be assembled when you open the file. A disk defragmenter stores files and applications contiguous to one another so that they can be fetched much more quickly than if they were spread out across your whole disk.

XP includes a built-in defragmentation program (sometimes called a *defragger*), which you can run by choosing Control Panel → Performance and Maintenance → "Rearrange items on your hard disk to make programs run faster." But there are ways you can use it more effectively, and there are third-party programs that do a more effective job of defragmentation as well.

Defragment Boot Files

One of the biggest improvements of XP's defragger over previous Windows versions is that it can perform a boot defragment, placing all boot files contiguous to one another so that you boot faster. The boot defragment option is usually enabled by default, but there's a possibility that it could be disabled, or enabled improperly. You can make sure it's enabled, using a Registry hack. Run the Registry Editor [Hack #68] and go to HKEY_LOCAL_MACHINE\ SOFTWARE\Microsoft\Dfrg\BootOptimizeFunction. Find the Enable string. If the String value is set to N, change it to Y. If it is Y, leave it as it is, since that means boot defragmentation is enabled. Exit the Registry and reboot. When you next defragment your disk, the boot files will be defragmented.

> You can also defragment the paging file, the hibernation file, and the Registry hives [Hack #68] using the freeware program PageDefrag (*http://www.sysinternals.com*).

Run Disk Defragmenter from the Command Line

If you prefer the command line to the graphical interface, you can avoid maneuvering through menus and dialog screens to defragment your hard drive. (Using the command line also gives you greater control over the defragmentation process, as you'll see in this hack.) To defragment a hard drive, type defrag C: at a command prompt, where C is the hard drive you want to defragment. When you use the command line, you won't see a visual display of the defragmentation process, and you won't be able to pause it or cancel it.

defrag also does work invisibly in the background to make sure that your programs load more quickly. It's set up so that every three days, when your computer is otherwise idle, it moves program code to the outside of the disk to make programs load more quickly. You can force it to do that manually, without having to do a full defragment, by using the –b switch, like this:

```
defrag C: -b
```

It takes only a few minutes for defrag to do this, in contrast with a full defragmentation, which can easily take more than 20 minutes, depending on how defragmented your system is and the speed of your processor.

There are several other command-line switches you can use with the defrag command:

/A   Analyzes the drive you want to defragment and shows you a brief analysis report, summarizing the hard disk size and total fragmentation. It only displays the report, however; it does not defragment the drive.

/V Analyzes the drive you want to defragment and shows you a comprehensive analysis report, detailing the size of the hard disk, percent of
free and used space, total fragmentation, and total number of fragments, among other details. It gives the analysis report, defragments the
hard disk, and then gives an analysis of the hard disk after defragmentation.

/F Forces the drive to be defragmented, even if there isn't a certain minimum amount of space. Normally, you can defragment the drive only if
your hard disk has at least 15% space free.

What to Do if the Disk Defragmenter Won't Defragment Your Drive

There will be times when the Disk Defragmenter won't defragment your
drive, or will defragment it only partially. It won't defragment your drive if
you don't have at least 15% of the drive's space free. To solve the problem,
as explained previously, type defrag C: /F at the command line, where C is
your hard drive.

There are also certain files and areas that the Disk Defragmenter won't
defragment: the Recycle Bin, the Windows page file, *Bootsect.dos*, *Safeboot.fs*,
Saveboot.rsv, *Hiberfil.sys*, and *Memory.dmp*. There's not much you can do
about it, though it's a good idea to empty the Recycle Bin before defragmenting.

Often, the Disk Defragmenter won't defragment every file on the first pass.
Your best bet here is to use brute force: run it again until it defragments the
files it missed the first time around. Also, keep in mind that the Disk Defragmenter won't defragment any files that are currently in use, so make sure to
close all programs; if there are files that won't defragment, it might be
because they're being used by an open program. Sometimes, programs may
seem to be shut down, but in fact may be running in a kind of phantom
mode. For example, Outlook sometimes stays running even after you've
shut it down. To make sure your programs are completely shut down before
running the Disk Defragmenter, run the Task Manager by pressing Ctrl-Alt-
Delete or right-clicking on the Taskbar and choosing Task Manager. Check
both the Applications and Processes tabs to see if any programs, like Word
for Windows (*Winword.exe*) or Outlook (*Outlook.exe*), are still running.
These two programs sometimes continue running even after you've shut
them down.

Get a Better Disk Defragmenter

For most purposes, XP's Disk Defragmenter works fine. But if you're a system administrator who needs to defragment multiple machines or defragment servers, you'll be better off with a better defragmenter. Even single users of XP might want a better disk defragmenter for purposes such as easy scheduling of defragmenting and the ability to defragment files that XP's defragmenter can't handle. Two of the best XP defragmenters are available as try-before-you-buy software:

Diskeeper

This defragmenter can automatically defragment a disk on bootup, allows you to remotely schedule boot-time defragmentation on multiple machines, will let system administrators create different defragmentation schedules for different groups of machines, will defragment disks that have little free disk space, and makes it easy to deploy on multiple machines. Get it at *http://www.execsoft.com*. It's free to download and try, but you'll have to pay if you decide to keep it. For an individual home users it's $29.95; for a single corporate user it's $44.95; and there are license packs available for multiple users. There's also a free version available, called Diskeeper Lite Freeware, which allows you to defragment only one volume at a time and doesn't allow scheduling.

PerfectDisk2000

Like Diskeeper, this defragmenter allows administrators to schedule defragmentation of machines across a network, and it can defragment disks with little free hard disk space. It can defragment files that XP's built-in defragmenter can't, such as the Windows page file. It also offers boot-time defragmentation. You can get it at *http://www.raxco.com*. It's free to download and try, but it is $44 per workstation should you decide to keep it. Figure 8-5 shows the options for using PerfectDisk2000.

H A C K   Build a Better Backup Strategy
#75

Don't be blindsided by disk crashes and other disasters. Here's how to have a backup ready at any time for any reason.

I used to use 3.5 inch diskettes for backup; to back up to disks today would take me approximately 98,000 diskettes. While we don't use diskettes for major backup procedures anymore, a lot of the thinking that goes into a backup is still pretty ancient.

I don't believe any users actually set out on a given day to destroy a functional operating system, but you know as well as I do that it happens. A lit-

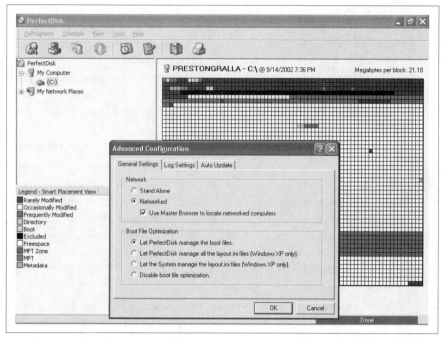

Figure 8-5. PerfectDisk2000 options

tle tweak here, a Registry edit there, a power surge or perhaps a badly behaved application that trashes the computer. We've all been there and when it happens I can almost guarantee you that if you listen closely you'll hear something approximating, "Darn. I meant to _____," where the blank is whatever backup task you have been putting off.

In addition to making yourself *do* the backup, there are a few steps I recommend to make your backup procedure easier, more convenient, and more effective.

Map Out a Backup Plan

I recommend separating the operating system and programs from the data when it's backed up. All three components—operating systems, programs, and data—have become huge over the years. In most cases, lumping them into a single, large backup is a waste of time, especially for home users.

Before you actually back up anything you need to ask yourself some questions:

How will the backup be saved? Many of today's computers come with devices that are suitable for backups; CD-R and CD-RW drives, tape drives, removable cartridge drives, and even a second hard drive can be used to store backups. With the exception of the second hard drive, any of those mentioned can be removed from the site where the system is located, and even the hard drive can be relocated by using specialty cradles that allow it to be plugged in and removed easily. There are a number of web-based hosting services that can be used for offsite storage for a monthly subscription fee. Business users normally back up to a company server, either local or remote, and the IS department takes over from that point.

The best system is one you think you'll actually use, so that you'll have the backup.

Where will the backup be stored once it's created? If fire, flood, or theft should strike where the system is located, the backup should be available from another location to restore the system and data files. Unfortunately, safe storage of the backup can be hard to get on-site. If you don't use an off-site service, consider storing your backups in one of the small fireproof chests that can be purchased at most department or office supply stores.

What files should be backed up? At one time, it was accepted, if not almost reasonable, to back up everything on a system at one time. But the amounts of data and the size of applications make that procedure very outdated. Here are three categories of data:

System files

> There is no need for the average user to back up operating system files. What *is* important is to protect the original media (i.e., the Windows XP CD and all of your program installation discs). Windows XP comes with System Restore, which backs up all of your system files automatically, or you can create a restore point whenever you prefer. System Restore is specifically designed to act in concert with the operating system to restore it in case of a system problem.
>
> If you don't like or trust System Restore, a number of programs are available that image the system and allow you to reinstall it in a fraction of the normal time. Ghost by Symantec is one of the popular choices (*http://www.symantec.com*).

Archive files

> These are files acquired through any number of methods, either downloaded or created by you, that don't change once they have been created. Image and audio files are good examples in this category. They are looked at and listened to for enjoyment, but as a rule they seldom if ever receive any modification once they have been added to your system. Don't back these up more than once.

Current data files

> More than anything else on your system, these are the files you most want backed up and protected on a regular basis. The list of included files will vary by user, but a few examples are text documents, spreadsheets, financial records, databases, email, Internet favorites, personal information managers (PIMs), web site projects, and any other type of data you create and work with or modify on a regular basis.

If the thought of losing one day's work makes the hair on the back of your neck stand upright, then you'd better have a tightly structured backup plan and ensure that it's adhered to without fail. If you have a computer full of spam and Freecell stats, it doesn't make much difference when, or even if, you back up.

System Organization Aids the Backup Process

How you organize your system can make backup a relatively painless process. Structuring the system so your data files are organized in one area facilitates pointing the backup program to one area rather than having to gather files from widespread locations. In Windows XP, the My Documents folder is an excellent choice for this purpose. Many programs default to saving created files in this location, including Office XP.

Many power users don't use My Documents because of its corny name; however, some of us have realized that it's a nice shortcut to have (along with My Pictures); because the applications default to these locations, you have less chance of spreading your documents and photos around the computer trying to find your chosen folder. If you don't like the name, change it [Hack #12]. Or, if you'd rather use your own organization structure but want to designate one of your folders as "My Documents," you can do that too [[Hack #8]].

Whatever location you choose, the important point is to use it for all the data you create and work with or modify on a regular basis that will be a part of the backup.

The Backup Utilities in Windows XP

While it isn't absolutely essential to have a utility specifically designed for backing up a computer system, it can make life easier. Both Windows XP Home and Professional come with what Microsoft calls the Backup and Restore Utility, better known as NTBackup. Unfortunately for XP Home users, Backup and Restore is not installed by default, nor is it as fully functional as the version installed by default in XP Professional. Supposedly, the reason it's not installed by default in XP Home is because XP Home does not support Automated System Recovery (ASR), which is a part of Backup and Restore. This in no way prevents you from making a full backup in Home Edition, but it does limit the recovery or restore options. Bottom line: if you have XP Professional, you're ready to go. If you have XP Home, follow these directions to install the Backup Utility manually:

1. Insert the Windows installation CD into your CD drive and navigate to *[CD Drive]:\VALUEADD\MSFT\NTBACKUP*, where *[CD Drive]* is replaced by *E:* or whatever letter represents your CD-ROM drive.

2. Double-click the *Ntbackup.msi* file to start the wizard that installs the Backup Utility.

3. When the wizard is complete, click Finish.

The "Restore" CD

A few years ago, I wouldn't even have had to add this sidebar, but a trend I heartily dislike has been gaining a foothold in the computer industry. That trend is the supplying of "restore CDs" by PC manufacturers. These useless little circles of plastic are used to restore a PC to factory specifications. "Factory specifications" means that the CD basically wipes your system clean and reinstalls XP and, along with it, all the other garbage (commercial sweetheart deals) that PC manufacturers use to pump up their coffers while depriving you of an unadulterated copy of a Windows XP installation CD. Unfortunately, if you fall into this group, you'll need to buy your own third-party backup program. Or, if you feel comfortable doing so, borrow a real Windows CD from a friend and install the Backup Utility on your system. The Backup Utility is something you should have received with your own copy of Windows to begin with. OK, kicking my soapbox back under the desk and moving on.

Here are a few things every hacker should know about NTBackup.

I Want My CDs! This really should go under the "you've got to be kidding me" category, but NTBackup does not allow you to back up directly to a CD-R or CD-RW drive. Allegedly the best, most stable, and advanced operating system Microsoft has offered, XP, has no CD burner support in backup. The solution is to back up to an alternative drive and then copy it to CD. There are many alternative backup programs available that do support direct backups to CD-R and CD-RW. Microsoft says their decision is by design. I say it's from a lack of design. Considering how popular CD-Rs and

CD-RWs have become as backup media—and how inexpensive they are—this lack of design presents a major problem for most people.

However, there is a way to store your backups on CDs (or DVDs, if you're in the early adopter wave and already have a DVD burner). First, back up as you would normally, and then copy the resulting file to a CD-R or CD-RW. If you have to restore a backup from the CD-R or CD-RW, you'll be able to do that directly; you won't have to first copy the file to another medium.

One problem you'll run across is that your backup might be larger than the 650 MB or 700 MB that CDs hold. To solve the problem, create two or more backup sets, each smaller than 650 or 700 MB (depending on your CD's capacity) separating data from programs or operating system files as suggested earlier will help you do this, and then copy each resulting set individually to a different CD.

Restoring a backup. When a backup is created the data is not saved in the same way you see it in the backup window where you select the files and folders. A backup is a single file that has to be broken apart during the restore process. To do so, it's necessary to use the same program that created the backup file to restore it to your system. Normally this is not a problem, except in one special circumstance. Restore will want to return your data to the location it occupied during the original backup. For example, if you backed up data from *D:* and no longer have a drive *D:* when you want to restore, the process will fail.

XP Home, NTBackup, and Automated System Recovery (ASR). Windows XP Home Edition does not support Automated System Recovery. I've been told this is why NTBackup is not installed by default in Home, but if that's the case, why include the item on the Home CD in the value-added directory? Whatever the reason, it's something you need to be aware of, in spite of the option for ASR that appears in NTBackup when installed on a XP Home machine. XP Professional users are good to go with ASR.

Get a Better Backup Program

XP's built-in backup program leaves a lot to be desired. But there are downloadable try-before-you-buy backup programs that offer you more features. Two of the best are Backup Plus and NTI Deluxe Backup Plus! Now.

Backup Plus
> One of the strengths of this program is its simplicity, particularly when restoring backups. Even though the program stores its backup file with a *.bac* extension, in fact, the backup files are *.zip* files. So, if you want to restore files or folders, you only need to rename the backup file so that

it has a *.zip* extension and then open the file with an unzipping program, such as the one built into Windows, or WinZip. Once you open the file, you can unzip it as you would any normal *.zip* file. The program also lets you schedule backups and, unlike XP's backup program, will back up to any kind of media, including CD-Rs and CR-RWs. Backup Plus is try-before-you-buy software. You can download it from *http://www.backupplus.net* and try it for free; if you decide to keep it, you should pay $39.95.

NTI Deluxe Backup Plus! Now

This is one of the more powerful and flexible backup programs you can find. It can back up to any media (including DVD-Rs), includes password protection for backup jobs, can span media and drives when backing up, and lets you make a complete image of your hard disk so that you can restore your entire system. NTI Deluxe Backup Plus! Now is try-before-you-buy software. You can download it from *http://www.ntius.com* and try it for free; if you decide to keep it, you must pay $79.99.

—*Jim Foley and Preston Gralla*

HACK #76 Extending Your Screen Real Estate with Virtual Desktops

Virtual desktops allow you to stretch your screen real estate well beyond its normal size, as well as to organize different views of your workspace.

At any point during the day, I might be writing software, listening to music, purchasing computer equipment, messing with my GPS and software, playing computer games with my son, or working with my editor. Sometimes, I'm doing all those things at once. It's a wonder that I can keep all the windows organized. Fortunately, I don't have to do all the organizing myself.

Virtual Desktop Manager (VDM) gives me a way to organize the work I'm doing, using up to four switchable desktops. VDM is part of the unsupported PowerToys collection from Microsoft that includes TweakUI [Hack #8].

Download VDM from *http://www.microsoft.com/windowsxp/pro/downloads/powertoys.asp* and install it on your machine. Once you have installed VDM, you will not notice anything new. You have to activate its toolbar before you can begin using it. To activate VDM, right-click on the taskbar at the bottom of the screen and select the Toolbars → Desktop Manager, as shown in Figure 8-6.

After you activate VDM, you will notice a new toolbar on the taskbar at the bottom of the screen, as shown in Figure 8-7. To switch between desktops, press one of the numbered blue buttons. At first, the desktops will appear the same, because you haven't done anything in them to make them unique.

Figure 8-6. Activating the Virtual Desktop Manager

Figure 8-7. The Virtual Desktop Manager toolbar

Click button 1 and then launch your web browser. Next, click button 2 and then open your email program. Next, click button 3 and then open the My Computer icon. Now, click the green button with an icon of a window on it. Your screen should look something like Figure 8-8. Click on one of the four images of the desktop to switch to that virtual desktop.

Without changing a single option, VDM is a very useful addition to Windows XP. But if you don't twiddle with it, you can't really call yourself a hacker, now can you? If you right-click on any of the buttons on the VDM toolbar, as shown in Figure 8-9, you will be able to configure VDM to suit your needs.

Your desktop has a background image that you can set as you wish. When you purchased your computer or installed Windows XP, the background image was a grassy hill with a blue sky. Since VDM provides you with four separate desktops, you can customize each with a different background image. If you choose the Configure Desktop Images item from the toolbar's menu, you will see the dialog box shown in Figure 8-10.

To change the background for one of the virtual desktops, specify which desktop area you want to change on the left side of the window. Then, locate a file from the list on the left. The list of images comes from both *C:\ WINDOWS\Web\Wallpaper* and *C:\Documents and Settings\<Your Name>\ My Documents\My Pictures*. If you want to use a picture not in the list, click the Browse button and locate the file. However, you might find that VDM changes your original background picture to a solid color when you first run it. Just change it back to your preferred background.

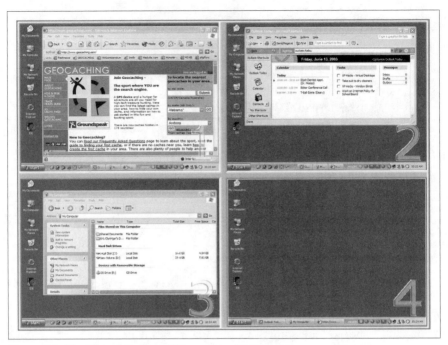

Figure 8-8. The Virtual Desktop Manager preview screen

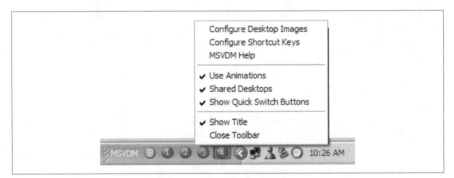

Figure 8-9. The Virtual Desktop Manager toolbar configuration menu

Look at Figure 8-10; notice that desktop 3 is shown in gray. This is how VDM informs you that you have no background image set for the desktop. When you switch to that desktop, the background will be whatever color you have selected in your display properties.

In addition to pressing the numbered buttons, you can use keyboard shortcuts to switch between the desktops. Hold down the Windows key (if your keyboard has one; if it doesn't, you can change the key assignments, as explained next) and the number keys 1 through 4 to switch to the appropri-

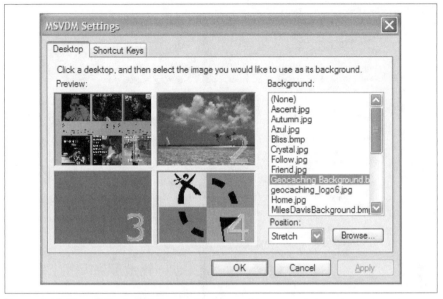

Figure 8-10. Virtual Desktop Manager background image settings

ate desktop. To switch to the VDM preview screen, hold down the Windows key and press V. To change the key assignments that switch between the desktops, choose Configure Shortcut Keys from the toolbar menu and use the dialog box shown in Figure 8-11.

> I'm not a big fan of animation on my computer when I'm trying to work. I don't like wasting CPU cycles and I don't like waiting for them to finish. (Also, it reminds me of the talking paperclip in Word.) So, I generally turn off all animation in the Windows desktop and Explorer. If you want to speed up the switch between virtual desktops, uncheck the menu item named Use Animations.

Look at Figure 8-8 again. Notice that each of the separate desktops has taskbar buttons for every program that is running. VDM does this so you can move running programs between the desktops. I prefer each desktop to have taskbar buttons for programs that run on that desktop. To do this, right-click on VDM on the taskbar and uncheck the menu item named Shared Desktops.

If you would rather rely on keyboard shortcuts and reclaim space on the taskbar, right-click on VDM and uncheck the Show Quick Switch Buttons menu item.

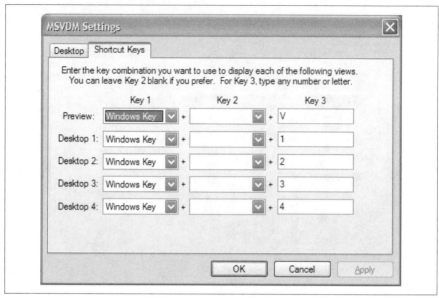

Figure 8-11. Virtual Desktop Manager shortcut key settings

The least useful bit about VDM is the fact that it actually wastes valuable space to tell you that it's there. If you uncheck the item named Show Title, the letters MSVDM will disappear from the toolbar.

Several things to keep in mind that when using VDM:

- If you choose a background image using the Settings dialog, the VDM settings will override the background image settings in the Display Properties dialog (your previous image won't be selected any more; you'll have to reselect it).

- If you use background images, the act of switching between desktops will be noticeably slower.

- Shortcuts and icons on the desktop will show up on all virtual desktops.

- If you have programs that float above all other windows on the screen (such as a program with an "Always On Top" option), they will show up on all desktops.

- Windows Media Player using the MiniPlayer skin is one of those programs that float above everything else. If you turn on the Windows Media Player toolbar and then minimize the player, a smaller version of the player appears on the taskbar and it is available to all desktops.

See Also

- Another popular product is the shareware application Cool Desk. It costs $24.95 and supports up to nine separate desktops. You can download Cool Desk at *http://www.shelltoys.com/virtual_desktop/index.html*.

- Also try Desks At Will. It costs $22.50 and also supports up to nine separate desktops. You can download Desks At Will at *http://www.idyle.com*.

- One of the more interesting desktop managers is Vern. Vern is free to download, but the author asks users who enjoy it to contribute. You can download Vern from *http://www.oneguycoding.com/vern/*.

—Eric Cloninger

HACK #77 Top Screenshot Tips

Capture any XP screen or portion of a screen and control the file format and output using these screen-capture tips.

Capturing good screenshots in XP takes a bit of work. If all you want to do is capture a screen for later reference, and don't care about the file format of the capture, and don't need to capture the cursor or only part of the screen, you can use XP's built-in capture capabilities. But if you need to create documentation, are a professional writer, an artist, or are a student preparing a term paper and need to get great-looking screenshots, you'll have to use a third-party program.

These screen-capture tips will help you capture just about anything you want, using built-in or third-party tools.

Built-In Screen Capture

XP comes with a built-in capability for capturing screenshots, though it's about as basic as screenshot capture gets. To capture an entire screen, press the Print Scrn button. To capture only the active screen, press Alt-Print Scrn.

Pressing those keys captures the screen to the Clipboard [Hack #73], but you'll have to paste the screen into a graphics program in order to save it. Use your favorite graphics program, such as Paint Shop Pro [Hack #86], or use XP's built-in Paint program by choosing Start → All Programs → Accessories → Paint. Paste in the graphic, and then choose a format for saving it.

If you have Microsoft Office, a better bet than Paint is pasting the screen into Microsoft Photo Editor (Start → Programs → Microsoft Office Tools → Microsoft Photo Editor). (Microsoft Photo Editor doesn't come with all versions of Office, or might not be installed by default, so it might not be available on yours.) It offers more control over file formats when you save the screenshot. For example, you'll be able to decide on the amount of compression to use on JPEG files, and you can choose among several graphics color depths and palettes. When you save a file, after you choose the format, click on the More button, and you'll get options for saving in that file format, as shown Figure 8-12. Of course, a graphics program like Paint Shop Pro offers even more options.

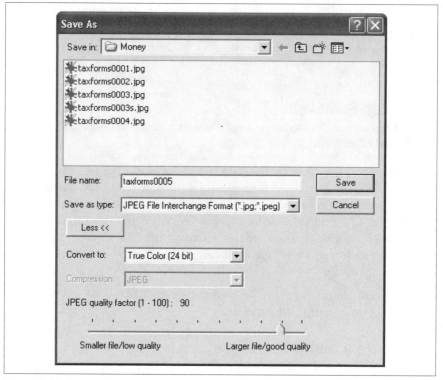

Figure 8-12. Saving screen captures with Microsoft Photo Editor

SnagIt

XP's built-in capture tool, while effective, has several drawbacks. It won't capture the cursor or portions of the screen, for example. To do that and more, get the ultimate screen capture tool, SnagIt from TechSmith (*http://www.snagit.com*). It's shareware and free to try, but it costs $39.95 if you decide to keep it. In addition to letting you capture the cursor and any portion of a screen, it will capture an entire scrollable area—such as a scrolling web page—gives you a wide variety of options for customizing file formats, and it will capture a screen and send it to the printer or a web page.

First, choose what you want to capture—the entire screen, the active window, a portion of the window and so on. Also, configure whether to capture the cursor. Figure 8-13 shows you the SnagIt menu options for capturing a screen.

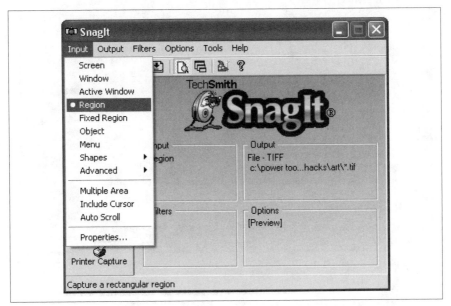

Figure 8-13. SnagIt screen-capture options

Next, set up the screen you want to capture and press SnagIt's hot key for screen capture. (The default is Ctrl-Shift-P, but you can change it.) If you've chosen to capture an area of the screen, you'll be able to define it using SnagIt's capture tools. If you've chosen the option of capturing a screen that scrolls, click on the scroll bar of the screen. Once you have the area you want, you get a preview of the screen, as shown in Figure 8-14. You can zoom in and out on any area of the screen to make sure it's what you want. When you decide the screen is what you want, click Finish, select a file format, name, and location, and you're done. To customize your graphics format—for example, to choose JPEG compression or change the color depth—click on the Options button that appears when you save a file, and make your choice.

See Also

- If you want to capture onscreen actions such as mouse movements, menu choices, and anything else you do on your PC, use the free Cam-Studio (*http://www.atomixbuttons.com/vsc/*), which will record all your actions and save it as a video file in either Windows *.avi* video format or Flash *.swf* format.

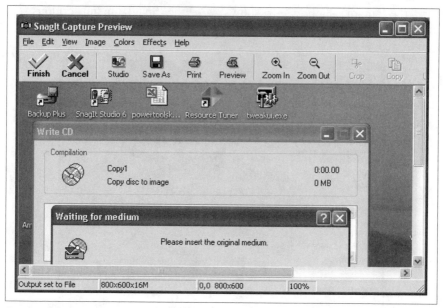

Figure 8-14. Previewing your screenshot with SnagIt

Going Beyond Messaging with Windows Messenger

HACK #78

Share a common whiteboard where you can collaborate on work in real-time over the Internet, and get alerts delivered to your desktop with Microsoft's instant messaging tool.

Windows Messenger can do far more than merely let you chat with other people. Hidden inside it are powerful collaboration tools for working with others over the Internet, as well as the ability to get automated alerts delivered to your desktop.

> Don't confuse the instant messaging program Windows Messenger with the XP Messenger Service, which is used to send notifications over local area networks—for example, when a network administrator wants to notify network users that a server is about to go down. They're completely separate programs with different purposes. The XP Messenger Service has been used by spammers as a backdoor way of sending spam pop ups. To see how to turn the XP Messenger Service off so you don't get spam, see "Stop Pop Ups, Spyware, and Web Bugs" [Hack #33].

Using .NET Alerts with Messenger

One of Windows Messenger's more useful features is its ability to deliver to you a variety of alerts called *.NET alerts*—messages, reports, or bulletins, such as weather reports, stock quotes, breaking news, and traffic reports. I'm a news junkie, and, where I live in New England, weather-watching is considered a contact sport (if you don't believe me, try making your way through a February Nor'easter with your body intact). So, I use .NET alerts to stay on top of breaking events and get the latest bad news about the weather. Here's how I do it.

First, sign up for alerts by clicking on the Alerts tab (the one that looks like a bell). If for some reason Messenger doesn't show you any tabs, choose Tools → Show Tabs → Microsoft .NET Alerts. You'll be prompted to sign up for an Alert provider, as shown in Figure 8-15.

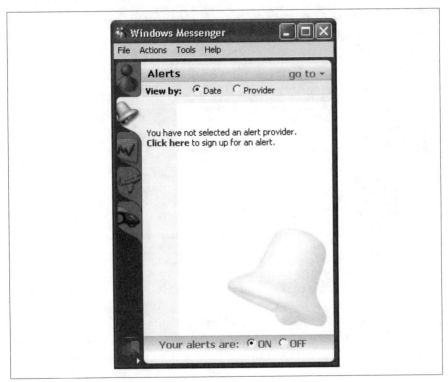

Figure 8-15. Signing up for .NET alerts

Next, you'll be sent to a web page where you can choose from a variety of alerts. Choose the alert you want, and fill out the form. The form for each alert is different and requires different information and different steps. In my instance, I signed up for MSNBC News to get its breaking news, and Weather.com alerts for the weather. I'm an eBay fan, so I signed up for alerts that will track auctions I'm interested in. And, like any long-suffering Bostonian with a taste for the tragic, I'm a Red Sox fan, so I also sign up for ESPN.com.

When you're done adding alerts, use the navigation on the web page to go to your My Alerts page, shown in Figure 8-16. From here you can edit, manage, add and delete alerts.

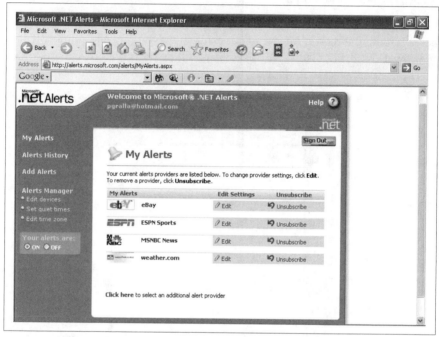

Figure 8-16. Managing all your alerts from your My Alerts page

Alerts will now be delivered to you on the schedule that you chose. They'll appear as a small window near the Notification area, as shown in Figure 8-17. As you can see, it's another lovely day in Cambridge, with a high reaching all the way up to a stratospheric reading of 30 degrees. To read the full alert, click on it and you'll be sent to a web page with the full alert.

If you want to read all your recent alerts, click on the Alerts tab. You'll be able to view them by date or alert provider.

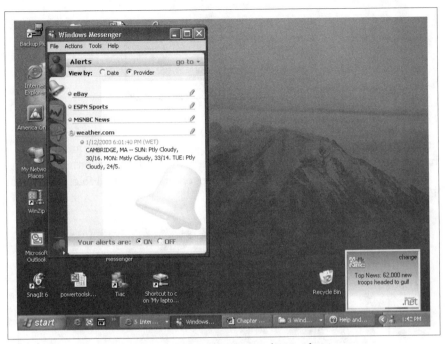

Figure 8-17. Alerts appearing as small windows near the Notification area

Collaborate Long-Distance with the Whiteboard

Chat windows are fine for simple communication, but when you're working with others at long distance, very often you need more collaboration than that. In particular, you might want to share drawings, images, and text. You can do that using the *whiteboard*, a tool that lets you collaborate in real time over the Internet or a network with other Windows Messenger users. It's a drawing program, similar to Microsoft Paint, that allows you to share drawings, diagrams, images, and text. The same whiteboard appears on the systems of both participants, and each person can draw, annotate, and mark up the whiteboard in any way they want. The other participant sees the markup, in real time, and can in turn mark it up as well.

To start a whiteboard with someone, double-click on their contact name and click on the Start Whiteboard link on the right side of the Messenger conversation screen. An invitation goes out to the contact, and, if he agrees, a small Sharing Session windows appears, as shown in Figure 8-18.

Click on the Whiteboard button, and the whiteboard appears. You can both now use the markup tools. They're largely self-explanatory and work like Windows Paint or another graphics program. You can see the whiteboard in

Figure 8-18. Launching a whiteboard session

action in Figure 8-19. Make sure, though, to use the remote pointer, a small hand that you can drag around the screen that helps you better highlight what you're currently working on together. If you look closely at Figure 8-19, you can see it.

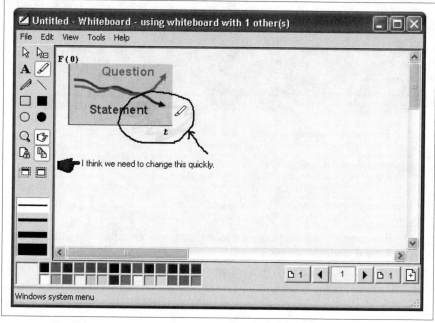

Figure 8-19. The whiteboard in action

The buttons along the lower right of the screen let you create new pages and navigate among those pages. When you create a new page and navigate among pages, the other participant comes along with you to those pages. Additionally, there are four buttons in the left part of the whiteboard that serve special purposes:

Lock Contents

When you click this button, it locks the whiteboard and prevents anyone else from making changes to it. To unlock the contents, click the button again.

Unsynchronize

When you click this button, you can jump to another page or create another page, and you'll do that privately; for the purposes of creating and navigating among pages, you're not synchronized with the other participant. When you click on the button again, other participants' whiteboards will switch to the page you're viewing.

Select Window

Click on this button, and then the next window you click on anywhere in XP or any application will automatically be pasted into the whiteboard.

Select Area

Click on this button, and you'll be able to select an area anywhere in XP or an XP application and paste it into the whiteboard.

When you're done using the whiteboard, click on the Close button in the Sharing Session window. You'll be given the option of saving the whiteboard. If you save it, it will be saved in its own proprietary format (as an *.nmw* file). To view that whiteboard again, double-click on it in Windows Explorer.

Share Applications with Messenger

The whiteboard is useful for basic collaboration, but an even more powerful tool is Messenger's application sharing. It allows two people to work in the same application on the same document. Whatever is on your screen appears on the other person's screen, and the two of you can work on the document together. I've found it to be ideal for collaborating on spreadsheets—it's easy to share "what-if" scenarios this way.

To start a whiteboard with someone, double-click on the contact name and click on the Start Whiteboard link on the right side of the Messenger conversation screen. An invitation goes out to the contact, and, if he agrees, a small Sharing Session windows appears, as shown previously in Figure 8-18. Once he agrees, click on App Sharing, and you'll be able to choose which file and application to share, as shown in Figure 8-20. You can share only programs and files that are already open on your PC.

Click on one or more programs and click Share; the applications open in a window on the other person's computer. You have full control over the application; they can only watch what you do. In that sense, it's not full collaboration. If you want the other person to also be able to control the document, click on the Allow Control button; they will be able to work on the application and document after they request your permission. Only one person at a time can control the document; you can pass control over it back and forth.

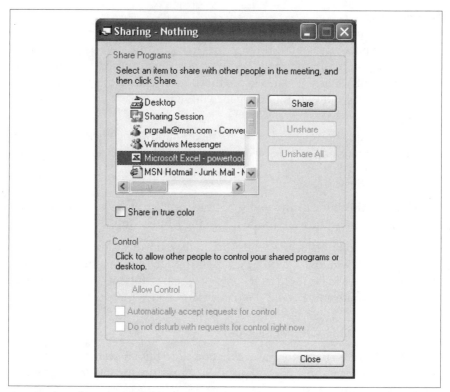

Figure 8-20. Choosing an application or applications to share

Universal Messaging: Trillian Unites AIM, MSN, Yahoo!, and ICQ
#79

It's the Esperanto of the Instant Messaging world; Trillian lets you communicate with all the major messaging programs.

I live, therefore I message. That's the credo of not just teenagers everywhere, but also for people like me. I use instant messaging to keep in touch with editors, friends, and other authors, as well as readers of my books. And I frequently use it along with conference calls; while the larger group is speaking over the phone, I instant-message others in the phone conference to get background information and make occasionally less-than-flattering remarks about speakers who revel in the sounds of their own voices.

But as all instant message users know, there's a big drawback to instant messaging: the major instant messenger programs, including Windows Messenger, can't communicate with one another. That's a bit like being able to make phone calls only to people who use the same brand of telephone as yours, but given the economics and ego that drives the instant messaging industry, that shows no sign of changing any time soon.

However, there's a great workaround, and it's free. The universal instant messaging program Trillian will let you communicate with users of with ICQ, Windows Messenger, Yahoo! Messenger, and AOL Instant Messenger as well as the old Internet chat standby IRC. You don't need to install any of those programs; just run Trillian (*http://www.ceruleanstudios.com*), shown in Figure 8-21.

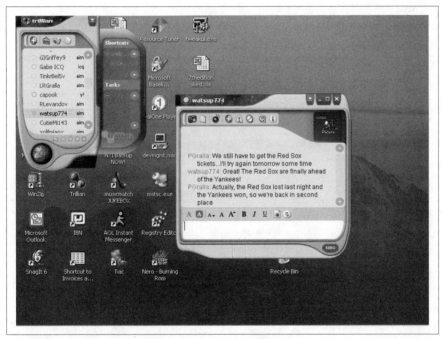

Figure 8-21. Universal instant messaging with Trillian

After you install Trillian, enter your usernames and passwords from your other instant messengers. When you do that, Trillian automatically uses those contact lists, so you don't need to reenter them. To enter a new contact from inside Trillian, choose the Add Contact button, tell Trillian which program your contact uses, and then fill in the contact information. Because instant messaging programs store your contacts on their servers, rather than locally on your PC, when you add contacts like this, these new contacts will not only be available in Trillian, but also when you use your instant messaging program.

If you have accounts on more than one instant messaging program, Trillian signs you into all of them when you log in, so you get a single sign-in and are then available everywhere.

Trillian lets you use some, but not all of the features of each individual instant messenger program. For example, you'll be able to send files as you can with instant messengers. But you can't, for example, use the Windows Messenger whiteboard or application sharing.

One problem with instant messaging with any program is the way that it leaves you open to the world: anyone who wants to contact you can, including increasingly aggressive messaging spammers. Each individual program gives you controls over who can contact you and how you want to be contacted, and Trillian also lets you customize your privacy for each of the programs. Right-click on the big Trillian icon near the bottom of the Trillian screen and choose Preferences. Then, scroll to the bottom of the list to where it says Chatting Services. You'll find ways to customize your privacy, which differ according to the service's capabilities, as shown in Figure 8-22.

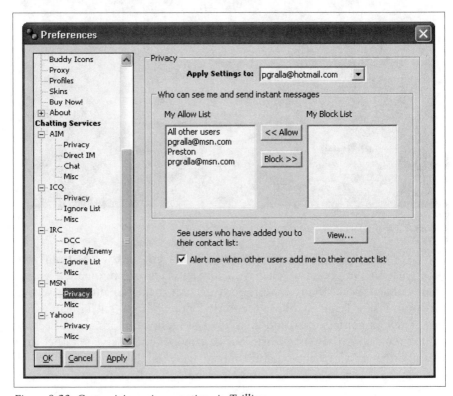

Figure 8-22. Customizing privacy options in Trillian

Trillian is skinnable, so you can easily change its appearance. To choose a new skin, select Skins in the Preferences screen shown in Figure 8-22, and choose either Launch Skin Chooser to choose from any skins already on your system, or Get More Skins to choose from skins online.

Trillian is one of the few programs that takes advantage of XP's transparency capabilities [Hack #18]. To make Trillian transparent, right-click anywhere in the program and choose Advanced Options → Transparency. You can then choose a transparency of anywhere from 10% to 90%, where 10% is the least transparent, and 90% is the most transparent. I'd suggest using 10%; any more than that and it becomes very difficult to see the program or chat with it.

There are two versions, one of which is free, and the other, called Trillian Pro, costs $25. The Pro version includes a plug-in system that allows third-party developers to create plug-ins that you can download for free. For example, there are plug-ins for delivering the weather and news, checking your POP3 email accounts, integrating with WinAmp MP3 software, and more. The Pro version has other features as well, such as the ability to videoconference using the Yahoo! portion of Trillian.

See Also

- Gaim (*http://gaim.sourceforge.net*) is another universal instant messenger. Earlier versions tended to crash unexpectedly on XP, but more recent versions are more stable. It's not as handsome-looking as Trillian, and it doesn't take advantage of as many of the built-in features as each of the instant messengers in the same way that Trillian does. But it's open source and runs on many other platforms, not just Windows.

Applications
Hacks 80–85

An operating system by itself is a paltry thing; applications do the real work. So, if you want to get the most out of XP, you need to hack the applications that run on top of it.

Some old programs have a hard time running under XP, so you'll see in this chapter how to get apparently incompatible programs to run under the operating system. You'll also find out how to remove applications and uninstall entries that you can't seem to get rid of, even when you thought you'd uninstalled the application. And we'll cover shortcuts for launching applications quickly and customizing them to the way you like them. There's more as well, including how to create and open Microsoft documents without having to spend hundreds of dollars for Office.

HACK #80 Remove Unruly Applications and Uninstall Entries

Uninstalling programs is sometimes tougher than you'd expect; even when you use built-in uninstallers, programs leave bits of themselves all over your hard disk and Registry. Here's how to remove them.

Uninstalling applications can be a tricky business. At a glance, it seems simple: choose Start → Control Panel → Add or Remove Programs, then choose the program you want to remove in the Add or Remove Programs dialog box, and click Remove.

But uninstall routines are generally only as good as the programmer that made them. And that means that unruly programs commonly leave bits of themselves behind, even after you uninstall them. They might leave behind DLLs that load every time you start Windows, as well as Registry entries, even though the original program is gone. In both instances, your system performance takes a hit loading resources for programs that no longer exist.

The programs also might leave behind unnecessary files and folders, which take up hard disk space.

There's a good deal you can do to clean up after these unruly applications, though. Follow this advice:

- After you've run the uninstallation routine, run the Registry Editor [Hack #68], search through the Registry for any keys and values the program left behind, and then delete them. Frequently, you can find the settings for the program at \HKEY_LOCAL_MACHINE\SOFTWARE*Publisher**Program Name* where *Publisher* is the name of the software company that made the program and *Program Name* is the name of the software package (in the case of companies with multiple products like Symantec or Adobe). For safety's sake, make a backup of Registry keys [Hack #71] before deleting them.

- Before uninstalling the application, look through your hard disk to see where the program stores its files and folders. Then, after you run the uninstallation routine, look for those files and folders and delete them if they haven't been deleted. Often, you'll find them in *C:\Program Files\ <Publisher>\<Program Name>*.

- After uninstalling the program, make sure that no parts of the program are still being run at startup. To do that, delete their entries from \HKEY_LOCAL_ MACHINE\SOFTWARE\Microsoft\Windows\CurrentVersion\Run and HKEY_ CURRENT_USER\Software\Microsoft\Windows\CurrentVersion\Run.

- Create a restore point so that you can restore your system to the state it was in before you installed the program. Choose Control Panel → Performance and Maintenance → System Restore and follow the wizard for creating a restore point. If you're testing out an application and aren't sure that you're going to keep using it, create a restore point before you install it. Then, after you've installed the application and decided not to use it, revert to that restore point instead of using the uninstallation routine; it's more thorough.

- Use RegSpy [Hack #72]. This downloadable program lets you watch and track changes made to the Registry whenever a program installs and runs, and it lets you roll back changes the program made.

Remove Stubborn Uninstall Entries from Already Uninstalled Programs

Inexplicably, even after you've uninstalled some programs, their entries still remain listed in the Add or Remove Programs dialog box. As time goes on, it's easy for you to forget what programs you've uninstalled, so when you see their entries there you'll assume the programs are still on your hard disk, but when you try to uninstall them you'll receive an error message. There's an easy way to remove those entries. First, try to uninstall the program from the Add or Remove Programs dialog box. If it doesn't uninstall, run the Registry Editor and open \HKEY_LOCAL_MACHINE\SOFTWARE\Microsoft\Windows\ CurrentVersion\Uninstall. Look for the entry of the uninstalled program (it will be the program name) and delete it. In some instances, instead of the program name, you'll see an entry like this: {3075C5C3-0807-4924-AF8F-FF27052C12AE}. In that case, open the DispayName subkey in that entry; it should have the name of the program—in this instance, Norton Antivirus 2002. When you find the proper entry, delete it. For safety's sake, make a backup of Registry keys [Hack #71] before deleting them,

Remove Access to Certain Microsoft Programs

As part of a settlement in a federal antitrust case, Microsoft was forced to allow non-Microsoft programs to be the default applications for certain uses, such as email, web browsing, and digital entertainment. Users also had to be allowed to remove access to Microsoft programs that accomplished those tasks. That ruling came well after Windows XP was shipped, though, so many copies of XP don't allow you to do that. However, if you have a later version of XP, or if you have installed the Windows XP Service Pack 1 (also called SP-1), your copy of the operating system has those capabilities.

To find out if you have SP-1, right-click on My Computer and look on the General tab. The words "Service Pack 1" will be there if you have SP-1 installed.

To remove access to Microsoft programs, first find out if your system has the capabilities. Choose Start → Control Panel → Add or Remove Programs and see whether the Add or Remove Programs dialog box contains a button in the left pane titled Set Program Access and Default. If it does, you can remove access to Microsoft programs. Click that button. You'll find three choices: Microsoft Windows, Non-Microsoft, and Custom. Click on the double-down arrow next to any choice to see more details.

If you choose Microsoft Windows, then your default programs for web browsing, email, instant messaging, digital entertainment, and accessing Java applications will all be Microsoft programs. If you choose Non-Microsoft, the defaults will be the non-Microsoft programs that your computer manufacturer installed on your PC. If you choose Custom, you can pick and choose between Microsoft and non-Microsoft applications, as shown in Figure 9-1.

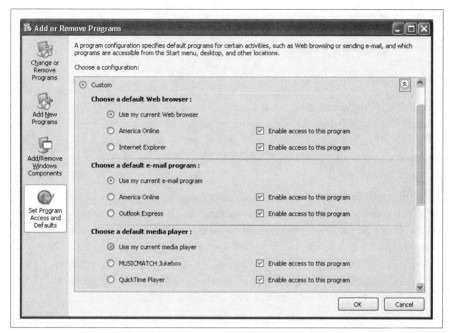

Figure 9-1. Choosing Microsoft or non-Microsoft applications for certain purposes

Keep in mind that "Remove access" doesn't mean the same as deleting the program. It only means that the icon for the program will be removed. For example, if you remove access to Internet Explorer, it won't actually be deleted from your hard disk; you merely won't be able to see its icon. Also, be aware that not all email, instant messaging, digital entertainment, and web browsing programs will show up on the non-Microsoft or Custom lists, so you won't necessarily be able to use this screen to set them as your defaults.

All this means that the best use for the Set Program Access and Default dialog box is to remove the icons of some Microsoft programs; it doesn't offer a lot of functionality beyond that.

See Also

- Remove "Uninstallable" XP Utilities [Hack #17]

Force XP-Incompatible Applications to Run
HACK #81

Don't throw away your old programs that can't run under XP. Use these hacks to force them to work.

Some older applications, including old games and programs written specifically for an earlier version of Windows, might not run properly or run at all under XP. But there's a lot you can do to make sure they run, including running an automated Compatibility Wizard and using a little-known Microsoft tool to solve compatibility problems.

Use the Compatibility Wizard

If you find a program that won't run under XP, start with the easiest step. Run the Compatibility Wizard: choose Start → Help and Support → Fixing a Problem → "Application and software problems" → "Fix a problem" → "Getting older programs to run on XP," then scroll down and click on Program Compatibility Wizard.

You'll be prompted to choose the software you want to fix and then asked a series of questions, including the operating system for which the software was written, or on which it last ran properly, and the screen resolutions recommended for the program. Figure 9-2 shows the wizard in action. The wizard then applies those settings and tries to run the program. If the settings work, the wizard will let you specify to always run the program using them. If they don't, try different settings until you get it working properly.

There may be some instances in which a program won't even install on your system. In those instances, run the Compatibility Wizard on the installation or setup program, commonly called *Setup.exe* or a similar filename. Then, after it installs, see if it works properly. If it doesn't, run the wizard again, this time on the installed program.

If you're not a fan of wizards, there's another way to set the program's compatibility settings. Right-click the program's shortcut icon and choose Properties → Compatibility. You can then manually configure compatibility settings, as shown in Figure 9-3. You can change the same settings as you can using the wizard. You may have to try several different settings before you find one that works.

At the bottom of the Compatibility dialog box shown in Figure 9-3, you'll notice a setting that lets you turn off "advanced text services." That setting is applicable if you use speech recognition and text services, so if you use them in the application that won't run, try turning them off for this application to see whether it helps. If the program doesn't use these services, don't bother using the setting.

If the Compatibility Wizard doesn't work, try these steps:

1. Check the software manufacturer's web site to see if an update, patch, or fix is available.

2. Use Windows Update to see if a fix is available, by choosing Start → Control Panel → Windows Update.

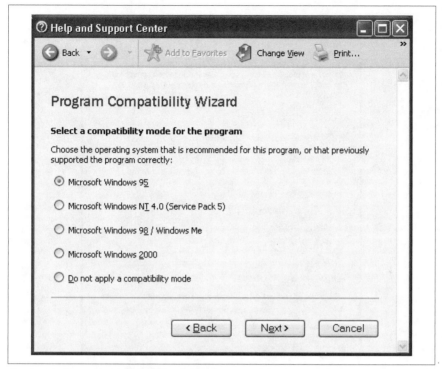

Figure 9-2. Using the Compatibility Wizard

3. Update your sound card and video card drivers by checking the manufacturer sites and downloading new drivers.

4. If the problem program is a game that uses DirectX, upgrade to the newest version of DirectX by going to *http://www.microsoft.com/downloads/* and clicking on the DirectX link or searching for DirectX.

Use the Application Compatibility Toolkit

If the wizard doesn't work, turn to a more powerful tool, a little-known free program, the Application Compatibility Toolkit from Microsoft. It will automatically apply fixes to hundreds of programs to enable them to run under XP. You can find it in the *\Support\Tools* directory of the XP CD, though a much better bet is to download it from *http://www.microsoft.com/windows/ appcompatibility/default.mspx* because newer versions are always being made available online.

Turn off your antivirus program before installing the Application Compatibility. The program makes many changes to numerous Registry entries, and antivirus software often interprets those changes as a malicious script.

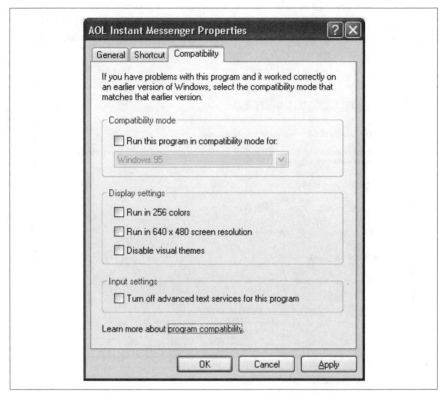

Figure 9-3. Setting compatibility settings directly in the Compatibility dialog box

After you install it, you don't have to do anything to fix the programs; the analyzer does it for you. It won't fix every program, though. To see if it fixed yours, go to *C:\Program Files\Microsoft Windows Application Compatibility Toolkit\Applications\Compatibility Administrator*, run *Compatadmin.exe,* and go to *\System Database\Applications*. You'll see a list of hundreds of programs that the toolkit has fixed. Scroll to see whether your problem application is on the list and, if it is, to see what fixes were applied. Figure 9-4 shows the fixes it applied to the MusicMatch Jukebox music software.

See Also

• Force Older Programs to Use XP Common Controls [Hack #82]

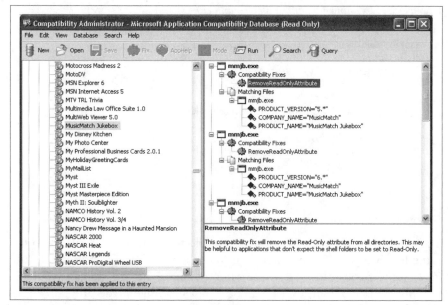

Figure 9-4. The Application Compatibility Toolkit

HACK #82 Force Older Programs to Use XP Common Controls

Older Windows programs look ancient and outdated in XP, because they don't use the newer-style buttons and check boxes. Here's how to make them use XP common controls.

When you run an older program in XP, the operating system applies an XP-type frame around it, with rounded title bars. But the older program itself still uses its older style interface. You can, however, force older programs to use XP-type common controls for things such as checkboxes and buttons. You'll have to create a manifest file (a specifically formatted XML file) and place it in the same directory as the older file.

Example 9-1 shows the code to put in your manifest file. For *Description of Program*, enter a description for the program, and for *Program Name*, enter the name of the program.

Example 9-1. Creating a .manifest file

```
<?xml version="1.0" encoding="UTF-8" standalone="yes"?>
<assembly xmlns="urn:schemas-microsoft-com:asm.v1" manifestVersion="1.0">
<assemblyIdentity
    version="1.0.0.0"
    processorArchitecture="X86"
    name="Program Name"
    type="win32"
```

Example 9-1. Creating a .manifest file (continued)

```
/>
<description>Description of Program</description>
<dependency>
    <dependentAssembly>
        <assemblyIdentity
            type="win32"
            name="Microsoft.Windows.Common-Controls"
            version="6.0.0.0"
            processorArchitecture="X86"
            publicKeyToken="6595b64144ccf1df"
            language="*"
        />
    </dependentAssembly>
</dependency>
</assembly>
```

To create the file, open Notepad, copy the text into it, and save it to the same folder as the executable file of the program you want to force to use XP common controls. Give it the same name as the program's executable file, but with an extension of *.manifest*. For example, if the program's executable file is named *oldprogram.exe*, give the manifest file the name *oldprogram.exe.manifest*.

See Also

- Force XP-Incompatible Applications to Run [Hack #81]

HACK #83   Launch Applications with Command-Line Shortcuts

Launch applications quickly and customize what they do when they run, by using command-line shortcuts, parameters, and switches.

Windows is a graphical operating system, but a lot of times all these pretty icons, menus, and clicking get in the way of getting work done. That's particularly true when you want to launch applications.

I started computing in the days of DOS, when real men and women didn't use mice and icons. (Sometimes because it wasn't an option.) So, I look for any chance I can get to use the command line, particularly when doing so saves me time and lets me take more control of my computer.

That's why I frequently launch applications using command-line shortcuts, along with parameters and switches. Parameters and switches let you customize the way programs launch. They're usually specific to each individual program, though some work on many or all programs.

An even bigger time-saver is to use the command line along with keyboard shortcuts. That way, you can press a key combination—such as Ctrl-Alt-W, for example—and launch Microsoft Word with a new document open, based on a specific template.

Create Keyboard Shortcuts for Running Applications

You'll first, create a desktop shortcut to the application, and then you'll customize the shortcut so that it launches when you use a specific key combination. Right-click on the Desktop and choose New → Shortcut. Enter or browse to the filename of the application for which you want to create a shortcut, including its path and surrounding it by quotation marks, such as "C:\Program Files\Microsoft Office\Office10\WINWORD.EXE". Click Next; then, in the "Select a name for the shortcut box," type the name of your new shortcut (such as Basic Word), and click Finish. Right-click on the shortcut you just created and choose Properties. In the Shortcut Tab, shown in Figure 9-5, put your cursor in the "Shortcut key" box and press the key combination you want to use to start the program. It has to be a combination of Ctrl-Alt, Shift-Alt, or Shift-Ctrl, plus a letter key, such as Ctrl-Alt-A, Shift-Alt-A, or Shift-Ctrl-A. In our instance, we're using Ctrl-Shift-W. Click OK. The program will now launch whenever you press the shortcut key combination.

There are a variety of entries on the Shortcut tab that let you customize how the program launches when you use the shortcut. The Run drop-down list lets you start the program minimized, maximized, or in a normal window. The "Start in" box lets you determine the start location for the application. You can even customize the ScreenTip that appears when you hover the mouse over the shortcut. In the Comment box, type the text you want to appear as a ScreenTip. Figure 9-6 shows how such a customized ScreenTip looks like when a mouse hovers over it.

Customizing Shortcuts with Switches and Parameters

Launching applications with a keyboard shortcut is a time-saver, but there's still a lot you can do to customize those shortcuts. For example, you can set up a number of separate keyboard shortcuts for Word—for example, to launch Word with new documents based on a different templates, or to open Word to specific already-created documents.

For example, let's say you want to launch Word and have it automatically open a specific document, one called *chapter 9.doc* in the *C:\Hacks* directory. Type this (all on one line) in the Target box displayed in Figure 9-5:

```
"C:\Program Files\Microsoft Office\Office10\WINWORD.EXE" "C:\Hacks\chapter
9.doc"
```

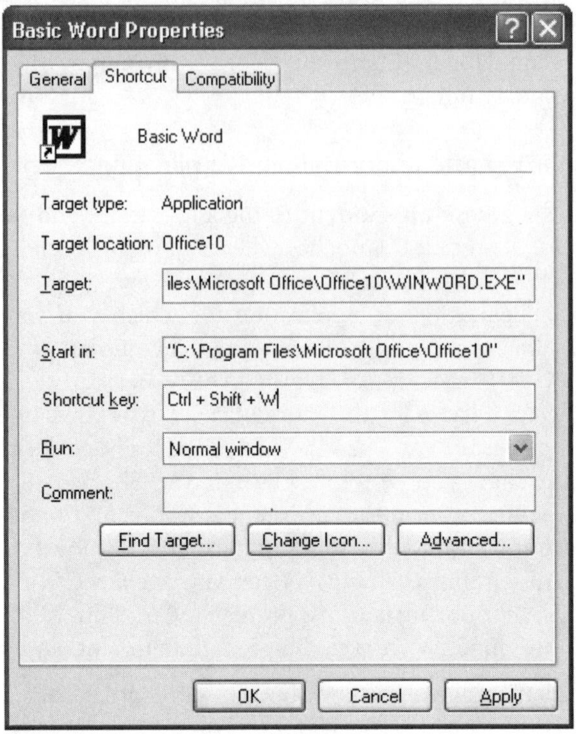

Figure 9-5. *The Shortcut Properties dialog box*

Figure 9-6. *A customized ScreenTip*

Doing this gives you much more control that double-clicking on the document or creating a shortcut to the document, because, in addition to launching individual files, you can use a variety of switches to customize how you launch those files. For example, let's say you want to launch Word without the splash screen. Use the /q switch, like this:

```
"C:\Program Files\Microsoft Office\Office10\WINWORD.EXE" /q
```

You can then combine switches with opening individual files, like this:

```
"C:\Program Files\Microsoft Office\Office10\WINWORD.EXE" /q "C:\Hacks\
chapter 9.doc"
```

This command opens the file and bypasses the splash screen. Use keyboard shortcuts along with these switches and syntax to create as many customized versions of Office applications as you like. Tables 9-1, 9-2, and 9-3 list switches for Microsoft applications Word, Excel, and PowerPoint, respectively.

Table 9-1. Switches for starting Word

Switch	What it does
/a	Stops add-ins and global templates, including the Normal template, from being loaded automatically. It also locks Word's settings so that they cannot be read or modified.
/l addinpath	Loads a specific Word add-in.
/m	Starts a new instance of Word without running AutoExec macros.
/m filen	Opens the file specified by number on the File menu's Most Recently Used list.
/m macroname	Runs a specific macro and prevents Word from running any AutoExec macros.
/n	Starts a new instance of Word without opening a document. Documents opened will not appear as choices in the Window menu of other Word instances.
/t templatename	Starts Word with a new document based on the specified template.
/w	Starts a new instance of Word with a blank document. Documents opened will not appear as choices in the Window menu of other Word instances.
/r	Opens Word, reregisters it in the Registry, and then quits. Use this switch if there have been problems with Word's settings and you want to reregister it. At times, certain Registry keys associated with Word can get corrupted. If you use this switch, you'll delete the corrupt Registry keys and recreate them from scratch. Your problems should then go away.
/q	Starts Word without the splash screen.

Table 9-2. Switches for starting Excel

Switch	What it does
/r workbook path/ file name	Opens the specified workbook as read-only.
/e	Opens Excel without a startup screen and without a new blank workbook.
/m	Opens Excel with a new workbook that contains a single macro sheet.
/p workbook path	Opens Excel and uses the specified path as the active path instead of the default path
/o	Opens Excel and then reregisters it in the Registry. Use this switch if there have been problems with Excel's settings and you want to reregister it.
/regserver	Opens Excel, reregisters it, and then quits.
/unregserver	Opens Excel, unregisters it, and then quits.

Table 9-3. Switches for starting PowerPoint

Switch	What it does
/s	Opens a presentation into the slide show window.
/p	Prints the presentation.
/n template_name.pot.	Creates a new presentation based on the specified template.

See Also

- Control Windows Explorer with Command-Line Shortcuts **[Hack #22]**

HACK #84 Open and Create Microsoft Documents without Microsoft Office

When it comes to word processing and spreadsheets, it's an all-Microsoft world. But you don't have to pay hundreds of dollars for Office to create and read Microsoft files; you can instead download a free office suite.

For better or worse, the Windows world has settled on Word and Excel as the word processing and spreadsheet standards. But as anyone who has recently bought a new computer can tell you, buying an office suite that includes them can push up the cost of your computer by several hundred dollars.

If you want to play well with others, you need to be able to create and read Word and Excel files. That doesn't mean, however, that you need to buy Microsoft Office. In fact, you can download a free office suite that includes a Word-compatible word processor, an Excel-compatible spreadsheet, as well as image-editing and photo album software. It's called the 602Pro PC SUITE, and it is available from 602 Software (*http://www.software602.com*).

The word processor, 602Text, reads Word documents, including all formatting, and can format and save Word documents as well. The spreadsheet, 602Tab, reads and writes Excel files. You won't get a number of Office extras, such as being able to use macros, but at least one feature of the program is superior to Word. When you open or save a document, you're shown file thumbnails that have the first several lines of the document, as shown in Figure 9-7. Look closely, and you'll see a small magnifying glass in the lower right of each document. Click on it, and you'll see even more of the text. It's a great way to preview information in files so that you know you'll be opening the right file.

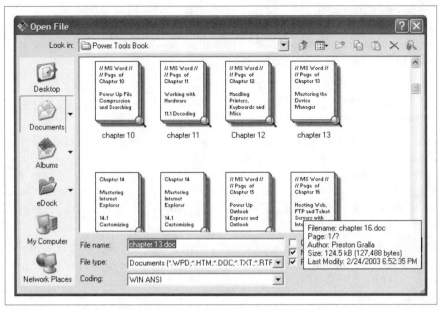

Figure 9-7. Opening a file with 602Pro PC SUITE

See Also

- The OpenOffice.org office suite (*http://www.openoffice.org*) is a free, open source software suite that includes a word processor, spreadsheet, drawing program, equation editor, and presentation software. It opens and saves Microsoft Office formats as well as many other formats. Versions are available for Windows, Macintosh, Linux, and Solaris.

HACK #85 Stop Hidden Fields in Word from Stealing Your Files and Information

Hidden fields in your Word documents can be used to peer into your PC and even grab your files. Here's how to prevent that from happening.

A little-known trick in Word can let malicious users steal your private information and can even allow someone to get access to the files on your PC. It does this by using Word Fields, which are used to insert self-updating information into Word documents, such as page numbers in a header or footer. Some fields, though, can be hidden, and, because you can't see them, you can't tell what they're doing.

One of these hidden fields, IncludeText, is generally useful; it can insert Word documents or Excel spreadsheets into other Word documents. However, the field can also be used maliciously. For example, let's say someone sends you a document, you edit it, and then send it back to the person who sent it to you. If it included a hidden IncludeText field with specific files and their locations on your hard disk, those files on your hard disk could be sent back to the document originator without your knowing it.

There are several ways to solve the problem. One is to install a Microsoft patch that fixes the vulnerability. For more information and to download it, go to *http://support.microsoft.com/default.aspx?scid=kb;en-us;329748.*

Another way to solve the problem is to download the free Hidden File Detector from *http://www.wordsite.com/HiddenFileDetector.html.* It adds a new menu item, Detect Hidden Files, to Word's Tools menu. When you choose it from the menu, a dialog box alerts you to any documents that have been inserted into the file by a Word Field that could be functioning as spyware.

You can also try to solve the problem yourself by choosing Edit → Links to see if there are links in your document to files. (If there are none, the Links option will be grayed out.) If you find them, delete them, and the problem should be fixed.

See Also

- Stop Pop Ups, Spyware, and Web Bugs [Hack #33]
- File Sharing without the Spyware [Hack #89]

Graphics and Multimedia

Hacks #86–90

XP is Microsoft's first attempt to truly integrate multimedia hardware and graphics-playing abilities. In previous versions of Windows, things such as movie making, music recording, CD burning, and graphics seemed an afterthought rather than a core part of the operating system.

But with XP, that changed. It's not only that Microsoft dressed up the operating system to make it look better; it also now offers Windows Media Player, a fully featured piece of music and entertainment software, and Windows Movie Maker, which lets you create home movies and videos.

In this chapter, you'll find hacks for improving your created movies, burning CDs more easily, converting graphics among formats, music sharing without spyware, and more.

HACK #86 Image Conversion in a Pinch

When you need to convert images from one format to another, or need to shrink the size of existing images, try these two graphics tools.

I frequently have to convert graphics from one format to another. For example, I may need to convert a high-quality, very large bitmap TIFF file to a much smaller GIF or JPEG for posting to the Web. Sometimes, I need to shrink the size of a file, while keeping the same format—for example, when sending a picture via email to relatives or friends. When I'm creating my own icons **[Hack #19]**, I need to convert graphics to the *.ico* format. There are also times when I work with an artist who needs a file in a particular format.

XP's built-in Paint program can't really do the trick. It can convert only a handful of graphics formats (for example, it can't handle *.pcx* or *.ico* format), and it won't let you customize the graphic; for example, you can't alter the compression of *.jpg* files to make them smaller. And it can't do batch conversions; to convert a file you have to open it and then save it in a different format.

For the kind of image conversion I do, I don't need a full-blown graphics program like Photoshop that carries a full-blown price tag of up to $600 (Photoshop Elements is another alternative, but that's not free either). Instead, I turn to the freeware and shareware programs detailed in the rest of this hack.

IrfanView

For most image-conversion chores, I turn to the free program IrfanView (*http://www.irfanview.com*), which is named after its creator, Irfan Skiljan. It lets you convert individual images or batches of images at a time, handles a wide variety of formats, and gives you a great deal of control over the conversion. For example, when converting to a JPEG, you can set the image quality, whether to save as color or grayscale, and whether to save it as a *progressive graphic*—one that gradually paints on the screen as it downloads over the Web.

To do a batch conversion, after you run the program, choose File → Batch Conversion, browse to the directory that has the files you want to convert, and select them. Choose the output format and any options you want to apply to the files. For example, for a certain project I needed to convert a group of large graphics in TIFF format to JPEG format, and the resulting files had to be very small, grayscale, and in progressive format. Figure 10-1 shows the options I chose in IrfanView.

If you need to convert only an individual file, then call up the file, save it in whatever format you want, and use options like those shown in Figure 10-1.

IrfanView does much more than image conversion. I use it as my all-purpose file viewer, for example. It also works with scanners to bring images into your PC, and it includes basic image-editing tools.

ImageConverter .EXE

One thing that IrfanView can't do is display before-and-after pictures of the graphic you're converting. For example, you can't preview what the converted picture will look like after it is converted. This can make image conversion a hit-or-miss affair: you'll first have to choose your conversion options, then convert the image, and then finally look at the output. If you're not happy with the results, you have to start back at the beginning, choose different options, and hope this one works.

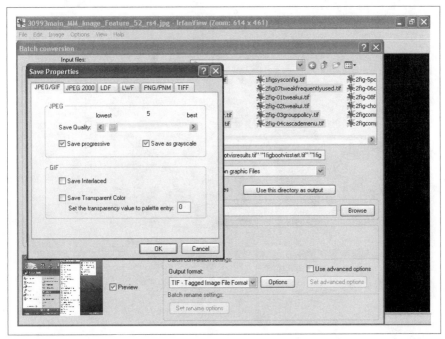

Figure 10-1. Converting a batch of files at a time with IrfanView

ImageConverter .EXE (*http://www.stintercorp.com/genx/imageconverter.php*) shows you a side-by-side comparison of the before-and-after images, before you do the actual conversion. It also shows you the size of each image. That way, before you do the conversion, you can keep tweaking it until you have the size and quality you want. Figure 10-2 shows an example of shrinking a JPEG file while still trying to retain as much detail and quality as possible. The image on the left is the original image and is 242 KB. The one on the right is only 36 KB, but there is very little difference in the quality of the two, so I chose to save this one.

The program does batch conversions, as well as letting you convert files one at a time. It also lets you edit and add a wide variety of special effects when you convert, such as changing the color depth and contrast, adding a motion blur, posterizing the image, and more. The program is shareware and free to try, but you're expected to pay $35 if you decide to keep it.

See Also

- Paint Shop Pro (*http://www.paintshoppro.com*) is an excellent all-around graphics program that also does image conversion, including batch image conversion. It's shareware and free to try, but it has a registration fee of $99.

Figure 10-2. A side-by-side comparison of image quality and size

Problem-Free CD Burning

XP lets you easily record digital music to your PC and burn music CDs. Here's how to make sure your digital music doesn't skip, pop, crackle, and hiss, as well as other advice on CD burning.

Windows Media Player lets you burn CDs, as well as "rip" digital music from CDs and put them on your hard disk; but, as anyone who has ever burned and ripped music knows, the process is never problem-free. When you rip music, you may find that your digital music files skip and pop. And when you burn CDs, you may find that those CDs skip and have similar problems as well.

I've had many problems like that myself, particularly when copying opera CDs, which, as you'll see later in this hack, suffer from a nagging problem that causes most copied CDs to skip at least several times per CD.

What to Do if Your Digital Music Files Skip and Pop

When you rip music from CDs or old LPs, you may find that the digital music you rip to your PC skips and pops. There can be many causes for skipping and popping, so this section provides a number of ways to fix a variety of problems.

Cleaning up .wav files. If you're recording from old LPs, the problem most likely isn't your computer. You're probably recording the music faithfully, but the vinyl on the LP has been damaged, so the resulting digital music suffers from skips and pops. You can solve the problem by cleaning up the skips and pops using downloadable software.

WAVClean (*http://www.excla.com/WAVclean/English*) and WaveCorrector (*http://www.wavecor.co.uk*) will both eliminate pops, skips, crackles, hisses, and similar noises from music you record from old LPs. Both programs require a several-step process. First, record the digital music using Windows Media Player or similar ripping software. You'll have to record in *.wav* format, because that's the only format these programs handle. Next, clean up the *.wav* files with one of the programs. Which one you use depends on whether you want to automate the cleanup or take a hands-on approach, and on how bad the problems are that you want to correct. WAVClean is the more automated of the two; load the *.wav* file, select Scrub, and choose from basic settings, and it eliminates hisses and crackles. It won't, however, clean up deeper scratches, so it's best for recordings that suffer from just hissing and crackling. With WaveCorrector, on the other hand, you see an actual oscilloscope view of the music files, with pops and similar problems highlighted in blue. You can either have the program make the edits to the file itself, or you can preview the edits and do the correcting yourself. WaveCorrector also includes a recording feature, so that you don't have to use Media Player or other ripping software, such as MusicMatch Jukebox (*http://musicmatch.com*). Once you've cleaned up the music, you can either convert it to *.mp3* or *.wma* digital music to save on your hard disk using MusicMatch Jukebox, or you can burn directly from a *.wav* file to a CD using Windows Media Player, MusicMatch Jukebox, or similar software.

Both programs are shareware and free to try, but you are expected to pay if you continue using them. WAVClean costs to register, and $30 WaveCorrector costs $45.

Other advice for reducing skips and pops. If you've recorded the digital music from a CD rather than an LP, the problem may be dirt and grime on the original CD, and physically cleaning it may solve the problem. Wipe the bottom of the CD clean. The bottom of the CD may be scratched, and that can cause problems as well. In that case, you can try some of the CD-cleaning devices sold at music stores and computer stores.

> Don't let your friends and family stomp around during recording! With enough movement, CD players can skip just like turntables, for those of you who remember such antiques.

Additionally, if the ripping software you're using allows it, try slowing down the speed with which you rip your music, or ripping it at a lower bit rate.

> Windows Media Player doesn't let you adjust the speed with which you rip music, but it does let you alter the music's bit rate. MusicMatch Jukebox lets you adjust the ripping speed as well as the bit rate.

Finally, if you have a very old CD drive, the drive itself may be a problem. With some older, slower drives, when you rip music, you'll frequently get skips. If that's your problem, the only solution will be to buy a newer drive.

What to Do If Your Burned Music CDs Skip

On occasion, your source and the digital music files will be free of skips, but when you burn a CD, the resulting CD skips. Sometimes, if you slow down the speed that you burn to a CD, you'll solve the problem. Most burning software will let you adjust your burning speed. In Windows Media Player, choose Tools → Options → Devices and highlight your CD drive. Then, click on Properties and choose the Recording tab, as shown in Figure 10-3. From the "Select a write speed" drop-down box, choose a slower speed than Fastest. Also, close all other programs when you're burning a CD, so that CPU, RAM, and system resources are all devoted to CD burning.

If that doesn't solve the problem, try using analog rather than digital CD writing. Choose Tools → Options → Devices, highlight the CD drive that you want to use analog playback, click on Properties, and go to the Audio tab. From the Copy section, choose Analog. If that still doesn't work, go back to the same tab and choose "Use error correction." This will slow down the CD burning process even further, but it may solve the problem.

What to Do if Long Selections Are Interrupted by Skips

On opera CDs, or any CD with particularly lengthy pieces, a single aria or other musical selection is sometimes spread out over two or more contiguous tracks. When a CD player plays the CD, the aria sounds as if it were one track; the music flows smoothly, without interruption. However, Windows Media Player and similar burning software, such as MusicMatch Jukebox, automatically adds pauses between tracks when you burn to a CD, so when you rip music from the opera CD and then burn it, the aria will be interrupted.

Some software lets you eliminate the pause between tracks when you burn to a CD. But then it eliminates *all* pauses, so the entire opera plays as if it were one long, single track, with no pauses, and you can't listen to it.

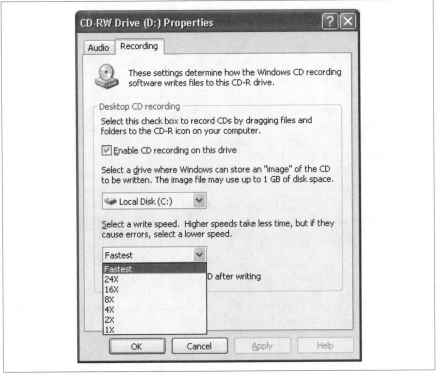

Figure 10-3. Slowing down CD burning in Windows Media Player

What's a Cecilia Bartoli or Renée Fleming fan to do?

You can solve the problem by using a program that makes an exact dupli-
cate of an entire CD, rather than copying individual files. Both Exact Audio
Copy (*http://www.exactaudiocopy.de*) and Nero Burning ROM (*http://www.
nero.com*) will do that. They'll make images of the CD and then let you use
those images to burn a CD. I've found that opera CDs burned with them
generally don't have the unnatural pauses. Exact Audio Copy is free, while
Nero Burning ROM is shareware and free to try, but $69 if you keep using it.

See Also

If you use Windows Media Player Version 9 to burn CDs, download and use
the TweakMP PowerToy for Windows XP from *http://www.wmplugins.com*.
(It's available for Version 9 only, not Version 8, of Windows Media Player.)
The PowerToy has a variety of tools, most of which are only moderately useful. But the feature that makes it worthwhile is its ability to level the volume
of files when you burn a CD. One problem with burning CDs is that the digital music files you're going to burn are frequently recorded at different levels.

Music from the Library

If you're looking to build up a digital music or CD collection, the Internet isn't the only place to turn. Another excellent place is the public library. Many libraries have excellent CD collections, particularly if you're interested in classical music, opera or jazz. While the legalities of the issue are questionable at best, technically you can rip music from your library's CD collection, and burn CD collections from the ripped music as well. Many libraries allow you to search the catalog and make request via the Internet, so you can make requests from home, and be notified via email when the CDs are in. In Cambridge, MA, where I live, I regularly make requests this way, and the library is part of a regional library network, so I have access to the entire library network's music collection. I frequently refer to the *Penguin Guide to Compact Discs* to find the best recording of a particular opera, request the CD, then add it to my digital music collection.

That means that when you play the CD, the music plays at different volumes, forcing you to constantly change the volume control on your CD player. The PowerToy automatically levels the volume of all files, so that the volume is the same on all tracks on the burned CD. After you install the plug-in, choose Tools → Plugins → TweakMP to run it. To do volume leveling, click on the CD tab and check the box next to "Automatically level the volume of files when copying to an audio CD."

Save Streaming Music to Your PC

Build up a digital music collection by saving files in MP3 format when you listen to Internet radio stations.

When I'm at my PC, I spend a fair amount of time listing to streaming Internet radio stations, such as you can find at *http://www.shoutcast.com, http://www.live365.com,* or the many radio stations available directly from Windows Media Player and MusicMatch Jukebox.

> To listen to radio stations with Windows Media Player, first launch it by choosing Start → All Programs → Accessories → Entertainment → Windows Media Player, then click on the Radio Tuner button.

Often, I'll want to listen to a particular song again after hearing it—for example, a pavan by the English Renaissance composer John Dowling that I don't have on my CD collection. But because radio stations stream music to your PC, that music apparently can't be called back up and listened to again. Same deal with sample clips on Amazon.com and other sellers of digital music—once you've listened to the clip, you can't save it like other files.

However, there is a way to save streaming music or any streaming audio to your PC as a digital music file. Super MP3 Recorder (*http://www. supermp3recorder.com*) lets you capture streaming music in MP3 and WAV formats. It's shareware and free to try, but if you continue to use it, you're expected to pay $19.95, or $29.95 for the Professional version, which lets you do sound editing and lets you automatically start recording at preset times.

To record streaming music, install and run the program, then choose Option, which will bring up the screen shown in Figure 10-4. This screen lets you choose which format to record your music. Unless you're planning to edit the sound file, choose MP3 as your recording format, because WAV produces files that are extremely large.

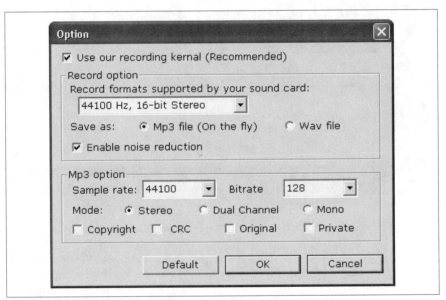

Figure 10-4. Choosing your file format and sound quality before recording

Click OK and return to Super MP3 Recorder's main screen. Now click Volume Control. This lets you not only set the volume control, but also to choose from which input you want to record. The program can record from a CD player, microphone, auxiliary input, and several other sources. By default, it's enabled to record only from a CD, so you have to choose the Wave Out option if you're recording from an audio stream.

By default, the recorded music files are stored in the *C:\Program Files\Super Mp3 Recorder Professional* folder. To change the location, click on the Browse button and choose a new folder.

Now you're ready to record. Listen to your radio station (or any other streaming input) and, when you want to record, click on the Start Recording button. The program will tell you that it's started recording, show you how long you've been recording, and display information about your recording format, as shown in Figure 10-5.

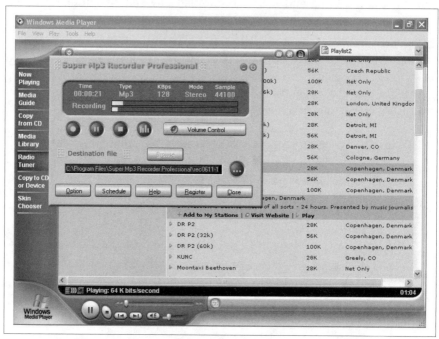

Figure 10-5. Recording an Internet radio station and saving to an MP3 file

The program's controls work like a CD player's, so you can pause and stop recording. When you've finished recording, go to the location where you've chosen to save your files, and the music file will be there, ready to play. The file will have an odd name, such as *rec0611-143130.mp3*. If you want it to have a more understandable filename, before you start recording, give it a filename of your choosing in the Destination file box, shown in Figure 10-5.

See Also

- Ripcast Streaming Audio Ripper is a similar program, but is designed to work with SHOUTcast servers that deliver streaming MP3 files, so won't work for all streaming audio formats. It's shareware and free to try, but you're expected to pay $9.98 if you continue to use it. It's available from Internet download sites and from *http://www.xoteck.com/ripcast*.

File Sharing without the Spyware

Finding and sharing music files doesn't mean that your system has to be filled with pop-up ads and spyware. Here's how to share files and entertainment files without the excess baggage.

If you're a fan of the Kazaa file-sharing and music-sharing software, you probably know that the biggest problem with the program is that it's full of pop-up ads and spyware. The spyware tracks your activities as you use the Internet, reports on them to an ad server, and you're then served ads based on your travels. Additionally, some of the spyware can be even more insidious and in the future could make use of your computer's spare CPU cycles without you knowing it.

If you try to track down and disable the program's associated spyware, as detailed in "Stop Pop Ups, Spyware, and Web Bugs" **[Hack #33]**, you'll disable Kazaa.

Kazaa Lite

One solution is to get an ad-free and spyware-free version of the program, called Kazaa Lite, shown in Figure 10-6. In all other respects, it looks and functions like Kazaa and taps into the same file-sharing network, but it doesn't carry the ads and spyware. It's free and available for download from *http://doa2.host.sk*.

Search and share files with it just as you do with Kazaa. As with Kazaa, if you're using a high-speed connection and fast PC, you may find that your PC will be turned into a *supernode*, which means you'll be subject to many searches and downloads from other Kazaa and Kazaa Lite users. In essence, your PC becomes a gateway into the entire file-sharing network for nearby users. This can be problematic and clog your bandwidth. If you don't want to be a supernode, choose Tools → Options → Advanced and check the box next to "Do not function as a SuperNode."

The program offers other benefits as well. When you run Kazaa, it calculates your participation level—how frequently other people download files from you. Based on that participation level, you may either have to wait in a long line to download files from others, or else immediately jump to the head of the download queue. Kazaa Lite automatically gives you the highest participation level, so that you need not wait in line to download. Additionally, it

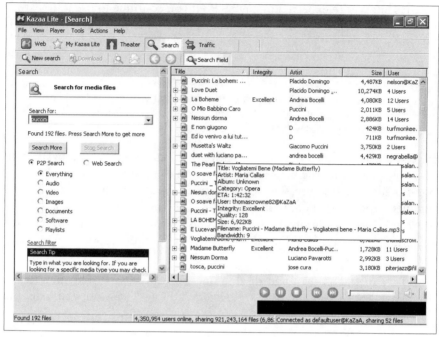

Figure 10-6. Kazaa Lite

will automatically find several sources for the file you want to download and then download from all sources simultaneously to save you download time.

By the way, don't look for the software in a popular download site such as *http://www.download.com*. The owner of Kazaa asked that the software be removed from that site, and the site complied. Instead, go straight to *http://doa2.host.sk/*.

Shareaza

Another ad-free and spyware-free alternative to Kazaa is Shareaza (*http://www.shareaza.com*), a front-end peer-to-peer client for the popular Gnu-tella file-sharing network.

HACK #90 Tips for Making Videos with Windows Movie Maker

Ways you can make better home movies and other videos with XP's built-in video maker.

XP is Microsoft's most media-aware operating system, and it comes with built-in software for making and editing videos and home movies: Windows Movie Maker. (To run it, choose Start → All Programs → Accessories →

Windows Movie Maker.) But making videos properly with it can be tricky, so check out these tips on how to make better home movies and videos.

Capture the Video Properly

Windows Movie Maker lets you edit movies and add special effects and titles, but it all starts with capturing the video properly. So, first make sure that you bring the video into your PC in the best way.

If you have an analog video camera or videotape, you need some way of turning those analog signals into digital data. You can do this via a video capture board or by using a device you can attach to your FireWire or USB port. If you're going the route of a video capture board, make sure the board has XP-certified drivers; otherwise, you may run into trouble. To find out whether a board has XP-certified drivers, search the Windows Compatibility List at *www.microsoft.com/windows/catalog.*

If you have a USB port, you can import analog video with USB Instant Video or USB InstantDVD, both available from *http://www.adstech.com.* They're hardware/software combinations; to get the video into your PC, connect the analog video device to the USB Instant Video or USB InstantDVD device, and then connect a USB cable from the device to the USB port on your PC. (A similar product, called the Dazzle Digital Video Creator 150, will do the same thing. For details, go to *http://www.dazzle.com.*)

Check your system documentation to see what type of USB port you have. If you have a USB 1.1 port, you won't be able to import high-quality video, and you'd be better off installing a video capture card. USB 2.0 will work fine, though.

If you have a FireWire-enabled PC, you're also in luck, because its high-speed capacity is also suitable for importing video. You'll have to buy extra hardware, called Hollywood DV-Bridge. Plug your RCA cable or S-Video cable into Hollywood DV-Bridge, and then plug a FireWire cable from Hollywood DV-Bridge into your FireWire port, and you'll be able to send video to your PC. For more information, go to *http://www.dazzle.com/products/ hw_bridge.html.*

Once you've set up the hardware and your camera, recording the video is easy. Open Windows Movie Maker, choose File → Record, start the camera or video, and click Record.

Capturing Video with a Digital Video Camera

If you have a digital video camera or WebCam, you shouldn't need any extra hardware in order to capture video from it, as long as you have a

FireWire port on your PC. These devices generally include built-in FireWire ports (the cameras might call the port an IEEE 1394 or an i.Link port). If you don't have a FireWire port on your PC, you can install a FireWire port card. These generally cost well under $100. Make sure that the card is OHCI (Open Host Controller Interface)–compliant.

When you plug your digital camera into a FireWire port and turn it on, Windows will ask you what you want to do with the camera. Tell it that you want to Record in Movie Maker, and it will launch Movie Maker to the Record dialog box, with a video showing in the preview window.

Best Settings for Recording Video

Before you start recording, you'll see a preview of your movie in the Record dialog box, shown in Figure 10-7. This is your chance to change your video settings, and choosing the proper setting is perhaps the most important step in creating your video.

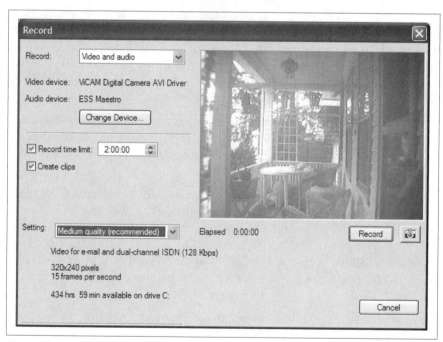

Figure 10-7. Options for recording video in Windows Movie Maker

Look at the Setting drop-down box in Figure 10-7. This box lets you choose the quality of the video you're creating, which is the most important setting. These setting will be dependent on the input source; digital video cameras, for example, let you record at a higher quality than analog video cameras, so they will give you a wider range of options. Movie Maker comes with a number of preset profiles, including three basic ones: High, Medium, and Low quality. When you make a choice of your profile, Movie Maker tells you how many hours and minutes of recording time you have, based on your disk space and the disk requirements of the profile. For example, you might have 193 hours of recording time based on the High setting, but 1,630 hours based on the Low setting.

Those three profiles aren't your only choices, though. You can choose from a much wider variety of profiles (as a general rule, I suggest doing that), based on what you plan to do with the eventual video. Do you plan to post the video on the Web? Just play it back at home? Run it on a personal digital assistant? These other profiles are designed for specific purposes like those.

To select the profile, choose Other in the Setting drop-down list. Underneath it, a new drop-down list appears, shown in Figure 10-8, with a range of profiles from which you can choose. They're prebuilt for specific uses— for example, recording video to post on the Web, for color PDA devices, and for broadband NTSC (National Television Standards Committee), which is standard TV.

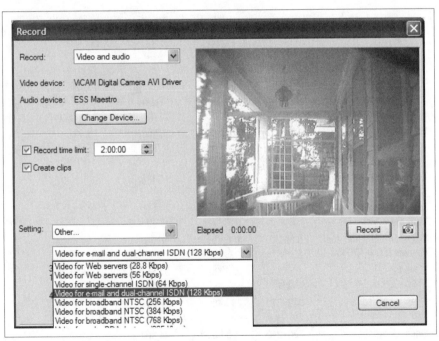

Figure 10-8. Choosing from additional preset profiles

Whenever you choose a profile, you'll see underneath it the frame size of the video, the frames per second, and if you choose a profile from Other, you'll also see the video bit rate. Here's what the settings mean:

Video display size

The size of the video, in pixels—for example, 740 by 480, or 320 by 240.

Frames per second

The number of frames captured per second. For smooth video, you need 30 frames per second, which is the "High quality" setting. The medium and low quality settings record at 15 frames per second.

Video bit rate

The bit rate of the recorded video—the higher the bit rate, the greater the quality.

Audio bit rate and properties

These settings aren't shown in the Windows Movie settings, but they vary according to which profile you choose. Audio properties are measured in kilohertz (kHz)—the higher the number, the greater the quality. Audio bit rate measures the bit rate—again, the higher the bit rate, the greater the quality.

To help you make the best choice among profiles, Table 10-1 shows the settings for every one of the Movie Maker profiles.

Table 10-1. Settings for Movie Maker profiles

Profile name	Video display size	Video bit rate	Audio properties	Audio bit rate
Video for web servers (28.8 Kbps)	160x120 pixels	20 kilobits per second (Kbps)	8 kilohertz (kHz)	8 Kbps
Video for web servers (56 Kbps)	176x144 pixels	30 Kbps	11 kHz	10 Kbps
Video for single-channel ISDN (64 Kbps)	240x176 pixels	50 Kbps	11 kHz	10 Kbps
Video for email and dual-channel ISDN (128 Kbps)	320x240 pixels	100 Kbps	16 kHz	16 Kbps
Video for broadband NTSC (256 Kbps)	320x240 pixels	225 Kbps	32 kHz	32 Kbps
Video for broadband NTSC (384 Kbps)	320x240 pixels	350 Kbps	32 kHz	32 Kbps
Video for broadband NTSC (768 Kbps)	320x240 pixels	700 Kbps	44 kHz	64 Kbps

Table 10-1. Settings for Movie Maker profiles (continued)

Profile name	Video display size	Video bit rate	Audio properties	Audio bit rate
Video for broadband NTSC (1500 Kbps total)	640x480 pixels	1,368 Kbps	44 kHz	128 Kbps
Video for broadband NTSC (2 Mbps total)	640x480 pixels	1,868 Kbps	44 kHz	128 Kbps
Video for broadband film content (768 Kbps)	640x480 pixels	568 Kbps	44 kHz	128 Kbps
Video for broadband film content (1500 Kbps total)	640x480 pixels	1,368 Kbps	44 kHz	128 Kbps
Video for color PDA devices (150 Kbps)	208x160 pixels	111 Kbps	22 kHz	32 Kbps
Video for color PDA devices (225 Kbps)	208x160 pixels	186 Kbps	22 kHz	32 Kbps
DV-AVI (25 Mbps)	720x480 pixels (NTSC) 720x525 pixels (PAL)	1,411 Kbps	48 kHz	16 Kbps

Tips for Making Your Own DVDs

If you use Movie Maker to make or copy your own videos and burn them to DVDs, consider these tips:

- The USB 1.0 standard is not fast enough to connect a camera or other video input to your PC. Its throughput of 11 Mbps isn't fast enough for capturing high-quality video, which is 30 frames per second with 24-bit color at a resolution of 640 by 480, and requires speeds of at least 210 Mbps. USB 2.0, which has a speed of 480 Mbps, and FireWire, which has a speed of 400 Mbps, will work, however.

- Make sure you have a substantial amount of free hard disk space if you're going to burn your videos to DVDs. The video will be cached onto your hard disk before it's burned to DVDs, so you'll typically need several free gigabytes.

- Defragment your hard drive [Hack #74] before creating and burning DVDs for best performance. If you have a second hard drive, use that for DVD creation rather than your primary hard drive. Regardless of the speed of your CPU, turn off any background applications that are running when you import video and create your DVD.

- If you're burning high-quality video to a DVD, figure that you'll be able to fit about an hour's worth on a single DVD. At a lower quality (lower bit rate), you can fit up to about two hours on a DVD. Keep in mind, though, that if you write at the lower bit rate, the DVD might not be able to be played on a set-top DVD player, though it will work on your PC's DVD player.

- There's no single accepted standard for DVD burning, so not all DVD disks that you burn will work on all set-top DVD players. Generally, most set-top DVD players will play DVD-R discs, but they may not all play DVD-RW or DVD+RW disks. Manufacturer information can't always be trusted, but check the web sites for the latest details.

- After you've created your video and you're ready to burn it to a DVD, set aside plenty of time. It can take up to two hours to burn a one-hour DVD, depending on your CPU and drive speed.

See Also

- If you want features beyond those offered by Windows Movie Maker, try Ulead DVD Movie Factory. In addition to basic video-editing tools, it lets you use transitions and add special effects and menus, and it includes backgrounds, preset layouts, and music you can add to your videos. In addition, it will burn to DVD, VCD, and SVCD and can save files in a variety of video formats. It's shareware and available to try for free, but you're expected to pay $44.95 if you keep using it. It's available from Internet download sites, as well as from *http://www.ulead.com*.

System Performance

Hacks 91–94

XP provides you with a variety of ways to hack your system to juice up its performance. Built-in tools, like the Performance Console, can monitor dozens of performance metrics and then take automated actions when those metrics fall below a certain level. You can make better use of your existing RAM by using a variety of different hacks, and the Registry offers many ways to speed up system performance as well.

In this chapter, we'll cover all those ways, as well as others, to help make sure that XP runs as efficiently as possible.

HACK #91

Track System Performance with the Performance Console

Before you can hack away at things to speed up your computer, you should know how to monitor system performance in the first place. As a power user, you'll like knowing what's causing those slow-downs and blips in performance. The Performance Console is a great hacker's tool for monitoring and tracking resources of all kinds.

Computers get faster every year, but somehow we still end up sometimes waiting around for them to finish a task.

To figure out what's slowing your computer down and get to the root of the problem, use the Performance Console (perfmon) to track and graph the activities of Windows XP and its components. First, I'll show you how to set up a log, and then I'll give you some ways to put the console logs to good use.

Setting Up Your Logs

Choose Start → Run and type perfmon. You'll see the Microsoft Management Console (MMC), with the Performance titlebar. In the left pane, click Sys-

Reducing Visual Effects

Windows XP's visual effects—such as fading and sliding menus, background images for folders, and drop shadows for icon labels—make it the snazziest-looking operating system that Microsoft has yet produced. But all those effects can take their toll on system performance, especially if you have an older computer.

XP gives you the option of balancing these visual effects against system performance. You can go full-bore and use all the visual effects, you can turn them all off, you can have your system decide which to use, or you can pick and choose which effects to turn on and off. Right-click on My Computer and choose Properties → Advanced → Settings (under the Performance section). To turn off all effects, choose "Adjust for best performance." To use all visual effects, choose "Adjust for best appearance." To turn on and off individual effects, choose Custom, then check the effects you want to use and uncheck the ones you don't. Experiment to see how they affect system performance.

tem Monitor to see a graph of your current system performance, including your processor, memory, and disk. You can use the toolbar buttons to configure the graph data and format. This graph is useful for seeing what's going on now, but it's useless for looking at the long-term picture.

To create log files of your system's performance, click Performance Logs and Alerts in the left pane of the MMC. You can create counter logs (with the values of performance indicators, measured on a regular basis), trace logs (with the values of performance indicators when something happens, such as a program crash), and alerts (an action for Windows to take when a counter hits a specified value). Log files stored in text format contain one line per observation, with values separated by either commas or tabs, and are usually stored in the *C:\Perflogs* folder. You can import these log files into a spreadsheet or database for analysis, reporting, and graphing. SQL and binary (nontext) log file formats are also available. (See article Q296222 in the Microsoft KnowledgeBase for how to log data directly to an SQL database.)

Create a counter log by right-clicking Counter Logs in the left pane and choosing New Log Settings from the shortcut menu. Specify the statistics you want to log by clicking Add Counters on the General tab of the Properties sheet for the log (see Figure 11-1). A nice feature of this utility is that you can choose whether to monitor the local computer or another computer on your LAN. Don't add more than a few counters, or your log file will grow quickly and be confusing to analyze. To select a counter, first select the performance object (i.e., the part of the computer system you want to monitor, such as memory or disks), and then choose counters from the list.

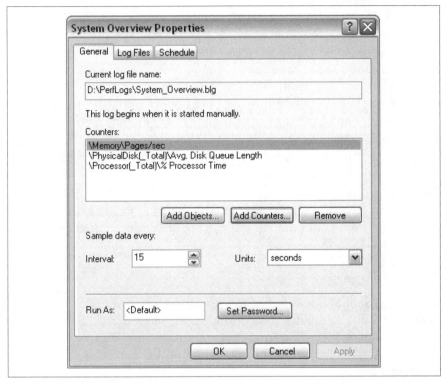

Figure 11-1. Creating or editing a performance log

Set the interval to the frequency you'd like to sample the data. Don't choose too frequent an interval, or your log file will take over your entire hard disk (start with once a minute). On the Log Files tab, specify the file type, name, and location. If you plan to import this file into a spreadsheet or database program, choose Text File (comma-delimited) for the type. On the Schedule tab, specify when the log start and stops—manually, or automatically on a schedule.

> The Performance console itself can slow down your computer considerably. Run it only when you need it, and don't set the logging interval to be too short. Set logs to stop after a day or two; otherwise, they'll run until your hard disk fills up.

What to Watch

These counters are often worth logging:

\Memory\Pages\sec
> Number of pages read from disk or written to disk when Windows runs out of memory. Swapping information to and from the disk can slow down your system significantly. Consider adding more memory.

PhysicalDisk\Avg. Disk Queue Length
> Number of read and write requests are waiting for the disk to respond. High numbers indicate that a faster disk drive would speed up performance.

PhysicalDisk\% Disk Time
> Percentage of the time the disk was busy. This is another indicator of a slow or overloaded disk.

Processor\% Processor Time
> Percentage of the time the processor was busy with all types of processes. This counter can tell you whether delays are caused by an overloaded CPU.

Viewing Performance Logs

With the System Monitor in the MMC, you can view a log as a graph. Click System Monitor in the left pane of the MMC window and click the View Log Data icon on its toolbar. Add the log file to the list. When you are looking at the graph, click the Properties button on the toolbar to change how the graph looks.

To look at the contents of a comma-separated (*.cvs*) log file in Excel or your default spreadsheet program, double-click the filename in Windows Explorer. Excel may complain that the file is still open (since the Performance Console is still appending information to it); click Notify to see what's in the file so far. In Excel, you can analyze, graph, and print the counters.

Performance Alerts

Create an alert to let you know when a counter exceeds a specified value. For example, the Performance Console can let you know when the idle processor time drops below 10%. Right-click Alerts in the left pane of the MMC window and choose New Alert Settings to create a new alert. Add one or more counters, and specify the limit (upper or lower) beyond which Windows should take action. On the Action tab, specify what Windows does when the alert occurs: specifically, you can have it add a note to an event log or run a program.

—*Margaret Levine Young*

Getting the Most Out of Your RAM

The best way to improve system performance is to make better use of your RAM. Here are several hacks to show you how to try this before you buy more.

No matter how much memory you have, you could always use more. Installing more RAM is generally the quickest way to better XP performance.

But you can also speed up XP by making better use of the RAM you already have. In this hack, we'll look at how you can speed up your system performance by using your RAM more effectively.

Make Better Use of Your Memory with the Task Manager

If your system doesn't have enough RAM, or if it uses what it has improperly, your system slows down. That's because in those circumstances it moves data and programs to a paging file on your hard disk, and your hard disk is slower than RAM. A certain amount of this is normal, but if you use a paging file too much, or if even your paging file can't handle the memory load, you'll run into system slowdowns and problems.

The Task Manager's Performance tab, shown in Figure 11-2, provides the best way to monitor memory use. To run the Task Manager, press Ctrl-Alt-Delete, then click on the Performance tab. With it, you can interpret the information and make better use of your memory.

The most important parts the screen shown in Figure 11-2 are the charts that report on paging file use and the tabular material below it that give a more detailed view of your current use of memory.

The charts relating to the Page File are self-explanatory; they show current usage, as well as usage over time. If you see that Page File use is frequently high, it means either that your system isn't making the most efficient use of RAM, or you need more RAM. In that case, follow the advice later in this hack for how to make better use of RAM.

The data below the Page File chart can be almost impossible to decipher. Table 11-1 details what the data means, and makes recommendations on how to use that information to make better use of RAM.

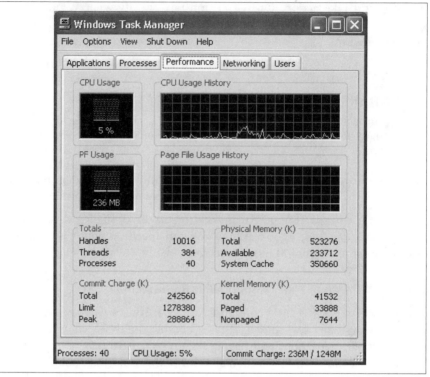

Figure 11-2. The Task Manager's Performance tab

Table 11-1. Understanding Performance tab memory reporting

Category	Subcategory	What the data means
Totals	Handles	Lets a program use system resources such as registry keys, fonts, and bitmaps. Sometimes, poorly written programs don't close their handles down when the program closes, leading to memory loss. As a practical matter, you won't need to monitor this number.
	Threads	A discrete portion of a program executing a single task independently of other parts of a program. Again, as a practical matter, you won't need to monitor this number.
	Processes	Reports on the number of programs and services (processes) currently running on your system. Monitor this to see whether you have too many programs and services running on your PC. To shut down unnecessary services, see "Halt Startup Programs and Services" [Hack #4].

Table 11-1. *Understanding Performance tab memory reporting (continued)*

Category	Subcategory	What the data means
Commit Charge (K)	Total	The total amount of physical memory (RAM) and virtual memory (page file) currently in use, in kilobytes. The more programs, files, and data you have open, the greater your commit charge will be. The greater the commit charge, the more demands will be put on your system. To reduce the commit charge, close programs and files, especially large files.
	Limit	Reports on the total amount of physical and virtual memory that is currently available for your PC, measured in kilobytes. To increase the limit, you can increase the Page File size (see article 4.9 "Optimize Your Swap File Size") or add RAM to your system.
	Peak	Reports on the highest total amount of memory, measured in kilobytes, that has been in use during your current session. Check this value each session to see whether the Peak value is frequently at or near the Limit value. If it is, you need to increase your memory, by either adding RAM or increasing your Page File size.
Physical Memory (K)	Total	Displays the total amount of RAM in your PC, in kilobytes. This number can be confusing; to find out the amount of RAM in megabytes, divide it by 1,024.
	Available	Reports on the total amount of RAM, in kilobytes, currently available. When available RAM is used up, your system begins to use its Page File.
	System Cache	Reports on the total amount of RAM, in kilobytes, that is being used for the most recently accessed data and programs. Programs and data can be in the system cache even after they have been closed down; the PC looks to the system cache first when opening a program or file, since it can be opened from the cache faster than from the hard disk.
Kernel Memory (K)	Total	The total amount of memory, in kilobytes, in use by the primary components of the XP kernel. The kernel is the core programs and files that make up the operating system.
	Paged	The total amount of memory in a Page File, in kilobytes, used by the primary components of XP.
	Nonpaged	The total amount of memory of RAM, in kilobytes, used by the primary components of XP.

Here's how to use the information on the tab to make better use of RAM:

If the Total Commit Charge exceeds the Total Physical Memory, you probably need more RAM. When the Commit Charge is regularly higher than the Physical Memory available, it means that you have to regularly use a

Page File, which slows your system down. Buy more RAM; it's inexpensive and will boost system performance.

Before running a memory-intensive application, use the Processes Tab to identify memory-hogging applications, and close them down. The Processes tab of the Task Manager lists every process and program in use and shows the total amount of memory each uses. Click twice on the Mem Usage heading on the tab to reorder the list of programs and processes so that those that require most memory show up at the top. Close down programs that you don't really need before running a memory-intensive application.

If the Peak Commit Charge is frequently at or near the Limit Commit Charge, you need to increase your memory. When this occurs, it means that your PC is frequently out of memory or close to being out of memory. Either add RAM or increase your Page File size.

General Advice for Making Better Use of RAM

So, you've learned how to use the Task Manager. Here are some additional tips for making better use of your existing RAM:

Remove DLLs from cache memory. If you notice your system running slowly after XP has been running for some time, or if your RAM seems to be getting low for some reason, the culprit may be left-behind DLLs from programs that are no longer running, but that XP still keeps in memory. Sometimes XP keeps DLLs in cache memory even when the program that required them is no longer running, and this cuts down on the memory available to other applications.

You can use a simple Registry hack to have XP automatically remove from cache memory DLLs that are no longer needed by programs. Run the Registry Editor **[Hack #68]** and go to HKEY_LOCAL_MACHINE\SOFTWARE\ Microsoft\Windows\CurrentVersion\Explorer. Create a new DWORD value named AlwaysUnloadDll, and give it a data value of 1. Exit the Registry and reboot for the new setting to take effect. Note that this setting may cause problems with some programs. Some Windows programs—especially older and 16-bit programs—may issue error messages with this setting in effect; so if that starts happening, delete the new key or give it a value of 0.

Reduce the number of colors. Using 32-bit color takes up a great deal more memory than 16-bit color, and it also puts a greater strain on your processor. If you primarily use business applications such as word processors and spreadsheets, you most likely won't notice a different between 16-bit and 32-bit color, so going with 16-bit color is a good bet. To change your color depth, right-click on the desktop, choose Properties → Settings, and in the Color Quality box choose 16 bit.

Avoid DOS applications. DOS applications don't allow XP to manage memory properly, and they hold onto the memory they use, not allowing it to be swapped out for use for other programs or processes. If you use any DOS applications, replace them with Windows versions.

Reduce the icons on your desktop. Every icon on your desktop uses up memory. Delete icons you don't use regularly. Run the Clean Desktop Wizard, which will automatically delete icons that you don't regularly use. Right-click on the Desktop and choose Properties → Desktop → Customize Desktop → Clean Desktop Now. A wizard will step you through the process of deleting unused icons. If you want the wizard to run every 60 days, check "Run Desktop Wizard every 60 days."

Reduce applications and services running in the background. You   may have many programs and services running in the background, without realizing it. Look at your Notification area, and see if there are any programs running that you don't require. Shut them down, and make sure that they don't load at startup. Also, XP frequently starts services on startup that you might not need **[Hack #4]**. For example, if you don't use a wireless network card, you don't need the Wireless Zero Configuration service.

More Power: Registry Hacks to Speed Up XP

#93 Put your Registry-hacking knowledge to good use: hack your way to running Windows XP at top speed.

Creating and marketing tuning and customization utilities for the Windows XP operating system is quickly becoming big business. A Google search will turn up hundreds of sites and programs dedicated to tweaking Windows XP. But no matter what type of interface is developed to make system tweaking easier and safer for the average user, the end result is that the changes are reflected in XP by modifying the Registry. For some people, commercial tweaking utilities may be the method of choice, but with a few precautions and safeguards it's possible to enhance system performance without any tools other than those supplied with Windows XP.

As you learned in Chapter 7, you can use Regedit **[Hack #68]** to edit the Registry. Make sure you take the precautions outlined in that chapter and back up your Registry **[Hack #71]**, no matter how comfortable you are editing the thing.

No single tweak is going to take an ancient PC and turn it into a gamer's dream machine. It's even unlikely that a number of tweaks will achieve substantial performance gains, but every little bit does help. As long as you keep your expectations realistic, you'll learn something about the Registry and hopefully see a performance increase in the process.

Menu Speed

When XP first appeared, there was a lot of conversation about the new interface, both good and bad. In spite of the initial complaints, most users stick with the default settings rather than reverting to the Classic interface found in previous Windows versions. But you may want to change the delay you notice when you click on the Start Menu. I see no reason for there to be any delay when I click on the Start Menu. Effects are pretty, but I wouldn't click on it if I didn't have business inside, so let's get it open and get moving. The default speed can be adjusted with a quick Registry hack.

Go to the Registry key `HKEY_CURRENT_USER\Control Panel\Desktop\MenuShowDelay`. The default value is 400. Set it to 0 to remove the delay completely, but if you do that it will be nearly impossible to move the mouse fast enough not to activate All Programs if you mouse over it en route to your final selection. Pick a number that suits your style, make the change, then test it until you find a good compromise between speed and usability.

Place Windows Kernel into RAM

It's a given that anything that runs in RAM will be faster than an item that has to access the hard drive and virtual memory. Rather than have the kernel that is the foundation of XP using the slower Paging Executive functions, use this hack to create and set the `DisablePagingExecutive` DWORD to a value of 1.

 Perform this hack *only* if the system has 256 MB or more of installed RAM!

Edit the Registry key `HKEY_LOCAL_MACHINE\SYSTEM\CurrentControlSet\Control\Session Manager\Memory Management\DisablePagingExecutive` to 1 to disable paging and have the kernel run in RAM (set the value to 0 to undo this hack). Exit the Registry and reboot.

Alter Prefetch Parameters

Prefetching (the reading of system boot files into a cache for faster loading) is a commonly overlooked component that can have a significant impact on system boot time. This tweak allows you to select which components will make use of the prefetch parameters. To see which files are gathered using each of the settings, clear the prefetch cache located at *C:\Windows\Prefetch* and then enable one of the settings listed in this hack. Clear the cache and repeat for each setting.

Set the Registry key HKEY_LOCAL_MACHINE\SYSTEM\CurrentControlSet\Control\ Session Manager\Memory Management\PrefetchParameters\EnablePrefetcher to 0 to disable prefetching, 1 to prefetch application launch files, 2 to prefetch boot files, or 3 to prefetch as many files as possible.

Disable 8.3 Name Creation in NTFS

Files that use the 8.3 naming convention can degrade NTFS drive performance. Unless you have a good reason for keeping the 8.3 naming convention intact (such as if you're using 16-bit programs), a performance gain can be achieved by disabling it:

Set the Registry DWORD key HKEY_LOCAL_MACHINE\SYSTEM\CurrentControlSet\ Control\FileSystem\NtfsDisable8dot3NameCreation to 1. Exit the Registry and reboot.

—Jim Foley

Repair and Recovery with the Recovery Console

If Windows won't start, use the DOS-like Recovery Console to make repairs.

The Recovery Console is one of the last-ditch tools you can use if your Windows installation doesn't start up at all. Before you resort to the Recovery Console, if Windows starts up, make sure you've already tried System Restore (especially if you've recently changed your hardware).

> To run System Restore, choose Control Panel → Performance and Maintenance → System Restore.

If it won't start, try running the Windows XP Setup Wizard from the installation CD and choosing its Repair option, or try starting Windows in Safe Mode.

If none of these easier paths work, you're stuck using the DOS-like Recovery Console to figure out what's wrong with Windows, your system or boot partition, or your disk's master boot record (MBR). You can use its DOS-like commands to look at the files and folders that make up Windows, and possibly repair them. You can also repair the master boot record and boot sector.

> You can configure the Recovery Console not to require the administrator password on login. In the Registry Editor [Hack #68], set the value of key HKEY_LOCAL_MACHINE\SOFTWARE\Microsoft\WindowsNT\CurrentVersion\Setup\RecoveryConsole\SecurityLevel to 1.

Starting the Recovery Console

To start the Recovery Console, boot your computer from the Windows XP installation CD and follow the prompts. When it asks which Windows installation you want, type the number of the installation (1, if Windows XP is the only operating system installed) and press Enter. Type the password for the Administrator account. When the Recovery Console is running, you see the prompt D:\WINDOWS>, which tells you the name of the current folder (directory).

> If you plan to use the Recovery Console often, add it to your boot menu (the menu that appears if you have a multiboot system). You must be logged in as an administrator. Choose Start → Run and type the command d:\i386\winnt32.exe /cmdcons (replace d: with your CD drive's letter if it's not D). The Recovery Console occupies about 7 MB of disk space and stores its program files in \Comdcons on your system drive.

Now you can type commands and press Enter, just like in the good old days of DOS! However, not all DOS commands work (see "Hacking the Hack" at the end of this hack), and you can't examine files in all folders. You are restricted to the Windows program folder (C:\Windows on most systems), its subfolders, the root folder of the Windows partition (C:\ on most systems), removable drives (including diskette, ZIP, and CD drives—but these are read-only), and the \Cmdcons folder (which contains the Recovery Console program itself, if you have added it to your boot menu).

If you know DOS, the Recovery Console's commands look familiar, though only a few are available and some work differently. To see a list of all the available commands, type help and press Enter. To find out how a specific command works, type the command, followed by a space and /? (for example, expand /?). When you are done using the Recovery Console, type exit and press Enter to reboot your computer.

Looking Around

Use these commands to examine your system:

cd *folder*
> Changes the current folder to the folder you name. In the folder name, two dots (..) represents the parent folder of the current folder. To move to a different drive, type its drive letter and a colon and press Enter.

dir *folder* or dir *filename*
> Lists the contents of the folder, including files and subfolders. For the filename, you can use * as a wildcard character (for example, dir *.dll). You see the last modification date and time, attributes, size (in bytes) and filename. The attributes are represented by letters: d (directory or folder), h (hidden), s (system), e (encrypted), r (read-only), a (changed since last backup), and c (compressed).

map
> Lists the drive letters with their file format (FAT32 or NTFS), size, and pathname.

type *filename*
> Displays the contents of the file as text. For executable, graphic, and other nontext files, you see garbage.

If a filename or pathname includes spaces, enclose it in double quotes.

Fixing the MBR, Boot Sector, or Boot Menu

If your system can't find a partition from which to boot, try fixing the MBR. Type fixmbr to rewrite the MBR on the boot partition (the drive or partition from which the computer starts up).

If the system finds the boot partition but the Windows boot sector is fouled up on the Windows partition (the drive or partition where Windows is installed), rewrite the Windows boot sector by typing fixboot. To specify which drive is the Windows partition, you can add the drive letter (e.g., fixboot c:).

Windows XP includes a boot menu that allows you to choose which operating system to start up. (It doesn't appear if your system has only one operating system.) To fix the boot menu, use the bootscan command. Type bootcfg /scan to look at all your partitions and drives, scanning for Windows installations. Type bootcfg /list to list the entries in *boot.ini* (the file that contains your boot menu entries).

Fixing Windows

If something is wrong with your Windows installation, use these commands to modify or replace the problematic files:

attrib *filename flag*
> Changes the attribute of a file (*filename*). The *flag* is + (adds, or turns on) or – (removes, or turns off), followed by r (read-only), s (system), or h (hidden).

chkdsk *drive*
> Checks and repairs files and folders on *drive*. Add the /p switch to check the drive even if no problems are marked.

copy *sourcepath1 sourcepath2*
> Copies the file from *sourcepath1* and names the new file *sourcepath2*. The asterisk wildcard (*) doesn't work, so you can copy only one file at a time.

diskpart
> Lets you add or delete partitions, though you can't resize or move them. (For that, you need a program like PartitionMagic; go to *http://www.partitionmagic.com*.)

expand *pathname*
> Decompresses files from a *.cab* file and puts the result in the current folder. If the *.cab* file contains more than one file, add /f:* to extract all the files. Or add /f:* /d to list all the files in the *.cab*, and then use expand *pathname* /f:*filename* command to extract just the one you want.

Hacking the Hack

By default, the Recovery Console doesn't allow you to use wildcards, copy files from local drives to removable media, or use the cd command to list files in subfolders in all folders on all local disks. It also issues a warning message every time you copy files that overwrite existing files.

However, if you have the Professional Edition, you can change that behavior using the Group Policy Editor. At a command prompt, type gpedit.msc to run the Group Policy Editor. Go to Local Computer Policy\Computer Configuration\Windows Settings\Security Settings\Local Policies\ Security Options. In the list of policies on the right, double-click on "Recover console: Allow floppy copy and access to all drives and all folders." Select the Enabled option and click OK.

Doing this won't actually make the changes; at this point, you'll have to use the Recovery Console itself to do that. Open the Recovery Console and use the following commands to customize its behavior:

`set allowwildcards = true`

This command lets you use the * and ? wildcards with the Recovery Console commands.

`set allowallpaths = true`

This command lets you use the `cd` command to list all files and subfolders on all folders on all local disks.

`set allowremovablemedia = true`

This command lets you copy files from local drives to removable media.

`set nocopyprompt = true`

This command lets you copy files that overwrite existing files, without getting a warning prompt.

—Margaret Levine Young

Hardware
Hacks 95–100

You probably notice your hardware only when it causes problems. When everything goes according to plan, it's invisible, which is the way we like it.

You can tweak your hardware in a variety of ways to make it run better, and you can use XP's built-in utilities to troubleshoot any problems. In this chapter, we'll look at hacks to help you troubleshoot hardware problems, remap your keyboard, make laptop and LCD screens more readable, and set up a cheap network by connecting two PCs.

Troubleshoot Hardware by Decoding Device Manager Error Messages

HACK
#95

The Device Manager is a great hardware troubleshooting tool, but you'll need this hack to make sense of the error messages it relays to you. Here's how to decode the cryptic messages and how to use the messages to solve hardware woes.

If you install and uninstall enough hardware on your system, error messages and system conflicts are a way of life. XP does a far better job than previous versions of Windows at keeping conflicts to a minimum, but on occasion they still pop up.

The first step in resolving these problems is to use XP's built-in Hardware Troubleshooters. Choose Start → Help and Support → Hardware → "Fixing a hardware problem" and under "Fix a problem" click Hardware Trouble-shooter. It's a wizard-style interface, so follow the prompts.

But that won't always solve the conflict. Luckily, XP includes a built-in way to resolve system conflicts by hand: using the Device Manager, XP's best all-around hardware-troubleshooting tool. Run it by typing devmgmt.msc at a command prompt or in the Run box. You'll see a list of all the devices installed on your system, as shown in Figure 12-1.

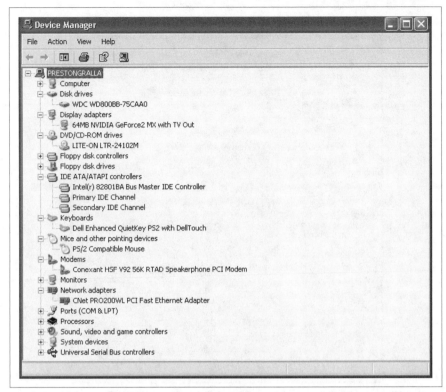

Figure 12-1. The Device Manager displaying all the devices installed on your system

To find information about any device, right-click on it and choose Properties. The device's multitabbed Properties dialog box appears, as shown in Figure 12-2. You'll be able to get comprehensive information about the device from here. You can also do troubleshooting by clicking on the Troubleshoot button.

When you open the Device Manager to the view shown in Figure 12-1, an icon will be displayed next to any device involved in a system conflict. A yellow exclamation point means that the device has a problem or conflict of some sort. A red "X" means that the device is disabled. A blue "i" (which stands for information) means that the device's resource configuration has been altered via the Device Manager.

The blue "i" icon shows up only when you choose one of two views: "Resource by type" or "Resource by connection." To switch to those views, use the View menu.

Figure 12-2. The Device Manager General tab

Only the yellow and red icons mean that there's a problem of some sort. To find out more details about the problem, double-click on the device that has an icon next to it, and an error message and error code will appear in the "Device status" section of the General tab shown in Figure 12-2. Those error messages are supposed to help you solve the hardware problem. Unfortunately, though, they're cryptic at best, and, as a general rule, you won't be any closer to resolving the problem after you read them.

However, armed with the right knowledge, you can resolve the problems based on the error message you see. The advice in Table 12-1 (adapted from MS Knowledge Base article 125174) tells you how to use the Device Manager to solve the problem.

Table 12-1. Device Manager error codes, messages, and potential solutions

Code	Error message	Recommended solution
1	This device is not configured correctly.	Update the drivers by choosing Update Driver from the Driver tab, and follow instructions in the Hardware Update wizard. You can also try removing the device in the Device Manager and running the Add New Hardware wizard from Control Panel.
2	The <type> device loader(s) for this device could not load the device driver.	Update the drivers by choosing Update Driver from the Driver tab, and follow instructions in the Hardware Update wizard. You can also try removing the device in the Device Manager and running the Add New Hardware wizard from Control Panel.
3	The driver for this device might be corrupt or your system may be running low on memory or other resources.	Update the drivers by choosing Update Driver from the Driver tab, and follow instructions in the Hardware Update wizard. You can also try removing the device in the Device Manager and running the Add New Hardware wizard from Control Panel. In addition, check memory and system resources by right-clicking My Computer, choosing Properties → Advanced tab, and then clicking Settings under Performance to see whether that is the problem. You might have to install more RAM to solve the problem. Also, try clicking Troubleshoot on the General tab of the device, in order to run the troubleshooting wizard.
4	This device is not working properly because one of its drivers may be bad, or your Registry may be bad.	Update the drivers by choosing Update Driver from the Driver tab, and follow instructions in the Hardware Update wizard. You can also try removing the device in the Device Manager and running the Add New Hardware wizard from Control Panel. If neither of these resolves the problem, get a new *.inf* driver file from the hardware manufacturer.
5	The driver for this device requested a resource that Windows does not know how to handle.	Update the drivers by choosing Update Driver from the Driver tab, and follow instructions in the Hardware Update wizard. You can also try removing the device in the Device Manager and running the Add New Hardware wizard from Control Panel.
6	Another device is using the resources this device needs.	Click on Troubleshoot on the General tab to run the Hardware Troubleshooter.
7	The drivers for this device need to be reinstalled.	Click Reinstall Driver.
8	Code 8 has many error messages associated with it.	Click Update Driver. You can also try removing the device in the Device Manager and running the Add New Hardware wizard from Control Panel.
9	Code 9 has several error messages associated with it.	Try removing the device in the Device Manager and running the Add New Hardware wizard from Control Panel. If that doesn't work, contact the manufacturer for the correct registry settings or updated drivers. You might also need to update your system's BIOS.

Table 12-1. Device Manager error codes, messages, and potential solutions (continued)

Code	Error message	Recommended solution
10	This device either is not present, is not working properly, or does not have all the drivers installed. This code may also have a manufacturer-specific error message associated with it, depending on the device.	Make sure that the device is physically connected to the computer properly. If that doesn't work, update the driver from the Driver tab.
11	Windows stopped responding while attempting to start this device and therefore will never attempt to start this device again.	Contact the hardware manufacturer for updated drivers.
12	This device cannot find enough free <type> resources that it can use. Note: <type> is a resource type, such as IRQ, DMA, Memory, or I/O.	Click Hardware Troubleshooter and run the troubleshooting wizard.
13	This device either is not present, is not working properly, or does not have all the drivers installed.	Click Detect Hardware. You can also try removing the device in the Device Manager and running the Add New Hardware wizard from Control Panel.
14	This device cannot work properly until you restart your computer.	Restart your computer.
15	This device is causing a resource conflict.	Click Troubleshoot on the General tab of the device, and run the troubleshooting wizard
16	Windows cannot identify all the resources this device uses.	Click the Resources tab and manually enter the settings as detailed by the manufacturer's documentation.
17	The driver information file <name> is telling this child device to use a resource that the parent device does not have or recognize. Note: <name> is the .inf file for the device.	Click Update Driver. You can also try removing the device in the Device Manager, and running the Add New Hardware wizard from Control Panel.
18	Reinstall the drivers for this device.	Click Reinstall Driver.
19	Your Registry may be bad.	Click Check Registry.
20	Windows could not load one of the drivers for this device.	Click Update Driver.
21	Windows is removing this device.	Wait several seconds and then refresh the Device Manager view. If the device appears, restart your computer.

Table 12-1. Device Manager error codes, messages, and potential solutions (continued)

Code	Error message	Recommended solution
22	This device is disabled.	Click Enable Device.
22	This device is not started.	Click Start Device.
23	Several error messages may appear with Code 23.	Click on Properties or Update Driver, depending on which button appears.
24	This device is not present, is not working properly, or does not have all its drivers installed.	Click Detect Hardware or Update Drivers, depending on which button appears.
25	Windows is in the process of setting up this device.	Restart your computer.
26	Windows is in the process of setting up this device.	Restart your computer.
27	Windows can't specify the resources for this device.	Remove the device in the Device Manager, and run the Add New Hardware wizard from Control Panel. If the device still does not work, get updated drivers or other assistance from the manufacturer.
28	The drivers for this device are not installed.	Click Reinstall Driver. You can also remove the device in the Device Manager and run the Add New Hardware wizard from Control Panel. If the device still does not work, get updated drivers from the manufacturer.
29	This device is disabled because the firmware for the device did not give it the required resources.	Check the device's documentation on how to enable its BIOS. If that doesn't work, enable the device in your computer's CMOS settings.
30	This device is using an Interrupt Request (IRQ) resource that is in use by another device and cannot be shared. You must change the conflicting setting or remove the real-mode driver causing the conflict.	Check Device Manager to see if another device is using the same IRQ and disable it. If you can't find another device using the IRQ, look for drivers loaded in a *Config.sys* or *Autoexec.bat* file, and disable them.
31	This device is not working properly because Windows cannot load the drivers required for this device.	Click on Properties. If that doesn't work, remove the device in the Device Manager, and run the Add New Hardware wizard from Control Panel. If the device still does not work, get updated drivers or other assistance from the manufacturer.
32	Windows cannot install the drivers for this device because it cannot access the drive or network location that has the setup files on it.	Restart the computer.

Table 12-1. Device Manager error codes, messages, and potential solutions (continued)

Code	Error message	Recommended solution
33	Windows cannot determine which resources are required for this device.	Contact the hardware manufacturer and configure or replace the device. Also try starting the trouble-shooting wizard by clicking on Troubleshoot on the General tab.
34	Windows cannot determine the settings for this device. Consult the documentation that came with this device and use the Resource tab to set the config-uration.	Change the hardware settings by following the manufacturer's instructions and then using the Resources tab to configure the device. Also try starting the troubleshooting wizard by clicking on Troubleshoot on the General tab.
35	Your computer's system firm-ware does not include enough information to configure and use this device properly. To use this device, contact your computer manufacturer to obtain a firmware or BIOS update.	Run the troubleshooting wizard by clicking on Trou-bleshoot on the General tab. If that does not work, get a new or updated BIOS from your computer manufacturer.
36	This device is requesting a PCI interrupt but is configured for an ISA interrupt (or vice versa). Please use the computer's sys-tem setup program to reconfig-ure the interrupt for this device.	Check your computer's documentation for how to reconfigure the IRQ settings in the BIOS. Also, try starting the troubleshooting wizard by clicking on Troubleshoot on the General tab.
37	Windows cannot initialize the device driver for this hardware.	Uninstall and then reinstall the driver. Also, try starting the troubleshooting wizard by clicking on Troubleshoot on the General tab.
38	Windows cannot load the device driver for this hardware because a previous instance of the device driver is still in memory.	Restart the computer. Also, try starting the trouble-shooting wizard by clicking on Troubleshoot on the General tab.
39	Windows cannot load the device driver for this hardware. The driver may be corrupt or missing.	Uninstall and then reinstall the driver. Also, try starting the troubleshooting wizard by clicking on Troubleshoot on the General tab.
40	Windows cannot access this hardware because its service key information in the registry is missing or recorded incor-rectly.	Uninstall and then reinstall the driver. Also, try starting the troubleshooting wizard by clicking on Troubleshoot on the General tab.

Table 12-1. Device Manager error codes, messages, and potential solutions (continued)

Code	Error message	Recommended solution
41	Windows successfully loaded the device driver for this hardware but cannot find the hardware device.	Uninstall and then reinstall the driver. Also, try starting the troubleshooting wizard by clicking on Troubleshoot on the General tab. If the device is non-Plug-and-Play, you may need to run the Add Hardware wizard. To do that, from the Control Panel, choose Performance and Maintenance -> System -> Hardware -> Add Hardware Wizard.
42	Windows cannot load the device driver for this hardware because there is a duplicate device already running in the system.	Restart the computer. Also, try starting the troubleshooting wizard by clicking on Troubleshoot on the General tab.
43	Windows has stopped this device because it has reported problems.	Check the hardware documentation. Also, try starting the troubleshooting wizard by clicking on Troubleshoot on the General tab.
44	An application or service has shut down this hardware device.	Restart the computer. Also, try starting the troubleshooting wizard by clicking on Troubleshoot on the General tab.
45	Currently, this hardware device is not connected to the computer.	Reconnect the device to the computer.
46	Windows cannot gain access to this hardware device because the operating system is in the process of shutting down.	No fix should be necessary; the device should work properly when you start your computer.
47	Windows cannot use this hardware device because it has been prepared for "safe removal" but it has not been removed from the computer.	Unplug the device from your computer and then plug it in again.
48	The software for this device has been blocked from starting because it is known to have problems with Windows. Contact the hardware vendor for a new driver.	Get and install a new or updated driver from the hardware manufacturer.
49	Windows cannot start new hardware devices because the system hive is too large (exceeds the Registry Size Limit).	Uninstall any devices you are no longer using. To see devices that are using drivers, but are no longer attached to your computer, see "Uncover Hidden Hardware with the Device Manager" [Hack #96]

See Also

- Uncover Hidden Hardware with the Device Manager [Hack #96]

Uncover Hidden Hardware with the Device Manager

HACK #96

Hardware ghosts and other hidden devices can cause system conflicts, and the Device Manager won't report on them. This hack forces the Device Manager to uncover all your hidden hardware so you can resolve any conflicts.

One of the strangest hardware problems you'll encounter in XP are hidden and *ghosted* hardware devices that are invisible to you but that may cause system conflicts. You won't be able to see them in the Device Manager [Hack #95]. When you use that troubleshooting tool, you won't be able to uncover any problems they may be causing.

There are several types of these hidden and residential gateways:optimizing- ghosted devices that are hidden by the Device Manager. Non–plug-and-play printers, drivers, and similar devices don't show up. Most newer devices are plug-and-play, so you'll most likely encounter this problem only if you have old hardware attached to your PC. (Plug-and-play devices are automatically recognized and installed in XP.) In this instance, the device is physically present on your PC, but the Device Manager doesn't show you that it's there.

Then there are the so-called *nonpresent* or *ghosted* devices—devices that you've removed from your system without doing an uninstall, or whose uninstallation did not work properly. These devices aren't physically present in your system, but XP treats them as if they were and devotes system resources to them. For example, if you physically remove an old network card without doing an uninstall, it may cause IP and other kinds of con- flicts, because XP treats it as if it were still in your system.

The Device Manager also may not give you details about USB devices that you only temporarily use and that you frequently attach and remove—for example, MP3 players that you attach to your PC only when you want to add or delete MP3 files from them. Even when these devices aren't present in your system, XP devotes resources to them. If you replace one USB device with another of the same model, it's best to go through the uninstall pro- cess rather than just swap them.

And then there are devices that you may have moved from one slot to another. XP may believe that they are actually present in two slots, so it devotes resources for both slots to them.

Displaying these hidden devices can help with troubleshooting. For exam- ple, a hidden device could possibly conflict with a nonhidden device. And there may be instances in which you will want to uninstall hidden devices—

for example, when you've moved a non–plug-and-play network card from one slot to another and want to uninstall it from one slot.

But to do this kind of troubleshooting you'll need to force the Device Manager to display information about the devices; otherwise, you won't know how to solve the problem.

Forcing the Device Manager to display non–plug-and-play printers, drivers, and similar devices is a simple matter. Run the Device Manager by typing devmgmt.msc at a command prompt and pressing Enter, and then choosing View → Display Hidden Devices, and they will appear.

Displaying ghosted or nonpresent devices takes a little more work. You'll set a system-wide environment variable that forces the Device Manager to display them. First, right-click on My Computer and choose Properties → Advanced → Environment Variables. The Environment Variable dialog box opens. This dialog box let you set system variables for the entire system or for individual users. Environment variables control a variety of XP features, such as the location of your *Windows* directory and *TEMP* directories and the filename and location of the command processor that will launch when you run the command prompt.

There are two sections in the Environment Variables dialog box: "User variables" and "System variables." To apply the variable to a single user, use the "User variables" dialog box; to apply the variable to all users, use the "System variables" dialog box. In this case, you'll want to create the variable system-wide, so click New in the "System variables" section. The New System Variable dialog box appears. For "Variable name," type devmgr_show_ nonpresent_devices. Once you've created the name, you need to give it a value. To turn the setting on, type 1 in the "Variable value" box. You can see the box filled out properly in Figure 12-3. Click OK and then OK again.

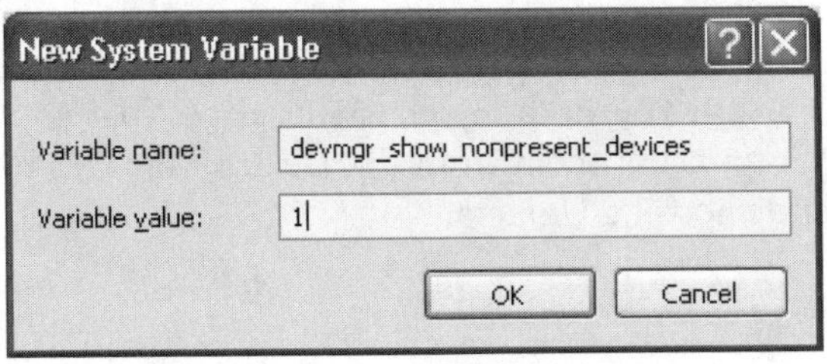

Figure 12-3. Setting the Device Manager to always show ghosted devices

So, now you've set the system variable properly, but the Device Manager won't display ghosted devices yet. You first have to tell it to display them. Run the Device Manager by typing devmgmt.msc at a command prompt or the Run box and pressing Enter. Then, choose View → Display Hidden Devices and the ghosted devices will appear, as shown in Figure 12-4. You should see quite a few devices now, including a lengthy list of non–plug-and-play drivers. Typically, devices that are not currently present on your PC will be shown as gray, rather than the black that connotes present devices. You may also see some devices listed more than once, as shown in Figure 12-4.

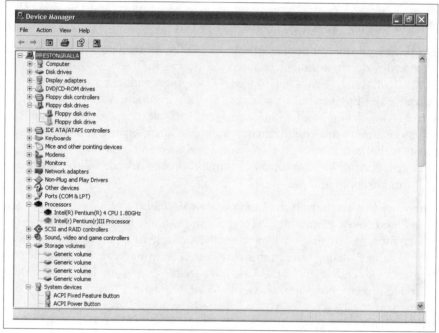

Figure 12-4. Displaying ghosted devices in the Device Manager

Now, use the Device Manager to troubleshoot any of those ghosted devices, as detailed in "Troubleshoot Hardware by Decoding Device Manager Error Messages" [Hack #95]. If you find any ghosted devices that you will no longer use on your PC, uninstall them from the Device Manager by right-clicking on the device and choosing Uninstall.

Hacking the Hack

If you want to use the Device Manger only on occasion to show ghosted devices and don't want to add another environment variable to your system, you can add the variable on an instance-by-instance basis—for example, for a single time that you run the Device Manager. At the command prompt, type set `devmgr_show_nonpresent_devices=1` and press Enter. You won't get a prompt in response; the command prompt will stay blank. At the same instance of the command prompt, type start `devmgmt.msc` and press Enter. The Device Manager will launch in a separate window. Now, enable the Device Manager to show ghosted devices in the same way you did previously in this hack.

Keep in mind that you have to run the Device Manager from the same instance of the command prompt in which you typed `devmgr_show_nonpresent_devices=1`. If you run the Device Manager outside the command prompt, it won't display ghosted devices.

HACK #97 Check Your PC's Pulse and Tweak It for Better Performance

Find out how well your PC performs, peer under the hood to get diagnostic information, and get advice on tuning it, with Sandra.

Do you know how well your PC is *really* performing? How well do you think it does compares to other systems? And do you have any idea of nitty-gritty information like its memory bank layout, the current video refresh rate, which currently running process consumes the most memory, or which services you can most likely safely disable [Hack #4]?

Better yet—how about using that information to get tips to get your PC to run faster?

My favorite hardware analysis and tune-up program, Sandra (*http://www. 3bsoftware.com*), will do all that and more. Sandra is shareware and free to try for 30 days, but if you use it beyond that you'll have to buy Sandra Pro for $29. Sandra Pro also gives you access to about a half-dozen analysis modules that Sandra doesn't have, such as modules about your network or fonts.

When you first run Sandra, you may well be overwhelmed, because you'll see several dozen icons, each of which runs a different diagnostic and benchmark test when double-clicked upon. For example, run the Memory Bandwidth Benchmark and Sandra returns results similar to the results shown in Figure 12-5, which measure the performance of one of my PCs. As you can see, it measures the speed of your memory and compares it to other memory chipsets. It also shows you the layout of your motherboard's memory bank, including the exact memory configuration in each bank. This is important when you want to add memory. Figure 12-5 shows me that I have two memory banks, each of which has a 128 MB memory chip in it. That means if I want to upgrade I'm going to have to take one of those chips out and essentially throw it away.

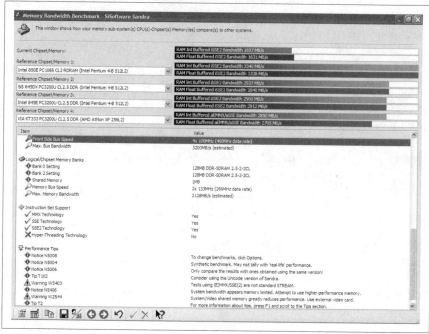

Figure 12-5. A memory bandwidth test and diagnostic for my PC

Sandra doesn't just give you diagnostics; it also offers recommendations on how you can fine-tune your PC. In this instance, it notes that my main system and my video system share memory, which reduces performance, and suggests that I install a video card with its own memory, as a way to improve performance.

The fastest way to get an overview of your system—as well as to get comprehensive advice on fine-tuning every part of your system, not just one subsystem—is to run the Performance Tune-Up Wizard. It analyzes your entire system and offers tips on tuning up each subcomponent, as shown in Figure 12-6. For my PC, it offered about a dozen tips, including which background services I might want to disable, ways to make my video system perform faster, among other advice.

See Also

- Aida32 (*http://www.aida32.hu*) is a freeware diagnostic tool that gives you comprehensive information about your system.

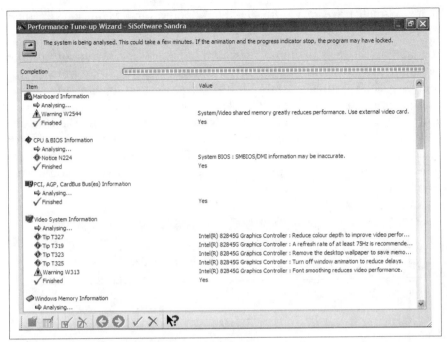

Figure 12-6. Sandra offers system-wide tips for fine-tuning your PC's performance

Remap Your Keyboard

#98

Create your own personalized, ultimate keyboard by remapping its keys to the way you want them to work.

Personal keyboard preferences are idiosyncratic; even a minor matter such as where the Alt or Ctrl keys should be located can inspire fevered debate. So, if you have personal preferences about where keys should be located, you can remap your keyboard to your own tastes using the TradeKeys utility from *PC Magazine*. It lets you map any key to any other key, including extended keys such as Right Ctrl, Right Alt, and the Windows logo key.

I find the utility particularly useful when I use one of my two laptops. Laptop keyboards are notoriously nonstandard, and I find the layout of my Dell Inspiron particularly maddening. The Windows key, for example, rather than being located on the lower-left part of the keyboard, where Nature intended it to be, is instead hidden away on the upper-right. Similarly, the Menu key, instead of being on the lower-right where all good Menu keys should be found, is also tucked away up on the right. So, I use TradeKeys to remap my Left Alt key to be a Windows key, and my Right Ctrl key to be a Menu key. True, it leaves me with only one Alt key and one Ctrl key, but that's a small price to pay to get the Windows and Menu keys in their proper places.

Remapping the keys is simple, as shown in Figure 12-7. After you run the program, choose the key you want to change from the "Map from:" area, and then choose the key you want it mapped to from the "Map to:" area. For example, to remap my Left Alt key to be a Windows key, I chose Left Alt in "Map from:" and Left Window in "Map to:" Then, I clicked on "Map → ". Keep on mapping keys in this way until you're satisfied with your new keyboard; then choose Save.... The new mapping will not take effect until you log off and then log back on. On some systems, you'll have to reboot.

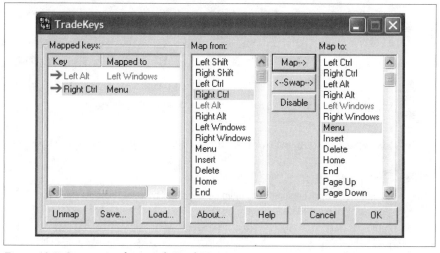

Figure 12-7. Remapping keys with TradeKeys

You can also create different keyboard layouts and use each depending on how you're using your computer. Some simple games, for example, use letter keys to control motions and actions. If you prefer using other keys, such as the larger Ctrl and Alt keys, for those motions and actions, you can create one keyboard layout for that game and another layout for your normal use. To create a new keyboard layout, first map it, then choose Save. Give it a descriptive name. Create multiple keyboard layouts that way. Then, when you want to use one, call up TradeKeys, choose Load, and choose the layout you want.

TradeKeys is free, but only if you pay an annual fee for access to *PC Magazine* utilities. You'll have to pay $19.97 for a year, or $14.97 for a year if you're a *PC Magazine* subscriber. Go to *http://www.pcmag.com* and click on Downloads to download it and other "free" utilities.

HACK
#99

Use ClearType for Better Laptop and LCD Resolution

Stop squinting at your laptop or LCD screen. Make any laptop and LCD screen easy to read.

Many people who use laptops complain that text is particularly difficult to read on LCD screens. Making matters worse is that many laptops are designed to work at very high resolutions (for example, 1400 by 1050 pixels), and at those resolutions the small type is particularly problematic on an LCD. The problem gets increasingly worse, because laptop screens keep getting larger and their resolutions keep increasing. On my 15-inch laptop with 1400-by-1050 pixel resolution, it's almost impossible to read text. Desktop-style LCD screens also have the same problems.

A simple hack will make text easier to read on both laptops and LCD screens; use Microsoft's ClearType technology, built into XP. To enable ClearType, right-click on the Desktop and choose Properties. Select Appearance → Effects. The Effects dialog box appears. Check the box next to "Use the following method to smooth edges of screen fonts." Select ClearType from the drop-down box, click OK, then click OK again. You'll notice the difference in how type is displayed.

You can use ClearType on a normal desktop PC monitor as well as a laptop, but I don't recommend it. On a normal monitor, it makes text appear blurry, and people have complained that using it gives them headaches. I've tried it and can vouch for that—headaches quickly ensue.

One problem with ClearType is that XP doesn't offer any apparent way to customize its appearance. However, there is an online tool that lets you fine-tune its appearance so that it's best for you. To tune ClearType, go to *http://www.microsoft.com/windowsxp/pro/using/howto/customize/cleartype/ tuner.* You'll be asked whether you want to install and run the Microsoft Cleartype Tuning Control. Click Yes. From the page that opens, make sure the Turn on ClearType box is checked. There are two versions of the control; depending on your version of XP and whether you have certain XP service packs installed, you might get one or the other. In one of them, from the opening page, you click on Next; in the other, from the opening page, you click on "Move on to Step 2: Tuning ClearType Settings." Depending on the version of the control, the next page may display two versions of the same text and ask which looks better (One version is for RGB monitors, and the other version for BGR monitors). Choose the text that looks better and click Next. (One version of the control skips this page entirely, so you may not see it.)

Next, you'll come to a page that displays a block of text in six different ways. Click on the text that looks best and then click on Finish. You're done; you've tuned ClearType.

One thing you need to watch out for is that the text Microsoft displays isn't real text at all; it's a series of graphics that have been made to appear as if they were text. So, the tuner won't necessarily reflect what you'll actually see on your system. To more accurately tune your settings, while you're going through the tuning process, open a Word document in another window and look at the text in the document after you've tried different settings. The text in that window will more accurately show you how the text will appear with various settings.

> Some users think ClearType looks better on some LCD screens than others. If you're creating screenshots for printing, you might try turning it off, since the effect doesn't always work as well on paper.

Hacking the Hack

When you enable ClearType, it's available only after you log on. So, the fonts displayed before log on won't benefit from ClearType. You can, however, use a Registry hack to enable Clear Type fonts even before logon. Run the Registry Editor [Hack #68] and go to go to HKEY_USERS\.DEFAULT\Control Panel\Desktop. Open the FontSmoothingType entry and change its value data to 2. (The default is 1, which means that font smoothing is enabled, but ClearType isn't. A value of 0 turns off both font smoothing and ClearType.) Exit the Registry Editor and reboot.

HACK #100   Networking on the Cheap: Set Up a Direct Cable Connection

You don't need a full-fledged network to connect two PCs using XP. Here's how to create a fast, cheap connection that's great for sharing files and other network needs.

If you are reading this book, which is (as you know) called *Windows XP Hacks*, then you probably get questions and pleas for help from your friends and family all the time (or you will, now that you've read the book!). You're the "computer guy" (women can be computer guys too, my female editor tells me) and you have the ability to "make it better." If that's a fair assessment of your situation, let's go through a scenario that happens to us hacker-types quite often.

It's 8:00 on a Sunday evening, and the phone rings. Your neighbor is panicking, because his computer is acting crazy and he just finished working on a huge PowerPoint presentation for work the next day. You grab your trusty laptop and your bag of computer parts and go next door.

You sit down at the computer and play with it a bit. Sure enough, it's got problems. The CD burner doesn't work, and the floppy drive is shredding disks. How's he going to transfer his file to his work machine? He doesn't have a dial-up account or Internet access, so you can't upload his file somewhere and download it to your computer—or perhaps it's just too big for his 28.8 bps modem to send.

Lucky for you (and for him), he's running Windows XP and so are you. Since you've read this book, you have exactly what you need on hand to save the day. You transfer his files to your laptop, burn a CD of the contents, and yet again save the day. He offers you money, but you refuse, because you'll keep him in mind the next time you need to move your piano.

Remember the Boy Scout Creed: "Be Prepared"

Before you can be the hero in this story, you need to have the proper tools. You might not have all the parts you need on hand, but you can get them with a quick trip to your computer store. There are three different cables you could use: a null serial cable, a parallel data cable, or a null Ethernet cable. All three cables are shown in Figure 12-8.

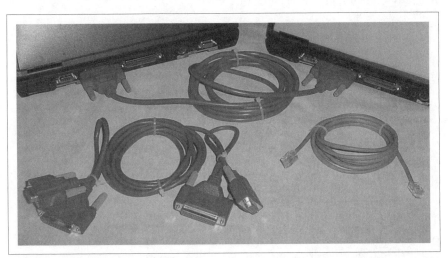

Figure 12-8. Null serial cable with DB-9 and DB-25 connectors (left), null Ethernet cable (right), and parallel data cable (back)

A *null serial cable* is the most universal cable; nearly every computer manufactured in the last 10 years has a serial port. The disadvantage is that serial transfer speeds are slower than parallel or Ethernet speed.

A null serial cable is *not* a serial modem cable; they look the same, but the connections are different. For this purpose, you want a cable that has female connectors on both ends. Serial cables can have two different connectors on the ends: DB-9 and DB-25. The DB-25 is an older connector that has 25 pins. If a computer has a DB-25 connector, it is probably too old to run Windows XP. I own a serial cable that has a DB-9 and a DB-25 connector on each end but I haven't used the DB-25 connectors for years. If you want to carry a serial cable, it is probably safe to buy one that only has DB-9 connectors.

> If you have cable and some connectors lying around your office, you can make a null serial cable by connecting the same numbered pins on each connector, starting from the upper left, except for pins 2 and 3. Those pins are crossed so that pin 2 on one connector goes to pin 3 on the other and vice versa.

A *parallel data cable* allows for faster data transfers than a serial cable. A parallel data cable is not the same as a parallel printer cable! What you are looking for has a *male* DB-25 connector on each end. It is often called a *LapLink* cable or an *FX* cable. LapLink and FX were commercial products that performed this function in the past. Since Windows XP has the functionality built-in, all you need is the cable.

A *null Ethernet cable* is your best bet in terms of speed and ease of use. The advantages are that it works with all modern Windows operating systems and will be the fastest connection you can get. The disadvantages are that older computers may not have an Ethernet card or they may not have TCP/IP installed. You can purchase a null Ethernet card at most computer stores for a few dollars.

> You can build a null Ethernet cable if you have a RJ45 crimper and RJ45 modular plugs by connecting the following pins with Cat-5 UTP cable: 1-3, 2-6, 3-1, and 6-2. The other pins are not necessary.

The null serial cable and the null Ethernet cable can be purchased for three or four dollars each from almost any computer store. The parallel data cable is a little more difficult to find, but it's still a good choice. No matter which of these you choose, you will be limited to connecting only two computers.

Cheap Networking with a Serial or Parallel Cable

Connect the computers using the serial or parallel cable. Make certain that you are connecting the same type of ports. Turn both computers on and log in so that both computers are waiting for you.

Decide which of the computers will be the host and which will be the guest. The *host* computer will be the one that supports the incoming connection. The *guest* will be the one accessing the remote computer.

On the host computer, open the Network Connections control panel. Click on the link labeled "Create a new connection." Click the Next button to get to the screen titled Network Connection Type. Choose the radio button labeled "Set up an advanced connection" and click Next. On the next screen, choose the radio button labeled "Connect directly to another computer" and click Next. When asked "Host or Guest," choose Host and press Next. You will be asked what device you wish to use to make the connection. If you are using a parallel cable, choose "Direct Parallel;" if you are using a null serial cable, choose the appropriate Communications Port (the one to which you connected your null serial cable—it should be labeled on your PC, but if not, check the documentation) and press Next. You will then be presented with the dialog box shown in Figure 12-9.

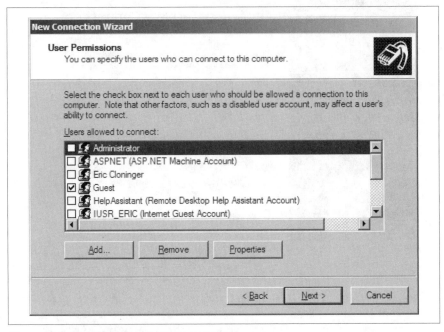

Figure 12-9. Host User Permissions screen

This dialog box asks you which users will have access to the host computer. If you are unsure about the security of the computer, you should choose an appropriate user. If you know the guest computer does not present a security risk, just choose the Guest account and press Next. The computer now has a network connection called Incoming Connections.

You need to know the network name of the host computer. If you do not know it, on the host computer right-click My Computer → Properties → Computer Name. The network name is the name next to the words "Full Computer Name."

Now it's time to configure the guest computer. Again, go to the Network Connections control panel applet and click the "Create a new connection" link. Select "Set up an advanced connection," click Next, choose "Connect directly to another computer," and click Next. This time, when given a choice of "Host or Guest," choose the Guest radio button and press the Next button. When asked for the connection name, type the network name of the host computer. If all goes well, you should see the dialog box shown in Figure 12-10. If you do, click the Finish button to close the dialog.

Figure 12-10. The New Connection Wizard

At this point, you have a physical and logical connection between the two computers. Activate the connection by double-clicking its icon on the desktop or in the Network Connections control panel of the guest computer.

When the computers recognize each other, you will be asked for the username and password. If you provided guest access on the host computer, you do not need to enter anything; just click the Connect button. If the connection is made, Windows XP will pop up a notification on the taskbar, as shown in Figure 12-11.

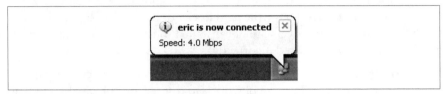

Figure 12-11. New connection notification

At this point, you have a network connection. You can use your Network Neighborhood window to browse or search for the host computer. Shared folders will work the same as if you were on an Ethernet network. If your folders and printers do not have permission for the user on the host computer, they will not have the ability to share files or print.

Keep in mind that this method is a one-way connection. One computer is specifically the host and the other is the guest. Those roles cannot be reversed without creating another connection. If you would like to be able to access the computers without designating one as the host, you will need to use an Ethernet connection.

Cheap Networking with an Ethernet Cable

If you need to connect two computers and you want a fast connection, you need nothing more than the null Ethernet cable described earlier. Both computers need an Ethernet card with correct drivers and the TCP/IP protocol installed. An advantage of the Ethernet option is that it works on all versions of Windows, as well as other brands of computers.

If your computer does not have an Ethernet card, you can purchase one for $30 or so. For most home applications, a 10BaseT Ethernet card is sufficient, though a 10/100 card is not much more expensive and can send 10 times as much data. There are also cards called *Gigabit* Ethernet, but they are considerably more expensive and very few manufacturers include this type of equipment in their consumer-grade equipment. My favorite Ethernet card is the 3Com 3C905BTX. It's reasonably priced and every operating system knows how to deal with it. The DLink DFE530TX and the SMC 1244TX are also widely recognized and can be found for less than $25. Installing an Ethernet card with the manufacturer's instructions in hand is not difficult, but if you aren't comfortable working with the hardware inside your computer, you should let a technician do the job.

Connect the two computers using the null Ethernet cable. If the drivers are installed on both computers correctly, a green or orange light will appear near the point where you plugged in the cable on each computer. These *link lights* indicate that there is a physical connection present between the two computers and that the two Ethernet cards recognize each other. If you do not see the lights, it means that the drivers are not installed correctly, the cable is not wired correctly, or the card does not have a link light. The most likely cause is that the drivers are not installed, but I find that about 1 cable in 10 that I purchase is wired incorrectly.

Once you have a physical link established between the two computers, it's time to make the TCP/IP protocol work. Go to the Control Panel folder and open the Network Connections section. (Under Windows 98 and Windows Me, this control panel is called Network.) Search for your connection in its list and double-click it. Then, open the item named Internet Protocol (TCP/IP). (Under Windows 98 and Windows Me, every card and every protocol are listed in the same dialog.) Search for the one that says TCP/IP and has the name of your Ethernet card next to it.

There are many ways to configure a local area network, but the quickest and easiest way to connect two computers using a null Ethernet cable is to set the values, as listed in Table 12-2.

Table 12-2. Suggested TCP/IP setting for null Ethernet connection

	Computer 1	Computer 2
IP Address	192.168.1.2	192.168.1.3
Subnet Mask	255.255.255.0	255.255.255.0
Gateway	192.168.1.1	192.168.1.1
Preferred DNS Server	Leave blank	Leave blank
Alternate DNS Server	Leave blank	Leave blank

At this point, the two computers will act is if they were on a larger network with routers and other equipment. You will not be able to access the Internet, but you will be able to share files and printers. The same restrictions apply here that apply to the other cabling options; the usernames on one computer must have appropriate permissions to access files and printers on the other computer.

If you plan to keep your cheap network connected all the time, use the Ethernet option. Ethernet has the advantage of being the fastest of the three cabling methods shown in this hack, and it is widely accepted as the high-speed networking choice. If you choose to add another computer at a later date or get broadband Internet access, the Ethernet option will be the easiest to adapt to the new network configuration.

—Eric Cloninger

Index

We'd like to hear your suggestions for improving our indexes. Send email to *index@oreilly.com*.

Colophon

Our look is the result of reader comments, our own experimentation, and feedback from distribution channels. Distinctive covers complement our distinctive approach to technical topics, breathing personality and life into potentially dry subjects.

The tool on the cover of *Windows XP Hacks* is an antique fan. Fans have been used to provide relief from the heat since the late 1880s. Antique fans that pre-date 1900 are quite rare and are highly sought after by collectors.

Darren Kelly was the production editor, and Brian Sawyer was the copyeditor for *Windows XP Hacks*. Colleen Gorman and Claire Cloutier provided quality control. Ellen Troutman-Zaig wrote the index. Jamie Peppard, Mary Agner, and James Quill provided production assistance.

Hanna Dyer designed the cover of this book, based on a series design by Edie Freedman. The cover image is a photograph taken from the PhotoSpin Power Photos Nostalgia CD, Volume 9, Disk 2. Emma Colby produced the cover layout with QuarkXPress 4.1 using Adobe's Helvetica Neue and ITC Garamond fonts.

David Futato designed the interior layout. This book was converted by Julie Hawks to FrameMaker 5.5.6 with a format conversion tool created by Erik Ray, Jason McIntosh, Neil Walls, and Mike Sierra that uses Perl and XML technologies. The text font is Linotype Birka; the heading font is Adobe Helvetica Neue Condensed; and the code font is LucasFont's TheSans Mono Condensed. The illustrations that appear in the book were produced by Robert Romano and Jessamyn Read using Macromedia FreeHand 9 and Adobe Photoshop 6. This colophon was compiled by Darren Kelly.

Other Hacks Titles Available from O'Reilly

By Paul Bausch
1st Edition
August 2003
304 pages
0-596-00542-3

By David A. Karp
1st Edition
August 2003
352 pages
0-596-00564-4

By Tara Calishain
& Rael Dornfest
1st Edition
March 2003
352 pages
0-596-00447-8

By Rob Flickenger
1st Edition
September 2003
304 pages
0-596-00559-8

By Rael Dornfest
& Kevin Hemenway
1st Edition
March 2003
432 pages
0-596-00460-5

By Raffi Krikorian
1st Edition
August 2003
288 pages
0-596-00553-9

How to stay in touch with O'Reilly

1. Visit our award-winning web site

http://www.oreilly.com/

★ "Top 100 Sites on the Web"—PC Magazine
★ CIO Magazine's Web Business 50 Awards

Our web site contains a library of comprehensive product information (including book excerpts and tables of contents), downloadable software, background articles, interviews with technology leaders, links to relevant sites, book cover art, and more. File us in your bookmarks or favorites!

2. Join our email mailing lists

Sign up to get email announcements of new books and conferences, special offers, and O'Reilly Network technology newsletters at:

http://elists.oreilly.com

It's easy to customize your free elists subscription so you'll get exactly the O'Reilly news you want.

3. Get examples from our books

To find example files for a book, go to:

http://www.oreilly.com/catalog

select the book, and follow the "Examples" link.

4. Work with us

Check out our web site for current employment opportunites:

http://jobs.oreilly.com/

5. Register your book

Register your book at:
http://register.oreilly.com

6. Contact us

O'Reilly & Associates, Inc.
1005 Gravenstein Hwy North
Sebastopol, CA 95472 USA
TEL: 707-827-7000 or 800-998-9938
         (6am to 5pm PST)
FAX: 707-829-0104

order@oreilly.com
For answers to problems regarding your order or our products. To place a book order online visit:

http://www.oreilly.com/order_new/

catalog@oreilly.com
To request a copy of our latest catalog.

booktech@oreilly.com
For book content technical questions or corrections.

corporate@oreilly.com
For educational, library, government, and corporate sales.

proposals@oreilly.com
To submit new book proposals to our editors and product managers.

international@oreilly.com
For information about our international distributors or translation queries. For a list of our distributors outside of North America check out:

http://international.oreilly.com/distributors.html

adoption@oreilly.com
For information about academic use of O'Reilly books, visit:

http://academic.oreilly.com

O'REILLY®

To order: *800-998-9938* • *order@oreilly.com* • *www.oreilly.com*
Online editions of most O'Reilly titles are available by subscription at *safari.oreilly.com*
Also available at most retail and online bookstores.